Teaching Exceptional Students in the Regular Classroom

Teaching Exceptional Students in the Regular Classroom

Raymond M. Glass
University of Maine at Farmington

Jeanne Christiansen
Education Resource Specialist
Kemmerer, Wyoming

James L. Christiansen
Consulting Teacher
Evanston, Wyoming

Little, Brown and Company
Boston   Toronto

Library of Congress Catalog Card No. 81-84675

ISBN 0-316-140600

9   8   7   6   5   4   3   2   1

HAL

Published simultaneously in Canada by Little, Brown & Company (Canada) Limited

Printed in the United States of America

Acknowledgments

Photographs by Ralph Granger, except: page 348, both photos courtesy of The Howe Press of Perkins School for the Blind; page 349, left, courtesy of Telesensory Systems, Inc.; page 349, right, courtesy of Martin L. Schneider/Associates.

Pages 107–108: Items reprinted by special permission from *Developmental Test of Visual Perception* by Marianne Frostig, Ph.D., and associates. Copyright 1961. Published by Consulting Psychologists Press, Inc., Palo Alto CA 94306.

Pages 114–116: Elimination diet testing for food allergy devised by William G. Crook, M.D. Reprinted by permission.

Pages 161–164: Items from the *Walker Problem Behavior Checklist* reprinted by permission. Copyright © 1976 by Western Psychological Services, 12031 Wilshire Boulevard, Los Angeles CA 90025.

Pages 164–165: Items from the *Devereux Adolescent Behavior (DAB) Rating Scale* reprinted by permission of the Devereux Foundation, Institute for Research and Training, Devon PA.

Pages 165–166: Items from *Pupil Behavior Rating Scale* reproduced by permission of the publisher, CTB/McGraw-Hill, Del Monte Research Park, Monterey CA 93940. Copyright © 1979 by McGraw-Hill, Inc. All rights reserved.

Pages 242–243: Pages from *World Geography Today* by S. Israel, et al., copyright © 1976 by Holt, Rinehart & Winston, Publishers. Reprinted by permission.

Pages 287–288: Quotations from Nicholas J. Long and Ruth G. Newman, "A Differential Approach to the Management of Surface Behavior of Children in School," *Teachers' Handling of Children in Conflict*, Bulletin of the School of Education, Indiana University, XXXVII (July 1961), pp. 47–61. Reprinted by permission.

To

Marc, Anna, and Matiana Glass
Harold and Joanne Stevenson
Raymond and Margaret Christiansen

Preface

Exceptional students are students who require some degree of modification in their educational programs either because they have intellectual, emotional, sensory, or physical impairments or because they are very bright. Some exceptional children have such severe handicaps or learning disabilities that they must be placed in special classrooms or in special schools, while many others have less severe problems and can succeed in regular classrooms. The success with which these children can be integrated — or "mainstreamed" — into the regular classroom depends a great deal on the willingness of teachers to make adjustments in their attitudes, goals, and teaching methods.

Whether you are an undergraduate elementary or secondary education major or a teacher already working in the regular classroom, this book will help you understand the nature and needs of exceptional children who are likely to receive much of their daily instruction in the regular classroom. It will also introduce you to methods for teaching these students. When you complete this text, you will be able to do the following:

- Describe the educational characteristics, needs, and placement alternatives for each category of exceptional student.

- Explain the basic requirements of federal law regarding the education of exceptional students.

- Identify and assess the educational needs of exceptional students who are likely to be placed in the regular classroom.

- Modify curriculum and teaching methods to help exceptional students make good academic progress in the regular classroom.

- Develop and implement techniques to promote positive classroom discipline and improve the behavior of disruptive students.

- Develop and implement strategies to help your other students develop positive attitudes towards their exceptional classmates.

- Participate in the Pupil Evaluation Team and in the development of Individualized Education Plans for exceptional students.

Organizing the body of information that you must master to meet these goals is a challenging task. Some texts present one chapter on each category of exceptionality and include teaching methods in each of these chapters. While this approach has some appeal, it reinforces the belief that a separate set of teaching methods exists for each category of student. Our experience suggests that this is not the case, especially when we work with students who are placed in the regular classroom. We believe that there is a core of critical teaching methods that applies to any student who demonstrates problems in learning or classroom behavior, and we present this core in Part III and Part IV of this book. The text begins with an overview of special education and the common categories of exceptionality. Students who have communication, sensory, or physical problems may need additional modifications to help them cope with life in the regular classroom, so separate chapters are devoted to these categories.

We have divided our seventeen chapters into six parts. Part I, "The Challenge and the Mandate," contains two chapters that introduce basic terms and concepts. In Chapter 1 we look at the categories of exceptionality, the educational alternatives for exceptional students, and the pros and cons of placing exceptional students in the regular classroom. In Chapter 2 we examine the evolution of attitudes towards the exceptional as well as the legal considerations regarding the education of exceptional students.

In Part II, "Students Who Have Learning and Behavior Problems," the chapters focus on students who are mentally retarded, emotionally disturbed, and learning disabled. In each chapter, we review definitions, characteristics, and educational needs to help you understand the nature and needs of these students. We group these chapters together because students in these categories have a number of common characteristics. In particular, these students most often demonstrate the learning and behavior problems that require classroom teachers to modify their instructional goals and teaching methods.

Part III, "Assessing Strengths and Weaknesses," introduces useful concepts and skills to help you determine the daily instructional needs of exceptional students, and specifically those who were introduced in Part II. These chapters will help you identify ways to assess a student's academic performance and classroom behavior. We also show you how to convert your assessment information into specific daily instructional objectives.

Part IV is "Teaching Exceptional Students." Once you have conducted an assessment and determined specific instructional objectives, you will need to identify techniques to accomplish your objectives. This part of the book introduces a variety of useful teaching techniques. In Chapter 9 we describe effective teaching practices for exceptional (and indeed for all) students. In Chapter 10 we introduce ways to modify existing curricula to help students learn more efficiently. In Chapter 11 we review specific strategies that promote positive student behavior and reduce inappropriate or disruptive behavior. In Chapter 12 we focus on strategies to improve interaction between exceptional and nonexceptional students.

Through Part IV, the text emphasizes concepts and techniques useful with those exceptional students who are likely to require a variety of modifications in teaching goals and methods. There are other exceptional students, in addition to the mentally retarded, learning disabled, and emotionally disturbed, who have impairments in communication, hearing, or vision, or who have actual physical or health problems. These children often require help from specialists such as speech or occupational therapists. In some cases adjustments in the classroom environment are needed to accommodate these students. Where these students demonstrate learning or behavior problems, the techniques presented in Parts II, III, and IV will apply. Part V, "Communication, Sensory, and Physical Problems," contains three chapters designed to help you understand the characteristics and needs of students with speech and language disorders, hearing and vision impairments, and physical and health impairments. In each of these chapters, we include teaching methods that apply specifically to the population under consideration.

Part VI, "Emerging Directions," consists of two chapters. In Chapter 16 we focus on the gifted and talented, a group often classified as exceptional, who are receiving increased attention today. We examine ways of identifying and teaching such students. The final chapter we devote to a review and synthesis of the critical teaching methods presented in the text.

Throughout this text you will find that we stress a problem-solving model of teaching. This model contains four critical steps, which you should observe regardless of the particular category of exceptionality you are teaching.

- *Step 1.*   Assess strengths and weaknesses.
- *Step 2.*   Develop specific goals and objectives.
- *Step 3.*   Select methods and modifications.
- *Step 4.*   Evaluate.

When you follow these steps, you can develop appropriate instructional activities for the exceptional students placed in your classroom.

This book is a collaborative effort, with all three authors sharing in the conceptualization, development, and writing of the text. We have been able to integrate our thoughts into a cohesive whole through the mutual endeavor.

Many people have helped us in the preparation of this text. We would like to thank our own mentors as well as our many undergraduate and graduate students who have helped to shape, evaluate, and refine the techniques presented in this book. We express our gratitude to Charlotte R. Clark, University of Kentucky; Nancy J. Kilpatrick, Estabrook School; Edwina Pendarvis, Marshall University; David E. Raske, California State University, Sacramento; Geraldine Scholl, University of Michigan; Melinda F. Welles, University of Southern California; and Nancy A. West, University of Colorado, who reviewed one or more drafts of this text and provided many useful suggestions for reworking.

Others contributed to the development and production of the book. Special thanks go to Viki Hellgren and Marjorie Bragg, who typed parts of the manuscript, and to Betty Gosselin, who typed the final draft of the text. Ralph Granger, our colleague and photographer, made an enormous contribution. Timothy J. Kenslea, our production editor, coordinated the many steps involved in converting the manuscript into a book. Mylan Jaixen, editor in the College Division of Little, Brown, assisted us every step of the way from the initial idea to the final product. We are indebted to him for his encouragement and assistance.

Finally, we wish to thank our parents and our families for their support and patience during the writing and production of this text.

R. M. G.
J. C.
J. L. C.

Brief Contents

Contents

Chapter 7
Assessing Student Behavior   **155**

Chapter 8
Developing Goals and Objectives   **178**

PART IV

TEACHING EXCEPTIONAL STUDENTS   197

PART VI

EMERGING DIRECTIONS   377

Chapter 16
Gifted and Talented Students   379

Chapter 17
Meeting the Challenge: The Problem-Solving Process   **401**

PART I
THE CHALLENGE
AND
THE MANDATE

A quiet revolution has been taking place over the past two decades. You, the classroom teacher; we the authors; and many students, parents, and professionals have been linked by this revolution. Just a few years ago the prospects for exceptional students were much dimmer than they are today. Certain groups of exceptional students were excluded from participation in regular classrooms or were denied the help they needed. A student with a speech or hearing impairment would have probably remained in the regular classroom but without any guarantee of receiving ongoing therapy to help in understanding and speaking with greater precision and clarity. A student with emotional or behavioral problems, one who learned at a slow rate, or one confined to a wheel chair might have been placed in a segregated special classroom, transported to a special school for handicapped children, or, perhaps worst of all, left to cope in a regular classroom without any special help. Today, because of the efforts of many people — parents, organizations for the handicapped, teachers, and legislators — exceptional students are beginning to receive the educational services they need without necessarily being excluded from participation in regular elementary and secondary classrooms.

The authors believe that schools must develop a range of placement alternatives for exceptional students. Some students need to be placed in self-contained special classrooms or special schools because their needs require unique kinds of instruction and continuous attention. However, we also believe that regular class placement is desirable for many excep-

1

tional students as well as beneficial for their classmates. Exceptional students can profit greatly from the intellectual and social stimulation provided by daily interaction with constructive models. Those who are not exceptional can also profit by learning how to view exceptional students for what they are: individuals who have special needs, but who also have feelings, interests, and talents that link them with all children. Ideally, both groups of students can learn how to interact with one another in increasingly positive ways.

Merely placing exceptional students in regular classrooms, however, is no guarantee that they will grow academically and socially or be accepted by their classmates. Teachers and administrators must develop a special set of understandings and skills to help these students reach their full potential. As consultants to many elementary and secondary teachers and as instructors in graduate and undergraduate courses that focus on teaching exceptional students in the regular classroom, we have learned that the following skills and understandings are most useful to classroom teachers who are faced with exceptional students:

1. Understanding the various definitions and legal concerns regarding exceptional learners.

2. Understanding how to recognize the basic characteristics and needs of each category of exceptional individuals.

3. Knowing how to use basic assessment techniques to determine some of the academic and social needs of exceptional students, indeed all students who are experiencing some type of academic or social difficulty.

4. Knowing how to make various adjustments in what students are to learn as well as how they can be taught.

5. Knowing how to promote positive peer interaction and help improve behavior of disruptive students.

6. Knowing how to interact effectively with parents and professionals who work with exceptional students.

This book has been written to help you develop these and other skills and understandings.

In Part I you will be introduced to basic definitions and legal considerations regarding exceptional students who are likely to be placed in regular classrooms. In the first chapter we will consider which students are classified as exceptional and why. We will also examine ways in which many exceptional students are currently educated, and we will introduce you to four exceptional students who are receiving much of their daily instruction in regular classrooms. In the second chapter we will review how attitudes towards exceptional individuals have changed over the years and then examine Public Law 94-142, The Education of All Handicapped Children Act of 1975. This act reflects current attitudes towards exceptional individuals and guarantees to all such individuals a free and appropriate education in the least restrictive environment.

Before proceeding, the terms "exceptional" and "handicapped" should be clarified. "Exceptional" refers to any individual who differs from the norm to the extent that specialized services are needed to adjust to the school environment and reach the full extent of his or her potential. Thus, a mentally retarded and an intellectually gifted student can each be considered to be exceptional since they both differ from the norm and require specialized services to reach their full potential. "Handicapped" tends to be a negative term in that it refers to what a person cannot do as a result of a specific disability and tends to overshadow the many things the person can do quite normally. "Handicapped" is, moreover, a relative term in that often a specific disability is not important unless there is an extraneous barrier. A wheelchair-bound person is not handicapped until he or she encounters a flight of stairs that must be ascended in order to reach a classroom. Similarly, a person with a facial disfigurement is not handicapped until he or she is denied a job as a clerk because the employer believes the disfigurement would cause prospective customers to go to another store.

We will use the term "exceptional" throughout this book because it is a more positive and inclusive term than "handicapped." Gifted individuals, for example, can be easily referred to as exceptional but could hardly be considered to be handicapped in a society that places such value on achievement. Despite our preferences, these terms are sometimes used interchangeably in the literature as well as in everyday practice.

As you read the first two chapters it will help to keep the following questions in mind:

1. Which students are exceptional?

2. What percentage of students are exceptional?

3. What types of school programs are available for exceptional students?

4. How do some classroom teachers feel about having exceptional students in their classrooms?

5. How have attitudes towards the handicapped changed over time?

6. What are some important implications of PL 94-142, The Education of All Handicapped Children Act, for classroom teachers?

7. What point of view do the authors take regarding the education of exceptional students in the regular classroom?

Chapter 1

The Challenge: Exceptional Students in the Regular Classroom

It was the beginning of another school year. Like all first days in the past, this one promised to be a mixture of excitement and anticipation of the responsibility of teaching one hundred seventh grade students to be competent in English. Jan Roberts was an experienced teacher who had seen many changes in the last eight years. This year something new was happening; the school district was making an all-out effort to provide appropriate services to junior-high-level exceptional students who would be obtaining all or part of their education in regular classrooms.

Walking in the front door, Jan noticed several dramatic changes. Ramps had been built to make the school barrier-free for wheelchair bound students. The library resource center had also undergone a major face-lifting. The center had received substantial funds from the district to purchase books, instructional kits, educational games, several typewriters, and other audiovisual learning devices to help exceptional students as well as their peers. Students could spend time working on special assignments in the resource center, or materials could be borrowed for use in the regular classroom.

Other important changes were less obvious to the eye. Two of the three special education rooms in the building were no longer to be used as self-contained classrooms in which exceptional students would receive all of their daily instruction. Instead, the ablest of these students would be integrated into as many regular English, science, math, language arts, home economics, shop, and other classes as possible. Two of the three special education teachers were now called resource teachers and were to help the integrated students cope with the demands of regular class placement through tutoring sessions, through extra periods of reading and math instruction, and by providing regular classroom teachers with additional learning materials and alternative teaching methods. One self-contained special education classroom was reserved for those students whose behavior and learning skills were not sufficiently developed to warrant regular class placement.

Not all of Jan Roberts's colleagues were pleased about the changes that were taking place. Indeed, summer staff meetings and in-service training sessions held to discuss ways to teach exceptional students in the regular classroom were marked by heated debates regarding the merits of placing exceptional students in these classes. A few teachers voiced fears that students with emotional and behavior problems would become disruptive when frustrated. Others were concerned that valuable teaching time would be taken away from the average learners by those students who required extra attention. A few teachers were misinformed and believed that even the most severely handicapped students would be forced upon them.

Jan was able to understand some of the fears voiced by her colleagues. Last year an experimental program was conducted in which four special education students were enrolled in her English class. She remembered being told at the beginning of the program that one student was classified as emotionally disturbed, one as learning disabled, another as mentally retarded, and another as hearing impaired. These labels had caused her a great deal of needless worry. Before meeting the students, she imagined herself having to cope with temper outbursts, threats to her authority, and students who could not read or write. Instead, she found the students to be more like their "normal" classmates than she expected. Although there were occasional outbursts of frustration, these students wanted to do well in class, to be seen as competent, and to enjoy the respect of their peers. Jan learned that labels, though needed for record keeping and administrative purposes, do little to tell what students are really like and the kind of help they need. She hoped her skeptical colleagues would also learn to look beyond labels and come to know their students as individuals.

The kinds of changes experienced by Jan Roberts and her colleagues are occurring in elementary and secondary schools throughout the United States. That is, exceptional students are spending increased amounts of time in regular classrooms, and classroom teachers are taking a more active role in the day-to-day instruction of many of these students. Let's take a closer look at some of these exceptional students.

Which Students Are Exceptional?

As you have probably noticed, there is a considerable range of variability among students in terms of learning rates, abilities, attitudes, interests, and behaviors in just about every classroom. Some students learn slowly and need extra amounts of drill and practice. Other students learn better when they receive a personalized explanation. Some students are easily frustrated and discouraged and need more than the usual amount of encouragement, while a few learn quickly and independently.

Indeed, a measure of variability in student learning and behavior is both expected and accepted by most teachers. Consider, for example, Karen and Dan, two sixth-grade students who differ from the average sixth-grader but still fall within the range of what most teachers consider to be typical.

KAREN

Karen is a socially outgoing student with many school friends. She enjoys painting and all forms of athletics. She reads at a fifth-grade level and has some difficulty remembering new information. She needs additional explanations and practice to learn new information but learns well with these simple adaptations.

DAN

Dan is a bundle of activity. He is frequently talking with his neighbors, out of his seat, or making funny comments. His academic work is average in most areas, although he excels in creative writing. Occasionally, Dan crosses over the line of acceptable behavior and requires a rather firm reminder from his teacher to get his work done or settle down. Dan generally accepts these reminders without becoming upset.

Obviously, both Karen and Dan need extra help and attention, but are they in need of special education? Probably not, since they seem to be making good progress with the minor adjustments made by the classroom teacher. In contrast, students who are classified as exceptional, and who therefore qualify for special education services, fall outside of the range of variability commonly accepted by classroom teachers and administrators. Such students demonstrate more serious learning and adjustment needs, which require continuous and carefully planned adjustments in their educational programs.

CATEGORIES OF EXCEPTIONALITY

Exceptional students are most often categorized by the unique characteristics they exhibit. The list below presents a brief thumbnail definition of each area of exceptionality using the authors' own informal definitions. A more formal study of the definitions, characteristics, and needs of each of these areas of exceptionality is presented in later chapters.

- *Mentally retarded.* Mentally retarded students have limited intellectual and academic potential. They learn at slower rates than their peers, have difficulty grasping abstract concepts, and may have some difficulty learning appropriate social behaviors.

- *Emotionally disturbed.* Emotionally disturbed students usually behave in ways that cause emotional conflict within themselves or with authority figures or peers. They often act in impulsive, aggressive, or overly withdrawn ways and have difficulty controlling feelings of frustration, anger, or disappointment.

- *Learning disabled.* These students usually have average or above-average intellectual potential, but demonstrate specific disorders in listening, speaking, reading, writing, arithmetic, or gross or fine motor coordination.

- *Speech impaired.* Students in this category have problems in one or more of the following areas: articulation, fluency, voice quality, and general language. These problems occur in such a manner as to call attention to the child's speech and impede communication.

- *Hearing impaired.* Students in this category have varying degrees of hearing loss ranging from mild to profound. Profoundly hearing impaired students are essentially deaf and do not learn to communicate through hearing. Students with lesser degrees of hearing loss (mild, moderate, or severe) require various aids and adjustments to help them learn and communicate by listening and speaking.

- *Visually impaired.* Some visually impaired students may be able to read with the aid of special print material or magnification devices. Others have impairments that are so severe that they must use nonprint materials. These students also need training in other areas of adjustment, such as mobility and travel.

■ *Physical and health impaired.* Included in this category are students with a wide range of conditions. Some may have special health problems such as asthma, epilepsy, or diabetes, while others have physical impairments such as cerebral palsy and muscular dystrophy. Some students are completely mobile while others may require wheelchairs and other devices to help them sit, stand, or walk.

■ *Gifted and talented.* Gifted and talented individuals are those who have outstanding abilities in one or more of the following areas: creative thinking, specific academic abilities, visual and performing arts, and leadership. Gifted and talented students are not included in federal legislation for the handicapped. However, many states are developing special education opportunities for these students.

Even from these brief thumbnail definitions it is easy to see that there is much diversity in the characteristics of exceptional students. Despite this diversity, there are common educational, social, and adaptive needs that tend to cut across categories. Many students who are learning disabled, mentally retarded, or emotionally disturbed have problems adjusting both to the curriculum and to the social requirements of the classroom. These students most often need help in academic areas and in their classroom and social behavior.

Students with speech and language disorders, hearing disorders, visual impairments, and physical or health impairments generally require specific forms of speech and language therapy, mobility training, or physical therapy, which is typically provided outside of the classroom. Many also require specific modifications or adaptations, such as wheelchair ramps, special seating arrangements, hearing aids or tape recorders to help them fully participate in and benefit from learning activities. Although some students in these categories learn and behave well, others may have learning or behavior problems similar to those demonstrated by mentally retarded, emotionally disturbed, or learning disabled students.

HOW MANY STUDENTS ARE EXCEPTIONAL?

It is difficult to provide a precise figure regarding the number of exceptional students in today's schools. As you might imagine, not all educators agree on who is exceptional. For example, one teacher may think a particular student has a learning disability or is emotionally disturbed, while another may consider the very same student to be within the normal range. As you will learn in later chapters, it is relatively easy to determine whether a student is blind or hearing impaired because diagnostic tools are relatively precise for such disabilities. It is, however, much more

TABLE 1.1
Estimated prevalence of exceptional students under 19

Category	Percentage	Number of students
Mentally retarded	2.3	1,507,000
Emotionally disturbed	2.0	1,310,000
Learning disabled	3.0	1,966,000
Speech impaired	3.5	2,293,000
Hearing impaired	0.6	372,000
Visually impaired	0.1	66,000
Physical and health impaired	0.5	328,000
Gifted and talented	3.0	1,960,000
Total	15.0	9,802,000

Source: Bureau of Education for the Handicapped, U. S. Office of Education, 1976.

difficult to determine whether some students are emotionally disturbed or learning disabled because diagnostic tools in these areas are more subjective, and there can be considerable overlap in the two disabilities. Many students who have learning disabilities also have emotional or behavioral problems. Conversely, many students who are emotionally disturbed also demonstrate marked learning problems. Putting these qualifications aside, a modest estimate that most experts would agree upon is that about 12–15% of the school-aged population is exceptional and requires some type of special education. The commonly used categories of exceptionality and estimated percentages of students in each category appear in Table 1.1.

Notice that the first four categories in Table 1.1 comprise the bulk of the 12–15% estimate. That is, students who are emotionally disturbed, learning disabled, mentally retarded, or speech impaired are the most prevalent. These are the exceptional students you will most often have in your classroom. The lowest incidence of exceptional students are those with sensory impairments or physical and health impairments.

The educational needs of gifted and talented students are now receiving widespread attention. Although these students are not included in PL 94-142, The Education of All Handicapped Children Act, many school districts are establishing services for these exceptional students.

HOW ARE EXCEPTIONAL STUDENTS TYPICALLY SERVED?

At one time many exceptional students were either excluded from school or placed in segregated classrooms. Most special educators now agree that a range or continuum of placement alternatives must exist for exceptional students (Deno, 1973; Reynolds and Birch, 1977; Lerner, Dawson, and Horvath, 1980). Some students can do well in a regular classroom, while others need more specialized settings. Legally, a school district must make available all or most of the placement alternatives shown in the inverted pyramid presented in Figure 1.1. This pyramid is an adaptation of Evelyn Deno's (1970) model of special education placement alternatives.

The upper portion of the inverted pyramid represents placements that are closest to the regular classroom and offer students maximum amounts of integration. The largest proportion of exceptional students can probably be well served in these placements. In the placements depicted farther down the pyramid, students become less integrated and more isolated from their normal peers. These placements are more appropriate for students whose needs are so pressing that they cannot be well served in the regular classroom. Much fewer students require the

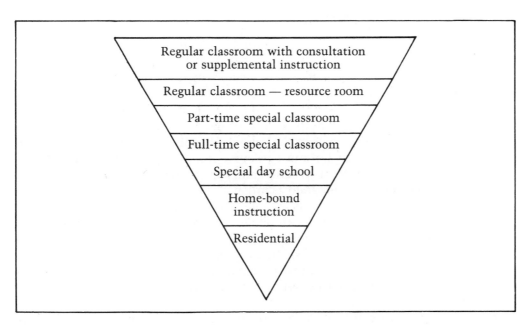

FIGURE 1.1
Continuum of placement alternatives from most to least integrated

placements shown at the lower end of the pyramid. Let's take a closer look at each of these alternatives.

Regular Classroom with Consultation and Supplemental Instruction   In this placement, the student remains in the regular classroom full-time and engages in all or nearly all class activities. The regular classroom teacher maintains primary responsibility for teaching the student but receives periodic consultation from a special educator. The classroom teacher and consultant work as a team, sharing information about the student's daily performance and unique needs. Together they determine the need for special adjustments or modifications that may be needed to insure appropriate student progress. The consultant may administer formal or informal tests, occasionally observe in the classroom, and help the classroom teacher identify and implement appropriate materials or methods for the student.

This alternative is most appropriate for students who can meet the majority of requirements for successful participation in a regular classroom. These students may require relatively minor adjustments in their programs through special forms of discipline, additional learning material, modifications in seating, changes in workload expectations, or special learning activities to help overcome specific weaknesses. It is important to note that relatively severe physical handicaps do not automatically require less integrated placements. For example, many blind or physically handicapped students can successfully participate in most regular classroom activities provided necessary adjustments are made.

Regular Classroom — Resource Room   In this alternative, the student receives the majority of instruction in the regular classroom and also receives help on a regularly scheduled basis in a resource room program. Depending upon the needs of the student, as little as thirty minutes a day or as much as half of the school day may be spent in the resource room. The main goal of most resource room programs is to provide students with intensive instruction and support while still keeping them in a regular education program as much as possible. Typical services offered by resource room programs include (1) daily remedial instruction in basic skills, such as reading, math, language, and fine and gross motor coordination; (2) intensive tutoring or small group instruction to help students pass content area subjects, such as geography, English composition, or history; and (3) intensive instruction in more effective ways of controlling behavior and interacting with peers and adults.

Part-time Special Classroom   In this plan, the student receives most instruction in a special classroom and limited instruction in the regular classroom. Both the regular teacher and the special class teacher share responsibility for providing instruction. This plan is often used for students who demonstrate considerable learning or behavior problems. Such students can be provided with large, concentrated doses of individualized instruction in the special class but still venture forth to participate in regular classroom activities in which they can experience success.

Full-time Special Class in a Regular School   For some students any participation in regular academic classrooms is too demanding. Because of extreme problems in coping with the academic or behavioral demands of the regular classroom, these students may require basic academic, social-emotional, and life skills instruction offered in a small group setting where they can progress at their own pace and receive highly individualized instruction. Some students in a full-time special class may participate with other children in routine nonacademic school activities such as art, recess, lunch, and extracurricular activities. They may take part in such activities as a separate class or join with regular classrooms.

Special Day School   A few students need comprehensive services that cannot always be provided in a regular school program. For example, students with multiple handicaps may need daily physical therapy to develop muscle strength and coordination. They may also need special adaptations in their environment to enable them to move about. Other students have severe emotional and behavioral problems that require supportive services from social workers, counselors, and music and art therapists, in addition to intensive academic instruction in a small group setting. Special day programs allow students to receive comprehensive services, such as counseling, physical and occupational therapy, special education, and vocational training, under one roof while still being able to live at home.

Home-bound Instruction   This type of service is typically offered to students with temporary or long-term chronic health problems who are confined to a bed or who have limited mobility. In some cases students with severe emotional problems may also receive home-bound instruction if no day school programs are available. If the health or emotional problem is relatively temporary, several months or less, the student may simply receive tutorial instruction with the goal of completing as much of the school curriculum as possible so that reentry into school will be facilitated. Students whose chronic health problems may prevent them from coming to school for prolonged periods may require more sophisticated forms of instruction. Two-way television systems or closed circuit television systems may be installed in homes and classrooms to enable students to take a relatively active part in class activities.

Residential or Hospital Program   For a few students almost total twenty-four hour care and programming is needed. Placement in a residential program or state or private hospital affords such care. The student both lives in and attends school at a facility away from his or her home. Ideally residential or hospital programs should offer a range of services in addition to special class instruction. These may include art, music, recreation, physical therapy, group and individual psychotherapy, vocational training, and instruction in daily living skills. However, because of lack of financial resources, some programs offer considerably less than an ideal program.

Since residential and hospital programs are so restrictive, they should be used only when community or regional services are inadequate to meet the needs of the student. Residential placement is often indicated when the student cannot be adequately cared for at home and therefore requires twenty-four hour supervision.

Exceptional Students: The Personal Side

Thus far our remarks have focused on the more traditional ways of introducing teachers and prospective teachers to exceptional students. While topics like definitions, numbers, and placement alternatives are necessary to achieve an overall understanding of the characteristics of exceptional students, they do little to tell what exceptional students are like face-to-face. Over the next few pages you will be introduced to some exceptional students who are in regular classrooms for significant portions of each school day. We hope that, by meeting these students and their teachers, you will gain a greater appreciation of the human qualities of exceptional students and the challenge they pose to their teachers.

A MENTALLY RETARDED STUDENT

Mentally retarded students vary in their degree of retardation and, of course, their academic and social skills. Until about twenty years ago, most educators believed that retarded students should be placed in self-contained classrooms. Now, most people believe that mildly retarded students can do well in regular classrooms as long as backup support is provided. The severely retarded students typically require more restrictive classroom placements. Let's meet Ed, a mildly retarded student.

ED

Ed is a ninth-grader who seems to enjoy his school program. He has a mixture of strengths and weaknesses. Tests of intellectual assessment place Ed in the mildly retarded range. He reads on a fourth-grade level and has almost mastered all math computation skills. Though he is slow to respond to questions and needs occasional reminders regarding his tasks, Ed is making a successful adjustment in school. He enjoys shop courses and almost any activity that calls for a "hands on" approach such as craftwork, lab demonstrations, and cooking.

Ed receives two periods a day of vocational training and participates in a regular general science and general math class. Ed goes to the special education resource room for two periods a day, where he receives intensive instruction to help meet the requirements of his math and science classes and where he also receives instruction in reading, filling out job forms, balancing a checking account, and other daily living skills.

Ed can understand and remember information best when it is presented in a concrete format. He has considerable difficulty understanding abstract concepts but can learn them when many concrete examples are provided. As long as teachers take a little extra time to introduce and review materials and ask him

Report card

General Math	D		
General Science	C		
Vocational Education	C		
Reading	C-		
Physical Education	B		
Art	B		

Math Teacher's Statement: I am just beginning to feel comfortable with Ed. At first I thought Ed would be a real troublemaker. I don't think I even talked to him for the first two weeks of class. I was so afraid he would act out in class that I gave him work that was far too easy. Now I am seeing that Ed is very teachable if I present things clearly and give him lots of reinforcement. I even know how to humor him to get him back to work when he is feeling discouraged. Ed enjoys working with other students, and I have started a buddy program for everyone. For brief periods each week, pairs of learners review basic facts or solve problems in teams. Ed enjoys this type of interaction and several students seem to enjoy having Ed as a partner. I hate to say this but the D Ed received was probably unfair. I think it reflected my initial discomfort with him and my inability to teach him.

FIGURE 1.2
Ed, a mentally retarded student

straightforward questions, Ed does quite well and fits in with his agemates. Like many of us, he becomes frustrated and discouraged when he doesn't understand what is being taught or when confronted with impatient peers or teachers.

Socially, Ed is a bit perplexing to some of his teachers. When frustrated or highly discouraged he sulks quietly and may ask to be left alone when offered help. However, some coaxing often gets him back to the task at hand. Ed is ignored by most of his classmates and accepted by one or two. Unfortunately, a few students make him the brunt of jokes and disparaging remarks, to which Ed sometimes reacts with shouting or crying. At home Ed is known as a helpful person who enjoys doing odd jobs for neighbors.

AN EMOTIONALLY DISTURBED STUDENT

Emotionally disturbed students range from extremely passive and withdrawn to extremely aggressive. As in the case of mentally retarded individuals, there are degrees of emotional disturbance ranging from mild to severe. A typical fear many adults have is that harm can be caused by saying the wrong thing to an emotionally disturbed student. This causes some teachers to feel reluctant to impose much-needed limits and expectations.

SARA

Two years ago Sara was in a self-contained special classroom all day long. Now a fourth-grader, Sara is making a good adjustment in a regular classroom. She can participate at an acceptable level in math, social studies discussions and science activities. She works in a resource room for an hour and a half each day where she receives intensive instruction in reading and, for a few minutes each day, discusses ways to control impulses and interact constructively with peers.

Sara's major difficulties are not in the area of academics, although she is reading one year below grade level. Instead, she has difficulty controlling her impulses. Sara becomes easily frustrated when she cannot quickly understand her work. She may yell out for help from the teacher or begin sobbing in quiet frustration. At other times she becomes overly aggressive, particularly in group games where she may lose self-control and hit others or grab

Teacher's Comment: At the beginning of the year I thought Sara didn't belong in my room. Having heard through the grapevine that Sara was very demanding, I was less than enthusiastic about her arrival in my class.

It is definitely quieter in my room when Sara is in the resource room, but I am beginning to see real progress. I have found that I can prevent many of her outbursts by spending a moment with her and getting her started on troublesome tasks. The resource teacher and I developed some management techniques that are effective, so Sara's self-control is improving. I complete her behavior chart each morning and afternoon, and this provides extra guidelines that Sara needs.

Right now I'm concerned about Sara's peer relationships. She has few positive interactions with her classmates. This is a goal I want to pursue with her resource teacher. I need a few ideas about how to get her working with groups in my classroom.

Daily behavior chart

Student ___*SARA*___   Date ___*TUESDAY*___

	Outstanding	Good	Needs improvement
1. Completed math, social studies, and science assignments on time.	X		
2. Worked independently. Didn't ask for help more than 3 times.	X		
3. Participated in recess without fighting.			X

FIGURE 1.3
Sara, an emotionally disturbed student

objects. Having to wait to take a turn, missing a word in an oral spelling test, not being first to line up, are typical situations that still cause Sara difficulty. Because she feels uncertain of her abilities, Sara seeks more than the usual amount of recognition and reassurance from teachers.

Because of her behavior problems, Sara has few friends in or out of school. She tends to be ignored by her classmates and made fun of by several students on the playground who know they can upset her through teasing.

A STUDENT WITH A LEARNING DISABILITY

The term "learning disabilities" refers to a wide range of academic, language, and math problems. Some students have specific academic problems in math or reading without any problems in oral language or gross and fine motor coordination. Others have a combination of problems in all the above-mentioned areas. Such students are often a source of frustration to parents and teachers. Because they often look, or speak, and reason in normal ways, their failure to learn or perform in specific academic areas is sometimes perceived as defiance or laziness. Scott is a fairly typical student with a learning disability.

SCOTT

Scott is a sixth-grader who spends nearly all of his time, except one hour a day, in the regular classroom. An alert youngster, Scott does

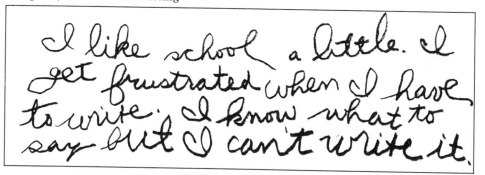

Sample of Scott's handwriting

I like school a little. I get frustrated when I have to write. I know what to say but I can't write it.

Teacher's Comment: Scott is a riddle to me. I can't understand how such a bright student can have so many difficulties. I enjoy the challenge of teaching Scott. He eagerly approaches science, math, and social studies as long as the lesson is discussion- or activity-oriented.

It does take extra effort to help Scott succeed. I have learned that it is better to highlight important passages in chapters for Scott to read instead of having him read the entire chapter. I also give him his test orally because he has such difficulty writing. I now understand that Scott isn't lazy at all. In fact, he seems to be a very bright youngster who is learning despite his problems. He seems to be very sensitive to people's feelings and reactions and definitely wants to be viewed as a capable person.

FIGURE 1.4
Scott, a student with a learning disability

well in math, social studies, and science. He speaks well, uses a good vocabulary for his age, and possesses an excellent fund of knowledge. He is athletic and relates easily to boys and girls in his classroom.

Scott learns well by listening, watching television or filmstrips, experimenting with concrete materials, or participating in discussions. His greatest difficulties are in reading and writing. Scott reads at about a third-grade level in a halting, word-by-word manner. He seems to forget words easily and confuses words that look alike. He has significant problems with spelling and writes in a near scrawl. Scott has almost always avoided written tasks, claiming that his hands and eyes get tired and tense. In earlier grades, Scott was sometimes accused of being rebellious. One teacher thought he was simply too lazy to write correctly. She accused him of being defiant on a number of occasions, which caused Scott to feel quite discouraged as a student.

Scott works in the resource room for an hour each day, where he receives intensive instruction in reading, spelling, and handwriting. In addition, the resource teacher helps Scott with his reading assignments in social studies and science.

A HEARING-IMPAIRED STUDENT

Hearing losses can range from mild to quite severe. The time of the onset of a hearing loss has much to do with an individual's ability to understand language and communicate orally. A loss at or near birth will likely restrict one's ability to hear and then accurately produce speech sounds. Children with mild hearing losses are able to learn to hear and speak quite effectively. Others, with more severe losses, may need to learn alternate forms of communication, such as sign language.

KEVIN

A fifth-grader, Kevin was born with a moderate hearing loss. Because the hearing loss occurred at birth, he was unable to hear and then reproduce sounds and words accurately. Fortunately, Kevin's hearing loss was detected before his first birthday. With the help of a hearing aid, which allows him to hear some tones a little more loudly, and a great deal of language stimulation provided by his mother, Kevin has learned to hear, understand, and use many words.

With the exception of an intensive hour of speech therapy provided each day, Kevin now participates in all aspects of his

"When I Grow Up"

> I like school a lot People in my classes are fun. Sometimes I get frustrated when they don't understand me. When I grow up I want to be a builder or an architect.

Teacher's Comment: Kevin has forced me to examine how I teach. He has taught me that many things cannot be taken for granted. In fact, I think I had a far greater adjustment to make than Kevin or any of his classmates. I had to remember to speak clearly and in complete sentences, to face Kevin whenever I wanted his attention, and to write assignments and directions on the chalkboard. These adjustments forced me to be much more organized in my teaching than I had ever been.

I made a few blunders with Kevin at the beginning of the year. I would give the entire class directions and then feel that Kevin was being unruly when he did not begin to work. I also became quite anxious whenever he spoke, since he slurred many words and spoke in a halting fashion. There were several occasions when I wanted to pass over him during oral reading. I soon realized that most of the students were far more patient than I was. Now I can understand how insensitive we can be and how we can do injury to the self-esteem of many students when we don't understand their special needs.

Although I'm sure I will make mistakes, I look forward to the challenge of teaching Kevin. He is a bright and highly motivated student and gives much to all of us.

FIGURE 1.5
Kevin, a hearing-impaired student

fifth-grade classroom. Kevin reads at a third-grade level and uses fewer words in his written and oral language than his peers. He still slurs some words and speaks in a somewhat garbled tone. However, he is improving in all areas. Kevin's speech therapist helps him to articulate more clearly and expand his general use of oral language.

Kevin has become an inspiration of sorts in his classroom. Many of the students have begun to appreciate his efforts to succeed in school. Kevin enjoys art and athletics and has several friends with whom he plays on a regular basis. Many students have learned to make a few simple but crucial adjustments to help Kevin feel included. For example, they look at him directly when speaking to him and check to make sure he has understood directions given to him. As in Ed's case, a few students treat Kevin as an oddity, either avoiding him entirely or mocking his speech patterns.

A Perspective on Mainstreaming

Mainstreaming is an often used and frequently misunderstood term. To some educators, mainstreaming means complete integration into the regular classroom. Others draw upon Deno's model (1970) and consider any form of integration with regular students as mainstreaming. We believe in the latter interpretation. That is, any attempt to integrate exceptional students in the regular classroom or in school activities is a form of mainstreaming. In this context, students may be mainstreamed for very brief periods or activities each day while others may be mainstreamed for longer periods. Thus, regular class placement is one form of mainstreaming, while placement in a part-time special classroom represents another form.

TOWARDS EFFECTIVE MAINSTREAMING

Although we believe that mainstreaming is appropriate for a large percentage of exceptional students, it must be approached with caution. Regular class placement needs to be accompanied by backup support to classroom teachers through consultants and extra help for exceptional students through special education teachers. Training in how best to approach exceptional students is certainly needed by current and future classroom teachers.

Support for mainstreaming is needed from the entire administrative staff from superintendent to building principal. It is commonly accepted that the building principal plays a significant part in shaping teachers' attitudes. Thus, whether teachers accept students with special needs grudgingly or in a truly accepting manner will depend on the degree of commitment, enthusiasm, and support provided by the administrator.

In addition to administrative support, ongoing communication between special education and regular classroom teachers is critical. These individuals should meet on a regular basis to review objectives and student progress. Indeed, a major pitfall of the resource room and part-time special class placement is the failure of such communication because of the busy schedules of all teachers involved. When communication breaks down or never develops, the regular classroom teacher may become confused about the nature and value of the services the student receives in the special education room. Similarly, the special education teacher may not be able to tell whether the student is applying newly learned skills in the regular classroom. Despite these potential communication problems, the resource room plan is a widely used option for delivery of service because students may receive relatively intense instruction in problem areas but still profit from the experiences a regular class provides.

PROS AND CONS OF MAINSTREAMING

As long as appropriate support is provided, mainstreaming has several notable advantages for both exceptional and nonexceptional students.

For the exceptional student, the stimulation provided by the regular classroom can be of great benefit. Expectations for learning may be higher than in special education classrooms, thus offering students more opportunities and greater challenges to learn important academic and social skills. When the majority of students function effectively, they provide models for appropriate social, academic and personal behavior. Being placed in a regular classroom for as much of the school day as possible may also help exceptional students to avoid the stigma of being different as a result of being placed in a segregated special class or special school.

There are clear advantages for nonexceptional students as well. These students can learn realistic and constructive ways of interacting with exceptional students. They can also appreciate the unique abilities and needs of their exceptional classmates and perhaps become more caring, accepting individuals in the process. Certainly, learning how to offer help when it is needed and learning that exceptional individuals can do many things well are lessons that will have lasting value.

The many advantages should not blind us to the potential disadvantages of mainstreaming. The classroom teacher must be willing to make special adjustments so that exceptional students can experience success. Simply placing an exceptional student in a regular classroom offers no guarantee that the student will be accepted by his or her peers or be well educated by the teacher. Teaching exceptional students requires extra effort on the part of the classroom teacher. With the ever-growing number of duties that classroom teachers must shoulder, it is no wonder that some may shudder at the thought of having to work with exceptional students as well.

There is also a tendency to be overzealous about the advantages of regular class placement. The authors have learned of some administrators who take pride in the fact that nearly all of their exceptional students are in regular classrooms, sometimes at the expense of the mental health of the teacher and the needs of all of the students! Some exceptional students, who are highly disruptive and whose academic skills are very low, may be an unreasonable drain on the resources of regular classroom teachers and still not get the help they need. If the student is not learning and the teacher is suffering, what possible good can come out of such a placement? In these cases, teachers and administrators should realize that it may be in the best interest of the student to be placed in a less integrated arrangement, such as a part-time or full-time special classroom.

The point that we must all remember when it comes to mainstreaming is that a range of placements should be available for students. While the regular classroom is a beneficial placement for many students, it may be unable to provide other students with the degree of support and structure that is needed to promote growth. In these cases, such a placement is not in the best interests of the student.

Summary

In this chapter we have presented brief thumbnail descriptions of each category of exceptionality, reviewed the statistics regarding the prevalence of exceptional students, discussed common placement alternatives, introduced you to several exceptional students who are in regular classrooms, and examined some considerations regarding mainstreaming. Major points that were considered are as follows.

1. Exceptional students constitute a diverse group. Included are those who are mentally retarded, emotionally disturbed, learning disabled, speech impaired, hearing impaired, visually impaired, physically and health impaired, and gifted and talented.

2. Exceptional students differ from their "normal" peers to the extent that they require special education services to help them achieve their full potential.

3. It is difficult to pinpoint exactly what percentage of all students are exceptional, but a modest estimate is 12–15%.

4. Students who are mentally retarded, emotionally disturbed, learning disabled, and speech impaired constitute the largest proportion of exceptional learners.

5. A variety of special education placement alternatives exist for exceptional students. Every school district must make available a range of special education placement alternatives, ranging from full-time placement in a regular classroom to placement in a private or hospital facility.

6. Mainstreaming refers to full-time or part-time placement in a regular classroom.

7. Simply placing an exceptional student in a regular classroom is no guarantee that the student will be accepted by his or her classmates or make good academic progress. Effective mainstreaming requires that support and training be given to classroom teachers and that teachers, administrators, and special educators communicate effectively with one another.

8. Regular class placement often provides exceptional students with increased expectations for academic and social performance as well as constructive role models.

9. Regular class placement of exceptional students may require more work on the part of the classroom teacher.

10. Not all exceptional students should be mainstreamed. Some students have such severe learning or behavior disorders that they may require intensive supervision and instruction.

Activities

1. Visit an elementary or secondary school to determine the type of special education placement alternatives that are used. Try to observe one or two students in each setting to determine how they are similar to and different from what you would consider to be average students.

2. Take an informal poll of prospective teachers. Using the categories and descriptions in Table 1 ask them which categories of students they would feel comfortable teaching in a regular classroom and which categories they believe can be placed successfully in such a setting.

Study Questions

1. List and define briefly each category of exceptionality.

2. Approximately what percentage of school-aged students are exceptional?

3. Define what is meant by a continuum of special education placement alternatives.

4. What general kinds of support should be provided to make mainstreaming work?

5. List several advantages and disadvantages of placing exceptional students in regular classrooms.

Questions for Further Thought

1. Think of your own elementary and secondary school experiences. Can you recall any exceptional students from these settings? Focus on one or two of these individuals. What were their strengths? What adjustments needed to be made for these students? How did other students feel about them?

2. As a prospective teacher, list your concerns about placing exceptional students in your classroom.

Additional Resources

BOOKS

Blackhurst, A. E., and Berdine, W. H. (Eds.). *An introduction to special education.* Boston: Little, Brown and Company, 1981.

Deno, E. *Instructional alternatives for exceptional children.* Reston, Virginia: Council for Exceptional Children, 1973.

Chapter 2

The Mandate:

Attitudes and

Legal Considerations

The idea of educating exceptional students in regular classrooms did not emerge in isolation from other social changes. Rather, it is a result of a gradual but fundamental shift in public attitudes towards people who differ from the majority in terms of race, religion, political beliefs or educational needs. The result of this shift in attitudes is a tendency to reject programs that segregate individuals in favor of programs that bring individuals into the political, economic, social, and educational mainstream. In this chapter we will trace the general shift in attitudes towards exceptional individuals and then examine Public Law 94-142, which guarantees a free and appropriate education for all exceptional individuals except the gifted and talented.

Attitudes Towards Exceptional Individuals

The status of exceptional individuals in society has evolved throughout history. In general, many such individuals were met by a combination of superstition and harsh treatment during early periods. These harsh and punitive practices have given way to more enlightened approaches (Hewett and Forness, 1974). Yet even today the status of exceptional individuals is not entirely secure. Difficult economic conditions and reductions in government expenditures may threaten some of the educational and social gains secured during the 1970s.

SURVIVAL AND SUPERSTITION

In primitive societies many people who had physical and sensory handicaps were plagued less by attitudes of others than by the all-consuming task of day-to-day survival. Concern with finding food, shelter, and protection from the elements probably left little if any time to care for those who were blind, physically disabled, or severely retarded. Thus, individuals with severe sensory, physical, or mental disabilities either died shortly after birth or rarely survived past childhood.

As civilization developed, survival became less of an issue. Early Greek and Roman civilizations tended to view exceptional individuals with a mixture of superstition and ruthlessness. In both Sparta and Athens, infanticide was practiced regularly. Fathers had the right to accept or abandon newborn infants. If deformed, such infants could be abandoned or even thrown from a cliff to certain death. Individuals with what is now known as epilepsy, mental retardation, and emotional illness were believed to be possessed by demons and evil spirits suffering the wrath of the gods, or blessed with special powers.

Superstition and mistreatment continued to plague the lives of many exceptional individuals throughout the Middle Ages and into the sixteenth and seventeenth centuries. Those who appeared deformed or who acted in strange ways were considered bewitched or under the spell of the devil. Since contemporary religious beliefs considered humans to be involved in a continuous struggle between good and evil, some exceptional individuals were thought to be suffering the consequences of evil behavior or conspiracy with the devil. Severe beatings, torture, and other forms of punishment were often administered by religious officials who attempted to exorcise evil spirits while setting an example for others should they consider succumbing to unconventional behavior.

HUMANE ATTITUDES AND TREATMENT

A more favorable trend in attitudes and treatment of exceptional individuals emerged in the eighteenth and nineteenth centuries. Superstitious views towards mental illness, blindness, mental retardation, deafness, and physical deformities gradually gave way to a more scientific perspective. As beliefs changed, so did treatment procedures. Extreme punishment, exorcisms, and other mistreatment in the name of religion gave way to attempts to provide basic custodial care in institutions. In some cases, basic education programs were established to help individuals learn to clothe and feed themselves and engage in basic living tasks.

The advancement of attitudes and treatment of exceptional individuals was stimulated by the contributions of a number of individuals. Jean-Marc Gaspard Itard, a French physician, became famous for his work with Victor, an abandoned, severely retarded boy who appeared to have been surviving on his own in the forest (Itard, 1932). Itard worked intensively with Victor between 1801 and 1806 and developed many methods for teaching retarded children, some of which are still in use today. Although Victor required custodial care until his death, Itard demonstrated to the medical and educational world that even severely retarded individuals could be taught basic skills to improve the quality of their everyday lives.

Dorothea Dix was a major force behind the reforms in institutions for the mentally ill in the United States. She made the public aware of the deplorable living conditions of mentally ill people housed in institutions. Her efforts helped to create thirty-two new hospitals between 1841 and 1881 and initiated an era of humane concern for the mentally ill. Thomas Gallaudet founded the first school for the deaf in Hartford, Connecticut, in 1817. Louis Braille opened new potentials for blind people by developing and refining what was to become a universally accepted tactile system for enabling blind people to read and write. A physician, Samuel Howe, established the Perkins School for the Blind in Watertown, Massachusetts, in 1842. Here new methods and techniques for blind and deaf-blind individuals were developed, refined, and shared with other interested educators. Anne Sullivan, a graduate of the Perkins School, taught Helen Keller, a blind, deaf, and mute child to communicate, a skill once thought impossible for people like Helen. Helen Keller eventually graduated from college, wrote several books, and served as a living testament to the untapped potential of many exceptional individuals. Edouard Seguin, a student of Itard, worked with Howe, Gallaudet, and other American educators to advance many of the techniques originated by Itard.

The early pioneers and their many dedicated but unsung colleagues helped shape a more humane approach to the treatment of exceptional individuals, an approach that set the stage for many advancements in the current century.

SEGREGATED PUBLIC EDUCATION

In the late 1800s and early 1900s exceptional individuals were gradually moved closer towards society's mainstream. Public school classes for the moderately retarded, the deaf, the blind, the hard of hearing, the emotionally disturbed, and the physically handicapped were established in larger cities. In less populated areas, regional or state schools were established for many of these individuals. The establishment of these services indicated the public's recognition of the need to provide education, not merely custodial care, for many exceptional individuals.

By the 1950s public school classes for the moderately retarded and other exceptional students were part of the educational establishment in most cities and towns. In most instances, the tendency was clearly towards segregating children into self-contained classrooms or special schools with little or no opportunity for interaction with their normal agemates.

Until about twenty-five years ago, students with milder forms of exceptionality received few or no special education services. Instead, they were often considered to be lazy, unmotivated, slow, or incorrigible and were passed along in regular classrooms from grade to grade. Many dropped out of school and some were expelled because of antisocial behavior. As public awareness increased, many of these students were found to have milder forms of emotional disturbance, mental retardation, or learning disabilities. The treatment model already established for students with moderate to severe needs was simply extended. Students with milder needs were often removed from their regular classes and placed into segregated self-contained classrooms patterned after those developed for more severely impaired students.

TOWARDS INTEGRATION

Although it can be argued that attitudes towards exceptional individuals have become more humane, there remains a tendency to exclude some students from regular school opportunities. Of particular concern has been the placement of students with milder forms of mental retardation, emotional disturbance, physical handicaps, and other problems into segregated special education classrooms or special schools created for exceptional students. These segregated placements came under severe attack by many special educators during the late 1960s and early 1970s (Dunn, 1968; Christopolos and Renz, 1969; Lilly, 1971). A major concern expressed by critics was that special class placement on a full-time basis was inappropriate for many students whose needs required only slight or moderate adjustments. Typical criticisms of restrictive placements included the following:

1. Many students with mild forms of handicaps showed greater academic growth in regular classrooms than in self-contained classrooms. Apparently, the regular classroom provided greater expectations and stimulation for some handicapped learners than self-contained classrooms.

2. The self-concept of some exceptional students was adversely affected by placement in self-contained classes. For some students, placement in self-contained classes created feelings of being isolated, different from, and less competent than their regular classroom peers.

3. Disproportionate numbers of Black, Mexican-American, Native American, and other minority-group students were placed in self-contained classes for the mentally retarded. Some critics argued that traditional intelligence tests were culturally biased against Blacks, Mexican-Americans, and other minority groups and resulted in the misplacement of large numbers of students into special classes.

4. Placement into self-contained classes sometimes resulted in a loss of educational opportunities in areas such as art, music, physical education, home economics, and industrial/vocational education. In many instances, the special education teacher was left to his or her own devices in offering instruction in these areas.

5. Students in self-contained classes lost contact with well-functioning peers who served as positive role models. For example, it was argued that placing students with emotional and behavioral problems in one classroom all day long provided too many examples of inappropriate behavior and attitudes which the students could model.

6. Students in regular classrooms were denied a unique opportunity to learn, by firsthand experience, how to get along with, accept, and understand their handicapped peers. Indeed, it was suggested that since many handicapped and nonhandicapped live and work side-by-side in adult society, they should not be segregated in school.

AN EMERGING VIEWPOINT

The critics of special class placement attacked the assumption that being exceptional automatically warranted a separate and special education. They urged their colleagues to consider the many ways in which exceptional students are similar to their nonexceptional counterparts. Nearly all students want to feel competent, experience success, be accepted by peers, make a contribution to the academic and social life of the classroom, and grow in their abilities to cope with the demands of everyday living. Exceptional students are no different in this respect. They need to learn the same basic academic, social, and gross and fine motor skills as their counterparts. While exceptional students are undoubtedly different in some ways, many of the social, emotional, and academic goals are quite similar to those established for all students.

This recent viewpoint, that the goals for educating many exceptional students are similar or identical to the goals for educating all students, is gaining recognition and is contributing to the belief that many exceptional students can receive a good part of their daily instruction in regular classrooms. It does not, however, disregard the special needs that exceptional students have. Some may need intensive instruction in certain academic, social, behavioral and gross and fine motor skills. Others may need special materials or apparatus, such as magnifying glasses, large-print books, or hearing aids to help them succeed in the curriculum of the regular classroom. Many materials and some types of individualized instruction can often be provided in the regular classroom by teachers or support personnel. Alternatively, students may leave the regular classroom for brief periods during the day to receive instruction. Special needs are not being neglected but are being provided for, increasingly, in the context of regular class placements.

The Legal Mandate

The public's general belief in the rights and basic worth of exceptional individuals has resulted in several major pieces of federal legislation. An early bill, signed by President Kennedy in 1963, provided federal dollars to train teachers and develop special materials for exceptional students. Since 1963, federal support has increased: some $875 million were appropriated to states in 1980 to help support public school programs for exceptional students. Moreover, $58 million were provided in 1981 to universities to train teachers and specialists to work with exceptional students. Although there has been a dramatic increase in federal aid for the education of exceptional students, it is doubtful that such increases will continue during the first part of the 1980s. Indeed, as the United States enters an era of fiscal conservatism, it is likely that reductions in federal aid will occur, and some services to exceptional students may be reduced.

During the 1960s and 1970s, nearly every state legislature mandated some educational services for exceptional children. Each state established its own definitions as to which exceptional students were eligible for services and then developed guidelines for local districts to follow. However, despite the provision of these state mandates, many exceptional students were not receiving needed services.

An all-out effort to guarantee rights and services to exceptional individuals was made during the mid-1970s with the passage of two pieces of major legislation, Section 504 of The Rehabilitation Act of 1973 and PL 94-142, The Education For All Handicapped Children Act. All states must now provide the services and assure the rights guaranteed by these two laws.

Section 504 guarantees certain civil rights to handicapped individuals. Among these are the following:

1. All school-age children are entitled to a free and appropriate public education.

2. All new public facilities must be accessible to handicapped people.

3. Discrimination in employment, compensation, job assignments, admission into institutions of higher education, or receipt of health, welfare, or social services is prohibited.

In a nutshell, Section 504 strictly forbids discrimination that would erect or maintain barriers to self-sufficiency. The establishment of barrier-free ramps, elevators, public telephones, and toilets; the appearance of handicapped individuals in the workplace; and the provision of needed social service and training programs can be largely attributed to Section 504.

The mechanics for providing a free and appropriate education were formally established in 1975 when Congress passed PL 94-142, The Education for All Handicapped Children Act. This act guarantees appropriate special education and supportive services, such as speech therapy and adaptive physical education, to all exceptional students (except the gifted) between the ages of 3 and 21. In some states it is not required that exceptional children under 5 years of age receive special education services. In these states the federal requirement to provide services for 3- and 4-year-old children does not apply. The sections of this act that bear most directly on the role and function of you, the prospective regular classroom teacher, are reviewed in this section.

THE LEAST RESTRICTIVE ENVIRONMENT

The Least Restrictive Environment section of PL 94-142, section 121a. 550(b), crystalizes the trend towards including exceptional students in local schools and, where possible, in regular classrooms.

> Each public agency shall insure:
>
> 1. That to the maximum extent appropriate, handicapped children, including children in public or private institutions or other care facilities, are educated with children who are not handicapped, and
>
> 2. That special classes, separate schooling or other removal of handicapped children from the regular educational environment occurs only when the nature or severity of the handicap is such that education in regular classes with the use of supplementary aids and services cannot be achieved satisfactorily.

Be careful to note that the law does not require that all exceptional students be placed in regular classrooms. This is a common misunderstanding that, if you recall, was voiced by some of Jan Roberts's colleagues and led to many apprehensive feelings. Instead, exceptional students should be educated in regular classrooms whenever such a placement is beneficial to the student. More restrictive placements, such as self-contained classrooms, should be used only when satisfactory progress cannot be achieved in the regular classroom. But "least restrictive" does not always mean "least segregated." Students with severe or unusual needs may find a regular classroom more restrictive than a special classroom that can better meet their needs. The idea behind the Least Restrictive Environment provision is to keep students in settings that are as normal as possible while still providing needed special education services. In this light, a regular classroom might be the least restrictive environment for one student while a special day school in the community may be the least restrictive environment for another student who needs very intensive instruction and the services of a variety of professionals (Schifani, Anderson, and Odle, 1980).

The effect of the Least Restrictive Environment provision is far-reaching. First, it requires each school district to make available a continuum of alternatives for special education placement. These alternatives were outlined in Chapter One. Second, it places regular classroom teachers in a more central position regarding the education of exceptional students and requires more systematic cooperation and interaction between regular classroom and special education teachers. Finally, simply being exceptional can no longer be reason enough to be removed from a regular classroom program.

THE PUPIL EVALUATION TEAM

Not long ago most critical decisions about what services exceptional students were to receive and what settings they would be placed in were made by building principals, superintendents, or other administrators, who often acted unilaterally. Parents and teachers were given little, if any, say in the decision-making process. The process of making decisions regarding the placement and services for exceptional students has been revolutionized by PL 94-142. Now, decisions must be made by a team, which must include an administrator, a regular or special classroom teacher, the parent(s) or guardian of the student, and, in some cases, the student. In some cases many other individuals, such as guidance counselors and psychological examiners, also serve on these teams. The teams operate under a number of titles, including Pupil Evaluation Teams, Educational Assessment Teams, Child Study Teams, Administrative Placement and Review Teams and Student Evaluation Teams. In this text we will use the term "Pupil Evaluation Team."

The function of the Pupil Evaluation Team is to make decisions regarding the education of each exceptional student. Three critical tasks usually consume the major portion of time of Pupil Evaluation Teams.

1. *Determining eligibility for services.* Students who may need special education services are referred to the Pupil Evaluation Team by classroom teachers, parents, or administrators. The team examines the referral and other test information gathered and then determines whether the student qualifies for special education services. To qualify for special education services, a student must show evidence of a particular handicapping condition such as mental retardation, emotional disturbance, learning disabilities, speech impairments, vision or hearing disorders, or physical disabilities. (More thorough descriptions and definitions of each of these handicapping conditions will be discussed in later chapters.)

2. *Development of an individualized education program.* Once it has been determined that a student qualifies for special education ser-

A pupil evaluation team. Parents, teachers, and administrators — and sometimes students themselves — plan the educational program for each exceptional student.

vices, the specific needs of the student must be determined and a plan for meeting the student's needs must be written. Included in this Individualized Education Program must be a description of the particular services the student is to receive and the type of setting in which the student will be placed.

3. *Annual review.* At least once a year the student's progress must be reviewed to determine whether the student is still eligible for services and to make sure that the student is making adequate progress. Another purpose for conducting annual reviews is to guard against locking students into restrictive placements, such as full-time self-contained classrooms, for any longer than is absolutely necessary.

Although it may often take more time for a team to make decisions, the team approach is often superior to the unilateral approach used in the recent past. Ideally teachers, parents, specialists, and administrators can share insights and expertise to make key decisions that reflect the best interests of the student.

THE INDIVIDUALIZED EDUCATION PROGRAM

PL 94-142 requires that an Individualized Education Program (IEP) be developed for every handicapped student. Developed by the Pupil Evaluation Team, the IEP is a written statement of the unique needs and special education services the student is to receive. While the specific items in IEPs may vary from state to state and from school district to school district, IEPs must have the following common components:

1. *Present level of educational performance.* The student's present level of educational performance is described by a summary of relevant test scores, classroom work samples, and teacher observations. Student strengths and weaknesses are derived from the assessment information on present levels of performance.

2. *Annual goals.* Academic, social, behavioral, language, motor, and other listed weaknesses and some strengths are converted into annual program goals for the student. These goals indicate the areas to be addressed by the special education program.

3. *Short-term objectives.* Annual goals are broken down into specific short-term objectives, which are usually written in behavioral terms. Since these objectives are often difficult to develop in a Pupil Evaluation Team meeting, one or more teachers who work closely with the student may be assigned the responsibility of writing these specific objectives. In many school districts, specific objectives are written for each new marking period or grading period. These objectives are stepping-stones towards the accomplishment of annual goals.

4. *Services.* The nature and amount of special education services and aids the student is to receive must be described (e.g., three twenty-minute sessions a week of articulation therapy; thirty minutes a day of instruction to increase sight vocabulary and word recognition skills, mobility training). In addition, the setting where the student is to receive the services as well as persons responsible for delivering the services must be listed.

5. *Evaluation.* Both procedures and timetables for evaluating the effectiveness of the special education services are specified. As mentioned previously, the IEP must be reviewed at least annually.

Other required information includes a statement regarding the expected length of time the special education services will be needed, the extent to which the student will engage in regular classroom activities, and assurances that the placement is consistent with the least restrictive environment provision. Figure 2.1 shows what a completed form might look like.

Though time-consuming to develop, the Individualized Education Program represents a crucial component of a student's special education

FIGURE 2.1
A completed IEP form

Individual Education Program

Student	PET Members
Name: Bob J.	
Grade: 5	Mr. Jones, Principal
School: Ingalls Middle	Mrs. J, parent
Current placement: Regular Class	Ms. Howard, 6th grade teacher
Age: 12 yrs. 3 months	Mr. Lennon, Resource teacher

Present level of educational functioning	Annual goal	Instructional objectives	Evaluation criteria
Math *Strengths* Bob is on grade level and is making good progress in all areas. He enjoys math. *Weaknesses* None **Reading** *Strengths* Based on Spache Diagnostic Reading Scales (administered 1/6/82) Bob read level 2^2 passages with 90% accuracy in word recognition and 80% accuracy in comprehension. Bob enjoys reading adventure and sports stories if the material is at or below third-grade level. *Weaknesses* Reads about 3½ years below grade level. Reads slowly, word by word. Does not consistently use sounds or blends to decode new words.	1. Increase all aspects of reading performance to mastery at the third-grade level.	1.1. Bob will read level 3^2 passages with at least 90% accuracy and 80% comprehension. 1.2. Bob will orally read third-grade level passages at a rate of at least 100 correct words per minute. 1.3. When presented with new third-grade level words, Bob will accurately use initial, medial and final sounds and blends to decode words at least 80% of the time.	Spache Diagnostic Reading Scales will be readministered by resource teacher in May. Teacher will test at the end of each new story. Weekly timed tests will be administered by resource teacher.

Present level of educational functioning	Annual goal	Instructional objectives	Evaluation criteria

Science and Social Studies

Strengths

Participates actively in class discussions.
Understands concepts when presented orally or when demonstrated.

Weaknesses

Completes only about half of written assignments and tests because of low reading skills.	2. Increase completion of written work and tests in science and social studies.	2.1. Complete an average of 90% of all modified science and social studies assignments with at least 75% accuracy.	Classroom teacher will maintain daily record of assignments completed.
		2.2. Obtain a test score average of at least 80% in science and social studies.	Classroom teacher will use teacher-made criterion tests at the end of each unit. Tests modified to suit reading level or given orally.

Spelling and Language Arts

Strengths

Can spell simple words having regular patterns (e.g. hall, tall, ring, sing, etc.)
Enjoys listening to and composing stories.

Weaknesses

Using a fourth-grade level spelling book, has an average weekly test score of six words correct out of fifteen. Misspells almost a third of words in themes and other written assignments.	3. Increase overall spelling skills.	3.1. Using grade level words, Bob will correctly spell at least twelve of fifteen words on weekly tests.	Weekly spelling test will be administered from fourth-grade text.
		3.2. By using a dictionary and increasing his spelling ability, Bob will reduce spelling errors to less than 10% per theme.	Classroom teacher will analyze errors on themes.

FIGURE 2.1 (Continued)

Present level of educational functioning	Annual goal	Instructional objectives	Evaluation criteria
Social Behavior *Strengths* Enjoys doing chores for teachers. Works with sustained attention when receiving one-to-one instruction.			
Weaknesses			
Needs continual reassurance and reminders to finish written seatwork tasks.	4. Increase ability to work independently.	4.1. Bob will complete seatwork activities with no more than two reminders each period.	Classroom teacher will keep daily frequency count of out of seat behavior during seatwork periods.
		4.2. Bob will complete a thirty-minute seatwork period without getting out of his seat more than once.	Classroom teacher will keep daily frequency count of reminders issued during seatwork.
When frustrated with spelling or reading work, gets tense and says "I hate this; I don't want to do it anymore." May also make self-deprecating statements such as "I'm stupid."	5. Improve selfconcept and ability to cope with frustration.	5.1. When frustrated, Bob will select and use appropriate coping measures such as asking for help, breathing deeply, or reminding himself to relax at least 80% of the time.	Classroom teacher will observe.
Often pushes, yells at, or makes derogatory comments about others, particularly when they make mistakes in playground or gym activities.		5.2. Bob will decrease self-deprecating statements to no more than two per week and, when asked, will verbalize positive aspects of his work or behavior at least 90% of the time.	Classroom teacher will observe.
	6. Increase positive interpersonal behavior with peers.	6.1. Bob will decrease pushing, yelling at, or making derogatory comments about others to less than two per week.	Classroom teacher will observe.

Present level of educational functioning	Annual goal	Instructional objectives	Evaluation criteria
		6.2. When asked, Bob will describe and demonstrate at least one constructive way to offer encouragement, resolve a dispute, and ask to play in a game.	Discussion and role-playing will be conducted by resource teacher.
		6.3. During playground and game activities, Bob will offer encouragement and praise to other students at least once each day.	Classroom teacher will observe.

Educational Services to be provided	Date initiated	Duration of service	Persons responsible
Regular classroom			
Science and Social Studies assignments will be modified to increase Bob's chances for success. Emphasis will be placed on oral tests and modified reading assignments. Frequency counts of work completed, out-of-seat behavior, and other relevant behaviors will be maintained. Bob will receive classroom privileges (e.g., time to listen to tape recorder) for in-seat behavior and appropriate playground behavior. A good behavior contract will be used.	1/16/82	6/1/82	Ms. Howard with weekly consultation from Mr. Lennon.
Resource room			
Bob will receive one hour a day of instruction in the resource room. Emphasis will be placed on improving reading, spelling, independent work habits, self-concept, peer interaction, and the ability to cope with frustration. Good-behavior contracts will be reviewed each day.	1/16/82	6/1/82	Mr. Lennon with Ms. Howard helping Bob to apply newly learned special and academic skills in the regular classroom.
Home—school coordination			
Mrs. J. will make Bob's weekly allowance and other special privileges contingent upon improved academic and social behavior.	1/23/82	6/1/82	Mrs. J. will implement a weekly allowance program from Mr. Lennon.

FIGURE 2.1 (Continued)

Justification for educational placement

1. It is believed that Bob can
   succeed in most regular class
   assignments provided the
   work and evaluation procedures
   are adjusted to his strengths.

2. Removal from class for one hour
   a day is necessary to provide
   intensive individual and small
   group instruction in academic
   and social-behavioral areas.

I have had the opportunity to participate in the Pupil Evaluation Team and to help develop this Individual Education Program.
   I agree with this program. (   )
   I disagree with this program. (   )

Parent's signature _____

---

program. Because goals, objectives, and services the student is to receive are put into writing, parents can be better informed about their child's program. For example, it is no longer sufficient to say a student will receive "special help" or "special education" or will be placed in a "resource program." These terms convey no information at all regarding the specific kinds of assistance the student is to receive. Instead, the kinds of help the student is to receive must be spelled out in detail. Teachers and students can also benefit from clearly written IEPs since they provide a concrete set of goals and methods to follow, thus helping to insure that a student's specific educational needs are addressed each day.

The role of the regular classroom teacher in the development of the Individualized Education Program is a critical one, particularly if the student is in the regular classroom for significant portions of the school day. The teacher, working daily with a student, is in an excellent position to help determine that student's present level of educational performance in all areas. Also, the classroom teacher and special educator must work together to develop, implement, and evaluate specific teaching objectives and methods. Although the actual writing of the IEP is typically up to special educators (Price and Goodman, 1980), the classroom teacher should take an active role in all aspects of the IEP.

DUE PROCESS FOR PARENTS AND STUDENTS

Just as PL 94-142 gives parents and guardians a right to participate on the Pupil Evaluation Team, it also ensures their right to approve or reject any or all parts of the IEP. In the great majority of cases, there is little or no parental disagreement. When initial disagreements do occur, they can usually be attributed to reasons such as the following. (1) The parent may believe that insufficient special education services are being recommended. (2) The parent may believe that an overly restrictive setting has been selected (e.g., a self-contained special class). (3) The parent may be unsure or confused regarding the value of the IEP. (4) The parent may reject the suggestion that any special education services whatsoever are needed. Parents may even refuse to authorize any special testing to determine whether their child has needs that require special education services.

Such disagreements can often be resolved if parents and school personnel discuss their concerns in a spirit of respect, cooperation, and compromise. In a limited number of cases, however, disagreements over the need for services, placement, or the exact nature of the services may persist. A sequence of procedures exists to help resolve these disagreements. Although specific procedures vary from state to state, the disagreement is usually reviewed by an independent hearing officer identified by the state department of education and selected by both parents and school officials. The hearing official reviews testimony presented by the school and the parents and then offers a nonbinding ruling. If the parents wish to contest the ruling, an appeal may be filed and a second review conducted by a different hearing officer appointed by the state department of education. Finally, the case may be taken to the courts for a legal ruling. It should be mentioned that many services for exceptional children have been won by parents or parent organizations willing to bring disputes concerning the adequacy of special education services or practices to the attention of the courts.

HOW DO CLASSROOM TEACHERS REACT TO THE LEGAL MANDATE?

There is little doubt that PL 94-142 has influenced profoundly the role of the regular classroom teacher. Many teachers serve on Pupil Evaluation Teams, instruct exceptional students in the regular classroom, and consult regularly with specialists who provide medical, recreational, psychological, and other services. It is reasonable to wonder how teachers react to these responsibilities.

In general, the response has been cautious but supportive. For example, in 1978 the National Education Association fully endorsed the concept of the least restrictive environment but asserted the need for ample support and training for classroom teachers. In her article "A Classroom Teacher Looks at Mainstreaming," Ellen Kavanaugh (1977) insists that classroom teachers need adequate materials, training and support personnel if exceptional students are to receive appropriate instruction in the regular classroom. She also warns that care must be taken to place such students in classrooms where teachers are able to individualize instruction.

The concerns expressed by Kavanaugh appear to be reflected in several studies about teachers' attitudes towards integrating exceptional students. Hudson (1979) surveyed elementary teachers in one region and found that significant numbers of teachers did not support the placement of handicapped students in regular classrooms. Many of these teachers reported little access to consultation and other services to assist in the process of integrating such students. Working with a different sample of teachers, Graham (1980) found generally positive attitudes towards integration. The teachers in Graham's study reported adequate assistance and support from resource teachers who assisted them on a regular basis.

Assistance and support may not go far enough to ensure positive attitudes of classroom teachers. Specific training in special education is also essential. Stephens and Braun (1980) found that regular classroom teachers' willingness to integrate exceptional students increased as the number of special education courses they took increased. Many school districts have developed in-service training programs to help teachers and administrators develop necessary skills in the areas of understanding and providing for the needs of exceptional students. Universities and colleges are now requiring training in special education for all elementary and secondary education majors. In fifteen states, undergraduate education majors are mandated by state legislatures to take course work in special education and, as of 1980, eleven more states were considering such a mandate (Smith and Schneider, 1980).

Towards a Point of View

As we consider the challenge and legal mandate of teaching exceptional students in regular elementary and secondary classrooms, it may prove helpful to share several beliefs we hold regarding how to best approach exceptional students. These beliefs have been shaped by our own experiences as teachers of exceptional students and, more recently, as consultants to regular classroom teachers who are faced with the responsibility of teaching exceptional students.

THE USE OF LABELS

Many college students and professional educators react strongly to the practice of labeling and categorizing students as mentally retarded, emotionally disturbed, or learning disabled. An often cited argument against the use of labels is that they create anxiety and negative expectations in the minds of some teachers and administrators (Gillung and Rucker,

1977). Jan Roberts, the teacher you met at the beginning of Chapter 1, suffered considerable anxiety when told, rather bluntly, that she would have one mentally retarded and one emotionally disturbed student in her classroom. Another argument is that labels provide only minimal amounts of information to the teacher regarding what special adjustments need to be made for an individual. Indeed, it can be said that there is as much variation in learning needs and styles among students who are classified as "learning disabled," for example, as there is among so-called normal or average students.

Despite the strong arguments against their use, labels are probably here to stay, because they are required for administrative purposes. Most special education programs receive state and federal support that is based on the number of exceptional students they serve. State and federal regulations require districts to identify by category the number of students they serve. Thus, local school districts are compelled to define, identify and categorize students for administrative purposes. Such requirements assure the continued use of labels despite the fact that many professionals would be pleased to do away with them.

Our position on the use of labels is a rather practical one. Labels seem to be here to stay and will likely be used by administrators and some teachers to categorize students for administrative requirements. However, we urge restraint in the use of labels to describe individual students. When individuals are concerned, it is far more practical and ethical to describe students in terms of how they learn and behave, rather than to assume that a label can fairly and accurately describe their abilities and needs.

TEACHING EXCEPTIONAL STUDENTS — A MASTERY VIEWPOINT

Our position on the use of labels translates directly into a point of view about teaching exceptional students. The point of view is this: Beyond some global considerations, there is no one way to teach mentally retarded students that is distinctly different from how we might teach learning disabled, emotionally disturbed, physically handicapped, or normal students. This point of view is particularly relevant when considering students with milder forms of exceptionality who can receive some or much of their instruction in regular classes with backup support.

If labels do not tell what exceptional students need to learn and how they can be best approached, how then can we plan instruction for such students? We believe that, regardless of the particular label a student may have been given, six interrelated concerns about each exceptional student must be addressed.

1. *Goals.* Will I need to adjust my instructional goals for this student? Should the student be expected to master the same skills and knowl-

edge as his classmates, or will I need to modify my expectations of how much the student will be able to learn?

2. *Methods.* Will I need to adjust my teaching and testing methods for this student? Will the student learn as a result of the way I teach most other students, or will I need to use different methods, materials, or techniques?

3. *Motivation.* Will I need to use any special techniques to motivate the student to learn and behave? Will the student respond to the typical incentives I use in my classroom, or will I need to tailor the incentives to this student's needs?

4. *Environmental Adaptations.* What special considerations do I need to be aware of to help the student adapt to the classroom and school? Does the student have any special needs, such as hearing aids, visual aids, or prosthetic devices, that I should know about?

5. *Acceptance.* What can I do to help the other students understand, accept, and interact favorably with the student?

6. *Communication.* What resources, such as parents and specialists, should I consult or communicate with to better understand and teach the student?

In different words, teaching exceptional students requires a readiness to modify instructional goals, teaching methods, or motivational techniques to help students experience success in academic and social areas. For some students, particularly those with sensory and physical impairments, other modifications may be needed to help them adapt to the classroom and school environment.

The idea of modifying goals, methods or motivational techniques to help students experience success is rooted in a mastery approach to teaching. The basic elements of mastery learning were introduced in the 1970s by Benjamin Bloom (1971, 1976). A noted educational psychologist, Bloom believes that both exceptional and nonexceptional students have a better chance of learning when teachers clearly state their instructional objectives and then take specific steps to help students accomplish these objectives.

Given the assertion that more students will achieve when mastery techniques are used, a question arises about what role ability or aptitude plays. Most of us, for example, have been taught to believe that ability is one of the most, if not the most critical factor related to achievement. Bloom and his followers (Block and Anderson, 1975) assert that aptitude or native intelligence matters most when instruction is uniform and no special adjustments or provisions for individualization are made. For example, when a teacher presents new information at a rapid pace and makes few adjustments for students who learn at a slower pace or who require supplemental methods, aptitude is very important. Here, the brightest students are most apt to succeed and others, including many exceptional learners, will fall by the wayside.

Aptitude is but one of several critical variables that influence achievement. Student perseverance and the quality of instruction are other variables that contribute to school success. Aptitude by definition cannot be changed by teachers. But perseverance can be influenced by providing incentives to learn, and the quality of instruction can be improved by making sure that appropriate methods are used to help students learn. The intelligent setting of goals can enhance both perseverance and the quality of instruction. Thus, teachers can directly influence learning by altering goals, methods and motivational techniques for specific students.

The argument that all students can learn what they are taught has its logical limitations. By no means are we suggesting that all students be in college-preparatory programs or that students with severe intellectual limitations be expected to learn the same material as their brighter agemates. Putting these extremes aside, it seems reasonable to expect that nearly all students can master important skills whether they are handicapped or not, as long as these skills are presented step by step and are taught using methods and motivational techniques suitable to the learner.

What are the advantages of mastery learning? Block and Anderson (1975) assert that when teachers use mastery learning procedures, more students accomplish designated objectives and earn higher grades. Their data show that as many as two or three times the usual number of students achieve the equivalent of A's and B's, while the proportion of students receiving D's and F's similarly diminishes. These genuine gains in achievement and success would likely have a positive effect on any student's self-concept and would probably lead to a heightened interest in those subjects in which the student achieves well. There is no reason to believe that exceptional students would be immune to these effects. They should make more satisfactory progress in regular classrooms in which mastery learning practices are used than in classrooms where instruction is uniform for all learners.

Summary

In this chapter we have considered the evolution of attitudes towards exceptional individuals, which culminated in PL 94-142, The Education For All Handicapped Children Act. We have also introduced you to a point of view regarding the education of exceptional students in the regular classroom. Key ideas presented are listed below.

1. Attitudes towards exceptional individuals have evolved from harsh treatment and superstition to acceptance.

2. Attitudes and treatment of exceptional individuals were advanced by a number of educators and physicians during the mid-1800s.

3. Early special education programs were for individuals with relatively severe impairments.

4. Students with milder forms of problems were often excluded from school or placed in segregated settings.

5. Recent federal legislation has guaranteed many rights for exceptional individuals.

6. Exceptional students should be educated in the least restrictive environment.

7. Every student who receives special education services must have a written individualized education program.

8. Parents have a legal right to participate in all aspects of the Pupil Evaluation Team.

9. Exceptional students may be classified and labeled for administrative purposes, but teachers must focus on helping individual students to learn and to adjust to classroom expectations.

10. A mastery approach to teaching exceptional students is advocated.

Activities

1. Interview one or two classroom teachers to determine their perceptions regarding advantages and disadvantages of mainstreaming as well as the degree of support they receive from special education personnel and administrators.

2. Find a teacher who uses mastery learning procedures and observe how these procedures differ from more traditional practices. Find out how slow learners and exceptional students fare in this type of classroom.

3. Examine several buildings and walkways on your campus to determine what provisions have been made for handicapped individuals.

Study Questions

1. Describe how attitudes towards exceptional individuals have changed from early times to the present.

2. What were the contributions of Jean-Marc Gaspard Itard, Dorothea Dix, Thomas Gallaudet, Louis Braille, Samuel Howe, Helen Keller, and Edouard Seguin?

3. What are three reasons critics believed that full-time special class placement is inappropriate for some exceptional students?

4. List the civil rights guaranteed by Section 504 of The Rehabilitation Act of 1973.

5. Discuss the meaning of the "Least Restrictive Environment."

6. What is the composition and function of the Pupil Evaluation Team?

7. Describe conditions under which teachers are likely to react favorably to placing exceptional students in regular classrooms.

8. What are several questions a teacher should consider when planning instruction for exceptional students?

9. What is mastery learning and how can it benefit exceptional students?

Questions for Further Thought

1. Do you think federal legislation was needed to advance opportunities for exceptional individuals or would advancements have occurred without such legislation?

2. List the personal and professional qualities you possess that may help or hinder your ability to teach exceptional students in a regular classroom.

Additional Resources

BOOKS AND JOURNAL ARTICLES

Hewett, F. M., and Forness, S. R. *Education of exceptional learners.* Boston: Allyn and Bacon, 1974.

Dunn, L. M. Special education for the mildly retarded: Is much of it justifiable? *Exceptional Children,* 1968, 35, 5–22.

Lynn, J. J., Woltz, D., and Brush, W. *The individual education program (IEP) manual.* Hollister, California: Argonaut Publications, 1977.

PART II
STUDENTS WHO HAVE LEARNING AND BEHAVIOR PROBLEMS

Now that you have been introduced to exceptional students and some of the legal requirements regarding their education, it is time to develop a deeper understanding of the characteristics and needs of some of these students. In part two of this text, we will focus on students who have special needs in learning academic skills and behaving appropriately. Students classified as mentally retarded, emotionally disturbed, and learning disabled often represent the greatest proportion of exceptional students in community schools. We introduce them in three successive chapters because each group presents a common set of instructional problems to classroom teachers.

A number of introductory texts on exceptional students present one category of exceptionality in a chapter and then include teaching methods and approaches in the same chapter. This approach makes a great deal of sense when the emphasis is on students with relatively severe problems. For example, there are different methods for educating the severely retarded, the blind, and the deaf. When the emphasis, however, is on students with less severe problems — those who are likely to be placed in regular classrooms — differences in teaching methods are far less obvious or significant. Thus, while we present information to help you understand the basic characteristics of mentally retarded, emotionally disturbed, and learning disabled students in the next three chapters, we will not focus on specific teaching methods in any of these chapters. Instead, appropriate teaching methods and practices for students in these and other categories will be presented as a whole in Parts III, IV, and V of this text.

The three chapters of Part II are similar to each other in design and purpose. Each chapter begins with case studies to help you appreciate students as unique individuals rather than labels or abstract definitions. These case studies are based on real students we have taught or known over the past several years. Then, we proceed to more traditional topics such as common definitions, characteristics, prevalence, educational and social needs, and theoretical approaches to teaching these students.

As you read each chapter, it may help to keep the following questions in mind:

1. What are the common definitions used to classify mentally retarded, emotionally disturbed, and learning disabled students?

2. What are some common behaviors and characteristics exhibited by these students?

3. What percentage of the school-age population falls into each of these categories?

4. What general goals should be established for students in each of these categories?

5. What are some theoretical approaches to teaching these students?

Chapter 3

Mentally Retarded Students

Who are the mentally retarded? Sit back for a minute, close your eyes, and visualize someone who is mentally retarded. You may see someone who is physically different; that is, the person may have facial or other physical characteristics that set him or her apart from other people. You may see someone who is intellectually and academically slower than others of the same chronological age. Your image may be of a person who is socially immature and exhibits behaviors like those of someone much younger. Or you may see someone who is uncoordinated in large and small muscle movements such as running, skipping, cutting, and writing.

What are your feelings about the images you visualized? Are you comfortable with the people who came to mind? Are you able to detect the unique characteristics of each person? Do you think you could work with a mentally retarded student in your classroom?

The term "mental retardation" covers a variety of physical, intellectual, academic, and behavioral characteristics. We find, for example, some retarded students who are about three grade levels behind their peers in school and social achievement. These students eventually become self-sufficient, contributing members of society. There are also people in this category, though, whose intellectual and physical impairment is so great that they must be assisted by others all their lives, often in residential facilities. While the focus of this chapter is on the mildly or educably retarded, some mention of the more severely retarded will be made in the definition of retardation.

DEREK

Derek is nine years old. He is currently enrolled in the second grade in a public school, having repeated kindergarten once. Derek has been identified as mildly retarded and receives help from special education personnel as well as instruction in a regular class setting.

When Derek entered kindergarten, his mother reported that he had developed normally, although he learned to walk and talk a little later than normal. He was toilet trained, fed himself, and took care of his other personal needs independently. In other words, he had acquired needed self-help skills. Derek, however, had not learned many of the readiness skills most children have mastered prior to entry into public school.

When assessing Derek's skills at the beginning of his kindergarten year, his teacher found problems in several areas. First of all, he was small for his age; his gross and fine motor skills were not as developed as those of his age peers. This limited his ability to complete tasks that required the use of pencils, crayons, and scissors. Second, Derek had not acquired many of the pre-academic skills most children have prior to entry into school. He was unable to count, recognize alphabet letters, or identify colors and shapes. In addition, he had not formed many of the concepts expected of children at that age: meanings of prepositions, spatial relationships, classes (such as one would use in animal identification), and numerical value. Socially, Derek was labeled as immature. He was unable to relate successfully to his age peers. It was noted that he seemed to choose companions who were about two years younger than he when playing in his neighborhood. He exhibited many of the behaviors associated with children of that age.

Throughout Derek's first year of school, a concerted effort was made to assist him in learning the skills needed for success in school. His classroom teacher designed programs for him in each of the areas of concern. She structured the kindergarten sessions so she could spend a minimum of ten minutes per day providing Derek with one-to-one instruction. She also utilized peer tutors and enlisted the help of parent volunteers to provide direct instruction for Derek. Derek's progress was carefully monitored; by the end of the year, he had increased his skill level in all areas, particularly in pre-academic skills. However, he still did not have the skills necessary for success in the first grade and it was recommended that he repeat kindergarten.

Derek was assessed when he entered school the next fall. The classroom teacher found that, although Derek had made progress during the preceding year, he still lacked many of the skills necessary for school success. Once again, his academic program focused on areas of need: fine and gross motor coordination, pre-academic skills, and social skills. At the end of his second kindergarten year, Derek was able to use fine motor skills in the completion of tasks requiring writing, coloring, and cutting. He could count from memory and was beginning to understand number concepts. He knew his alphabet and had increased his language skills. Derek had also developed skills for appropriate social interactions with his peers. Derek was promoted to the first grade.

Derek had enough experience to be successful during the first few weeks of first grade. Gradually, though, he began to experience failure once new skills were introduced. He could learn the skills, but at a much slower rate than his peers. Although he had learned gross and fine motor skills in kindergarten, he still had deficits in the areas of language and concept development. These deficits affected his progress in skills such as reading and arithmetic. He continued to choose playmates who were much younger than he during unstructured play time. The first-grade teacher referred him to the Pupil Evaluation Team for evaluation and possible special education help. The team found that Derek did, indeed, have needs requiring specialized instruction and developed an Individualized Education Program for him. The program consisted of continued placement in the classroom for art, music, physical education, social studies, health, science, and group experiences, such as field trips, show and tell, recess, and lunch. In addition, Derek was to spend two hours per day with the special education resource room teacher for direct instruction in reading, arithmetic, and language development. This plan was in effect through the remainder of the school year.

Although Derek made progress during the first grade, he did not have all the skills necessary for complete reintegration into a full-time classroom placement in the second grade. The Pupil Evaluation Team reviewed Derek's progress towards some of the stated objectives, and structured a program similar to the one used during the first grade. He again spends two hours a day with the special education teacher, where he receives instruction in reading, arithmetic and language development. At nine years of age Derek is currently about two years below his age peers in both academic achievement and social skill development. He also remains small for his age and has some motor development problems. Derek has been classified as mentally retarded for administrative purposes.

The case study of Derek provides us with a realistic perspective of the needs of mentally retarded students at the elementary school level. As these students progress in school, they continue to lag behind their age peers in academic, social, and physical development. By the time the students enter secondary school programs, their needs and their ability to interact in the school environment have usually changed. Let's return for a moment to Ed, the mentally retarded student presented in Chapter 1.

ED

Ed is in the ninth grade. He is enrolled in vocational courses, general science and math classes, and in the resource room for reading, daily living, and tutorial instruction. Although Ed experiences success in most of his learning activities, he does not have the necessary academic background to participate in most regular classes. He reads at fourth-grade level; he can say most of the words he encounters at that level and can tell someone else what he has read. He has difficulty, however, when the level of the reading material increases and when he is expected to explain higher level concepts in what he has read. Ed's reading skills are not adequate for him to participate in secondary classes such as English or social studies, which require a great deal of reading. Ed is receiving reading instruction from the resource room teacher, who is focusing on improving Ed's reading level and ensuring that Ed can read the words necessary for his daily survival.

Although Ed is currently enrolled in a general math class, he still has difficulty in this area. Ed is just mastering his division skills; once he has mastered this area, he will be able to perform all basic math computations. Since Ed is required to use these skills in his general math class, the resource room teacher tutors him each day in both computational skills and in the new skills being taught in the math class. In addition, the resource room teacher is reviewing math-related skills like handling money, so Ed will be able to be self-sufficient in these areas.

The most significant aspect of Ed's program is a focus on vocational preparation. Ed is learning many job-related skills, such as completing job applications, obtaining a social security number, banking, and social behaviors needed on the job. Some of Ed's reading and math instruction is centered around vocational preparation as well. Next year, Ed will be placed in several job settings where he will have an opportunity to utilize the skills he is being taught this year as well as develop some specific job skills he will be able to use once he leaves the public schools.

Socially, Ed is not as readily accepted as Derek. Ed has some behaviors that his peers find inappropriate for their social settings. Sometimes, Ed is too pushy. He tries to make a good impression, but ends up offending his peers. Because his peers do not understand the reason for Ed's somewhat clumsy attempts at socialization, they tend to shun him. A few students in the school mimic Ed and other retarded students, poking fun at them when they see these students in the school. Ed is unable to find female students who are willing to talk with him and to acknowledge him socially in the school. At the present time, Ed associates with two other students from his vocational program who are also enrolled in the resource room.

What Is Mental Retardation?

As you can see from the information presented on Derek and Ed, students who are mentally retarded have some similar intellectual, academic, physical, and social characteristics. For the most part, these students perform at a level significantly below that of their age peers. Because of the lag in development in these areas, mentally retarded students require assistance from special education personnel throughout their school career. Who are these students?

DEFINITION

The basis of the current definition of mental retardation originated in work done in the early 1900s by a committee of the American Association on Mental Deficiency (AAMD). This committee developed some of the first standardized mechanisms for classifying the mentally retarded. These original standards have been revised and have evolved into an approach to the classification of the mentally retarded that emphasizes the etiology, or causes, of retardation and behavioral characteristics. The current AAMD definition and classification system emerged from these efforts.

> Mental retardation refers to significantly subaverage intellectual functioning existing concurrently with deficits in adaptive behavior, and manifested during the developmental period. (Grossman, 1977, p. 5)

PL 94-142 uses this definition, with the addition of the words, "which adversely affects a child's educational performance." Although the definition may appear to be very technical, it can be broken into three major units for clarification.

The first major part of the definition refers to intellectual functioning. "Significantly subaverage general intellectual functioning" means that an individual who is mentally retarded can be expected to perform at a lower level on tasks that purport to measure intelligence than others of his or her age. In most cases, intelligence tests are used to measure this area. An intelligence quotient (IQ) of 100 is considered to be average; an intelligence score of 68 to 70 serves as an approximate cutoff for classification as mentally retarded.

Adaptive behavior is also cited in the definition. Adaptive behavior refers to the individual's ability to exhibit behavior appropriate to a given situation. It includes self-help skills, such as feeding, dressing, toilet training, and travel, and age-appropriate social behavior in school, at home, and in the community. For instance, a nine-year-old student who looks up when a visitor enters the classroom and then returns his attention to the task at hand is likely exhibiting appropriate adaptive behavior. When Derek, though, leaves his seat, greets the visitor with a hug, and leads the visitor by the hand to the teacher, he is not demonstrating appropriate adaptive behavior for that classroom. When Derek bursts into the middle of games at recess, "hogs" the ball, and consistently chooses to play with the kindergarten children, he is again demonstrating a lack of adaptive behavior appropriate to his age. By the same token, a twelve-year-old retarded student who is unable to find his way around a school he has attended for three years has not developed appropriate adaptive travel behavior.

Finally, the definition states that the retardation exists or is manifested during the "developmental period." This means that the retardation occurs prior to age eighteen, rather than as a result of some impairment during adulthood. The skills and behaviors of the retarded student are compared to the skills and behaviors of other students who are developing within the normal range.

Retardation, then, is characterized by low intellectual functioning and deficits in adaptive behavior, manifested before age eighteen. Let's return to Derek. Although a specific IQ figure was not presented, it is apparent that Derek functions well below his peers in school achievement. When IQ testing was done, the results indicated an IQ score of 63, placing Derek's score significantly below the average IQ range of approximately 85 to 115. Academic achievement test results placed Derek about two grade levels below his age peers. Derek has developed necessary self-help skills; however, he demonstrates deficits in adaptive behavior through his choice of playmates and responses to some school and social situations. Finally, the retardation manifested itself during the developmental period, or prior to the age of eighteen. Thus, Derek could be considered a mentally retarded student.

The AAMD goes on to subdivide the area of retardation into categories representing progressively more severe forms of retardation. These

TABLE 3.1
Categories of mental retardation

Level	IQ score
Mild	55–69
Moderate	40–54
Severe	25–39
Profound	14 and below

Source: Grossman, 1977.

are listed in Table 3.1. There are certain characteristics and expectations associated with each of these categories.

Mildly retarded students, sometimes referred to as the educable mentally retarded, will usually be self-supporting participants in a community. To that end, the curriculum for the mildly retarded often resembles that of other students their age. While these students will often be performing at a level two or more grades below their peers, they may participate in many of the classroom activities with their peers. They will likely receive special education assistance from a resource room teacher or from a part-time special class teacher in basic academic skills like reading, arithmetic, and oral and written expression. As these students progress through school, their program may emphasize prevocational and vocational training at the secondary levels.

The moderately retarded, also known as the trainable mentally retarded, on the other hand, will usually be somewhat dependent on others all their lives. They will receive the bulk of their instruction in a full-time special education setting, with some social interaction with age peers. The curriculum for the moderately retarded focuses on basic academic work (reading, basic arithmetic, and writing), self-help skills, communication skills, and prevocational and vocational skills. Many moderately retarded adults work in sheltered workshop settings and live in supervised settings with family members, in group homes, or boarding homes.

The severely and profoundly retarded will usually require sheltered work and living situations. The basic goals for this population are to provide them with the skills to care for their personal needs and contribute in a sheltered work or home setting. The school curriculum often focuses on the training of self-help skills, communication skills, and some prevocational skills. These students are usually educated in self-contained special education classes or in residential settings. Because of their very limited skills and their special educational needs, these students seldom participate in regular classrooms.

These brief descriptions of the categories within retardation have been provided to illustrate the range of needs the mentally retarded possess. While the more severely retarded students will not participate in regular classrooms, they may be present in the school. It is important that classroom teachers understand the educational needs of these students and how they might interact in school settings.

CHARACTERISTICS

At the outset, it should be noted that mentally retarded students as a group are as diverse as any other group of students. It is possible to describe characteristics for the group, but these will not always be present in every student who is labeled mentally retarded. The following characteristics should serve as guideposts rather than absolutes when identifying and teaching the mentally retarded.

The definition of retardation itself leads us to some of the characteristics of mentally retarded individuals. That is, many characteristics are directly related to intellectual functioning. Others are related to adaptive social behavior. Finally, some characteristics are related to adaptive skills necessary for successful learning in school.

Mentally retarded students function intellectually at a significantly lower level than their age peers. Since the development of skills such as basic academics, language and vocabulary, thinking, and memory are related to intellectual functioning, we find that mentally retarded students, as a group, demonstrate some similar characteristics in this area.

1. *Academic retardation.* A mentally retarded individual performs well below average in academic subjects such as reading, arithmetic, science, and social studies (Hutt and Gibby, 1976). Performance is almost always consistently low in all academic areas. As you will recall, Derek performed about two grade levels below his peers in academic achievement testing.

2. *Language deficits.* Many retarded students have language skills below that of their peers. Since language functioning is often related to intellectual development and school achievement, it is not difficult to understand the nature of this characteristic. Retarded students may not understand as much as their peers or be able to express their thoughts as well as their peers.

3. *Deficits in conceptualization and generalization.* The development of abstract concepts and conceptual thinking is a high-level skill. Many retarded students are unable to identify common concepts, such as prepositions, building types, and land forms. In addition to deficits in conceptual thinking, many retarded individuals have difficulty generalizing from the learning situation, or classroom, to "real life" settings. For example, the student may be able to read a particular word when presented

in a word list, but be unable to identify it on a billboard on the way to school.

4. *Deficits in attention.* Many retarded students show deficits in the area of attention. They seem unable to orient themselves to the critical cues necessary to properly utilize what is being presented. For example, Derek relies on the pictures in his reader to provide him with the cues for reading stories rather than utilizing the printed words. He also uses coin size rather than coin value when he counts money. On occasion, Derek begins to make a correct response, but waits for cues from his peers to reinforce his own answer.

5. *Problems with memory.* A common characteristic of the retarded student is difficulty with short-term memory. Such students frequently have problems remembering newly acquired information from day to day. It should be noted, however, that there is some research that indicates that long-term memory of the retarded does not significantly differ from that of normal students. Thus, because of short-term memory deficits, it may take retarded students longer to learn a skill. However, once they have mastered or learned the skill, they should retain it over a long period of time (Payne, Polloway, Smith, and Payne, 1981).

Ed provides us with a good example of memory problems in the mentally retarded. As you recall, Ed has difficulty in math. He is able to respond to combinations of numbers when he has practiced them during a class period in the resource room. When he gets to the classroom later in the day, though, he does not seem to be able to remember skills he practiced earlier. However, once Ed is finally able to use the skill in the general math class, he rarely forgets it.

The second part of the AAMD definition focuses on adaptive behavior, the skills necessary to successfully interact in various school, home, and community settings. The following characteristics are related primarily to adaptive skills.

1. *Gross and fine motor coordination.* Many mentally retarded students, like Derek, have deficits in fine and gross motor development. They learn such skills as running, walking, skipping, and other gross motor skills later than their age peers. They may also show delayed progress in fine motor skills, such as writing, cutting, drawing, and painting. It should be noted, however, that some mentally retarded students are quite proficient at these tasks.

2. *Social skills.* Because of below-average functioning in intellectual areas and social skills, most retarded students tend to exhibit social behavior appropriate to a younger age level. They tend to choose younger playmates and behave at levels approximately two or more years below their chronological age. As you will recall, Derek frequently made this choice. In addition, some retarded students may be ostracized by their

age peers because of their intellectual, academic, and social differences. Such rejection may result in a lower self-concept (Hutt and Gibby, 1976).

3. *Self-help skills.* Some retarded students, especially those who are more severely retarded, show deficits in self-help skills. These individuals are unable to perform such tasks as feeding, dressing, and cleaning themselves, as well as taking care of their toilet needs. These individuals need training in all of these areas. While most mildly retarded students have acquired many of these skills, they may need work in areas such as independent travel, telling time, counting money, and homemaking.

4. *Skills related to learning.* Mentally retarded children frequently have not developed some skills that are needed for successful learning. For example, they often have a short attention span and may become easily frustrated when attempting academic and social tasks. They require many concrete examples when learning a new skill, although abstractions can be learned with sufficient examples (Chinn, Drew, and Logan, 1979). Motivation may be a problem if the student has previously experienced failure on learning tasks. The teacher must allow more time for the acquisition of skills, using drill and repetition to ensure that learning does take place (Payne and Patton, 1981).

It should again be emphasized that these characteristics apply to the retarded as a group. Individuals who fall within this category may exhibit some of these characteristics, but not necessarily all of them. A mildly retarded child may enter school with nearly normal language skills because of an enriched environment in his or her home. Another child may have social skills appropriate for his or her age as a result of past experiences and instruction. In general, though, mentally retarded students will have deficits in intellectual functioning, including academic skills; and adaptive behavior, including gross and fine motor skills, self-help skills, and social behavior.

IDENTIFICATION

The identification of mentally retarded students is based upon the concepts developed in the AAMD. definition and the characteristics of the retarded. Intellectual functioning (as measured through IQ tests), adaptive behavior (as measured through rating scales), and classroom behavior (as measured through observations of classroom behavior) are keys used in the identification of mentally retarded students.

Most students who are categorized as mentally retarded have been given an individual intelligence test. Although federal and many state guidelines do not specify an IQ score for retardation, it is still used by many professionals as one measure for determining a student's handicapping condition. Tests such as the Stanford-Binet Intelligence Scale (Terman and Merrill, 1960) and the Wechsler Intelligence Scale for Children—Revised (WISC-R) (Wechsler, 1974) are used to obtain an indication of the student's intellectual functioning.

Since PL 94-142 requires the use of more than one measure when identifying exceptional students, the IQ score cannot be the sole criterion for placement in a special education program. The use of IQ alone may result in placement errors since IQ tests seem to favor white, middle-class students. Group and individual achievement test scores are also used frequently to corroborate the level of classroom performance demonstrated by the student. Most retarded students perform well below average on both measures.

In addition to measuring intellectual functioning, most professionals who are identifying students as mentally retarded rely on measures of adaptive behavior. Since both deficits in intellectual functioning and adaptive behavior must exist concurrently, both should be measured. The utilization of both measures provides educators with a broader perspective of the student's strengths and weaknesses and allows for more accurate identification of mental retardation (Huberty, Koller, and Brink, 1980).

Adaptive behavior is typically measured through the use of published checklists and observation. A number of such checklists exist. One example is the AAMD Adaptive Behavior Rating Scale (American Association on Mental Deficiency, 1977). This scale consists of a series of items with indices of behavioral development. For example, the rater (a classroom teacher, specialist, or parent) is asked to note which utensil the child uses and rate how well it is used when eating. The rater observes the child in several areas over a period of time, rates each area of behavior, and then develops instructional plans based on the ratings. Some rating scales provide the examiner with a norm-referenced score for the child. Such a score indicates how that student compares with normal age peers rated on the same scale. The results obtained from the use of these scales may also lead directly to the development of goals and objectives.

In addition to intelligence and achievement testing and adaptive behavior scales, observation plays an important role in the identification of mentally retarded students. Skills such as gross and fine motor coordination, the choice of playmates, some social interactions, and day-to-day performance in the classroom can best be noted through work samples and actual direct observation. This is often done by the classroom teacher and/or specialist, and should occur over a period of time, rather than on a one-shot basis or over a very short amount of time.

The classroom teacher's role in the identification process is very important, especially in day-to-day observation. Often the teacher is the first to realize that the student has special needs. The teacher can observe the student for a period of time, noting academic performance in the classroom, social behavior in and out of the classroom, and other areas of concern. The teacher may also review pertinent school records.

The student would then be referred to the Pupil Evaluation Team for further consideration. In most cases, a licensed examiner will administer any needed IQ test and possibly other measures of student performance. Other specialists may also administer some tests to the student, including an adaptive behavior rating scale, with which the classroom teacher may be asked to assist. The combination of all this information is used by the Pupil Evaluation Team to determine whether the student is mentally retarded and qualifies for special education services.

EDUCATIONAL AND SOCIAL NEEDS

The educational and social needs of the mentally retarded vary depending upon the degree of retardation found in the individual. This discussion will focus on the needs of mentally retarded students who are mainstreamed into regular classes for some portion of their school day.

The educational needs of the mentally retarded fall into two major areas, academic skill development and vocational development. Important goals in these areas include the following:

1. Instruction in basic skills, such as reading, writing, arithmetic processes, money, and telling time.

2. Instruction in concepts, language, and the generalization of skills to other settings.

3. Expansion of general knowledge to broaden educational scope and increase social interaction skills.

4. Prevocational and vocational training in appropriate job areas.

In addition to the major educational needs, the mentally retarded need instruction in adaptive behavior. While the goals differ for each student, the following may be appropriate for training in an educational program:

1. Developing social skills that are appropriate for school, home, leisure, and work settings.

2. Developing self-help skills, if needed.

3. Developing skills for leisure-time activities.

4. Increasing gross and fine motor coordination.

5. Increasing skill level in such areas as attention to tasks, memory, and frustration tolerance to facilitate learning.

The social needs of the mentally retarded have already been presented to some degree in the section about characteristics of the mentally retarded. Appropriate social behavior is necessary for success at work and success in developing and maintaining interpersonal relationships. Since many mildly retarded individuals can and will be self-sufficient and must rely on their own skills, it is important that social skills be emphasized in their educational programs.

If you reflect for a moment on the Individualized Education Program developed for Derek, you will recall that many educational and adaptive goals are contained in the program. Derek receives instruction in reading, arithmetic, and language from the resource room teacher. As Derek's language skills improve, his vocabulary and general information skills also improve. Since Derek has acquired the self-help skills he needs at his age, the goals emphasized in adaptive behavior include social skills, gross and fine motor coordination, attention to tasks in school, and memory. As Derek acquires some of these skills and progresses in school, some of the current goals will be dropped; new, more appropriate goals will be added as they are needed.

The educational and adaptive goals the school has established for Ed differ somewhat from those set for Derek. While Ed still receives instruction in basic academic skills, the focus is on those necessary for daily living. Ed has acquired many of the academic skills he must use in school and vocational settings, so these are not emphasized at the present time. The major focus in educational programming for Ed is vocational training. Since Ed will soon be leaving the school environment, the vocational goals are a necessity. The adaptive goals for Ed were also selected on the basis that Ed would soon be leaving school. The emphasis in this part of his program is on social skills, leisure-time activities, and the improvement of his short-term memory. As Ed finishes his high-school program, the emphasis of his program will shift more and more towards the development and improvement of daily living, vocational, and leisure-time skills.

PREVALENCE

The most common estimate given for the percentage of people in the population classified as mentally retarded is 3%. Although it is likely that 3% of the newborn population will be diagnosed as mentally retarded at some point during their lifetime, this figure has been challenged (Mercer, 1973; Tarjan, Wright, Eyman, and Keeran, 1973). In the past, professionals relied primarily on IQ scores to diagnose retardation. When IQ is the sole basis for determining whether retardation exists, approximately 3% of the population are identified. The addition of adaptive behavior as a second criterion for classification changes the perspective on mental retardation. When both measures of IQ and adaptive behavior are used, approximately 1% of the population may be considered mentally retarded. Whatever the diagnostic measure, approximately 75–80% of those classified as mentally retarded are mildly retarded and may be placed in a regular class setting.

How Are the Mentally Retarded Educated?

Up to this point, we have introduced the characteristics and educational needs of mentally retarded students in public school settings. We have not, however, discussed how the educational needs of these students are met in the context of the regular and special class. What curriculum models do we follow with retarded students? Should we provide a "watered down" curriculum? Can they even participate in the type of curriculum approaches utilized in public schools? As we have seen with Derek and Al, the answer to the last question is yes; mildly retarded students are able to participate in public school programs. Because these students do have some intellectual and academic limitations, it is important to understand how they are able to participate in the curriculum offerings of the school.

Once the curriculum issues have been addressed, it is also necessary to review the types of settings under which the curriculum will be delivered. Most mildly retarded students are able to participate in the classroom for some portion of their school day. The student will receive instruction from a special education teacher in some skill areas. This instruction may supplement that being provided in the classroom. In some cases, it may replace classroom instruction in basic skill areas like reading and arithmetic. The placement option selected for an individual student will depend upon the specific needs of the student and how those needs can best be met in the total school program.

CURRICULA FOR MILDLY RETARDED STUDENTS

In the previous section of this chapter, we introduced the educational and social needs that exist in mentally retarded students. Basically, the primary educational concerns for mentally retarded students who participate in classroom programs are basic skill development, the acquisition of general information (concepts, vocabulary, information), career and vocational training, and social and emotional growth. While all of these skill areas are important through the student's school career, the emphasis changes as the student progresses through the curriculum.

The Elementary School Curriculum   While in elementary school, most mentally retarded students enjoy a curriculum very similar to that of their age peers. The students receive instruction in reading, arithmetic, social studies, language arts, science, health, physical education, art, and music. Any curriculum areas offered for the students in the classroom are open to mentally retarded students as well. There are some differences, though. While the mentally retarded student may indeed receive instruction in reading, the instruction may be provided by a special educator. Since it takes longer for mentally retarded students to acquire skills, the pace of instruction may be adapted to ensure mastery of the content. Mentally retarded students may require individual tutoring in some content areas, such as social studies and science, to gain the maximum benefit from the instruction.

Let's return to Derek for a moment. As you recall, Derek is enrolled in a second-grade classroom and receiving instruction from a special education teacher and his classroom teacher. The special education teacher provides all of Derek's instruction in the basic skill areas of reading, arithmetic, and language arts. Derek is currently learning new reading skills in word recognition and attaching meaning to words and sentences. In arithmetic, he is continuing to practice his addition skills and is beginning to work on the subtraction facts. The special education teacher ties language development to Derek's new reading and spelling words, incorporating oral and written expression into reading lessons. Derek's classroom teacher reinforces these basic skills as Derek uses them in the classroom. She focuses her efforts with Derek on his social and emotional growth by including him in all class activities and by seeing to his physical development. Learning activities in areas such as social studies and health are structured to promote maximum success for all students. Recess, physical education, and art activities are selected to assist Derek and three other students in developing their gross and fine motor coordination. While these approaches are successful at the present, Derek's teachers are concerned that his low reading and arithmetic levels will soon limit his participation and success in some academic areas.

As the student progresses through the school program, the gap between his or her skills and those of other students the same age usually grows increasingly greater. This gap, particularly in reading, arithmetic, and language arts, makes it more difficult for mentally retarded students to participate in the classroom experiences designed for their age peers. There will be a gradual change, in most cases, to a somewhat differentiated curriculum; that is, retarded students may receive more instruction from a special educator, and the instruction provided in the classroom will become more adapted to accommodate their skill level. While students may have initially received instruction from a special educator only in reading, arithmetic, and language arts, they will likely see the specialist for additional help in some content areas before the end of their elementary school program.

The Secondary School Curriculum　As mentally retarded students progress through school, the emphasis on some skill areas changes. While the students may still participate with their age peers in some content areas, the principal goals are to develop basic academic skills and social skills that will be used in vocational placements. The vocational component of the students' program is emphasized with a goal of employment at the conclusion of the school program. Academic skills and social skills that are included in the curriculum are often related to job situations and practiced on the job as the students work in various job settings.

The participation of mentally retarded students in regular classroom activities often diminishes as they move through secondary programs. As mentioned previously, the students' skill level is well below that of their age peers. Much more work is dependent upon reading and math abilities that are up to grade level; since the mildly retarded students are unable to perform at these levels, they often experience failure in classroom settings. In some school systems, the mildly retarded are enrolled in vocational programs and receive instruction from special education personnel in basic skill areas. While this setting is more restrictive for the student than a regular class placement, it is less restrictive in facilitating the development of skills necessary for successful employment and daily living outside the school setting.

PLACEMENT OPTIONS

Mentally retarded students are usually educated by classroom teachers, special educators, and vocational instructors. The amount of time the student spends with these people depends upon the instructional needs of the individual student. Some retarded students who are enrolled in an ordinary school are able to spend the majority of their school day in a regular classroom, experiencing a moderate amount of success, while other retarded students are successful if they spend most of their school day with a special education teacher, returning to the classroom for art, music, physical education, and social activities.

In order to meet the diverse educational needs of these students, several options are available for the delivery of instruction. The selection of a particular option for a student is based upon the student's educational needs, his or her ability to interact in social settings, and the goals and objectives developed for the student by the Pupil Evaluation Team. In reviewing these options, it is important to note that some variation may exist in your school district; the basic models, though, are used nationally.

The Resource Room   The resource room is used for students who require instruction in specific skill areas, but are able to participate in most classroom activities. When a retarded student is placed in a resource room, the student generally receives instruction in reading, arithmetic, and language arts from the special education teacher. The remainder of the school day is spent with the regular classroom teacher. Many students in kindergarten through third grade receive special education assistance under this model.

The Part-time Special Class   When retarded students require more instruction of a specialized nature, they may be placed in a part-time special

Some exceptional students are able to spend most of the day in a regular classroom, while others are taught by the special education teacher.

education classroom. In this setting, the special education teacher provides instruction in the basic skill areas taught by the resource teacher as well as instruction in many of the content areas, such as social studies, science, and health. The student participates in the regular classroom during art, music, physical education, and social activities. If possible, the student is mainstreamed in other activities in the classroom; however, the lack of necessary basic skills often precludes such integration.

The Special Class   Some retarded students have special needs that require full-time placement in a special education class. These classes may be located within a school building, but all instruction comes from the special education teacher. Some secondary-school programs are based upon this model; students have educational needs that are quite different from those of their age peers and that can best be met in a self-contained special education program. In these cases, the student does not have the skills necessary to participate in the regular classroom and needs specialized instruction in vocational skills to be as independent as possible in a job setting.

The program that Ed is enrolled in is an example of the need for flexibility in providing services for the mentally retarded. Ed is currently enrolled in two regular classes, general math and a general science course. The remainder of the day, Ed participates in the special education program and in the vocational program. When Ed is a sophomore in high school, he will be enrolled in a physical education course with his age peers. The remainder of the school day, Ed will spend in the special education program receiving instruction in basic academic and social skill areas and participating in the vocational work-study program. This program was developed to provide students like Ed with the opportunity to learn vocational skills prior to graduation from high school. Many of the students who demonstrate appropriate job skills during the work-study program find permanent employment at one of the participating businesses.

Summary

In this chapter we have presented an overview of one category used to identify exceptional students, mental retardation. Through the descriptions of Derek and Ed and the content provided in the text, we have attempted to provide you with the background information necessary to help you understand the definition of retardation, the characteristics of mentally retarded students, and the educational and social needs of these students that must be met in the public school setting. Let's review the major concepts and ideas presented in the chapter.

1. The term mental retardation refers to a population of people who function intellectually at a level significantly lower than that of their age peers and who are unable to respond to some social situations in a manner appropriate to their age.

2. Mentally retarded students are characterized by the way in which they interact in the school setting. These students have specific academic, social, and physical needs that require specialized instruction.

3. Intelligence test scores and measures of adaptive behavior are usually used to determine the students who are mentally retarded and will benefit from special education services.

4. Educational programs for mentally retarded students contain the following components: instruction in basic academic skills, the development of concepts and skills for generalization, the development of gross and fine motor skills, instruction in social skills, and vocational training.

5. Mentally retarded students who participate in the regular classroom will have some academic, and possibly social, skill limitations that will prevent total integration into the regular

classroom program. The classroom teacher will have to adapt instruction to increase the likelihood of success in these learning activities.

6. The curriculum for mentally retarded students who participate in the regular class program will resemble that of other students; the delivery of the instruction may be somewhat different to meet the needs of the individual student.

7. Mentally retarded students are usually placed in a resource room or a part-time special class to receive instruction from a special education teacher. Some secondary programs, though, are self-contained for the mentally retarded with an emphasis on vocational education.

8. Mentally retarded students are unique individuals who can participate in the regular classroom and benefit from the opportunities provided by the classroom teacher.

Activities

1. Develop a relationship with a mentally retarded student. There are organizations such as Special Olympics and Big Brother/Big Sister programs that sponsor activities for students who may be retarded. If you enjoy the relationship, you may want to seek summer employment in a camp for exceptional students.

2. Research the development of tests of mental ability (IQ tests). Note the initial purpose of these tests. Compare and contrast this purpose with the current use(s) of intelligence tests.

3. Visit a special education class that serves mildly retarded students. Note the curriculum, the activities used to teach skills, and the relationship of the curriculum in the regular classroom and in the special education class.

4. Talk with a classroom teacher who has mildly mentally retarded students mainstreamed in the classroom. Discuss the advantages and disadvantages of mainstreaming, noting at least one gain and one drawback to the integration of these students from the teacher's perspective.

Study Questions

1. List and briefly describe the three major components of the definition of mental retardation.

2. Why is it important to use both intellectual functioning and adaptive behavior when classifying students as mentally retarded?

3. Briefly describe the relationship between the development of language skills and performance on intelligence and achievement tests.

4. What are the strengths of mentally retarded students in the area of memory? What memory skills should the classroom teacher accommodate when teaching new skills to mentally retarded students?

5. List two characteristics of mentally retarded students related to adaptive behavior.

6. Identify at least one way of assessing each of the following areas: (a) intellectual functioning; (b) adaptive behavior; and (c) classroom performance.

7. What are the instructional needs of mildly mentally retarded students?

8. What are two special education placements commonly used for mildly mentally retarded students? Briefly describe the role of the special education teacher and the classroom teacher in each.

Questions for Further Thought

1. A number of states have laws that allow for involuntary sterilization of the mentally retarded. What are some of the moral, civil, religious, and ethical issues involved in such a decision?

2. Many mentally retarded students are ostracized socially in school. As a classroom teacher, what steps could you take to increase positive social interaction among students in your classroom?

3. What efforts should be made towards improving the education of more severely retarded students? Should these students be included in regular public school programs?

Additional Resources

BOOKS

Blatt, B., and Kaplan, F. *Christmas in Purgatory: A photographic essay on mental retardation.* Boston: Allyn and Bacon, 1966.

Goldstein, H. *Readings in mental retardation.* Guilford, Connecticut: Special Learning Corporation, 1978.

Neisworth, J. T., and Smith, R. M. *Retardation: Issues, assessment, and intervention.* New York: McGraw-Hill, 1978.

Payne, J. S., and Patton, J. R. *Mental retardation.* Columbus, Ohio: Charles E. Merrill, 1981.

Robinson, N. M., and Robinson, H. B. *The mentally retarded child* (2nd ed.). New York: McGraw-Hill, 1976.

PROFESSIONAL JOURNALS

American Journal of Mental Deficiency

Education and Training of the Mentally Retarded

Mental Retardation

CHILDREN'S LITERATURE

Brightman, A. J. *Like me.* Boston: Little, Brown and Company, 1976.

Byars, B. *The summer of the swans.* New York: Viking Press, 1970.

Friis-Baasted, B. *Don't take Teddy.* New York: Scribner, 1967.

Luis, E. W., and Millar, B. *Listen Lissa.* New York: Dodd, Mead and Company, 1968.

Reynolds, P. *A different kind of sister.* New York: Lothrop, Lee & Shepard Company, 1968.

PROFESSIONAL ORGANIZATIONS

American Association on Mental Deficiency, 5201 Connecticut Avenue, Washington, D.C. 20015

Division on Mental Retardation, Council for Exceptional Children (CEC), 1920 Association Drive, Reston, Virginia 22091

National Association for Retarded Citizens (NARC), 2709 Avenue E East, Arlington, Texas 76011

Chapter 4

Emotionally Disturbed Students

At one time or another, each of us has probably experienced relatively intense feelings of frustration, anger, jealousy, or loneliness. We may have also suffered the debilitating consequences of these powerful emotions in terms of our ability to function in work, social or academic situations. Yet, it is also likely that we were not labelled "emotionally disturbed," because we were not continually paralyzed by these emotions. Similarly, many school children exhibit behaviors and emotions such as oversensitiveness, overactivity, destructiveness, defiance, and temper outbursts; but not all of these children are labelled "emotionally disturbed." Emotionally disturbed students demonstrate the same kinds of problem behaviors as most other students. However, students classified as emotionally disturbed display these behaviors more frequently and more intensively than their normal counterparts (Hewett and Taylor, 1980).

In this chapter we will examine how emotionally disturbed students are identified and what approaches are commonly used to understand and teach them. Before proceeding with formal definitions, let's meet some students who have been labelled emotionally disturbed.

BOB

Bob Jones entered Alfred Elementary School this past September and was placed in the third grade. At Alfred, there is a resource room program for children with learning and behavior problems and it was soon evident that Bob needed the additional support of this program. Bob's initial school performance and behavior could be summarized as follows:

1. He was reading at a first-grade level and showed a substantial degree of anxiety and concern about reading. Bob's math skills were quite low. He was just beginning to learn basic addition facts. His handwriting was nearly illegible. In general, Bob was weak in all academic and skill areas.

2. His classroom behavior could be characterized as overactive with a short attention span. Frequently, Bob would get out of his seat, roam about the room, talk out loudly, or hit other pupils. On the playground he was often seen running about and almost randomly hitting or knocking down other pupils. It appeared that Bob had few social skills and may have been engaging in these behaviors as a means of playing with or making contact with other pupils. Bob's thinking seemed to be somewhat disorganized, and he appeared to have a lot of difficulty remembering what behavior he engaged in just a few minutes ago. It was difficult to have a conversation with Bob for any length of time, because he would wander from the topic and introduce topics that were momentarily interesting to him. Many of Bob's initial contacts with teachers were characterized by loudness and a façade of anger or hostility.

During the course of the year, Bob has shown steady improvement and progress in almost all areas. The following represents a summary of the steps taken to provide an Individualized Educational Program:

1. A schedule was designed to provide a balance between time spent in the regular third-grade classroom and time spent in more individualized instruction. This schedule was developed because Bob's learning needs required a great deal of individual attention, and his overactive behavior was difficult to tolerate in the regular classroom for long periods of time. Bob is scheduled for 30 minutes of remedial reading each morning and one and one-half hours of daily instruction in the resource room where reading, language, math, and behavioral skills, such as paying attention and taking turns, are stressed.

2. Much of Bob's work in the third-grade class is highly individualized. It was found that short, clear, and well-defined learning tasks help him to achieve success. Each morning, Bob is presented with his work folder. The folder usually contains a page of math problems and activities, a page of word-study skills and activities, and a short reading assignment with comprehension

questions. Bob now participates in spelling, handwriting, and math lessons with his third-grade classmates.

3. Expectations for Bob's classroom behavior are very clear and are backed up by a combination of rewards and daily reports that are sent home to his parents. Rewards include tokens that can be exchanged at the end of the activity period, hour, or day for special free-time activities such as watching a filmstrip, listening to a record, working on an art project, and so on. In general, it appears that a highly structured learning program utilizing rewards and praise is most helpful. Since it was known that Bob has a history of negative experiences with adults, every effort is made to respond to Bob with understanding, acceptance, praise, and warmth, while adhering to a basic policy of structure and consistency. For example, when initially confronted with a learning task, Bob may exhibit negativism or defiance that could be misperceived as a threat to the teacher's authority. We have learned that it was helpful to ignore this and allow Bob a moment or two to settle down before reminding him of his task.

JANE

Although Jane Cox fully participates in most seventh-grade classes, her school experience has been marked by relatively extreme behavior problems that impede her current performance. Interviews with Mrs. Cox, Jane's mother, indicate that problem behaviors occurred as early as age three. While many basic needs such as food, shelter, and attention were provided, Mrs. Cox found it difficult to establish and maintain consistent limits and routines, often giving in to Jane's pleas to stay up later, have extra stories read to her, or receive toys and treats during shopping trips. By age four Jane exhibited tantrum-like behaviors such as shouting and fist pounding when she did not have her wishes met. Her mother alternately responded to these tantrums with spankings or pleas to "behave" but ultimately gave in to her daughter's wishes. Some difficulties with neighborhood playmates were reported, with Jane being accused of hitting other children, taking toys, or refusing to cooperate in games.

Jane's problem behaviors were magnified by the demands of school. In kindergarten she was unable to share materials or engage in basic routines, such as lining up, sitting in a circle and listening to a story, or playing group games. When her wishes were not immediately met, crying, screaming, or hitting others, including the teacher, were likely to occur. In an effort to appease her, limits were removed and Jane was allowed to engage in only those activities that she desired. This strategy reduced the number of tantrums but did not help her learn basic readiness or group participation skills.

Jane's needs became apparent during the first grade. Her lack of readiness skills led to an inability to complete basic academic tasks, which added to the frustration she experienced. Her aggressive outbursts and tantrums increased to three or four incidents per day, with each incident requiring considerable individual attention from the teacher to help her regain composure. Jane's teacher reported feeling anxiety about her ability to conduct the class and ensure adequate learning in the face of these outbursts. By October, Jane was referred for special education placement.

Jane was placed in a resource room for one hour a day so that she could receive individual help in reading and learn to respond appropriately to limits. The resource teacher developed a plan for managing and reducing tantrums. This plan was in effect for two months but did not improve Jane's behavior. With consent from Jane's mother, Jane was placed full-time in a class for emotionally disturbed children, remaining in her regular first grade class for opening exercises, lunch, recess, art, and music. This arrangement continued through the first, second, and third grades, with Jane gradually spending more time in her regular class.

From the fourth through sixth grades, Jane received special education help in the resource room for one hour each day. Emphasis was placed on improving academic skills and developing more constructive responses to frustration.

Now a seventh-grader, Jane attends all of her junior-high classes and spends one forty-minute period a day in the resource room. Jane's major difficulties are in the area of self-concept and peer interaction. Although she no longer becomes upset when she is stuck on a problem, she continues to denigrate her work and her abilities, sometimes saying "I'm just too dumb to do this" or "I'll never be good at anything." Jane has few positive interactions with classmates. She sometimes perceives laughter from other students as being directed towards her and has told me that no one likes her.

Jane's current resource teacher reports the following general description of the special goals and considerations established for Jane.

> As her resource teacher, my energies are directed towards reassuring Jane about her abilities. I try to praise her good work and use humor when she denigrates her abilities. She has actually smiled several times, and I know she is starting to think better of herself. I also have

Jane work with two other girls each day. They write and share creative stories and discuss topics of interest to each other. This activity provides Jane with an opportunity to relate to others in a positive manner. I know that Jane also attends an evening therapy group at our local mental health center. The focus of the group is on developing social skills.

What Is Emotional Disturbance?

As you can observe from reading about Bob Jones and Jane Cox, there is no typical emotionally disturbed student. Rather, the term "emotional disturbance" refers to a wide variety of emotional and behavioral problems that interfere with daily academic and social performance. In this section we will examine some of the ways in which professionals view emotionally disturbed students.

DEFINITIONS

There are several widely accepted definitions applied to the emotionally disturbed, but most seem to incorporate some or all of the factors appearing in Bower and Lambert's (1962) definition, which appears below:

The emotionally handicapped child is defined as having moderate to marked reduction in behavioral freedom, which in turn reduces his ability to function effectively in learning or working with others. In the classroom, this loss of freedom affects the child's educative and social experiences and results in a noticeable susceptibility to one or more of these five patterns of behavior:

1. An inability to learn which cannot be adequately explained by intellectual, sensory, neuro-physiological, or general health factors . . .

2. An inability to build or maintain satisfactory interpersonal relationships with peers and teachers . . .

3. Inappropriate or immature types of behavior or feelings under normal conditions . . .

4. A general pervasive mood of unhappiness or depression . . .

5. A tendency to develop physical symptoms, such as speech problems, pains, or fears, associated with personal or school problems. (Bower and Lambert, 1962.)

The expectations of teachers also plays a key role in the definition of emotional disturbance. Hewett and Forness suggest that in the classroom a child who is inattentive, withdrawn, or nonconforming to such a degree that he or she consistently fails to meet the expectations of the teacher and the school is a likely candidate for the label "emotionally disturbed" (Hewett and Forness, 1974, p. 58). Similarly, Graubard and Miller (1973), who prefer the term "behavioral disabilities" to "emotional disturbance," define behavioral disabilities as a variety of chronic, excessive deviant behaviors, ranging from impulsive and aggressive to depressive and withdrawal acts, which violate the perceiver's expectations of appropriateness, and which the perceiver wishes to see stopped (cited in Dunn, 1973, p. 246).

We prefer the definition provided by Bower and Lambert, because it appears in PL 94-142 as well as in several state definitions of the emotionally disturbed. However, the important considerations regarding teacher expectations offered by Hewett and Forness (1974) and Graubard and Miller (1973) must be kept in mind. While some professionals use IQ scores to determine who is retarded, there are no similar test scores that can be used by themselves to identify the emotionally disturbed. Thus, the expectations, perceptions, and observations provided by classroom teachers assume a significant role in determining whether a student is emotionally disturbed and therefore qualifies for special education services. No doubt, some teachers have a much higher level of tolerance for problem behavior than other teachers. In fact, what appears to be problem behavior in one teacher's classroom may be within the limits of acceptability in another room. This phenomenon makes it difficult to place the entire responsibility for the label "emotionally disturbed" on the student alone. Rather, any consideration of emotionally disturbed students must take into account both the student's behavior and the teacher's values, expectations, and ability to manage problem behavior.

Some educators add further subdivisions to the definition of emotional disturbance according to the degree of severity of problem behavior. For example, Kelly, Bullock, and Dykes (1977) outline three levels of severity of emotional disturbance, each level relating to commonly used special education service delivery categories. These levels are the following:

1. *Mild behavioral disorders.* Students who can receive all or most of their instruction in the regular classroom with periodic assistance from resource teachers, counselors, and other helping persons.

2. *Moderate behavioral disorders.* Students who remain in the regular classroom but who need intensive, ongoing help from specialists, such as resource teachers or counselors.

3. *Severe behavioral disorders.* Students whose needs are such that they must be placed in special classrooms or special schools.

These levels of disorder provide some help in describing the student's ability to function in classroom settings. Again, however, one must be aware of the relativity of these subdivisions. Some regular classroom teachers demonstrate unique skills and are able to experience success with students who exhibit rather extreme behavioral difficulties.

Finally, as we conclude our discussion of definitions of emotional disturbance, it may be apparent that the terms "emotional disturbance," "behavioral disorders," and "behavioral disabilities" have been used somewhat interchangeably. There is disagreement among some professionals regarding which terms are most appropriate. Some prefer the label "behavior disorders" since it is the student's overt behavior rather than emotions that are of the most immediate concern to teachers. Other labels that are sometimes used include "emotionally handicapped," "emotionally impaired," and "behaviorally impaired." Although labels may vary, the same problem behaviors are almost always used when the label is defined. The term "emotionally disturbed" has been used and will continue to be used in this text because it is commonly used in federal and many state laws and regulations regarding exceptional students.

CHARACTERISTICS AND DEFINITIONS

A wide variety of problem behaviors are exhibited by emotionally disturbed students. Typically, one or more of the following clusters of behaviors are demonstrated at a relatively frequent and intense level:

1. *Hostile, aggressive responses.* Reactions towards peers or adults that are marked by suspicion, hostility, anger, shouting, hitting, or impulsiveness.

2. *Defiance of authority.* Disregard for or defiance of school or classroom rules; rejection of teacher suggestions.

3. *Feelings of inferiority.* Expressions of inability to meet academic or social expectations, extreme devaluation of one's abilities and work efforts.

4. *Withdrawal/isolation.* Withdrawal from interaction with others, excessive shyness, unwillingness to talk or participate in class activities.

5. *Overactivity.* Restlessness, difficulty working with sustained attention, easily distracted from learning activities, irritable.

6. *Dependence and anxiety.* Excessive clinging, fearfulness, in need of frequent reassurance, perfectionistic, inability to relax, frequent complaints of physical symptoms such as headache and stomachache.

7. *Inappropriate affect.* Expressing laughter, crying, sadness, and other emotional responses at inappropriate times.

Although students labelled as emotionally disturbed may be average or above in intelligence, most mildly or moderately disturbed students score in the low average range on measures of intellectual performance (Kauffman, 1981). These students are likely to have academic deficiencies that place them one or two years below grade level in academic areas (Morse, Cutler, and Fink, 1964; Rubin and Balow, 1978). No doubt, these academic deficiencies often contribute to a cycle of frustration, anger, and inappropriate classroom behavior.

While most children have developed coping skills that allow them to successfully meet the demands of classroom life, emotionally disturbed students are noted for their inability to cope with stress in appropriate and acceptable ways (Redl and Wineman, 1951; Long and Dufner, 1980). Ambiguous assignments, work that takes too long to complete or seems too difficult, new learning activities, or the need to share learning materials or wait one's turn may result in excessive anxiety or frustration. This anxiety or frustration may lead to inappropriate responses, such as hostility, defiance, withdrawal, and impulsiveness. Indeed, one of the primary goals of teaching disturbed students is to help them learn more appropriate coping behaviors.

What causes emotional disturbance? Many teachers want to know the exact cause or reason for a student's emotional or behavioral problems. Although it is natural to search for causes, it is often very difficult to attribute a student's difficulties to any one cause. Generally, one or more of the following factors may be involved in a student's emotional or behavioral disorders.

1. *Emotional and physical deprivation.* Prolonged deprivation of basic needs such as food, shelter, and love may cause some children to develop mistrust of others and a preoccupation with meeting basic needs (Maslow, 1943). This preoccupation may interfere with learning appropriate responses to the environment.

2. *Temperament and abuse.* At early ages, children have been noted to exhibit different temperament levels. Some are difficult to manage from birth (Thomas, Chess, and Birch, 1968). Parents of these difficult children may use increasingly more abusive tactics in an effort to calm or control their children. Such abused children may, in turn, act in hostile and aggressive ways towards their peers and teachers (George and Main, 1979).

3. *Parental insensitivity.* Parents who continually demand perfection, prevent their children from exploring their environment, denigrate the contributions of their children, and use excessive punishment may generate feelings of mistrust, shame, guilt, and inferiority (Erikson, 1963).

4. *Conditioning.* Many children learn unconstructive behaviors through a gradual reinforcement process. For example, a parent who invariably gives attention to a child who whines or hits when he wants something may teach the child to use whining or hitting as a means of gaining attention (Becker, 1965).

5. *Modeling.* Related to conditioning is learning through imitation. The child who lives in a family or neighborhood in which aggressive responses such as shouting, yelling, and hitting are used to solve conflicts is likely to learn to use these same tactics. Patterson and colleagues (Patterson, Reid, Jones, and Conger, 1975) found that interactions in families with aggressive children were marked by frequent exchanges of negative, hostile behaviors. Here, children demonstrated high levels of hitting, shouting and other aggressive responses. Parental efforts to control their children's behavior relied on many of these same negative behaviors.

6. *Physiological factors.* Physiological factors such as inadequate diet, food allergies, lack of sleep, neurological impairment, and chemical imbalances, have been investigated and found to be potential contributors in a small percentage of children (Feingold, 1976; Rapp, 1978; Ritvo, 1977).

7. *School failure.* While school failure per se may be a result of emotional disturbance, it must also be considered a contributor. Since most students who are emotionally disturbed experience academic difficulties, it is likely that these difficulties contribute to a cycle of failure and frustration.

8. *School insensitivity.* Some teachers and administrators overreact to the misbehavior of students or react in ways that provoke student misbehavior. Thus, some students may behave more or less appropriately depending on the strategies and techniques used by their teachers.

While there exists a desire to pin the blame for a student's problems on one factor, such as parental insensitivity, school failure, or nutrition, it is likely that a variety of causes are involved. In particular, caution must be exercised regarding the role of parents. As Kauffman admonishes, ". . . it would be extremely inappropriate for special educators to adopt an attitude of blame toward parents of troubled children. The special education teacher must realize that the parents of a disturbed child have experienced a great deal of disappointment and frustration and that they too would like to see their child's behavior improve." (Kauffman, 1981, p. 104). Blaming parents may avoid the issue of what can we do to help students improve their learning and behavior in school. In addition, such blame may prevent teachers or other school personnel such as psychologists and social workers from helping parents to develop more constructive child management techniques.

IDENTIFICATION

Standardized achievement and intelligence tests, behavioral observations, samples of class work, and recommendations from special educators, psychologists, and other specialists typically form the basis for identifying a student as emotionally disturbed. The regular classroom teacher plays a key role in the initial identification process. In addition to being in a position to describe academic functioning, teachers are often in an excellent position to provide information regarding classroom behavior and general emotional functioning.

What methods can teachers use to assist in the identification process? Typically, direct observation and behavior checklists are used to provide information regarding the frequency and intensity of characteristic behaviors listed in the preceding section. Direct observation is a valuable source of information providing the teacher reports events using descriptive instead of evaluative language. Consider the following evaluative and descriptive observations provided for the same student in Figure 4.1.

FIGURE 4.1
Evaluative and descriptive observations

Evaluative observation	Descriptive observation
John is a hyperactive boy with little ability to do independent work.	Today (October 15, 1981) John got out of his seat on ten different occasions during the 9:00–10:30 work period. Each time he got out of his seat, I had to ask him three or four times to return to his work. This pattern is typical of John's behavior and attention level throughout the day.
Karen is a hostile young lady with little interest in cooperating with teachers.	Karen is earning D's and a few C's in my eighth grade English class. She completes less than half of her class assignments and almost none of her homework. When I try to remind her to begin her work or attempt to help her, she frequently responds with an angry or sarcastic voice, saying "Get off my back" or "Leave me alone." She spends a great deal of time whispering with one friend or just glancing at magazines. I believe she is capable of doing much better work but seems to resist my attempts to help her.

Notice that evaluative statements do not describe student behavior. Rather, they represent the teacher's judgments and feelings about the student. Descriptive statements, on the other hand, provide a clear account of how the student behaves under specific circumstances. Such clarity can provide important information regarding the frequency and intensity of student misbehavior and will help determine whether a student's behavior is such that special education services may be needed.

Another commonly used identification tool is a problem behavior checklist to be completed by the teacher. Such checklists usually contain a list of problem student behaviors. Teachers are asked to rate the frequency or intensity with which the student demonstrates each of the problem behaviors appearing on the list. Items from one informal checklist appear in Figure 4.2.

FIGURE 4.2
Informal problem behavior checklist

Directions: This is an instrument to help describe the needs of students with behavior problems. After completing the general identifying information, read each item and circle the response that best characterizes how the student behaves or performs. Circle the **1** if the student demonstrates the behavior not at all or does the opposite of the behavior. Circle the **2** if the student demonstrates the behavior occasionally or with repeated help or warnings. Circle the **3** if the student demonstrates the behavior at least sometimes on his or her own initiative. Circle the **4** if the student willingly demonstrates the behavior.

Student's Name _____   Grade _____

Teacher _____   Date _____

1. *Academic Behaviors*

    1.1. Arrives on time for class.   1 2 3 4

    1.2. Begins tasks on time.   1 2 3 4

    1.3. Completes tasks on time.   1 2 3 4

    1.4. Works independently.   1 2 3 4

    1.5. Pays attention while teacher is delivering information.   1 2 3 4

    1.6. Follows written directions.   1 2 3 4

    1.7. Organizes work carefully.   1 2 3 4

    1.8. Other _____   1 2 3 4

2. *Group Participation Skills*

    2.1. Offers opinions and answers when asked.   1 2 3 4

2.2.	Enjoys group activities.	1	2	3	4
2.3.	Takes turns and shares.	1	2	3	4
2.4.	Complies with basic rules for group participation.	1	2	3	4
2.5.	Shows concern for others' feelings and property.	1	2	3	4
2.6.	Solves conflicts without shouting, fighting or intimidating.	1	2	3	4
2.7.	Makes constructive contributions during group activities.	1	2	3	4
2.8.	Other _____	1	2	3	4

3. *General Coping Skills*

3.1.	Follows classroom rules and routines.	1	2	3	4
3.2.	Follows rules and expectations during unsupervised periods.	1	2	3	4
3.3.	Accepts constructive criticism/feedback.	1	2	3	4
3.4.	Takes part in classroom housekeeping.	1	2	3	4
3.5.	Seeks help when necessary.	1	2	3	4
3.6.	Accepts help from teachers.	1	2	3	4
3.7.	Accepts help from peers.	1	2	3	4
3.8.	Is confident of own abilities.	1	2	3	4
3.9.	Seeks constructive or legitimate peer attention.	1	2	3	4
3.10.	Asserts own rights when appropriate.	1	2	3	4
3.11.	Is willing to try new activities.	1	2	3	4
3.12.	Maintains composure under mild frustration.	1	2	3	4
3.13.	Considers consequences before acting.	1	2	3	4
3.14.	Is physically alert and active.	1	2	3	4
3.15.	Changes assignments within class smoothly.	1	2	3	4
3.16.	Can work with normal distractions.	1	2	3	4
3.17.	Is generally positive about self.	1	2	3	4
3.18.	Other _____	1	2	3	4

To determine high priority behaviors, look over the behaviors for which you circled a **1** or a **2** and select the two or three behaviors that you feel are most in need of immediate attention. Write each behavior down.

1. _____

2. _____

3. _____

Several commercially developed checklists are available. Among these are the Walker Problem Behavior Identification Checklist (Walker, 1970), The Behavior Problem Checklist (Quay, 1967), and the Hahnemann High School Behavior Scale (Spivack and Swift, 1971). Several of these checklists are reviewed in Chapter 7.

EDUCATIONAL AND SOCIAL NEEDS

Because of their somewhat disorganized, anxious, and/or disruptive behavior, emotionally disturbed students have typically experienced frustration, rejection, failure, and inconsistent treatment from adults. Such students need to experience success in meeting the academic, social, and behavioral demands of everyday school life and to ultimately become

A day in the life of Jane (clockwise from bottom left): working alone in the resource room, where this seventh-grader spends one forty-minute period a day; conferring with her resource teacher; at her desk in the regular classroom; sharing stories with two other girls in the resource room.

productive, well-adjusted adults. Typical educational and social needs include the following:

1. Develop basic academic skills to successfully participate in all aspects of academic and/or vocational programs at both elementary and secondary levels.

2. Develop increasingly more constructive and socially acceptable responses to frustration and other forms of stress.

3. Develop basic group participation skills such as taking turns, sharing materials, and working cooperatively with classmates.

4. Develop increasingly positive attitudes about self and others.

5. Learn to comply successfully with basic classroom and school rules and routines.

Many emotionally disturbed children can be well served in the regular classroom provided teachers are given assistance regarding how to manage misbehavior and students are given some additional help from resource teachers (Wixson, 1980). Of course, students with more severe difficulties may require special classrooms or other specialized placements.

PREVALENCE

The question of how many school-aged emotionally disturbed students exist is an important one for local, state, and federal officials who are charged with planning programs for exceptional students. An early and often cited study of the prevalence of emotional disturbance was conducted by Wickman (1929), who surveyed elementary teachers to determine the incidence of abnormal behavior. Wickman concluded that 7% of the school population was seriously maladjusted and 42% of the students demonstrated mild adjustment problems.

More recent studies reveal considerable variety in prevalence figures. Mackie (1969) suggests that only 2% of the school-aged population is emotionally disturbed, while Bower's (1969) estimate reaches 10%. An examination of prevalence estimates established by each state department of education found figures ranging from 0.5% to 15% (Schultz, Hirshoren, Manton, and Henderson, 1971). More than likely, the great variation in prevalence figures can be accounted for by different definitions of emotional disturbance used by each researcher.

Rubin and Balow (1978) studied a group of approximately 1600 elementary children over several years in an attempt to determine the prevalence of teacher-identified behavior problems over time. Near the end of each school year, teachers completed questionnaires to identify students who demonstrated behavior problems during the year. An interesting pattern emerged. More than half of the children were identified as having a behavior problem by at least one teacher during their elementary school career. In any given school year, about 30% of the students were identified as having some type of behavior problem. Slightly over 7% of the students were consistently identified from year to year (and from teacher to teacher) as evidencing behavior problems. Of this 7%, boys outnumbered girls three to one.

Rubin and Balow's prevalence figures are strikingly similar to those presented by Wickman. It would appear that, while many students demonstrate behavior problems during the school year, about 7% consistently demonstrate problems from year to year. It is this latter figure that probably reflects the number of students who require special education services of some form or another. It should be noted, however, that this 7% figure is considerably higher than the 2% estimate offered by the federal government and presented in the table in Chapter 1. A reasonable explanation of the discrepancy is that the 2% estimate offered by the federal government pertains to more seriously emotionally disturbed students or those who require a highly restrictive placement, such as a self-contained special class. It is likely that when mild to moderately emotionally disturbed students are counted, the total percentage may near the 7% figure found by Rubin and Balow.

How Are Emotionally Disturbed Students Educated?

Most experts agree that there is no one approach to understanding and teaching the emotionally disturbed. As a classroom teacher it is likely that you will confer with special educators and other specialists who may hold widely different positions regarding how to best approach these students. To help acquaint you with this diversity, a synopsis of the most common positions follows.

PSYCHODYNAMIC POSITION

Historically, the psychodynamic position was the first clearly stated approach to the education of emotionally disturbed children. Rooted in the psychoanalytic tradition, a major feature of this approach is the belief that problem behaviors, such as aggression, anger, defiance, and withdrawal, stem from inner conflicts. These inner conflicts are caused by unsatisfactory or traumatic relationships with parents, siblings, and authority figures. The unfulfilling relationships cause students to feel basic mistrust, shame, and doubt regarding themselves and others (Erikson, 1963).

A basic goal of the psychodynamic position is to provide a means for expressing inner conflicts in the context of a caring, supportive teacher-student relationship. Berkowitz and Rothman (1960), leading proponents of the psychodynamic approach, define the teacher's role as one of making the child feel that the teacher accepts the child and can meet misbehavior with understanding instead of rejection. Thus, students are encouraged to express their feelings and impulses but are not allowed to harm others. It is believed that once disturbed children feel accepted and valued, they will begin to identify with the positive and constructive behaviors of their teachers and peers and change for the better (Bettelheim, 1950).

Educational applications of the psychodynamic approach are more likely to be found in psychiatric clinics and special schools than in the regular classroom. This is because public schools stress academics and tend to limit students' expressions of feelings and behavior. Some psychiatrists, social workers, and psychologists who provide consultation to schools regarding how to help specific students may use a psychodynamic orientation and emphasize the importance of understanding and accepting students' feelings and behaviors. Classroom teachers must search for ways to offer understanding while still maintaining basic limits and expectations.

PSYCHOEDUCATIONAL POSITION

An outgrowth of the psychodynamic position, the psychoeducational approach represents an attempt to combine educational and emotional considerations, thus making it a more practical approach for public school teachers. As in the psychodynamic approach, an important feature of the psychoeducational approach is an emphasis on the development of trust and acceptance between teacher and student. Such a relationship is viewed as a key factor in helping students develop more positive attitudes and expectations about themselves and others. Through an accepting relationship it is also believed that the student will feel increasingly valued and, therefore, more willing to learn new behaviors and attitudes (Long, Alpher, Butt, and Cully, 1971). William Morse (1971), a leading proponent of the psychoeducational approach, suggests that the ideal teacher combines the qualities of both teacher and therapist.

A second critical feature is an emphasis on developing self-control and group participation skills. Many students with learning and behavior problems function reasonably well in a one-to-one learning situation in which they can receive almost constant attention and help. However, these same students may experience considerable difficulty in group activities where they must exercise self-control and use various group participation skills such as sharing, taking turns, and offering opinions in a constructive manner. Thus, academic and social activities and games that involve gradually increasing amounts of group interaction are viewed as an important arena for learning many coping skills (Fagan, Long, and Stevens, 1975).

Finally, although academic remediation activities cannot be construed as a psychoeducational practice, efforts to remediate academic deficiencies are practiced by nearly every teacher who espouses the psychoeducational approach. Daily instruction in reading, math, language, and other areas in need of remediation is a common practice. Instructional materials are selected, when possible, on the basis of student interest. Since it is understood that many students have a fear of failure in addition to anxiety over learning, traditional testing is minimized and academic lessons are made as informal and relaxing as possible. Emphasis is placed on pointing out correct responses rather than incorrect responses. As the students' academic skills and self-confidence increase, more challenging academic tasks are provided.

HUMANISTIC POSITION

There is no single humanistic approach. Rather, humanistic approaches to students with behavior problems are quite varied. The thread that ties these approaches together, however, is the emphasis on individual choice, commitment, and decision making and the rejection of psychiatric terms and labels to define students. Many students with behavior problems are viewed as reacting to feelings of failure, isolation, and low self-esteem (Glasser, 1969; Rogers, 1969).

Humanistic approaches stress the importance of a facilitative teacher-student relationship. For example, Carl Rogers (1969) asserts that the quality of the interpersonal relationship between teacher and student significantly influences academic and social-emotional growth. A relationship that facilitates growth is characterized by conditions of positive regard and empathic understanding. "Positive regard" refers to a valuing of the student that is communicated through the genuine acceptance of many student ideas, opinions, and suggestions. Opportunities to demonstrate such acceptance may occur during class discussions, individual student conferences, and by providing students with an opportunity to engage in some self-selected activities.

"Empathic understanding" is the ability to detect and then convey awareness of conflicts and strong emotions a student may be experiencing at a particular moment. Empathic teachers have learned how to recognize verbal and nonverbal indications of student stress and how to convey their understanding in a supportive manner. Opportunities to demonstrate empathic understanding frequently occur when the student is angry, frustrated, confused, or happy.

Just as high levels of empathy and positive regard promote growth, Rogers believes that low levels of these conditions influence adversely self-concept and academic achievement. Thus, not only what is taught but how teachers relate to students is associated with learning.

Humanistic approaches also stress high levels of student choice and involvement in school activities. Glasser (1969) advocates the use of frequent class meetings in which students are encouraged to discuss academic, social, or other concerns, with the teacher serving in a nonjudgmental manner. Glasser believes that many students with behavior problems need to voice their concerns but also need to be encouraged to assume personal responsibility for learning and behavior in appropriate ways. Rogers believes that students can begin to experience commitment and self-actualization by being able to engage in some independent, self-directed learning activities each day.

BEHAVIORAL POSITION

The foundation of the behavioral position rests on the premise that student misbehavior is shaped and maintained by reinforcement from adults and peers. Reinforcement most typically comes in the form of attention and recognition. In some cases teachers, parents, and peers inadvertently pay far too much attention to the misbehavior of certain children while overlooking their positive behavior. Over a long period of time, children can actually learn to gain attention or recognition by misbehaving (Becker, 1971).

Behaviorists carefully apply positive reinforcement in the form of grades, praise, special privileges, and attention to help students learn appropriate behaviors. In some cases, reinforcers such as recess and special activities are removed in an effort to help a student decrease or eliminate inappropriate behaviors. A teacher may withhold an activity that a student enjoys (watching a filmstrip, going to the library) because of a problem misbehavior, such as getting out of one's seat too often, in a direct effort to decrease the frequency of that misbehavior.

Another distinguishing characteristic of the behavioral approach is its focus on observable behaviors. Adherents to the behavioral approach often reject internal conflict, brain injury, poor self-concept, and other unobservable or speculative explanations for learning and behavior problems. Instead, they believe that identifying and then rewarding specific academic and social behaviors is of the most immediate and practical value to teachers and students. For example, some educators propose that a student must first learn to feel accepted and valued before a significant amount of learning can take place. Acting on this belief, they present only minimal academic tasks to students. Most behaviorists, however, would be quick to suggest that students will automatically feel better about themselves as they experience greater academic success.

The role of a teacher who follows a behavioral viewpoint is fairly clear. The central concern is to identify specific academic skills for students to master, determine maladaptive behaviors to decrease, identify appropriate social behaviors that need to be taught, and then select and use appropriate learning materials and reinforcement principles to accomplish specific objectives (Hewett and Taylor, 1980). Of course, acting as a behavior modifier does not preclude showing interest in students, listening to them with empathy, and creating a warm classroom atmosphere.

Behavioral approaches have been applied successfully by elementary and secondary classroom teachers, special educators, counselors, and parents to help reduce disruptive behavior and promote more constructive behavior (O'Leary and O'Leary, 1972; Walker and Shea, 1980). Despite the favorable results often brought about by behavioral techniques, these procedures have not always been accepted by concerned adults. The use of praise, privileges, and other rewards has been thought of by some as bribery. This attitude has come about largely due to the use and misuse of reinforcers such as candy and various prizes. While these items may be necessary in a few situations, more conventional rewards, such as praise, teacher recognition, and enjoyable activities, can be used in the regular classroom. Some people who have used the techniques have been labelled as antihumanistic and unfeeling. This rather narrow view of behavior modification has begun to give way. Many teachers realize that the systematic application of reinforcers can bring about positive changes in student behavior and learning.

ECOLOGICAL APPROACH

In the ecological approach, considerable attention is placed on determining the various factors in a student's life that may contribute to emotional disturbance. William Rhodes is probably the most renowned spokesman for this approach. According to Rhodes (1967, 1970), significant agents in the student's life, such as family members, teachers, peers, and other community members, contribute to emotional health or emotional disturbance. When a child is identified as emotionally disturbed, the problem does not reside exclusively within the student. The attitudes, expectations, and behaviors of others usually contribute to the problem and must be considered.

If the attitudes and expectations of others contribute to problem behavior, then the focal point of who must change or who owns the problem must shift. We are probably accustomed to believing that it is the disturbed student whose behavior must change. Proponents of the ecological approach do not dispute this point. However, they would frown on any approach that views the student as the only person in need of change. Ecologists recognize that teachers have different tolerance levels and that what may be bothersome and disturbing to one teacher may be acceptable to another (Swap, 1974; Curran and Algozzine, 1980). Thus, how the teacher responds to the student may also need to be modified. This same logic is applied to parents, peers, and other community members who come in contact with the student. Emphasis is placed on helping these individuals develop constructive and supportive expectations and relationships regarding the emotionally disturbed student.

The ecological approach does not attempt to replace the psychodynamic, psychoeducational, humanistic, or behavioral positions. One can use techniques from any or all of these positions and still adhere to an ecological viewpoint. The distinguishing feature of this position is not so much the techniques that are used as the focus of the techniques. Since the ecological position recognizes the interdependence between the student and the other people in his or her environment, the attitudes and behaviors of all involved must be considered.

Because the ecological approach focuses on many individuals, a treatment team is needed to effect widespread change. This team may consist of social workers, teachers, special educators, and other workers dedicated to the welfare of children and families. To be completely effective, such teams need to develop common goals and work in a spirit of cooperation and mutual understanding.

Educators can apply some ecological principles in everyday practice. These principles might include the following:

1. Placing emotionally disturbed students with teachers who feel comfortable with problem behavior and who have developed effective management skills.

2. Providing consultation and support to teachers who work with students who demonstrate problem behaviors.

3. Making sure that all teachers and staff members develop and follow a consistent approach with each problem student.

4. Helping classmates to develop constructive responses to emotionally disturbed students.

5. Helping the disturbed child to feel welcome, safe, and successful in a variety of academic and nonacademic activities.

6. Developing constructive and ongoing communication with parents regarding expectations for their children.

Summary

In this chapter we have introduced you to the definitions, characteristics, identification, educational and social needs, and prevalence of emotionally disturbed students. We have also reviewed some of the major approaches towards the education of disturbed children. Key points are listed below.

1. A variety of definitions of emotional disturbance exist. The authors prefer the one developed by Bower and Lambert. This definition also appears in PL 94-142.

2. Any consideration of emotional disturbance must take into account the teacher's tolerance level for disturbing behavior.

3. Emotionally disturbed students exhibit a wide variety of characteristics. They often have academic problems in addition to a variety of behavior problems.

4. Emotionally disturbed students are identified through methods such as standardized tests, observation, and interviews with specialists.

5. The educational and social needs include the development of academic skills, self-control, group participation skills, and positive attitudes about the self.

6. Prevalence figures vary depending upon the definition used. Although the federal government uses a 2% figure, as many as 7% of the school-aged population may have behavior problems that require some form of special education assistance.

7. There is a variety of approaches to the education of emotionally disturbed children. These approaches are not necessarily mutually exclusive.

Activities

1. Select a student who demonstrates problem behaviors. Observe the student for about thirty minutes and write down specific instances of appropriate and inappropriate behavior, being careful to use descriptive instead of evaluative terms.

2. Locate a resource room or special classroom for the emotionally disturbed and arrange a visit. Observe several students and interview the classroom teacher to determine his/her goals and approaches to teaching.

3. Interview a regular classroom teacher who teaches several emotionally disturbed students. Determine what methods are used as well as the teacher's feelings about working with these students.

Study Questions

1. In your own words, provide a definition of emotional disturbance.

2. Why are teachers' attitudes and expectations so important in identifying emotionally disturbed students?

3. List several characteristics of emotionally disturbed students.

4. What methods are typically used by classroom teachers to identify emotionally disturbed students?

5. What is the difference between a descriptive and an evaluative observation?

6. Explain the discrepancy between the 2% incidence figure provided by the federal government and 7% figure offered by Rubin and Balow.

7. Identify the basic goals for educating emotionally disturbed children.

8. Briefly define the psychodynamic, psychoeducational, humanistic, behavioral, and ecological positions towards emotional disturbance.

Questions for Further Thought

1. Think of a time you were particularly frustrated, angry, or disappointed. In what ways were your feelings and reactions similar to and different from the feelings and reactions of an emotionally disturbed student?

2. What might be some advantages and disadvantages of placing emotionally disturbed students in regular classrooms?

3. In what ways can school be a helpful experience for emotionally disturbed students? A harmful experience?

Additional Resources

BOOKS

Hewett, F. M., and Taylor, F. *The emotionally disturbed child in the classroom.* Boston: Allyn and Bacon, 1980.

Long, N. J., Newman, R., and Morse, W. C., (Eds.). *Conflict in the classroom* (4th ed.). Belmont, California: Wadsworth, 1980.

JOURNALS

American Journal of Orthopsychiatry

Behavioral Disorders: Journal of the Council for Children with Behavioral Disorders

Journal of Abnormal Child Psychology

Psychology in the Schools

PROFESSIONAL ORGANIZATIONS

Council for Children with Behavioral Disorders, Council for Exceptional Children, 1920 Association Drive, Reston, Virginia 22091

National Association for Mental Health, Inc., 1800 North Kent Street, Arlington, Virginia 22209

CHILDREN'S BOOKS

Berger, T. *I have feelings.* New York: Human Sciences Press, 1971.

Clymer, E. *My brother Stevie.* New York: Holt, Rinehart and Winston, 1967.

Gold, P. *Please don't say hello.* New York: Human Sciences Press, 1975.

Krasilvosky, P. *The shy little girl.* Boston: Houghton Mifflin, 1970.

Little, J. *Spring begins in March.* Boston: Little, Brown and Company, 1969.

Simon, N. *I was so mad!* Chicago: Albert Whitman, 1976.

Chapter 5

Learning Disabled
Students

At one time or another almost every student has a difficult time mastering a skill. There are many reasons for these learning difficulties. The material to be learned may be perceived as uninteresting, leading to low motivation. The subject matter may be beyond what the student is ready to learn or it may be poorly taught. In some instances, however, motivation is high and the lessons are taught very well, but the student still has an apparent difficulty learning academic skills. While there are many possible reasons for low achievement in school, many low achievers have what have come to be known as learning disabilities. In this chapter we will examine definitions, characteristics, and various approaches to developing an understanding of learning disabilities.

IAN

Ian is a fourth-grader who has an ability to charm adults. His sense of humor and high level verbal skills enable him to engage almost anyone in meaningful conversation. Although he is having difficulty in math and other tasks that require writing or drawing, he is generally regarded as a "bright" student. The existence of his learning disability remained undetected during his first four years of school.

Ian, a learning disabled student, often appeared frustrated when involved in activities for which he had not mastered academic skills.

Ian's fourth-grade teacher was the first to suspect an actual learning disability. She observed a number of behaviors that she found puzzling. For example, during math periods Ian often appeared frustrated. That is, he made facial grimaces, rocked in his seat, and avoided his work by playing with objects in his desk or talking to others. On several occasions, when she reminded Ian to pay attention to his work, he pretended to begin working but soon began his nonproductive behaviors. When Ian's teacher examined his work, she noticed that his handwriting seemed immature, with letters written in an inconsistent manner.

As the year progressed, Ian's problems became more apparent. He not only refused to do math, but when he was coaxed into completing second-grade level math, which the teacher provided so that Ian could experience success, he made many errors. On an addition facts exercise, for example, he scored less than 20%. His teacher tried to provide some easier work with occasional one-to-one instruction with few positive results. Ian's classroom behavior deteriorated somewhat, with increased signs of tension during math periods and activities requiring extensive handwriting.

Ian's teacher referred him to the Pupil Evaluation Team shortly after Thanksgiving. The team met to consider the referral and decided that further assessment and evaluation were needed. Their investigation of Ian's educational needs provided some surprising results. Ian's score on an individually administered IQ test was 119. His reading score was above the sixth grade level. The examiner carried out other assessment procedures and found no evidence of visual or auditory problems. On an individually administered math test, he obtained a score on the 1.5 grade level. His knowledge of math concepts was almost nonexistent. Other formal and informal tests revealed that his fine motor skills were well below his expected level of performance. On the basis of these findings and other observational data collected by the teacher, Ian was classified as learning disabled and was placed in a resource room program for two hours of specialized remedial instruction each day.

During the Pupil Evaluation Team meeting someone questioned why Ian had not been referred in one of the previous years. It seems that the teachers in grades one and two had been convinced that Ian would grow out of his problem. They pointed out that it is difficult to gauge the severity of a skill deficit in the early grades. One teacher had remarked, "After all, how far behind can you be in the first grade?" By grade three, Ian had mastered basic math problems by developing an elaborate finger counting, tally mark system. He solved multiplication problems using a time-consuming process in which he converted them to long repeated addition. His teacher also assisted by providing easier work. It was in the fourth grade that Ian's problems became acute; his problem-solving techniques were too cumbersome to use with the more difficult problems. As each school year progressed, Ian's failures led to more problem behavior and emotional reactions, but his verbal abilities and natural "charm" obscured the severity of these problems.

Like Ian, many children struggle through school and experience unnecessary failure because of undetected learning disabilities. In many instances, academic failure also leads to emotional and behavior problems as in the case of Billy.

BILLY

Billy, a high-school sophomore, had stated many times that he wanted more than anything to play on the varsity basketball team at school. To maintain the grade-point average necessary to play on the team, Billy often spent as many as five hours per night on his homework. His parents often bragged about his high level of motivation. Despite Billy's desire to succeed and his willingness to work, his grades were barely above the minimum level required to remain eligible for sports. Oftentimes, however, the passing grades he received were based on attitude and effort more than his test scores.

Then several things happened. Billy received failing notices in English and mathematics. As a result he became ineligible for sports and unable to play basketball. While his parents knew this would be a severe problem for Billy, they were unprepared for his reaction. While he continued to study, he often appeared upset and frustrated, especially when working on English and math assignments. He began to say that he hated school. Finally, Mr. Ward, the principal, called for a parent conference. Billy had recently been quite disruptive in school, a change that concerned many of his teachers.

At the conference, several of Billy's teachers described him as extremely withdrawn at times, inattentive in class, and failing to follow directions. It seemed that these behaviors began to occur when Billy became ineligible to play basketball. Because of Billy's previous record for trying to learn and cooperating in school, most of his teachers had tried to help him. It seemed, however, that extra help did not result in an improvement in his academic work. Upon hearing from everyone present, a referral was made to the Pupil Evaluation Team.

The Pupil Evaluation Team met to determine whether Billy qualified for special education help as a learning disabled student. The assessment of his learning showed that Billy was of normal intelligence, three years below grade level in reading, and moderately handicapped in his ability to express himself in writing. Additional observations of his performance indicated that he seemed to learn more efficiently when presented with written material rather than an oral approach. An analysis of the tests and observational data led the team to classify Billy as learning disabled and to design a special program to help him achieve success in the classroom. Once Billy began to be successful, his problem behavior disappeared and he became happier at school and at home.

Many students, like Billy, achieve little or no success in school despite a great desire to learn. In some instances, the cause of learning problems is a learning disability. The identification of learning disabilities and the development of specialized teaching programs for disabled students can increase the likelihood of student and teacher success.

What Are Learning Disabilities?

In order to understand learning disabilities we must begin by learning how to identify the learning disabled. This is not an easy process. There exists no clear-cut procedure for determining whether or not a student is learning disabled. Given the current state of the art in detecting and treating learning disabilities, members of the Pupil Evaluation Team should be aware of the issues and philosophical concerns presented in this chapter. This insures that students who are eligible for special education services receive the help they need to become successful learners.

DEFINITION

It has always been recognized that some people have difficulty acquiring academic skills. In the past, explanations for such problems were likely to focus on limited mental capacity. Some students, however, did not seem to be retarded. Yet they showed a marked inability to learn. Early studies of children who had difficulty learning had occurred, but the widespread recognition of learning disabilities as a specific handicapping condition did not occur until the latter part of the 1960s. A movement started with the formation of the Association for Children with Learning Disabilities in 1963 and has grown until today learning disability programs are available in many of our schools.

The general acceptance of learning disabilities as a distinct classification of special needs has not occurred without some differences of opinion. After the movement was started, it became clear that one of the most difficult tasks would be to agree on a definition. The major controversy focused on whether or not the cause of learning disabilities was brain injury or a problem in the way in which the brain processes information (Hallihan and Cruickshank, 1973; Johnson and Morasky, 1977). Those advocating a brain injury approach believed that learning disabilities were caused by actual, although difficult to detect, brain damage. The psychological process advocates rejected the brain injury hypothesis and proposed that learning disabilities were caused by poorly functioning perceptual processes.

The outcome of the controversy over definitions would have a fairly dramatic impact on the field of learning disabilities. If the definition finally adopted was too narrow, many students who might benefit from special education would be automatically excluded. If the definition was too broad, then too many students might be included and students with significant problems might not receive assistance.

Several years after the definition controversy arose, the National Advisory Committee on Handicapped Children included a definition of learning disabilities in its report to Congress in 1968. The definition seemed to represent an attempt to accept both the brain damage and the psychological process approaches. While there has been some dissatisfaction with the definition, it has become the standard among special educators and is included in the Education for All Handicapped Children Act of 1975 (PL 94-142) as follows:

> "Specific learning disability" means a disorder in one or more of the basic psychological processes involved in understanding or in using language, spoken or written, which may manifest itself in an imperfect ability to listen, think, speak, read, write, spell, or to do mathematical calculations. The term includes such conditions as perceptual handicaps, brain injury, minimal brain dysfunction, dyslexia and developmental aphasia. The term does not include children who have learning problems which are primarily the result of visual, hearing, or motor handicaps, of mental retardation, of emotional disturbance, or of environmental, cultural, or economic disadvantage. (*Federal Register*, August 23, 1977, p. 42,478)

An analysis of the definition reveals that a child is learning disabled if there is evidence of a psychological process disorder or a brain injury. In order to identify a child as learning disabled using this part of the definition, the educator would first document the existence of a learning problem (an imperfect ability to listen, think, speak, read, write, spell, or do mathematical calculations) and then choose among the variety of tests that measure psychological learning processes or refer the child to a specialist who might document the existence of organic brain damage. As the psychological processes are not defined, the educator must choose from among the variety of tests available at this time.

It should be noted that the definition also excludes those who have learning problems that are primarily the result of visual, hearing, or motor handicaps; retardation; emotional disturbances; environmental, cultural or economic disadvantages. This part of the definition has led to some confusion. Some educators have asked, "Can a student who has one of the other handicaps, or is culturally or economically disadvantaged, be classified as learning disabled?" The answer is yes. A student can have more than one handicap and still be classified as learning disabled, as long as one of the handicaps is a learning disability. It is often very difficult, however, to determine which handicap is the primary one. Because of the difficulties in identifying specific learning disabilities in some cases, a student who is low in academic skills may be classified as learning disabled only when all other possible causes have been eliminated.

From time to time during the two decades or so that learning disabilities have been recognized as a discrete professional field, the proposed definitions have been criticized by one professional group or another. In an effort to overcome the problems inherent in the current definition, a joint committee representing a number of professional organizations has proposed a new one.

> Learning disability is a generic term that refers to a heterogeneous group of disorders manifested by significant difficulties in the acquisition and use of listening, speaking, reading, writing, reasoning, or mathematical abilities. These disorders are intrinsic to the individual and are presumed to be due to central nervous system dysfunction. Even though a learning disability may occur concomitantly with other handicapping conditions or environmental influences, it is not the direct result of those conditions or influences. (Maine Council for Learning Disabilities, 1981)

When this or some other new definition is adopted, some substantial changes may occur in the identification and education of students with learning disabilities. As these changes occur, it is important for educators to use any new developments as a basis for better programs for learning disabled students.

CHARACTERISTICS

There have been numerous attempts to determine what characteristics learning disabled students have that distinguish them from students who do not have learning disabilities. One article in a popular magazine advises parents to watch for the child who has an extraordinary attraction towards sweets or who may be a tip-toe walker (Hirshey, 1978). More helpful articles in professional literature cite such characteristics as attention problems, memory difficulties, and language deficits (Blackhurst and Berdine, 1981). One such list compiled by Gearhart (1977), however, contains several characteristics that represent *opposite* kinds of behavior:

1. hyperactivity
2. hypoactivity
3. lack of motivation
4. inattention
5. overattention
6. perceptual disorders
7. lack of coordination
8. perseveration
9. memory disorders

As you can see, there is some disagreement on the types of difficulties exhibited by learning disabled students; if you examine the characteristics in the lists you will likely see some that are present in students who do not have learning disabilities. Given the lack of agreement among existing lists it is likely that teachers who use lists to identify learning disabled students might make many errors.

Are lists of characteristics useful? In our view they are, in spite of the apparent contradictions between lists and within lists. Some easily observed behaviors can be used to justify a referral to the Pupil Evaluation Team and to determine if a learning disability is present. The following list, culled from our own work, is a set of traits that should lead a teacher to suspect that a student has a learning disability:

1. Pays attention to learning tasks for only short periods of time.

2. Demonstrates frequent, inappropriate behavior that replaces appropriate classroom learning behavior. Playing with objects, leaving his or her seat, and frequent bathroom breaks are examples of this type of behavior.

3. Does not learn from traditional instructional techniques.

4. Frequently becomes angry or upset when asked to perform academic tasks.

5. Rarely begins or completes assignments on time.

6. Appears nervous and overactive in some learning situations.

7. Is forgetful and frequently does not follow verbal or written instructions.

8. Exhibits confusion when recalling sequences of events.

9. Frequently selects the wrong word when speaking or writing.

10. Has significant problems with gross or fine motor skills, such as would be evident in physical education or handwriting.

The behaviors and characteristics of learning disabled students are sometimes misinterpreted. Students are incorrectly labeled as lazy or having a poor attitude, and punishment is substituted for proper instruction. Teachers who develop an awareness of the characteristics listed above are less likely to make such errors and more likely to take appropriate further steps to identify a student as learning disabled.

IDENTIFICATION

The broad, somewhat vague, definition has led to a variety of methods used to identify the learning disabled. The major types discussed here center around the psychological process and brain injury approaches, already mentioned above, and a third one, called the discrepancy approach.

The Psychological Process Approach Some researchers have theorized that learning disabilities are the result of specific deficits in mental processes. These researchers have hypothesized the existence of many different processes. Some widely adopted theories focus on visual and visual-motor perception and language processes. Efforts to utilize these process theories to understand learning problems have led to the development of tests such as the Purdue Perceptual Motor Survey (Roach and Kephart, 1966), the Frostig Developmental Test of Visual Perception (Frostig, Maslow, Lefever, and Whittlesey, 1964), and the Illinois Test of Psycholinguistic Abilities (Kirk, McCarthy, and Kirk, 1968).

The Purdue Perceptual Motor Survey assesses perception and motor performance by having the child perform tasks requiring coordination, balance, and specific movements such as jumping, following moving objects with the eye, and walking on a balance beam.

The Illinois Test of Psycholinguistic Abilities (ITPA) was developed for primary-grade students and measures abilities in twelve areas of language functioning including expressive, receptive, and organizing abilities. A student taking this test is asked, among other things, to repeat numbers from memory, count partially hidden objects, pantomime the use of common objects such as a pencil sharpener, and supply missing words in sentences.

The Frostig Developmental Test of Visual Perception has five subtests, which require the child to identify and outline specific shapes, draw curved, straight, and angled lines, and to match shapes. This test, like the ITPA, is designed for use with the younger child.

Identification of learning disabilities using tests based on the psychological process approach assumes that the processes examined actually underlie learning disabilities. If a student has a significant dysfunction as measured by any of these special tests, then, by definition, the student may be classified as learning disabled.

The Brain Injury Approach A number of psychiatrists, physicians, and educators believe that a mild form of brain injury or neurological damage is the probable cause of learning disabilities. Those adhering to this belief typically employ a variety of medically oriented test procedures in the identification process. Data obtained from sources such as electroencephalographs (EEGs) and/or tests for muscle imbalances, coordination, and reflexes might lead to a diagnosis of learning disabilities. Other tests, such as the Bender Visual-Motor Gestalt Test (Bender, 1938) may be administered by a trained psychologist in an effort to detect patterns that might suggest brain injury. Obviously, the testing procedures just mentioned must be conducted by highly trained medical specialists, such as pediatric neurologists, psychiatrists, and trained psychological examiners.

The Discrepancy Approach Another commonly used technique for classification has been called the discrepancy approach. In selecting this approach, the Pupil Evaluation Team collects data to document learning capacity and actual performance, usually an intelligence quotient and a set of achievement level scores. If the achievement levels are significantly below the level suggested by the child's IQ, the child may be classified as having a learning disability.

Developing criteria to determine who is learning disabled is not an easy task. If too many students are found to be learning disabled, any available special education services could be quickly exhausted and those with genuine learning disabilities might not get the intensive help they need. On the other hand, some identification procedures can be too rigorous, too costly, and of questionable value. For example, few school districts could afford to have every student suspected of having a learning disability receive a complete neurological examination. Ultimately, each school district must interpret state and federal guidelines and develop its own identification procedures. The authors suggest that the discrepancy approach represents the most direct and economical avenue towards the identification of learning disabled students. Assessment of psychological processes and neurological functions have substantial limitations that will be addressed later in this chapter.

EDUCATIONAL AND SOCIAL NEEDS

The effects of having a learning disability may go far beyond the failure to learn academic skills. Students who experience frequent failure often develop problems with their attitudes and behavior. They may engage in a variety of inappropriate behaviors that would lead some teachers to label them as lazy, angry, or hyperactive. Learning disabled students are likely to view themselves as incompetent or "dumb" and suffer as a result a lack of self-confidence and respect.

Despite the possibly serious nature of learning disabilities, most learning disabled students receive a majority of their education in a regular classroom with supportive help from an itinerant specialist or a resource room teacher. By developing an awareness of the needs of the learning disabled student, the classroom teacher can provide educational experiences appropriate to the student's needs. These needs can be expressed as the following general goals:

1. Developing essential academic skills.

2. Improving ability to pay attention, to remember and follow directions.

3. Developing effective listening, study, and note-taking skills.

4. Decreasing the frequency of distracting or disruptive behaviors, which are incompatible with the completion of assigned tasks and hinder academic success.

5. Learning ways of coping with the inevitable frustrations resulting from minor failures.

6. Improving fine and gross motor coordination.

7. Developing a sense of self-worth and positive regard for one's abilities.

8. Developing a sense of positive regard for others.

A learning disabled student is likely to experience many emotional, behavioral, and learning difficulties. It is sometimes too easy to use these side-effects as excuses for blaming the child. Teachers who say such things as "She could do it if she only tried" are merely absolving themselves of the responsibility to make sure learning takes place. By viewing the student's problems as instructional challenges the teacher will be more likely to play an active role in helping these students overcome both their educational and their behavioral problems.

PREVALENCE

Estimates of the incidence of learning disabilities have ranged from 1% to as high as 41% of the school population (Bryan and Bryan, 1978). The variability in these estimates is likely related to general differences of opinion regarding the definition of learning disabilities. Some professionals would consider only students with severe neurological problems as being learning disabled, while others would include those who are below grade level in academic subjects despite at least average ability. The United States Bureau of Education for the Handicapped has published a 3% estimated incidence figure (Heward and Orlansky, 1980). In some cases, however, the percentage of the school population that is classified as learning disabled is determined by state or local guidelines and will vary depending upon the local definition of learning disabilities.

How Are the Learning Disabled Educated?

There are many different approaches to the education of learning disabled students. Each of these is based on a different theory about the nature of the disability. Theories that emphasize internal factors, such as the psychological process approach and various medical approaches, usually result in methods designed to alter or compensate for the underlying causes of learning deficits. Theories that discount the effects of internal factors, such as the skill deficit approach, generally emphasize an approach that focuses on skill development.

THE PSYCHOLOGICAL PROCESS APPROACH

The belief that defects in thinking processes are responsible for learning disabilities has led theorists to attempt to identify these processes and to devise teaching methods to improve the way the brain handles sensory input. While many different processes have been postulated, the perceptual and perceptual-motor approaches have been widely adopted.

The overriding assumption of the perceptual approach is the belief that academic performance is based on perceptual abilities. Marianne Frostig is a well-known advocate of the perceptual approach. Frostig claims that visual perceptual skills, such as the ability to discriminate between figure and ground relationships and to identify basic shapes, are important prerequisites to learning basic academic skills. The perceptual theories of Frostig are representative of a number of others that hypothesize the existence of discrete perceptual functions.

A second assumption regarding the perceptual approach is that perception can be assessed. The testing of perceptual functions appears to be a major concern for adherents of this approach. A number of tests have been developed over the past decade that purport to measure discrete perceptual functions. Frostig's Developmental Test of Visual Perception (Frostig et al., 1963) is perhaps the most well-known test in this area. Her test measures five functions: eye-motor coordination, figure-ground perception, constancy of shape, position in space, and spatial relationships. Representative test items for each of the five functions appear in Figure 5.1.

Many learning programs have been based on the Frostig Test. Remediation activities resemble the test items and include such activities as matching shapes, sorting items according to size and shape, discriminating shapes, finding hidden figures, and drawing straight, curved, and angled lines between two or more points. The Frostig approach has had a fairly dramatic impact on early education. An examination of nursery school and kindergarten curricula reveals a large number of Frostig-like materials and activities. Remediation based on the Frostig theory is carried out both by special education and many regular classroom teachers.

Newell Kephart (1971) is a leading proponent of a perceptual-motor theory. He suggests that all perception is based on a foundation of motor skills learned at an early age. Mastery of skills such as balance, movement, laterality, and directionality allows the child to explore the environment perceptually by correlating motor and perceptual information. This process is called perceptual-motor matching. Only when the child is able to collect accurate perceptions from the environment can conceptualization occur. Thus, according to Kephart, the child must first attain appropriate perceptual-motor development before academic skills such as reading and writing can be learned. Failure to learn academic skills adequately is considered evidence of a failure to develop adequate perceptual-motor

FIGURE 5.1
Selected items from the Frostig Developmental Test of Visual Perception

1. *Eye-motor coordination.* The child is asked to draw lines between two points on a page. The ability to draw lines within established boundaries is said to reflect eye-motor ability.

2. *Figure-ground.* The child is asked to outline a particular shape, which is presented with backgrounds of other figures.

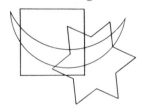

2. *Constancy of shape.* The child is asked to recognize basic shapes under varying stimulus conditions.

4. *Position in space.* The child matches shapes when given several distractors. The skill tested is the ability to match shapes.

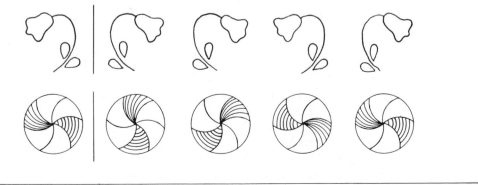

(continued)

FIGURE 5.1 (Continued)

5. *Spatial relationships.* The child copies patterns using dots as guide points.

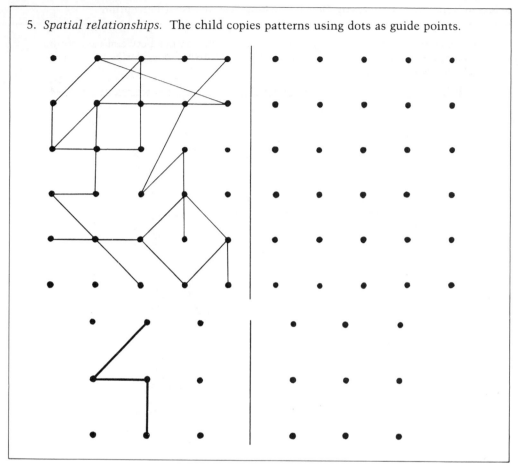

skills. Kephart (1971) has developed a variety of remedial activities to improve the student's ability to learn. Tracing forms, walking balance beams, identifying body parts, completing puzzles, and engaging in rhythm activities are but a few of the many tasks suggested by Kephart. In most cases, such exercises are carried out by a specialist trained in learning disabilities. In some cases, the classroom teacher carries out specially designed activities by integrating perceptual-motor activities into the regular curriculum.

Proponents of perceptual and perceptual-motor theories believe that the training of perceptual functions will lead to improvement in the ability to learn. When perceptual deficits are detected by low scores on perceptual tests, specialized remediation activities are selected to improve perceptual performance. The expectation is that academic skills will improve as perceptual problems are eliminated. This belief markedly influences the role of the special education teacher whose principal task is to assess and then remediate specific perceptual-motor deficits. In most cases, perceptual-motor remedial activities that occur in the regular class are carried out under the direction of a special educator.

Of utmost concern to the classroom teacher who may be considering the use of perceptual or perceptual-motor training activities is the question of validity. Do perceptual deficits underlie learning problems, and will perceptual or perceptual-motor training activities improve academic performance? Unfortunately, research has not conclusively demonstrated that students who receive perceptual-motor training activities increase specific academic skills. Although students who receive perceptual-motor training may improve their scores on perceptual-motor tests, corresponding gains in academic skills rarely occur (Salvia and Ysseldyke, 1978; Hammill, 1975; Ohleson, 1978).

The general failure of research to support the perceptual-motor approach seems to bear little relationship to school practices. Specialized perceptual-motor tests and related teaching materials continue to be widely sold, and many teachers are still trained in methods whose efficacy has not been supported. Perhaps the relative popularity of these materials lies in the fact that they offer a medically oriented explanation regarding the cause of learning problems.

As the basic assumption that training motor responses will have an effect upon perceptual abilities has not been established, there seems to be little reason for adopting perceptual training as the primary approach for helping children with their academic problems. It has been proposed, however, that some perceptual-motor exercises might be adopted in order to assist children in developing fine motor skills, balance, and general motor proficiency (Salvia and Ysseldyke, 1978). If the teaching materials and practices are carefully selected with motor skill development as a goal, then they may be useful to the teacher. Some perceptual exercises are also helpful to teach concepts like shapes and size to the beginning learner. It may be, too, that continuing research in the area of perception will lead to new methods and materials to help the learning disabled. However, at this point, the authors fail to discern any advantage to using perceptual-motor training activities to improve academic performance.

THE MEDICAL APPROACH

The medical approach to dealing with learning disabilities is a consequence of the brain-injury approach to identifying the disabilities. The view that learning disabilities are caused by an actual physical impairment within the brain has been widely accepted. Early work by Orton (1937) and Strauss and Lehtinen (1947) provided a foundation for the belief that neurological impairments were responsible for the learning problems exhibited by some children. Because many children with learning problems exhibited behavior similar to that of adults with verifiable brain damage, the link between brain damage and learning disabilities became widely accepted. Later, others hypothesized a relationship between hyperactivity and brain damage (Cruickshank, Bentzen, Ratzburg, and Tannhauser, 1961).

The kind of brain damage that leads to learning disabilities is implied only by circumstantial evidence. The damage is considered so slight that direct evidence is unlikely to be found. It is conceivable that some method may one day be found to detect microscopic damage or subtle chemical imbalances in the brain. But for the moment, the fairly widespread acceptance of the brain-injury approach remains based on circumstantial evidence.

The medical approach is based on internal causes, and therefore involves internal remedies—attempts to modify or ameliorate organic problems. Typical of the approach is the use of drug and diet therapies. The use of these therapies has captured the interest of many parents and educators.

Drugs are currently given for a wide variety of problems that may affect learning. For example, when a child's activity level is too high (commonly called hyperactivity), he or she may be treated by stimulant drugs, which apparently have the effect of slowing the child down and increasing attention span.

Diet therapy, on the other hand, is based on the idea that an inappropriate diet may alter physiological functioning to the point that the brain is affected and academic or behavior problems begin to occur. Some suggestions that have come out of research in this area would have students avoiding artificial preservatives, white flour, and sugar, and eating organic foods. Another aspect of the diet approach is the recommendation that large doses of particular vitamins and/or minerals will have a positive effect upon physical functioning.

Stimulants and Hyperactivity   The use of drugs in the treatment of exceptional children has become widespread only during the last twenty years. This relatively late development came about partly because of the development of new drugs and partly because drugs have become immensely popular in our society as a cure for a variety of problems ranging from depression to obesity.

Although stimulants arouse or activate the central nervous system, they actually induce a calming effect on many, but not all, students who are judged by physicians to be hyperactive. This somewhat paradoxical effect of a stimulant actually calming children probably occurs because the stimulant helps the child focus and maintain attention on important tasks. Stimulants commonly prescribed by doctors include Ritalin, Dexedrine, and Cylert. These drugs usually have an immediate effect that lasts for two to five hours (Gadow, 1979).

A number of studies have described beneficial effects of drugs for many hyperactive children. These effects include a reduction in activity level, improvement in handwriting, a greater ability to listen and pay attention, and, in some instances, more appropriate behavior. Grades may improve because students behave more appropriately or complete more work. While the short-term effects of stimulants are evident for some hyperactive students, the long-term effects of drug use are less clear. Some students continue to make good progress, while others still demonstrate learning and behavior problems.

Although there are advantages to the use of stimulants, there are also unwelcome side effects. At the initiation of drug treatment, insomnia, loss of appetite, and nausea may occur. In addition, some students may experience increased heart rate, drowsiness, headache, irritability, or a pale facial expression characterized by dark hollows under the eyes. Perhaps little is known about any deleterious effects from prolonged use of stimulants.

The use of drugs to control student behavior, particularly hyperactivity, is a source of controversy. Some critics regard the prescription of drugs to be an inexpensive way of avoiding problems that should require a range of special education services that could be costly both in terms of dollars and time. Others are concerned with the possible long-term effects of prolonged drug use, including the possibility of teaching students to rely on drugs as a solution to all problems. Finally, lack of teacher involvement in the process of monitoring the impact of drugs on classroom behavior and learning can be a disadvantage. Teachers are often in an excellent position to provide observational information and work samples to help document a drug's effect or lack of effect. However, they are rarely called upon to contribute such information.

Although drugs are useful for some hyperactive children, the question of whether this approach is overused is important. It is fairly widespread: Krager, Safer, and Earhardt (1977) reported that 2% of all the elementary-age children in one school district were receiving drug therapy of some form. But there are other treatments that should be tried before resorting to drugs. Educators and psychologists have identified a number of approaches, many of which are reviewed in Chapter 11, to help hyperactive and other children with behavior problems. These approaches typically involve the setting of clear limits and the use of rewards for appropriate behavior. Although these and related techniques have been used effectively to manage students with problem behaviors, they can be difficult to carry out. Parents and teachers must learn to set clear rules, reward appropriate behavior quite frequently, and maintain consistent schedules, routines, and expectations. For some teachers and parents, the approach is perceived as too difficult or too time-consuming. Drugs, and to a lesser extent, diet hold the promise of an immediate and relatively simple intervention. They are perceived by some as a more effective solution because they are more likely to be carried out.

We share many of the concerns voiced by the critics of drug intervention, particularly when drugs are used as a substitute for special education or when they are prescribed without first trying other educational approaches. At best, drugs can be an adjunct to special education, but they cannot be a substitute for sensitive, skillful teaching. Even if a student is receiving medication for hyperactivity, the teacher should not be excused from setting clear expectations, rewarding appropriate behavior, and adjusting the learning environment to help the student learn.

Since drugs are commonly used and will likely continue to be prescribed by physicians in the treatment of hyperactivity, what role can teachers take in this process? Ideally, teachers should be consulted by parents and physicians when the use or termination of drugs is under consideration. As teachers, we are often in the best position to observe and monitor the effects of drugs on behavior, mood, and academic performance. Actual work samples can be used to help judge the effects of initiating, modifying, or terminating specific drugs. Handwriting samples, math papers, weekly quiz scores, and related work products can provide concrete evidence regarding the effects of drugs on school performance.

Another tool for judging the effects of drugs is a behavior rating scale. Any of the scales introduced in the chapter on assessing student behavior would be useful. A teacher rating scale for specific use in drug studies was developed by Connors (1969). This scale can be completed before and after the initiation of drug treatment to assess the impact of drugs. It can also be used to determine the effect of modifying dosage levels or of terminating the use of drugs. A copy of the scale appears in Figure 5.2.

We hope that your role in a drug therapy program will be an official one, as a member of the team of people who are trying to help the exceptional student. If one or more of your students are being given drugs, and you have not been made a part of the team, there are at least two things you can do. First, you can ask your school administrators to help in making you a member of the team. Second, you can provide parents and school administrators with information about any changes you observe in the students' academic work or classroom behavior. Keep your reports informal but brief and based on observable facts. You may not find it necessary, or perhaps even advisable, to mention the drug therapy as part of your reports.

Special Diets   The fear of unwanted side effects of drugs, as well as a concern that drugs may avoid or even mask the cause of some learning and behavior disorders, has generated considerable inquiry into the role of nutrition in learning and behavior. Common sense tells us that nutrition plays some role in learning. We all know that it is difficult to work or pay attention when hungry. But from that observation it requires a great leap of logic to assume that diet or nutrition is an actual cause

FIGURE 5.2
Rating scale for observing children on drugs

Connors' Abbreviated Teacher Rating Scale

Child's name _____

Completed on _____ by _____
                    (date)   (teacher's name)

Instructions:
Please consider the last _____ (day, week, month) only in filling out
the checklist. Check the appropriate box for each item, *Not at all, Just a
little, Pretty much,* or *Very much,* which best describes your assessment of
the child. Please complete all ten items.

Observation	Degree of activity			
	Not at all 0	Just a little 1	Pretty much 2	Very much 3
1. Restless (overactive)				
2. Excitable, impulsive				
3. Disturbs other children				
4. Fails to finish things he/she starts (short attention span)				
5. Fidgeting				
6. Inattentive, distractable				
7. Demands must be met immediately; gets frustrated				
8. Cries				
9. Mood changes quickly				
10. Temper outbursts (explosive and unpredictable behavior)				

of learning or behavior problems, particularly in a society where hunger and malnutrition are hardly visible.

Perhaps the most well-known advocate of special diets is Benjamin Feingold (1975), a physician who claims that a number of hyperactive and emotionally disturbed children may be allergic to specific foods. The detection and treatment of food allergies is nothing new, of course. Most of us are familiar with the physiological symptoms of food allergies: skin eruptions, asthma-like symptoms, bowel problems, and so on. Feingold adds to these a number of behavioral symptoms: moodiness, hyperactivity, poor attention span, and related behavior problems.

A common method of detecting food allergies is the elimination diet. On an elimination diet, a group of foods is totally cut out of the diet and any changes are observed. If there is any noticeable improvement, the eliminated foods are added back to the diet one by one. That way the allergic effect of any one food can be detected. If there has been no improvement, a new group of foods is selected for elimination. Among the items on Feingold's list of potentially harmful foods are citrus fruits, which are high in salicylates; food colorings; artificial preservatives; milk; chocolate; cola; sugar; wheat; and eggs. The Kaiser-Permanente diet (Feingold, 1975), sometimes known as the Feingold diet, eliminates all or most of these foods. Parents who follow this elimination diet must become careful shoppers and meal planners, as it is difficult to obtain food without food colorings, preservatives, and sugar.

Others have proposed that other foods may also result in problem behavior. William C. Crook, M.D., has devised procedures to help parents use an elimination diet to discover if allergies are causing inappropriate behaviors.

1. Before beginning a trial diet, keep a diary or symptom inventory for at least three days. Continue to keep the symptom inventory while your child is on the diet.

2. Before starting on the diet, make up menus for all meals, including snacks and school lunches. Then go to the store, market, or garden and restock your pantry and refrigerator.

3. In general, avoid all prepared or mixed foods since most contain hidden ingredients.

4. Read all labels.

5. An elimination diet should be followed for seven days (occasionally longer). During the test period, your child must completely avoid the foods being tested.

6. If your child is allergic to the food or foods which have been eliminated, his symptoms should improve after he has been on the diet for

three to five days. However, an occasional child may not show significant improvement until he has been on the diet for a full two to three weeks.

7. Sometimes your child will show "withdrawal" symptoms. He might feel worse for the first two or three days on the diet. These withdrawal symptoms may include headache, fatigue, and irritability. Part of these symptoms may be caused by hunger; part of the symptoms may occur because he craves or is addicted to some of the common foods which have been eliminated.

8. If your child feels dramatically better on the elimination diet, you can determine which foods have been causing the symptoms by returning the eliminated foods to your child's diet. Add one new food back each day and notice any reaction. A reaction may occur within a few minutes or it may not occur for several hours or until the next day. If a reaction occurs, wait at least twenty-four hours before re-adding another food.

9. If the results of the test diet suggest food allergy, yet are not clear-cut, repeat the test diet once or twice to see if he's really allergic to the suspected food.

10. Although during the test period the child will need to avoid a suspected food completely, after avoiding a food for four to six weeks, he can usually take smaller amounts of a food he's allergic to without reaction.

11. A good elimination diet is one that avoids sugar, food colors and additives, milk, chocolate, wheat, corn, eggs, and citrus fruits. You can offer any meat but bacon, sausage, hot dogs, ham, and luncheon meats; any vegetable but corn, and any fruit but citrus. You may have rice and oats, nuts in shells, honey, pure maple syrup, and sugar-free peanut butter.

Further information on this procedure can be found in *Tracking Down Hidden Food Allergy*, Professional Books, Box 3934, Jackson, Tennessee, 38301.

Diet and Behavior   Generally, the scientific community is skeptical about the claims made by Feingold and others. Feingold has been faulted for not conducting carefully controlled studies to back up his claims. Instead, he has tended to collect testimonials from parents whose children have followed the diet. A growing number of parents claim the diet does, indeed, reduce hyperactivity and other behavior problems.

Good research, however, is not entirely absent. Connors and his associates (1976), in a carefully controlled study, demonstrated that the elimination of certain food additives did reduce the hyperactive behavior of some, but not all, children. Rapp (1978), a physician, studied twenty-four children who were diagnosed as hyperactive by either a physician or a psychologist. These students were given doses of food dyes and were then observed by trained observers who did not know which of the students had received the food dyes. Nine of the twenty-four children showed a marked increase in activity level immediately after consuming the food coloring. Rapp then put all twenty-four children on an elimination diet. Twelve of the children showed marked improvement. A few of these students had been receiving medication for hyperactivity and were able to stop taking their medication as a result of the diet.

High doses (megadoses) of certain vitamins such as C, E, and Niacin have also been linked to behavior. Rimland (1974), for example, found that megadoses of certain vitamins helped some, but not all, psychotic children. Rimland believes that some seriously disturbed children have severe vitamin or mineral deficiencies that may cause learning or emotional problems.

The research on special diets and vitamin therapy is in its infancy. Generally speaking, the claims outweigh the scientific evidence. Yet there appears to be enough evidence to suggest that diet is an area worthy of continuing investigation. What if a parent should ask your opinion about investigating an elimination diet such as the Feingold diet? Adler (1978), a researcher and clinician, suggests that no harm can occur from the short-term elimination of certain foods. Thus, the interested parent should not be discouraged from trying an elimination diet. Indeed, teachers can help evaluate the effects of the diet by using many of the same procedures suggested for studying the effects of drugs.

Finally, despite the popular claims, drug and diet treatments are not a panacea. Not all children respond to drug or diet treatments. Thus, while these approaches should not necessarily be discouraged, they should not be allowed to serve as a substitute for the good instructional and behavior management practices outlined in this text.

THE SKILL DEFICIT APPROACH

Educators have long been concerned about students who have specific learning deficits. As a result, a number of educational approaches have been developed which are based on assessing student strengths and weaknesses. Two approaches, diagnostic-prescriptive teaching and diagnostic-remedial teaching, are probably the most widely accepted in education.

Both approaches are based on the measurement of strengths and weaknesses. They differ in that the teacher who uses the diagnostic-remedial approach assesses the psychological processes that underlie academic skills and plans instruction to overcome ability deficits. The diagnostic-prescriptive approach places a greater emphasis on academic strengths and weaknesses. In reality the teacher might choose to combine approaches and give both types of tests in an effort to determine the best instructional technique; it may therefore be only an academic exercise to try to differentiate between the two.

The teacher who desires to use the skill deficit approach can choose from a wide variety of tests. *Diagnostic tests* can be used to discover and analyze a student's specific weaknesses in an academic area. A diagnostic reading test, for example, would indicate whether the student's reading problem was in phonics, syllabication, comprehension, or some other skill area within reading. *Psychological process tests* are used to test abilities that allegedly underlie the learning of academic skills, such as memory and perception. *Standardized achievement tests* are used to compare a student's score with others of the same age or grade level. These tests are also called *norm-referenced tests* and provide us with grade-level scores. We can use standardized tests to determine whether a student is below, at, or above grade level in a given area. The selection of the tests used to discover strengths and weaknesses is usually made by a specialist in the school or by the Pupil Evaluation Team.

One additional type of test has recently become more widely used by all teachers to measure specific strengths and weaknesses. These tests, known as *criterion-referenced tests*, can readily be used in the classroom to measure specific knowledge the student has attained. These tests may be contrasted to norm-referenced tests, in which a student's performance is compared with that of others in the same grade. If a seventh-grader was below average on an achievement test in geography the teacher might receive a score that indicated that the student scored on the fourth-grade level. On a properly constructed criterion-referenced test, however, the teacher would be able to identify specific skill deficits and know how far the student was from mastering specific skills.

Criterion-referenced tests used in the classroom are typically devised by the classroom teacher, using the curriculum taught to identify instructional objectives. At the heart of the approach is the belief that nearly every student can learn if learning tasks are broken down into small enough component parts or subskills. This process of breaking down larger areas of skill into smaller steps is known as *task analysis*. For example, the mastery of high-school algebra can only occur after the systematic learning of a series of concepts and operations. The student who has a skill deficit in algebra might be tested on each specific subskill beginning with simple operations and systematically moving towards more difficult complex computations. If the student has difficulty learning new tasks, then the skill area may have to be divided into smaller subskills so that the student would essentially have less to learn at any one time. The smaller the step, then, the greater likelihood that it can be mastered by the student.

Related to criterion-referenced testing is the emphasis on individual learner progress. While teachers carefully instruct their students to master specified goals, systematic attention is not often paid to individual student progress in achieving specific goals. That is, if a student does not master objectives within the allotted time period or by the particular method used by the instructor, the student is likely to fail. In the deficit approach, the teacher takes deliberate steps to make sure that students achieve objectives at a reasonable rate. This emphasis often requires varying teaching methods for specific students.

A third characteristic of the criterion-referenced skill deficit approach is its emphasis on specific, observable learning objectives. In nearly all instances, teachers must carefully analyze and then list the specific skills and/or knowledges they wish their students to demonstrate. This approach is particularly suited to developing basic academic skills and fundamental knowledge and understanding in content areas.

It shows its limitations when teachers try to deal in attitudes, such as a love for reading and an appreciation of fine art. It would be difficult to analyze love and appreciation and come up with teaching goals leading to measurable results. The deficit approach is somewhat limited to areas where it is practical to identify subskills. Some desired outcomes are simply not observable in the precise and measurable way demanded by criterion-referenced testing.

Flexibility is an important characteristic of the skill deficit approach. The number of tasks or subskills to be mastered can vary according to the needs of the individual. In teaching an advanced learner to acquire a body of information, the task may not need to be broken down into a large number of steps. In teaching the student who is functioning on a lower level, however, a large number of very small subskills may need to be identified and then systematically developed if success is to be achieved. Teachers need to relate task analysis to each student's needs and capabilities.

When students are given objectives they can master, they are more likely to participate in learning activities. The use of specific goals also helps the teacher to be accountable. Every objective mastered by a student becomes documentation of what has been learned. Thus, the system allows the teacher to be more precise in articulating a student's goals and accomplishments. Statements like, "Well, I think he's a better reader," give way to more descriptive evaluations like, "John can now read at the fifth-grade level at 95% accuracy and 120 words per minute."

Task analysis can provide an important dimension to the skill deficit approach. It gives the teacher an understanding of what to teach that leads to success with the learning disabled as well as with a variety of other types of handicapped children. Breaking a skill into small steps may benefit the child with limited mental capacity as well as the easily frustrated emotionally handicapped students.

The skill deficit approach does have some limitations that may affect its use in some classrooms. It is time-consuming. Effective implementation requires that the teacher have the time, resources, and training to carry out some individualized instruction. The skill deficit approach also places a greater burden of responsibility on the teacher for learner success. If the philosophy that everybody is ready to learn something is totally accepted, then the teacher is faced with the likelihood that anyone who fails to make progress does so because of inadequate teaching.

Teaching the learning disabled child does not require that the teacher select only one approach. The use of the skill deficit approach does not preclude the use of the perceptual or medical methods. In selecting the proper solution to a student's learning problem, the teacher should carefully evaluate what each theory has to offer and utilize procedures that promote successful learning.

Summary

In this chapter we have presented an overview of the field of learning disabilities. It should be apparent that there still exist major differences of opinion regarding the causes and treatment of the problem. While no single approach to the problem has provided all the answers, research into the causes and solutions to learning problems continues. Perhaps in the near future, the contributions of researchers in a variety of areas will be combined to provide a clearer understanding of the field of learning disabilities. For now, however, we believe that an understanding of the following ideas and concepts will help the classroom teacher understand the current state of the art in learning disabilities:

1. The widespread acceptance of learning disabilities as a type of handicapping condition is a recent development.

2. The majority of explanations of the cause of learning disabilities fall into one of two categories, brain injury or psychological processes.

3. The most widely used definition of learning disabilities appears in PL 94-142; it appears to accommodate a variety of philosophical approaches. The definition is vague, however, and is difficult to interpret.

4. The identification of learning disabled students can be made by using a variety of specific tests and procedures. The type of methods used for classification depends on the philosophy of those doing the labeling.

5. Learning disabled students often exhibit special characteristics that go beyond the failure to learn and that must be accommodated in the educational program if the student is to be successful in the classroom.

6. A variety of treatments have been proposed to help students with learning disabilities. The effectiveness of some commonly used interventions has not been conclusively proven.

7. The skill deficit approach to helping students requires the teacher to identify and measure weaknesses and provide instruction for specific educational deficits.

Activities

1. Visit a material resource center and examine several teaching materials designed for LD students. Try to determine whether the material teaches basic skills or psychological processes.

2. Conduct a library research project investigating the contributions of such pioneers in the field as: Helmer Myklebust, Samuel Kirk, Kurt Goldstein, Samuel Orton, Marianne Frostig, Newell Kephart, and William Cruickshank. Present your findings to the class.

3. Volunteer some time in an LD resource room. Familiarize yourself with the instructional practices carried out there. Try to identify methods and materials that you might use in your class to help students learn new skills.

4. Interview several professionals regarding their philosophy of learning disabilities. Compare and contrast their views. Discuss your beliefs with several others in your class.

Study Questions

1. According to the definition, how would a student be identified as having a learning disability?

2. What characteristics might lead a teacher to suspect that a student has a learning disability?

3. Compare and contrast the psychological process, brain injury, and discrepancy approaches to identifying learning disabilities.

4. Why might a learning disabled child be described as lazy?

5. What are the typical needs of learning disabled students?

6. In a school system of 1,000 students, how many students might be learning disabled?

7. Why is it that proponents of the medical approach frequently rely on drugs and/or diet to help students overcome their learning problems?

8. What role does the teacher play in assisting the physician when drugs are used to help the student?

9. Describe the skill deficit approach to working with learning disabled students.

10. Why are criterion-referenced tests useful in carrying out the skill deficit approach?

Questions for Further Thought

1. Recall an experience where you had difficulty mastering new knowledge or skills. What attitudes and behaviors did you develop?

2. To receive special services, a student must be labeled or classified. How could you minimize the possible negative effects of being labeled as learning disabled?

3. The existence of learning disabilities has been widely accepted. Why is it important that regular classroom teachers learn about teaching learning disabled students?

4. Learning disabled students may exhibit problem behaviors as well as academic deficits. Given the variety of remediation approaches available to educators, how might you select the best methods to help students in your classroom?

Additional Resources

BOOKS

Faas, L. A. *Learning disabilities: A competency based approach.* Boston: Houghton Mifflin, 1981.

Lerner, J. *Learning disabilities theories, diagnosis and teaching strategies.* Boston: Houghton Mifflin, 1981.

Mann, L., Goodman, L., and Wiederholt, J. L. *Teaching the learning disabled adolescent.* Boston: Houghton Mifflin, 1978.

Ross, A. O. *Learning disability: The unrealized potential.* New York: McGraw-Hill, 1977.

PROFESSIONAL JOURNALS

Academic Therapy

Journal of Learning Disabilities

PROFESSIONAL ORGANIZATIONS

Association for Children with Learning Disabilities, 5255 Grace Street, Pittsburgh, Pennsylvania 15236

Division for Children with Learning Disabilities, Council for Exceptional Children, 1920 Association Drive, Reston, Virginia 22091

CHILDREN'S LITERATURE

Albert, L. *But I'm ready to go.* Scarsdale, New York: Bradbury Press, 1977.

Gardner, R. *The children's book about brain injury.* Framingham, Massachusetts: Massachusetts Association for Children with Learning Disabilities, 1966.

Hayes, M. *Tuned in — turned on.* San Rafael, California: Academic Therapy, 1974.

Lasker, J. *He's my brother.* Chicago: Albert Whitman, 1974.

PART III
ASSESSING STRENGTHS AND WEAKNESSES

We have talked about exceptional students and the new legal mandate to provide an appropriate education for each of these students. The next two parts of the book are devoted to presenting information that we believe will provide you with the skills to be an effective participant in the design and implementation of appropriate educational programs for exceptional students. When you finish the next two parts, you will have been presented with the skills listed below.

1. You will be able efficiently to gather educational and behavioral data that can be used to identify and measure student deficits.

2. You will have the knowledge to select appropriate long-term goals and short-term objectives for individual students.

3. You will be able to select appropriate teaching methods, materials, and behavior management techniques to insure accomplishment of goals and objectives.

4. You will understand the role and importance of ongoing and final evaluation of all teacher attempts to educate handicapped children.

The major purpose for assessment is to provide the teacher and the Pupil Evaluation Team with a data-based rationale for placement and instructional decisions. In our minds, assessment represents the beginning of an instructional delivery system that ultimately provides the best possible program for the exceptional student. We have called this system a *problem-solving model*. Each step is designed to provide solutions to the following problems:

1. What are the student's educational and behavioral needs?
2. What should the student be taught?
3. How should the student be taught?
4. Have the placement and teaching methods resulted in positive changes?

As you review the material, keep in mind the basic problems you are trying to solve. This will help you synthesize the parts of the problem-solving model into a whole. The first two steps of the problem-solving model will be emphasized in the next three chapters. These include (1) the assessment of academic and behavioral problems, and (2) the development of goals and objectives based on the assessment data. In the problem-solving model, goals and objectives become the bridge that links assessment to instruction.

The problem-solving model

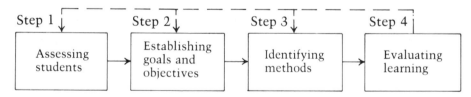

The assessment process is focused on academic performance and classroom behavior. Since most exceptional students have needs in both these areas, any assessment process used by the classroom teacher must incorporate means for collecting data in each area.

Our focus on academic assessment is on the collection of data from a variety of sources, beginning with informal classroom observations and the information in the student's cumulative record folder and going on to norm-referenced and informal criterion-referenced tests.

As in the evaluation of academic skills, classroom behavior may also be assessed through norm-referenced tests and direct observation in the classroom. The assessment of behavior should also result in specific goals and objectives that can be implemented in the classroom.

Once you have collected the assessment data necessary to determine that students are in need of special education assistance and the nature of their individual learning problems, it is necessary to set a direction for their instruction. Goals and objectives become the basis of our instructional programs for exceptional students and can serve as part of the evaluation plan when you review their progress.

As you study the material in this part of the book, keep in mind the necessity of conducting a thorough assessment to obtain sufficient data to develop goals and objectives for exceptional students in your class. Successful implementation of these first two steps of the problem-solving model can ensure greater success as you teach the exceptional student in your classroom.

Chapter 6

Assessing
Academic Performance

Assessment of academic skills can provide you with important information that can be used to plan a student's academic program. Determining exactly what the student knows and doesn't know in any academic area allows you to concentrate your teaching efforts in areas where they will do the most good. Careful assessment of the academic skills of exceptional students is particularly important, as many of these students have deficits in certain academic skills that require concentrated teaching efforts, specialized methods and materials, or other changes in their educational program.

Why should assessment be a responsibility of the classroom teacher? First, the classroom teacher usually spends more time with the student than any other professional. Data obtained are likely to be more valid because the teacher has the opportunity to collect more representative information than someone who may see the child for an hour or two. Second, assessment can become an ongoing process that is part of the act of teaching. By collecting, recording, and evaluating information on a frequent schedule, the teacher has a constant awareness of the success of each student. This allows the teacher to adjust the student's program if the student is experiencing some problems.

This chapter is divided into two major parts. In the first section, we will examine commonly available sources of information that can be used to assess academic performance. Procedures that can be used to measure academic deficits precisely are presented in the second part of the chapter.

Using Assessment Data Available to Teachers

Teachers are bombarded with data about their students. Observations, tests, cumulative records, interviews with parents, medical reports, and psychological evaluations may all provide information that has some relevance to the process of education. In order to use such information, however, you must be able to select useful data and to provide accurate interpretations as to the implication of the data. By carefully selecting and assessing the data from various available sources, you will be able to make informed decisions about how to teach each student.

STANDARDIZED ACHIEVEMENT TESTS

One of the most widely used type of test is the standardized achievement test. In many schools these tests are given each year to measure student growth in academic areas such as reading, arithmetic, social studies, and science.

Tests of this type derive their name from how they are administered. The tests are given to large numbers of students nationwide. Directions are read verbatim from a manual, and certain procedures and time limits are followed. This following of a standard procedure was to insure that all students taking the test, no matter where they lived, had the same opportunity to understand the directions and respond to the questions. This is an important consideration because such tests are norm-referenced; that is, each student's score is compared to the scores of all the students, or a specific subset of students, taking the test. Fourth-graders are compared with all fourth-graders, tenth-graders are compared with all tenth-graders, and so on. The group the student is compared to is called the norm group. Standardized test scores are expressed in several ways. The most primitive is the *raw score*, usually a simple percent-correct figure for a test or subtest. Without further interpretation, raw scores are not particularly useful. The most useful scores you will see are probably *percentiles, stanines, and grade equivalents.*

Percentile scores tell you what percentage of the students taking the test obtained lower scores. If a fifth-grader obtained a score that was at the 40th percentile it would mean that 40% of all fifth-graders who took the test scored lower. Similarly, a student who scored in the 95th percentile would be above 95% of his or her peers. A score at the 50th percentile is the *median* score. It means that half of the students scored above it and half of them below it. The median is not necessarily the *average*, or *mean* score, but many people think of the median as a kind of average score. Percentile scores may be used to compare a student to

Subject area	Raw score	Percentile	Stanine	Grade equivalent
Social studies	24	41	5	9.5
Language arts	14	13	3	6.1
Mathematics	31	52	5	10.1
Science	19	62	6	10.7
Reading	20	46	5	9.9

Student got 20 questions correct in reading.	The student's score is above 46% of all others who took the test.	The score falls in the middle stanine.	20 is the score obtained by students in the ninth grade, ninth month.

FIGURE 6.1
Sample achievement test score report

a large national group of students, to the students within your district or school, or any combination of the three.

Stanines are like percentiles except that students' scores are divided into nine ranges with a specified percentage of scores in each range. A score that falls in the fifth stanine would be in the middle 20% of all students taking the test. (The relationship between stanines and other standardized test scores will be shown in Figure 6.2.)

Grade equivalent scores translate the raw test scores into grade levels. They are expressed as a numeral plus a decimal; the numeral is the grade year, and the decimal is the month. Thus, a score of 4.2 on a test or subtest means that the student did as well as a typical fourth-grader in the second month of the school year.

Figure 6.1 shows how a typical achievement test report for a tenth-grader might look. Can you find the percentile score and grade equivalent score that represents the student's weakest area?

Interpreting Standardized Tests   As has been mentioned, a norm-referenced test may compare a student to a large population or to a group as small as, say, all fourth-graders in a single school. Test scores are often

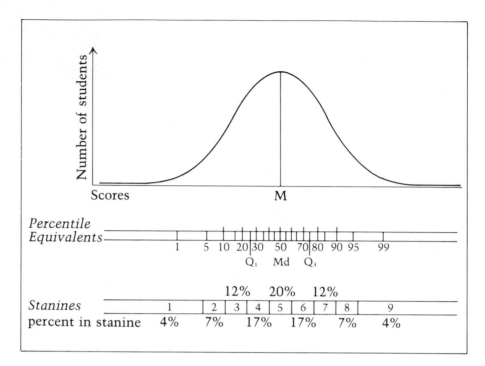

FIGURE 6.2
A normal distribution

reported for two or more different norm groups. There are important implications for you when you interpret these scores.

Let's say, for instance, that you are investigating the scores of a student with a suspected math problem. On the math section of her test scores, you see that she was in the 60th percentile in math for the national norms. That doesn't look so bad. But when compared with her fellow fourth-graders in your school, the same raw score in math was assigned to the 20th percentile. Does your student have a math problem or doesn't she? The discrepancy in percentile scores may mean that your school does a much better than average job at teaching math, when compared to the nation as a whole. It also means that your student is probably not doing very well in math as it is taught in your school. You should, therefore, look for further evidence of a problem in math for this student. Generally, the closer a norm group is to your local situation, the more weight you should give to the percentile or stanine scores.

The size of the norm group can be another consideration. When norm groups are very large, as they are for national norms, the score distributions tend to even out so that they would fit what is called a normal distribution. The normal distribution looks like a symmetrically shaped bell, as in Figure 6.2.

In a normal distribution, such as that in Figure 6.2, the median score, M, is the same as the average of all scores, and is also the most frequent score.

When the norm group is quite small, however, the scores may not be distributed so neatly. It is quite possible for the median score — 50th percentile or 5th stanine — to be rather far above or below the average score for all test scores. This makes interpretation far less certain. If the norm group of all fourth-graders in your school amounts to only twenty or thirty students, the percentile scores should not be accepted without further investigation.

Even the most sophisticated tests will have some statistical error built into them. You should look for a figure whose label is Standard Error of Measurement (SEM) or something expressing a range of error. This can be particularly revealing for grade equivalents. A score of 6.7 with an SEM of 0.7 means that a student's true performance would fall between 6.0 and 7.4. A beginning seventh-grader who got this score might be a year below grade level or more than half a year above it. The SEM tells us the range within which a student's true performance can be placed. It helps us make more accurate estimates of a student's actual achievement level.

Standardized achievement tests have limitations more directly related to teaching. First, the scores do not tell you what to teach. Knowing whether a student is below or above grade level does not lead to the identification of appropriate instructional objectives. Second, some students do not obtain scores that reflect their knowledge in an area. Test anxiety, lack of motivation, and errors in filling out the answer sheets may lead to inaccurate scores in some instances. Third, nationally normed tests may not reflect the content of the local school curriculum. The test may be measuring skills the students have not had the opportunity to learn.

Despite the limitations of standardized achievement tests, they can provide you with a general indication of the level of performance of each individual student. You can use such data to identify areas of relative strength and weakness in the curriculum. Administrators might use these tests to evaluate their school's educational programs or to place students in remedial or enrichment programs.

Types of Achievement Tests   There are several major types of achievement tests. These tests differ in their purpose and use. Some tests are designed as screening instruments; others are diagnostic tests that assess discrete subskills within an academic area. Achievement tests may be individually administered or administered to a large group. Table 6.1 contains a listing of some achievement tests used in schools.

TABLE 6.1
Common achievement tests

Name of test	Purpose/use	Typically administered by:
California Achievement Test (CTB/McGraw-Hill, 1977)	Norm- and criterion-referenced test. Multiple skills battery. Grades K through 12.9. Group Test.	Classroom teacher
Iowa Test of Basic Skills (Hieronymus, Lindquist & Hoover, 1978)	Norm- and criterion-referenced test. Multiple skills battery. Grades K through 9.	Classroom teacher
Metropolitan Achievement Test Survey Test (Prescott, Balow, Hogan & Farr, 1978)	Norm- and criterion-referenced test. Reading, Mathematics, Language, Social Studies and Science. K through 12. Group Test.	Classroom teacher
Peabody Individual Achievement Test (Dunn & Markwardt, 1970)	Norm-referenced test. Math, reading, spelling, general information. K through 12. Individually administered.	Specialist
Stanford Achievement Tests (Madden, Gardner, Rudman, Karlsen & Merwin, 1973)	Norm- and criterion-referenced test. Multiple skills battery. Grades 1.5 to 9.5. Group Test.	Classroom teacher
Wide Range Achievement Tests (Jastak & Jastak, 1978)	Norm-referenced test. Reading, spelling, and arithmetic. Elementary and high school. Individually administered.	Specialist

SPECIALIST REPORTS

It is a common practice in many school districts to employ a variety of outside specialists to evaluate students with problems. In most cases, outside experts write reports that are included in the student's records.

Psychologists may administer specialized instruments and interview the students in an attempt to determine the cause of a learning problem. An IQ test may help to determine if the child's learning difficulties are caused by limited intellectual capacity. Similarly, certain psychological tests, such as the Bender Visual Motor Gestalt Test or the Draw-A-Person Test, can be given to determine whether or not a child has a brain dysfunction or possible organic brain damage. Results from other instruments, such as the Thematic Apperception Test or the Rotter Incomplete Sentence Test, may lead to the determination that the basis for the child's problem is emotional disturbance. Various tests commonly used by specialists are summarized in Table 6.2.

TABLE 6.2
Tests used by specialists

Tests of personality and emotional development	Typically administered by:
Bender Visual Motor Gestalt Test (Bender, 1938)	Trained specialist in all cases
Draw-A-Person Test (Urban, 1963)	
Rorschach Ink Blot Test (Rorschach, 1966)	
Sixteen Personality Factor Questionnaire (Cattell, Eber & Tatsuoka, 1970)	
Thematic Apperception Test (Murray, 1943)	

Intelligence tests	Typically administered by:
Slosson Intelligence Test (Slosson, 1971, 1981)	Special educator or trained examiner
Stanford Binet Intelligence Scale (Terman & Merrill, 1973)	Trained examiner
Wechsler Intelligence Scale for Children (Wechsler, 1974)	Trained examiner

Tests related to learning disabilities	Typically administered by:
Illinois Test of Psycholinguistic Abilities (Kirk, McCarthy & Kirk, 1968)	Learning disabilities specialist
Memory For Designs Test (Graham & Kendall, 1960)	Learning disabilities specialist
Purdue Perceptual Motor Survey (Roach & Kephart, 1966)	Trained examiner

In some cases, physicians are called upon to provide assistance to educators as certain diseases and physical abnormalities have educational implications. For example, a student who has repeated *petit mal* (mild) epileptic seizures may be unable to concentrate at times. Heart problems may lead to a lack of stamina, and defects in vision and hearing often have an effect on learning.

You should evaluate medical data carefully. The effects of even serious medical conditions on a student's ability to learn are difficult to assess. Some students with seemingly severe physical problems are able to learn quite well, while others with seemingly minor problems may have extreme difficulty. Medical reports may help you understand the student but should be carefully evaluated along with other available data.

Other specialists who may be called upon to evaluate students include psychiatrists, physical therapists, occupational therapists, social workers, and special educators. These and others who write reports usually have a specialized repertoire of instruments and evaluation procedures and often may write reports that are difficult for you to understand and evaluate. It is a good practice to find someone who can translate the meaning of the specialist's report into understandable, educationally meaningful terms. Reports should be carefully analyzed to insure that all useful information is understood by educators who use the information to improve educational programming.

Information found in specialist's reports should be carefully weighed. The opinions of "outside experts" should be considered in light of what is already known about the student. Information that seems irrelevant or illogical should not automatically replace your own common sense. Because of the amount of time you spend with your students, you are often more able than anyone to provide accurate information to be used in assessing student needs.

Using outsiders to find possible causes of problems is only useful when finding the reason for a problem helps you teach a child more effectively. You should be careful not to let causes become excuses for a student's lack of achievement. If you are too ready to accept such diagnoses as brain damaged, mentally retarded, or perceptually disabled, you may be tempted to minimize or discount your role in providing special help.

GRADE REPORTS

Most schools maintain ongoing records of grades students earn in the various subject areas. Such records are usually available in a student's cumulative educational folder. Grades are good, general indicators of the student's success in school and can be used to understand more clearly a student's educational needs.

Grades allow you to understand a student's general strengths and weaknesses and performance over time. A stronger performance in a specific class can be weighed against what is known about the subject matter and teaching style of a particular teacher. In this way, you may get some idea about what the child has mastered and what kind of teacher seems to be the most successful.

Analysis of grades over a long period of time can show whether a current academic difficulty is a chronic problem or of more sudden onset. A sudden, precipitous drop in grades may indicate that the student is reacting to a specific problem at home or has developed a health problem. In any case, a sudden change should alert you to a potential problem area to be investigated further. A chronic problem may lead you to question the adequacy of the student's educational program.

Cumulative grade reports may be useful if the data are used appropriately. Because of the subjective nature of the data, there is always a danger of misinterpretation. Grade data should always be considered along with other data before making important educational decisions.

CLASSROOM PERFORMANCE

Careful observation and documentation of classroom performance can provide you with a fairly objective source of data. In most instances, your observations center around academic performance and general behavior.

Academic performance can be assessed by collecting data that indicate whether or not the student has mastered the necessary skills in the subject area and the degree to which the student carries out assigned tasks. You can use informal tests and assignments to discover academic strengths and weaknesses. A record showing percentage of assignments completed and degree of participation in class activities can be used as a fairly accurate indication of current level at which a student is functioning. By carefully observing and measuring academic skills and classroom behavior, you can begin to understand individual educational needs. Figure 6.3 shows two possible kinds of teacher-made records. The first uses tally marks to record a student's voluntary contributions to class discussions. The second is a weekly summary of how faithfully the student has been handing in written assignments.

A common problem with classroom performance data is that some teachers fail to describe the data accurately. Rather than saying, "John scored 63% on his language assignment," they might state, "John got a low score on his language assignment." While both statements might reflect a significant problem, the first one is less subject to misinterpretation and can be used to gauge future performance. John may improve his score to the 75% level and the teacher may still say he gets low scores even though an improvement has been made. Classroom data reported

Class participation — Number of contributions _John H._					
Day	Mon.	Tues.	Wed.	Thurs.	Fri.
Frequency	~~HHT~~ I	//	~~HHT~~ I	///	///

Assignments completed Ratio = number completed/number assigned. _John H._					
Week of	9/15	9/22	9/29	10/5	10/12
Ratio	5/10	7/12	8/11	10/10	7/7

FIGURE 6.3
Individual student records

in measurable terms are more objective and therefore more useful to the Pupil Evaluation Team.

Classroom performance is an important data source to teachers. The lack of objectivity is a problem that can be minimized by seeing that all observational reports in a student's records are written in measurable terms. As a general rule, the less measurable the data, the less they should be used to make important decisions about a student's educational program.

SUMMARY OF USING AVAILABLE ASSESSMENT DATA

We have so far discussed sources of assessment data that may already be available to you in our initial search for information about a student who is having academic or behavior problems. Standardized achievement tests give you a general idea of where a student stands with respect to other students, either nationally or locally. The tests may be quite general, or they may focus diagnostically on a fairly small subskill. Specialist reports may include medical data or the results of personality tests, IQ tests, or tests designed to diagnose specific learning disabilities. Grade reports from past years may reveal a chronic problem in one or more subjects, or they may show a sudden problem caused by trouble at home, illness, or incompatibility with a specific teacher. Finally, your own classroom observations of academic skills and classroom behavior can be collected. This requires accurate, written descriptions of measurable events.

The sources of assessment data we have already examined can have significant value in forming a general idea about a student's problems and deciding where to place the student. Though the data may sometimes be contradictory, they usually paint a reasonably consistent, compelling picture.

None of the data, however, seem to lead in a natural way to the second element of our problem-solving model: establishing goals and objectives. It is one thing to determine whether and where to place a student. It is quite another to determine in detail what the remedial program is to be. The remainder of this chapter is devoted to a measurement technique that does lead naturally to the establishing of goals and objectives of a student's academic program.

Criterion-Referenced Measurement

As is the case with many educational innovations, the elements of criterion-referenced measurement have existed long before there was a special term for it. Its most familiar manifestation is probably the pretest – teach – posttest sequence followed by many good teachers. A related notion, with more emphasis on the instructional element, is called teaching to mastery.

The term used here, criterion-referenced measurement, is intended to contrast with norm-referenced measurement. A norm-referenced test measures a student against other students whose scores have been pooled to establish a norm. The criterion-referenced test compares a student's test scores against a criterion of performance that indicates mastery of a skill.

The classroom teacher is often in a unique position with regard to criterion-referenced measurement and its implications. It is likely that no one knows better than you what skill areas a student may need special help in. From your daily observations you should be able to analyze and define the specific subskills to test, devise informal tests for the subskills, and establish criteria for mastery.

Let us take a brief look at a typical application of criterion-referenced measurement, analyze some of the underlying procedures, and then examine more carefully two case histories of criterion-referenced testing in action.

CRITERION-REFERENCED MEASUREMENT IN THE CLASSROOM

Samantha's written reports are a minor disaster. You can make out her handwriting with supreme effort and a little lucky guessing, but then her logic begins to escape you. The basic thoughts are there, but they're poorly organized, the grammar is shaky, and some sentences seem to get detoured before they reach the end punctuation — if there is any. Curiously, Sam is fairly articulate in her speech, and some small intuition tells you that her grasp of written punctuation could stand a closer look. So, you devise a short test. It consists of ten sentences that lack all punctuation, and Sam's task is to provide the punctuation. You know that almost every one of your other students would get a perfect score on this test, so you set the criterion level at 90% (to allow for a momentary lapse of attention, Sam's second-guessing an item, or even a poorly constructed test item). If Sam scores 90% or better, you will look elsewhere for her problem. If she scores under 90%, you will conclude that punctuation is one of her problems and provide her with some extra help.

Of the twenty-five places requiring punctuation, Sam provides correct punctuation in fifteen. The percentage score, 15/25 = 60%, is far below your criterion level. You plan a set of special lessons and a retest after three weeks.

Sam retests at 92%; she has placed the correct punctuation in twenty-three out of twenty-five places in a test similar to the first one. And you have already begun to notice that her writing assignments make more sense (once you've deciphered her handwriting, of course).

By stating the standard or criterion for mastery and by assessing each student's performance, you should be able to pinpoint strengths and weaknesses for each student. Criterion-referenced tests, then, provide data that allow you to compare a student's performance with desired performance standards that you establish. Information from criterion-referenced tests tell you exactly what the student can and cannot do relative to a specific skill. Specific teaching activities can be geared towards helping students reach criterion levels you establish.

Some typical skills taught in school and their possible criterion or mastery levels are shown in Table 6.3. It should be noted that the mastery levels are selected by the teacher and may vary according to the teacher's beliefs as to how well a student must perform to master a specific skill area.

The criterion or mastery level represents the minimum level of performance the student must exhibit before you can say that he or she is competent in a given skill. Analysis of the mastery level criteria for seventh-grade reading in Table 6.3 shows that the student must read at 125 words per minute above the 95% accuracy level before you can say his or her skill is adequate. A lower speed or accuracy level would mean that the student was not yet reading at the criterion level.

Criterion-referenced assessment encourages you to be objective about students. If the minimum criterion for a student using the metric system is 100% in chemistry class, then the student who measures accurately 95% of the time is below mastery. By observing and measuring such behaviors you avoid the possible communication problems that can come from saying such things as "That student is not very good at metric measurement." Statements such as, "She doesn't know her fraction concepts," give way to more objective statements like "She is now able to

TABLE 6.3
Typical skills and criteria

Skills	Criterion (mastery level)
Kindergarten: recognizing alphabet letters	The student orally reads all alphabet letters within 90 seconds at 100% accuracy.
Fourth grade: writing addition facts	The student adds 40 digits per minute at 100% accuracy.
Seventh grade: oral reading	The student orally reads at 95% accuracy level at an average rate of 125 words per minute.
High-school shop: making a wooden bowl	The student constructs a bowl of the correct size and shape within 10 class periods.

match the fractional parts ½, ¼, ⅓, ⅙, ⅛ with their printed name 100% of the time." By describing a student's behavior or skill level in measurable terms, you can be relatively sure that others understand the nature of the student's strengths and weaknesses.

The use of criterion-referenced procedures does not usually require you to purchase special tests; each regular assignment given is a potential test. Moreover, many textbook and workbook programs already contain tests or other materials that are criterion-referenced. Look for detailed scope-and-sequence charts and such terms as "behavioral objectives," "criterion level," "objectives," and so on.

By paying attention to individual students' skills, the use of criterion-referenced test procedures can become a routine part of your instructional program of all students. You need only take the extra step of establishing mastery criteria and writing down performance data that show accuracy and the time it takes to complete a specified task.

By advocating criterion-referenced assessment, the authors are not rejecting norm-referenced assessment procedures. Norm-referenced assessment data can be used as a basis for some important decisions, such as placement or identifying general strengths and weaknesses. Criterion-referenced tests provide the teacher with the data to make instructional decisions and clearly identify specific academic objectives for our students. Both types of tests have their uses in education.

Identifying What to Test   Once you decide to use criterion-referenced measures, the first step is to decide what ought to be tested. Typically, you begin by listing all the discrete skills taught in a subject area. Analyzing an academic area to determine its component skills is a process known as task analysis. Most general academic skills can be broken down into a hierarchical sequence of subskills. An example of one breakdown of basic mathematics is shown below.

1. The student writes the correct sum while adding multidigit numbers with carrying.

$$\begin{array}{r} 3428 \\ + 1989 \\ \hline \end{array}$$

2. The student writes the correct difference when subtracting multidigit numbers with borrowing.

$$\begin{array}{r} 8425 \\ - 5439 \\ \hline \end{array}$$

3. The student writes the correct product in multidigit multiplication with carrying.

$$\begin{array}{r} 9282 \\ \times 4931 \\ \hline \end{array}$$

4. The student writes the correct answer to multidigit division problems with remainder.

$$64 \overline{) 98265}$$

If a student was able to carry out the correct operations listed in the skill breakdown, you would be able to state that, according to our definition of basic math, the student had mastered the required skills for the particular instructional unit. If the curriculum in your class contained only addition, subtraction, multiplication, and division, the four-part skill breakdown might serve your needs. It is likely, though, that further skill breakdowns would be necessary. If you found that the student could not add multidigit numbers without carrying, you might need to identify more precise subskills to determine where in addition the student's problem exists. A more precise skill analysis might look something like this.

1. The student writes the correct sum for all one-digit plus one-digit problems.

$$\begin{array}{ccc} 2 & 4 & 8 \\ +9 & +3 & +6 \\ \hline \end{array}$$

2. The student writes the correct sum for two-digit plus one-digit numbers without carrying.

$$\begin{array}{ccc} 32 & 55 & 71 \\ +4 & +3 & +6 \\ \hline \end{array}$$

3. The student writes the correct sum for two two-digit numbers without carrying.

$$
\begin{array}{r} 23 \\ +\ 32 \\ \hline \end{array}
\qquad
\begin{array}{r} 17 \\ +11 \\ \hline \end{array}
\qquad
\begin{array}{r} 43 \\ +45 \\ \hline \end{array}
$$

4. The student writes the correct sum for two two-digit numbers with carrying.

$$
\begin{array}{r} 89 \\ +\ 19 \\ \hline \end{array}
\qquad
\begin{array}{r} 73 \\ +29 \\ \hline \end{array}
\qquad
\begin{array}{r} 98 \\ +56 \\ \hline \end{array}
$$

5. The student writes the correct sum for two three-digit numbers with carrying.

$$
\begin{array}{r} 392 \\ +\ 678 \\ \hline \end{array}
\qquad
\begin{array}{r} 985 \\ +576 \\ \hline \end{array}
\qquad
\begin{array}{r} 642 \\ +589 \\ \hline \end{array}
$$

By identifying the subskills and arranging them in a logical order, you can systematically assess all skills necessary to master a basic academic task.

The teacher of basic math is usually faced with teaching more than the four basic operations, but the procedure is the same: each area is broken down into its component parts. Fortunately, many school text-books are designed to teach basic skills systematically in a logical order leading to mastery of the larger skill area. And, as has been mentioned, the texts are sometimes a part of a system that provides criterion-referenced tests. It is not usually necessary for you to carry out your own task analysis unless you design your own curriculum. In that case, the process of identifying what to test consists of listing the discrete behaviors the student must exhibit in order to achieve success.

THEORY INTO PRACTICE

Task Analysis

Bob Chambers had been teaching sixth-grade reading for a number of years. During that time he had collected a great number of excellent teaching pro-grams and materials. He had found during the years that no single program worked with all students. Older students seemed to become easily disen-chanted with lessons that were repetitive even though he felt they needed practice and a lot of review. He decided to do a task analysis of oral reading and then select a wide variety of activities and materials for each skill. In thinking about his task analysis he wanted something simple that at the same time included all important skills. After a lot of deliberation he decided on the following list of subskills, which begins with the most basic competencies and progresses to the most complex oral reading skills.

Skill	*Criterion (Mastery)*
1. Each student will say individual letter sounds when presented with a list containing all letter sounds.	100% accuracy at 40 per minute
2. Each student will orally read single-syllable words.	100% accuracy at 40 per minute
3. Each student will orally read phonically irregular words selected from the student's own reading materials.	100% accuracy at 40 per minute
4. Each student will orally read sentences in grade-level material.	95% accuracy at 100 words per minute
5. Each student will orally read paragraphs in grade-level material.	95% accuracy at 100 words per minute

When Bob used his task analysis for testing, he used instructional materials he had on hand. By testing students he was concerned about on each phonic sound, he was able to identify students who needed extra work in phonics. Each student's ability to blend these phonetic elements into syllables was determined by having them read single-syllable words. As Bob proceeded through the hierarchy of skills he was able to identify specific skill deficits and to select a variety of materials for each student.

When he showed his task analysis to other reading teachers he was surprised to find that others had constructed task analyses that contained many more steps and were much more detailed. In talking to the teachers who had made them, he decided that while his simple task analysis worked for him, a more complex task analysis worked well for others. He decided that the task analysis needed to be individualized and reflect the philosophy of the instructor using it. In any case, the task analysis ought to reflect what the teacher teaches. The analysis should contain only the skills that the teacher believes are necessary to achieve mastery in the subject area. There is little use in selecting areas to test that do not appear in the curriculum.

The preceding example of a task analysis is representative of a large number of basic academic areas. Skills required for reading, language arts, woodworking, chemistry, and the like can usually be analyzed and broken down into a logical hierarchical sequence. This is not true with all subjects, since there is no logical sequence of steps in some content areas. While mastery of all steps might be necessary to achieve success, the order in which they are taught makes little difference. For example, students learning about South American countries could begin by studying Argentina or Brazil or any other country. The order would be up to the teacher's discretion. Similarly, if the major topics covered included agriculture, culture, economic systems, and government, the order of teaching is determined by teacher preference. In cases where the subject matter has no set order, the teacher need only identify and list the specific behaviors the student must display in order to demonstrate mastery.

In order to identify what to test in an academic area, the teacher needs to identify what skills the student must master. By listing these skills in the order they are logically taught, the teacher is ready to determine how to measure performance for each basic skill.

Selecting Appropriate Measures   By selecting the subskills in an academic area, you have identified what is known as a skill domain. If you have selected World History as the subject area, then the list of subskills should represent all important knowledge in that area. By knowing the skill domain, you have identified what to assess. By stating what the student should learn in an area, you have a standard to judge how many skills the student has mastered so you can determine which skills need to be taught.

Another important reason for determining the areas in which a child lacks competence is that some deficits will lead to almost guaranteed failure. For example, the student who does not master writing complete sentences will almost certainly fail to master the content in an English class where the skill domain is writing essays. Failure to master phonetic elements in reading will lead to probable failure later on. Some education majors experience the same problem when they attempt to understand research methodology without first understanding the fundamentals of statistics. Skills that serve as a foundation for later success should have high priority.

Once the skills have been selected, you must decide how well a student must perform the skill. The problem is to determine what standards represent minimum competency. In some cases you use common sense. If the student is learning the correct form for a business letter, you might demand 100% accuracy as your standard minimum. If a student is identifying minute structures in a human anatomy class we might

TABLE 6.4
Measures of school performance

Measurement term	How expressed	Examples	Mastery level	Mastery?
Accuracy	% correct	a. John scored 100% on a math test.	a. 95%	Yes
		b. Mike's shop project was 50% completed.	b. 100%	No
Rate	number of correct answers in a given unit of time	a. Chris reads at 100 words per minute.	a. 120 per minute	No
		b. Lois answered times tables problems at 50 per minute.	b. 40 per minute	Yes
Time Limit	time required for a behavior	a. It took Derek 30 minutes to complete a workbook page.	a. 20 minutes	No
		b. Vince solved a quadratic equation within 60 seconds.	b. 60 seconds	Yes

accept a lower accuracy level and feel comfortable that the student knows the material well enough.

In order to determine whether or not a student achieves mastery on a skill, you must select an appropriate means of measuring student performance. In most cases, you can select from among three measures — accuracy, rate, and time limit. Accuracy refers to the degree to which the student's answers are right or wrong. Rate is described as frequency or how often a correct answer is given within a given time period. Time limit refers to the time allotted for an operation to be completed or a series of correct answers to be given. These measures are illustrated in Table 6.4.

In the following case study the selection of appropriate measures is demonstrated. Note how Mr. McCarrie systematically uses the principles of criterion-referenced testing to solve his instructional problem.

Decide what skills ought to be tested, and then decide what the mastery level should be. Skills that serve as a foundation for later success should have a high priority, with careful testing and a high mastery level.

THEORY INTO PRACTICE

Selecting Measures of School Performance

Mr. McCarrie, a third-grade teacher, was concerned about the oral reading skills of some of his students. He had several students who seemed to be below par when they were asked to read out of their reading textbook. He knew that oral decoding of grade-level reading material was dependent upon several basic skills. He decided to list these skills to determine what to test. The list he devised was as follows:

1. The student should read words in a text on the student's grade level.

2. The student should pause at commas and punctuation at the end of sentences.

3. The student should use proper inflection.

He reasoned that if the students could master the skills in his list they would be good readers. He knew, however, that he would have to decide how well the students would have to perform each skill. He then selected mastery criteria for each identified skill. His list of skills was refined somewhat and looked like this:

Skill   *Mastery criteria*

■ Decoding words in the grade   Accuracy: 95% words pronounced
  level test.   correctly

                                               Rate: 110 words per minute

■ Pausing at punctuation   Accuracy: 95%
  appropriately.

■ Using inflection: emphasis of   Accuracy: 75%
  appropriate words and
  syllables.

He reflected on his choice of criteria. He had determined his accuracy and rate criteria for oral decoding by listening to several students who seemed to have no difficulty reading and then recording their rate and number of errors. He felt that these readers represented the minimum level he hoped his problem learners would achieve by the end of the year. By setting his mastery criteria for rate and accuracy at their level, he was setting a fairly reasonable standard. In selecting his criteria for appropriately pausing at punctuation, he determined the percentage of time his adequate readers paused appropriately. He found that the average was above 95% so he selected the 95% as a fair minimum standard. When he looked at inflection he found that most third-graders did not always use what he considered to be appropriate inflection. So he determined that he would be pleased if they achieved a 75% level. He did not use rate or time limit as measures because they seemed to be impractical for the skills of pausing appropriately or using inflection.

Having selected important skills and determined the minimum standards for mastery, Mr. McCarrie was ready to assess his problem students. He decided that for efficiency he would tape-record a three-minute reading sample from each student's basal reader and then analyze the skills by playing the tape several times. On the first playing of the tape for each student, he marked down words read incorrectly and counted the total words read in three minutes. He determined accuracy level by dividing the total number of words in the passage read into the number of words read correctly. Joe read 160 total words and missed 30. Mr. McCarrie computed his accuracy as shown: $130 \div 160 = 81\%$. Joe was below the minimum criterion for mastery. In order to compute rate, Mr. McCarrie decided only to count the number of words read correctly. Joe read 130 words in three minutes, which meant that his rate was 43 words per minute $(130 \div 3)$. Mr. McCarrie decided not to assess Joe's skills on punctuation and inflection until his accuracy and rate were increased. He felt that it would be impractical to work on these skills until Joe achieved more success on decoding.

Mr. McCarrie tested his other students and found different problems. Stephen's accuracy and rate for oral reading were above the criteria; his problem was that he frequently ignored punctuation. In fact, out of the 40 punctuation marks in his three-minute passage that required a pause or hesitation, Stephen only stopped on 4. This was only at the 10% accuracy level (4 ÷ 40), which was well below the minimum criterion of 95%.

Mr. McCarrie continued his informal testing program with his other problem students and found that he was able to pinpoint the nature and degree of each student's specific problem. By investing less than two hours he felt that he could accurately describe each student's reading weaknesses. He did not bother to use this precise criterion-referenced procedure on all students. Instead, he focused mainly on those students who seemed to be having problems. He did, however, administer the test to Jamie, a very advanced student who was able to progress to the eighth grade reading level before dropping below the criteria in the three skill areas. Mr. McCarrie was able to use this finding to support Jamie's referral to an enrichment program.

Selecting Mastery Levels   Educators are almost always concerned about accuracy as a measure of performance. Accuracy alone, however, is not sufficient. Some students can get the right answer or complete the project with appropriate accuracy but work so slowly that you cannot say they are performing well enough. Consider the student who is asked to add six plus seven and takes forty seconds to say "thirteen." You would want to teach the student to say the correct answer within a shorter time. But accuracy is likely your most important goal. When you teach any skill or idea, you first try to have the student make the right response. Once that is achieved, then you can teach the student until she or he is able to give correct responses within a reasonable time. You would select rate (frequency of responses in a given time) or time limit depending on which measure is appropriate for the task being measured. It should be pointed out that just because you use time limit or rate as one measure of behavior it doesn't mean that you are trying to make all students perform faster. You only want to make sure that they perform tasks quickly enough to experience success when applying their knowledge and skills in other areas. In addition, the rate of response and time limit are often the aspects of a task that are most appropriate to modify for an exceptional student.

There are some practical considerations that should guide your choice of mastery levels. If you are concerned about a student's mastery of spelling, you will not select rate as an appropriate measure. You are not usually interested in how many words a student can write in one minute. It would not be logical to require that the student write five words per minute. Also, as spelling achievement is usually measured by the teacher

Rate of response and time limit are often the aspects of a task that are most appropriate to modify for an exceptional student.

saying the words one at a time, the student cannot control the rate at which the words are given. The fast and slow students' responses are controlled by the speed at which you dictate the words. Rate would also be an inaccurate measure of each student's capabilities. Time limit would be the better measure. The criterion might be writing each word within 15 seconds after you say the word. Thus, if the student's written response was inaccurate or if it was not completed within 15 seconds, it would be considered an errror. The mastery criteria for spelling might be at the 80% accuracy level with each response occurring within 15 seconds of your verbal cue. This would allow a majority of the students to achieve mastery. If mastery were set at 100%, very few students would experience success.

In most instances, rate or time limit criteria are set at levels that are reasonable for the individual student and the type of skill being learned. You would certainly want to adjust your criteria if the student was physically handicapped. For example, the student who has cerebral palsy might learn to type five words a minute which would represent an appropriate mastery level.

It is important to realize that while you are concerned with how quickly a student performs a particular skill, you cannot always say that faster is better. You might settle for an oral reading rate of 80 words per minute as being sufficient. A student who reads so fast that clarity and meaning suffer is not reading well. In most instances, once the minimum rate or time limit or mastery level has been reached, you do not continue to emphasize speed.

The three measures used in establishing criteria for specific skills form the basis for the criterion-referenced testing process. By identifying the important skills and determining the appropriate measures for establishing competency levels, the only remaining step is to assess the student's level of mastery for each skill. By selecting appropriate worksheets, chapter exercises, flash cards, and other materials readily at hand, the teacher is ready to begin the criterion-referenced testing process. The following case study illustrates testing being used in the classroom setting.

THEORY INTO PRACTICE

Using Criterion-Referenced Test Procedures

It had been another long day in Mr. Garrett's ninth-grade general math class. He had just spent the fourth day trying to teach how to compute interest rates. He had planned to spend two days on it, but a quarter of his class clearly did not understand the basic concepts. The entire first month of school had been that way; a small group of students always seemed to take too much time. It was clear that the extra time he had spent already would prevent him from meeting all the course objectives. It seemed to him that he was being forced to choose between teaching only what the poorest students could master or accepting their failure if he met the needs of the more advanced students. He was not comfortable with either option. He was not going to accept failure to teach anyone. But, how could it be done? He decided to consult with Mr. Mozden, the new resource teacher in the building, to see if he might offer some suggestions.

Mr. Mozden had dealt with similar problems before and spent a considerable amount of time listening to Mr. Garrett's description of the problem. He determined that the problem was not in teaching. Mr. Garrett had used a variety of approaches and apparently used some good instructional techniques. He was also adept at motivating students to want to learn. The basic problem, then, was that some students were not able to learn the materials at an adequate rate.

Mr. Garrett and Mr. Mozden decided on a plan to determine what to do about the students who seemed unable to learn. The first step consisted of several short observations. It was clear that Mr. Garrett's teaching methodology was not at fault. He covered the subject matter very thoroughly and clearly; his teaching should have resulted in better performance than he was obtaining from some students.

At their next meeting Mr. Mozden asked about the students' mastery of prerequisite skills. He wondered if it was possible that the underachieving students had not built a solid foundation of math concepts and operations. He reasoned that it was possible that the students did not have a readiness to learn consumer math. Of course, the first question was, what skill concepts are necessary to be able to understand the subject area?

The first step was to analyze the math book used in the class. Mr. Mozden and Mr. Garrett brainstormed and came up with the following list.

1. Reading skills
   a. decoding the words
   b. understanding the special vocabulary words
   c. following directions

2. Basic math skills
   a. number concepts
   b. operations with whole numbers
   c. operations with fractions
   d. operations with decimals

The second step was to identify basic skills in each area. Mr. Mozden carried out a readability analysis on the test and found that it had been written at the ninth-grade level. He noted that a student who did not read somewhere near that level might not be able to read and comprehend word problems or directions. Mr. Garrett went through the text and wrote down specialized vocabulary words, beginning with words like *divisor, dividend,* and *factor,* and moved on to more difficult concept words like *compounded interest, sine,* and *tangent.* By using the text and his own knowledge, he was able to devise a list containing over one hundred words, which he felt represented important concepts in math.

Mr. Mozden's expertise in task analysis led him to develop a hierarchical list of math skills. Together the two teachers had completed a fairly comprehensive analysis of math skills taught in ninth-grade math. They were ready to determine the appropriate measures and minimal standards for mastery. They were also able to determine quickly what test materials to use and who would do the testing. Their assessment plan was as shown below.

Skill area	Mastery criteria	Materials	Who tests
1. Reading	9th-grade material at 95% accuracy.	7th-grade reading book	Mozden
2. Vocabulary	Identify the definition for each word on the test at 100% accuracy within one hour.	Teacher-made multiple-choice test of fifty of the key terms	Garrett

3.	Basic math skills	Accuracy above 90% and rate or time limit where applicable.	Worksheets, elementary level text, or workbook	Garrett

Using materials already available, plus a test devised by Mr. Garrett, the teachers were able to assess readiness skills among the few students who were slowing the class down. The results they obtained were extremely helpful. A few students were assigned to the reading teacher, who taught reading skills and math vocabulary. Mr. Mozden worked with two students on basic math skills during study halls, and Mr. Garrett provided special instruction for several students during part of his math class. The precise data obtained on the criterion-referenced tests served as a basis for effective program changes. Several students were able to make adequate progress once their difficulties were remediated. By removing skill deficits that were prerequisite to, or the cause of, later achievement problems, the teacher was able to be more effective in the classroom.

CRITERION-REFERENCED ASSESSMENT IN ACADEMIC AREAS

The assessment of most academic areas may differ in the fact that the selection of skills is generally up to your discretion. For example, one teacher who decides to teach nutrition may use the competencies listed below.

1. Identifying the basic food groups (90% accuracy).

2. Being able to place selected foods within their appropriate groups (100%).

3. Planning a nutritionally balanced weekly menu (90%).

Another teacher may add other competencies, such as planning a nutritional weekly menu with vegetarian foods or planning a shopping list for which the student must plan nutritionally balanced meals within particular budget limitations. There are, of course, many other competencies that might logically be added to the list. Whatever the form of the final list of competencies, it should reflect what you teach.

A United States history class may have competencies much like these.

1. Each student will write a one hundred word essay describing how the isolationism trend which followed World War I led to the Four Power Agreement.

Criteria:
Length: at least 100 words; Content: three accurate reasons stated; Form: complete sentences, no more than one spelling error.

2. Each student will orally name each of the original thirteen colonies.

Criteria:

100% accuracy within three minutes of teacher request.

Whatever your area of specialization, the basic procedure for carrying out criterion-referenced assessment remains the same.

1. List important subskills.
2. Select appropriate measures.
3. Establish minimum performance standards.
4. Select test materials.

The informal testing of academic skills relies on your developing efficient procedures that are practical in your particular class. In some cases, you may need to use some outside assistance. But if each student's skill deficits are precisely described, you will be able to determine a starting point — a beginning that allows you to teach what the child needs to learn in order to achieve success in mastering academic skills.

Summary

This chapter presented a broad overview of assessment procedures used to provide for the needs of students in a variety of classroom settings. While it was our intention to describe assessment procedures for exceptional students, we believe that the application of the ideas presented can be used to benefit all students. Assessment based on an analysis of educational tasks results in the teacher seeing more clearly what skills are being taught. Establishing measurable goals provides the students with a clear understanding of what they must learn to achieve success. Finally, the careful assessment of student skills and behavior allows the teacher to make appropriate decisions regarding placement and selection of teaching methods and materials. Simply put, we believe assessment to be the starting point of good instruction. The major ideas presented in the chapter are as follows:

1. There are many data sources for assessment available to you. Among these are standardized tests, specialist reports, grade reports, and observation of classroom performance.

2. When selecting data sources you should keep in mind the purpose of the assessment and the possible limitations of some types of data.

3. Criterion-referenced tests have several advantages over norm-referenced tests for the classroom teacher. They provide instructional objectives and objective measures of academic skills.

4. Criterion-referenced assessment can be carried out on an ongoing basis in the classroom if you routinely collect performance data on assignments.

5. Selecting the essential skills to be tested can be done by using task analysis procedures to identify teaching objectives within a curricular area.

6. Selecting appropriate measures for academic performance almost always requires measuring the accuracy of a student's performance. Some measure of rate of response or time to complete a task is also important.

7. Criterion-referenced assessment can be used in all academic subjects. You need to identify instructional steps through task analysis, identify appropriate measures and performance standards, and select the test materials.

Activities

1. Obtain a copy of an achievement test. Using the test manual, find the standard error of measurement. Try to determine whether or not the possible error on the test is significant.

2. Using one of your classmates as a subject, practice administering and scoring an achievement test such as the WRAT. Interpret the results by determining grade-level placement.

3. Devise a criterion-referenced test in your area of study. Administer the test and see if you can use the test to identify and measure specific strengths and weaknesses.

4. Visit a special education classroom and find out how the teacher uses norm-referenced tests for classification and placement.

5. Familiarize yourself with the Buro's *Mental Measurement Yearbooks*. Read the review of a commonly used test and report your findings to the class.

Study Questions

1. What is the primary purpose of standardized achievement tests?

2. Why is it unrealistic to expect every student to be on grade level?

3. What does the standard error of a test tell us?

4. If a student is on the 50th percentile what percentage of all students taking the test scored lower?

5. How should reports from outside specialists be evaluated?

6. What useful information can teachers obtain from grade reports?

7. Why should classroom observations be reported in measurable terms?

8. In what way do norm-referenced tests differ from criterion-referenced tests?

9. Why are criterion-referenced tests used to determine whether or not a student is at the mastery level?

10. Describe the process of task analysis.

11. Describe a skill that could be accurately assessed using each of the following measures: accuracy, rate, and time limit.

12. In some instances task analysis is not used to select the necessary skills for criterion-referenced testing. In your area of study identify several examples.

13. List the steps necessary to construct a criterion-referenced test.

Questions for Further Thought

1. Some people have advocated the elimination of all norm-referenced tests. If this were to occur what changes would take place within education?

2. If criterion-referenced assessment were used to measure academic performance, would our current concept of grading have to be changed? In what way?

3. When we administer norm-referenced tests to a large group of students we expect that half of the students tested will be below average. In your opinion, how might this lead many students to view themselves as stupid or less worthy?

4. Large amounts of money are used to administer norm-referenced achievement tests to students. Is this a worthwhile practice? Explain your response.

Additional Resources

BOOKS

Hammill, D. D., and Bartel, N. R. *Teaching children with learning and behavior problems* (2nd ed.). Boston: Allyn & Bacon, 1978.

McLoughlin, J. A., and Lewis, R. A. *Assessing special students: Strategies and procedures.* Columbus, Ohio: Charles E. Merrill, 1981.

Salvia, J., and Ysseldyke, J. E. *Assessment in special and remedial education.* Boston: Houghton Mifflin, 1981.

Chapter 7

Assessing
Student Behavior

As a teacher, you must be concerned about student behavior. You would be pleased if all students behaved in such a way that classroom activities took place exactly as planned. However, despite your wishes for desirable classroom behavior and your efforts at good planning, it is likely that you will have some students who interrupt, refuse to participate in planned activities, or engage in other behavior that disrupts the teaching or learning process. When misbehavior consistently interferes with learning, it is necessary to develop a program to meet the student's needs.

The degree to which you manage behavior problems effectively in the classroom often determines how successfully you are able to teach your students. Teachers who manage student behavior successfully are generally looked upon as "good teachers" and are likely to be happier and feel less stress. The first step in an effective behavior management program is the careful identification and description of student behavior in the classroom and other school settings. This assessment provides you with the information necessary to identify specific objectives, make decisions about the management of student behavior and, if appropriate, make recommendations regarding special education services.

Data Sources Available to Teachers

As in the assessment of academic skills, there is a wide variety of instruments and procedures available to help you obtain data related to student behavior. When reviewing a student's record, it is possible to find   155 specialist reports, anecdotal records from previous years in school, and completed behavior rating scales that give an indication of the student's past behavior in school. You may also receive reports from other school personnel and outside consultants on students in your classroom. It is important to be aware of the types of information you may locate or receive about a student and how you might utilize that information in developing a plan for managing the problem behavior.

SPECIALIST REPORTS

Students who consistently behave in ways that disrupt the learning environment are sometimes referred to other professionals for evaluation. These professionals, or specialists, may assist the Pupil Evaluation Team in making classification decisions and in developing effective behavior management programs for the student. The outside opinion offered by a specialist can be helpful in both parts of the decision-making process.

The classroom teacher is always aware of the particular problems presented by students in the classroom. You may suspect that the problems are consistent with certain handicapping conditions and that the student may benefit from the special services offered by special education personnel. The specialist may be able to confirm your suspicions, using various assessment tools, and arrive at the appropriate classification for the student's problem. In the case of behavior problems, the specialist will often be a school psychologist, clinical psychologist, or a special educator.

Another service provided by specialists can be in the form of specific recommendations for working with problem behaviors in the classroom. Because specialists can usually invest more time and collect more data on an individual student than the classroom teacher can, they are in a position to provide a unique perspective on the student, which may lead to a number of suggestions for classroom implementation. The specialist who provides these kinds of data and suggestions should be able to help you develop goals and objectives for the individual student, as well as overall classroom management plans.

Specialists present their findings in formal reports (Figure 7.1). These reports usually include the results of any formal testing done with the student, observations of the student in the school setting, and some specific recommendations. The information contained in the reports can be most helpful to the classroom teacher when the specialist uses clear, descriptive language, objectively reporting the findings on the student. This objectivity can lead to the development of programs designed to meet the specific needs of the student in question.

Even though specialists can provide assistance in many cases, teachers have a tendency to minimize their own professional judgment and expertise when confronted with information gathered by a specialist. Input provided by outside experts should be utilized to confirm and sup-

FIGURE 7.1
A specialist's report

November 10, 1981

TO: Mrs. L. Y.

FROM: George Allen, Ph.D.

RE: Summary of observations for Martin

1. <u>Reason for observation</u>: Mr. B, Martin's fourth-grade teacher expressed concern regarding Martin's difficulties with completing assigned work, daydreaming, and not paying attention during class activities.

2. <u>Summary of observations</u>:

   2.1. First observation period: 11/4/81, Individual Seatwork Activity, 8:50-9:40. During most of this period students have seatwork in math or spelling to complete. Mr. B circulates about the room to provide help where needed.

      2.11. From 9:00-9:20 Martin remains at his desk with his math work in front of him. However, he spends very little time working. Rather, there is a high frequency of turning around, looking at Mr. B when he talks with other students, as well as fixing his eyes on his hands and making rolling movements with his fingers.

      2.12. On two occasions during the above-mentioned period, Mr. B offered Martin a reminder ("Come on, Martin, let's get back to work"). Martin puts his eyes toward his work and appears to begin working but after about 30 seconds begins to look around the room again.

      2.13. At 9:20, Mr. B walks to Martin's desk and issues a firm expectation, "Martin, let's get ten more facts done before recess" (Apparently Martin has not yet completed any math facts.) Between 9:20 and 9:40, Martin's attending behavior increases, although he still looks about the room every one or two minutes. Martin has nine problems completed when the recess bell rings.

   2.2. Second observation period: 11/7/81, Social Studies Activity, 2:00-2:35. Mr. B organizes the class into three groups. Each group has one person assigned to read a segment of the text, the other group members expected to follow along in their texts. Mr. B circulates from group to group asking comprehension questions, etc. For the duration of this activity Martin appears to be task oriented. He appears to follow along in his text book and volunteers several answers to questions raised by Mr. B. Martin appears to maintain his attention (following along in textbook) even when Mr. B is working with another group.

3. <u>Impressions</u>: Based on the above-mentioned observations, as well as discussions with Mr. B, the following impressions occur to me:

   3.1. Martin does have attending difficulties. However, these difficulties seem more pronounced when Martin has individual seatwork to complete than when he is in a reading activity.

   3.2. Martin appears to be responsive to Mr. B's reminders to complete his work although these reminders seem to influence Martin for only a moment or two.

(continued)

FIGURE 7.1 (Continued)

3.3. Clear expectations such as "Let's get ten math problems done before recess" appear to have a more lasting impact on Martin's attending behavior than more general reminders such as "Let's get to work."

3.4. Martin appears to be somewhat willing to please Mr. B. He seems to volunteer answers to questions and one might take this to mean that Martin is concerned with gaining some recognition from Mr. B.

4. Recommendations: It appears that Martin may need specific help in learning to be a more independent student. Objectives should focus on helping Martin to increase his performance in independent seatwork activities, completion of assigned work, etc. The following types of methods used alone or in combination may prove helpful.

4.1. Clear expectations: It may be helpful to clarify expectations for Martin, particularly during seatwork activities, by telling him exactly how many problems he is to complete within a specific time limit. At first, the time limit and the number of problems should be relatively brief (e.g., five problems in five minutes) but can be extended as Martin's skill improves.

4.2. Clear consequences: When Martin completes an assignment (e.g., five problems in five minutes) one or more of the following consequences might occur:

4.21. Martin is warmly praised by Mr. B.

4.22. Mr. B awards Martin a smiling face sticker or similar token that is placed on a daily rank card to go home or a chart that remains in the classroom.

4.23. The use of backup rewards at home (e.g., allowance, special TV) or at school (time to read, play a checker game, etc.) in exchange for tokens might be considered if praise alone does not seem to help Martin accomplish these specific objectives.

4.24. Other feedback devices, such as having Martin keep a daily performance chart that records the number of math problems completed within a specified time period, may prove motivating. The use of such a performance chart could eventually lead to Martin's establishing (with Mr. B's assistance) daily performance goals.

4.3. Praising positive behaviors: Where possible, it may be helpful to point out appropriate behaviors that Martin demonstrates. For example, Mr. B may wish to "catch Martin being good" by occasionally praising him for things such as keeping his eyes on his work, working hard, etc.

5. Summary: It would appear that a great deal of structure and guidance will be needed to help Martin become more capable of completing work under self-directed conditions. Mr. B's apparent warmth towards Martin as well as his ability to structure learning expectations for Martin seem to be very positive qualities. The addition of even clearer expectations and consequences should help Martin to see the value of self-directed work. At the same time, it must be recognized that Martin's behavior patterns appear well established and that change will occur gradually, with occasional setbacks.

plement the current knowledge about the student. Because a specialist spends a limited amount of time with a student, the student may not display "typical" behaviors. This results in an inaccurate analysis of the student's real needs. The specialist's objectivity in a particular case, however, may result in a better understanding of the student's needs, and so should be given full consideration.

ANECDOTAL RECORDS

An anecdote is a written record that is a precise description of a behavioral incident. Anecdotal records provide a documentation of student behavior when they contain all necessary information and are stated in descriptive terms. A record that states "Joey was terrible in class today" may be subject to misinterpretation by others. A better description might be stated as follows: "Joey interrupted the half-hour lecture five times by dropping his books on the floor."

Anecdotal records are useful in determining the types of problem behaviors a student is exhibiting in the classroom. Frequently, students who are disruptive or interfere with the instructional process have exhibited the same behaviors in other classes with other teachers. If these teachers have kept anecdotes on the student, the records will appear in the student's cumulative record. A review of these anecdotal records will give you a perspective on the present behavior in the classroom. You would certainly want to supplement these records with your own observations and records of the student's current behaviors.

A good anecdotal record has several characteristics. The date, time, and setting of the observation should be clearly stated. The name of the person making the observation and writing the anecdote should also be part of the record. Most important, the behavior(s) of concern should be described in objective, descriptive language. Anecdotal records should be kept over a period of time if they are to serve as representative samples of the student's performance.

When reviewing existing anecdotal records, you should examine them carefully to determine whether they contain the necessary information. If they do, you should also assess the objectivity of the statements. Judgmental statements may not be helpful in obtaining a clearer picture of the student's behavioral needs. Consider the two examples of anecdotal records in Figure 7.2. Both describe the same behavior incidents. Which record gives a clearer picture of Bart's behavior problems? Mr. Holmes's report is, of course, the better example. When keeping anecdotal records be sure to collect information over at least a one-week period to insure your descriptions represent typical behaviors. Also, don't overlook the possibility of keeping records of positive behaviors, which can be used to document improvements in behavior.

FIGURE 7.2
Two examples of anecdotal records

Student name _Bart S._   Grade _5_   Observer _Mr. Holmes_

Date _1-6-82_   Time _9:00_   Setting _Reading-Classroom_

Behavior _Bart refused to come to reading group. After two requests he
came but knocked Mary's papers on the floor on the way._

Date _1-6-82_   Time _9:15_   Setting _Reading-Classroom_

Behavior _Bart began reading but stopped after two sentences.
(He seemed to be upset after making a mistake.)_

Date _1-6-82_   Time _9:30_   Setting _Reading-Classroom_

Behavior _Bart refused to begin seatwork assignments. Did not
attempt to fill out worksheet._

Date _1-7-82_   Time _11:40_   Setting _Lunchroom_

Behavior _Bart threw his milk at another student. He cried
when he was escorted to the principal's office._

BEHAVIOR RATING SCALES

In an attempt to quantify problem behaviors and examine their relative
importance and frequency, a number of rating scales have been developed
to assess common behaviors present in the school environment. Teachers
are asked to note the relative frequency with which some behaviors occur
and compare that frequency with norms taken from a large sample population. This allows educators to determine if a student's behavior significantly deviates from that which is accepted as a norm for students of
that age.

Behavior rating scales are developed around the theory that students
can be ranked according to the types and/or the frequency of the behaviors
in which they engage for any behavior trait. For example, if you were to
measure social withdrawal you would begin by identifying specific characteristics and behaviors that represent this trait. The Walker Problem
Behavior Checklist (Walker, 1970) lists the following:

Student name _Bart S._ Grade _5_ Observer _Mr Weatherbee_
Date _1-6-82_ Time _9:00_ Setting _Reading Classroom_
Behavior _Bart created a disturbance in reading group. He ruined half the lesson._

Date _1-6-82_ Time _9:15_ Setting _Reading Classroom_
Behavior _Bart didn't do his work again._

Date _1-6-82_ Time _9:30_ Setting _Reading Classroom_
Behavior _No work still._

Date _1-7-82_ Time _11:40_ Setting _Lunchroom_
Behavior _Bart got angry at lunch again. He threw things around; had to be removed._

- Tries to avoid calling attention to himself
- Does not engage in group activities
- Has no friends
- Doesn't protest when others hurt, tease or criticize him
- Does not initiate relationships with other children

Teachers using the Walker Problem Behavior Checklist are asked to note whether or not they have seen the behaviors exhibited by the student being rated. The degree of withdrawal is then determined by adding up the weighted scores for each item. As the average student would likely have few of these behaviors, the rating for a majority of students would be near zero. If the results using the rating scale on an average population were graphed, the figure would resemble a normal curve although it would be asymmetrical because most students would not have withdrawal be-haviors. See Figure 7.3.

The assessment of information obtained on behavior rating scales like the Walker is based on normative principles. This means that scores that fall close to the average, or mean, are considered to be normal and scores that are farther away are said to represent a significant problem. Norm-referenced assessment of behavior is based on the normal curve concept. The idea is that specific types of behaviors are distributed in varying degrees throughout a population. Within this population some people display a lot of the behavior, some very little of it, while most individuals exhibit an "average" amount. When the frequency of such behaviors is graphed the result is a normal curve (see Figure 7.4). In any normal population distribution the average range encompasses the 68% of the population that is within one standard deviation of the mean. In the case of withdrawal all students whose scores fall more than one standard deviation above the mean are said to be withdrawn. The farther from the average their score lies, the more socially withdrawn they are said to be.

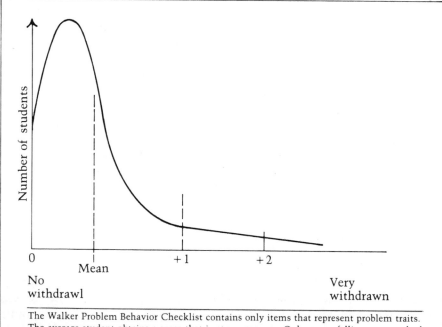

The Walker Problem Behavior Checklist contains only items that represent problem traits. The average student obtains a score that is at or near zero. Only scores falling one standard deviation *above* the mean are considered to be out of the normal range.

FIGURE 7.3
Theoretical distribution of behaviors representing withdrawal

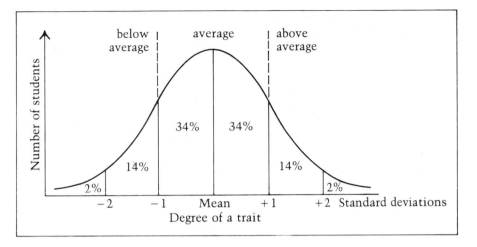

FIGURE 7.4
Standard deviation and the normal curve

Behavior rating scales, then, are norm-referenced instruments that allow the teacher to evaluate whether or not a student's behavior falls within the normal range. If a student's behavior consistently falls outside the normal range, the Pupil Evaluation Team can determine that the student requires special education assistance. These scales can also be used to evaluate student progress in behavior problems. Ratings spaced several months apart can be used to supplement direct observations when substantiating improvements in behavior.

When behavior rating scales are present in a student's record, it is important to note the behaviors that were identified as significant problems. While this knowledge may be helpful in planning for the student at the present time, you may find that some behaviors have improved and are no longer of concern. If more than one rating has been done over a period of time, you should look for trends in the student's performance. Both pieces of information can provide a general picture of the student's behavior in the past. Following are some examples of behavior rating scales you may encounter.

Walker Problem Behavior Checklist   The Walker Problem Behavior Checklist (1970) is intended to measure disturbance in grades 4, 5, and 6. The scale provides a total score as well as measuring the following five factors (Walker, 1970, p. 4):

1. Acting out (disruptive, aggressive, defiant).

2. Withdrawal (restricted functioning, avoidance behavior).

Filling out the Walker Problem Behavior Checklist.

3. Distractability (short attention span, inadequate study skills, non-attendance).

4. Disturbed peer relations (inadequate social skills, negative self-image, compulsive).

5. Immaturity (dependent).

To use this scale teachers are asked to indicate whether or not they have observed particular behaviors for the student being rated. The severity of the problem is assessed by how far the student scores from the average.

Devereux Adolescent Behavior Rating Scale   The Devereux Adolescent Behavior Rating Scale (Spivack, Spotts, and Haimes, 1967) allows the teacher to rate the student on items that are grouped in twelve behavior factors. The analysis of the obtained score can be made by determining whether or not the student's score falls out of the normal range as measured by standard deviation. The twelve behavior factors on this test are as follows:

1. unethical

2. defiant, resistive

3. domineering, sadistic

4. exhibits heterosexual interest

5. hyperactive, expansive

6. has poor emotional control

7. needs approval, dependent

8. emotional, distant

9. exhibits physical inferiority, timidity

10. schizoid, withdrawn

11. exhibits bizarre speech and cognition

12. engages in bizarre action

Specific statements to which the rater responds include items such as the following:

(Compared to normal adolescents his age, how often does the youngster . . .)

- Look puzzled or confused by things happening around him?

- Express anger in a poorly controlled fashion?

- Rock back and forth while sitting or standing?

- Daydream?

- Talk rapidly or hurriedly?

Pupil Behavior Rating Scale   The Pupil Behavior Rating Scale (Lambert, Hartsough, and Bower, 1978) is designed to screen and assess entire classrooms to appraise psychological, social, and emotional functioning for grades kindergarten through seven. Scores can be analyzed by determining how far above or below the norms the students are rated. The students are rated on eleven scales. These are as follows:

1. This pupil fights or quarrels more often than the other pupils do.

2. This pupil has difficulty following directions.

3. This pupil makes immature or inappropriate responses during school activites.

4. This pupil is too dependent on the teacher and becomes uneasy without continual supervision.

5. This pupil has to be coaxed or forced to work or play with others.

6. This pupil is easily distracted.

7. This pupil behaves in ways that are dangerous.

8. This pupil has no enthusiasm for school and does not respond to or maintain interest in learning.

9. This pupil has difficulty in learning skills.

10. This pupil becomes sick or upset or may stay home from school when faced with a difficult problem or situation.

11. This pupil seems unhappy or depressed.

When behavior rating scales are present in a student's records or appear in a report from a specialist, you should analyze the scores in terms of planning in the classroom. Does the scale identify specific behaviors to be concerned about? Can you determine the behaviors that interfere with learning and develop a mangement program for them? If you can answer in the affirmative, the data can ultimately lead to specific objectives when supplemented by your own or others' observations. Data from these instruments may also be used to corroborate beliefs about a student, but a more direct observational plan will have to be developed to determine behavioral needs.

Assessing Problem Behaviors in the Classroom

When a student has been identified as presenting a behavior problem in the classroom, and existing information such as anecdotal records, specialist reports, and the results of behavior rating scales have been evaluated, you will want to collect current data on the behavior of concern. In order to collect such data, it is important first to determine the types of behavior that are of concern in the classroom. When this is done, you can pinpoint the exact problems of any particular student and collect data on the problem. This data collection process can result in specific statements of concern that can, in turn, become the basis for writing objectives and developing intervention plans in the classroom.

IDENTIFYING BEHAVIORS TO ASSESS

Because there is such a wide variety of appropriate and inappropriate behavior present in the classroom, you must collect precise behavior data on the students whose behavior deviates the most from the norm. These are typically the students who are overly aggressive, destructive in the classroom, distracting or distractable during lessons and seatwork time, or extremely immature or withdrawn. As a rule of thumb, you should be primarily concerned about inappropriate behaviors that (1) cause harm to others, (2) interfere with the management of the classroom, or

(3) interfere with the successful academic performance of the student. Here are five of the behaviors frequently found in classrooms and that pose significant instructional problems.

1. *Behaviors that interfere with learning.* In order to be a successful learner, the student usually needs to engage in such behaviors as paying attention, writing, reciting, and taking tests. Any behavior that replaces these learning behaviors will likely impair the student's ability to master content in the subject area. Thus, any behavior that frequently replaces the desired learning behaviors should be assessed.

2. *Behaviors that result in the destruction of property.* Some students willfully destroy school property, such as books, furniture, teaching devices, or the property of other students. Such behavior usually ends in others' feeling angry or attempting some retaliation. The result is an atmosphere permeated with tension and not conducive to good teaching. The destruction of property that occurs fairly regularly is something that should be dealt with.

3. *Acts of physical violence.* Some students have learned to obtain gratification by physically harming others. Because such behaviors tend to escalate in severity over time, and there is a possibility of significant or permanent injury, acts that result in physical harm should be a concern of highest priority.

4. *Social withdrawal.* When a child consistently refuses to join in social activities or obviously withdraws to avoid interaction, a significant problem may exist. While it is important to realize that the level of social interaction among peers and teachers varies greatly, when there is a total lack of interaction and the avoidance of a majority of normal childhood activities, the problem likely deserves further attention.

5. *Interruptive attention-getting behavior.* Acts that disrupt the ongoing teaching and learning activities and interfere with the normal school activities deserve careful scrutiny. Such behaviors include inappropriate statements, being a clown, making fun of others, stealing, and not following instructions.

The types of problem behaviors students exhibit are almost limitless. When a student consistently calls attention to himself or herself as a result of inappropriate behaviors, it is important to collect the type of data that will confirm any problems that do exist and lead to the development of a program to increase the occurrence of appropriate school behaviors.

COLLECTING BEHAVIORAL DATA IN THE CLASSROOM

The first step in assessing the nature of a behavior problem in the classroom is to pinpoint the exact problem. This can be done in a descriptive statement that isolates a particular behavior. For example, rather than saying, "Carlos causes problems on the playground," you might say, "Carlos started at least three fights at noon recess each day this week." The latter statement provides the observer with a behavior that can be observed as a basis for data collection. All behaviors of concern in the classroom can be stated similarly.

Once the precise behavior has been pinpointed, it is necessary to determine the most effective technique for collecting data on the behavior problem. Since different techniques yield different types of information, it is important to select the type of measure that will assist you in adequately describing and documenting the occurrences of the behavior.

Using Direct Observation   Anecdotal records, which were described earlier in this chapter, are useful in determining the types of problem behaviors a student is exhibiting in the classroom. Since these records are more reliable than mere memory and can provide a "running record" in descriptive terms of the student's behavior, they are very useful when documenting behavior.

Once a behavior has been defined precisely, you should decide when you wish to collect data on the behavior. You will want to select the time period(s) during the day when the behavior seems to occur most frequently. Anecdotal notes should be made at the time of occurrence of the behavior or as soon as possible thereafter. For example, if the behavior occurred during seatwork activity, you could make a note of it at the

Student _____

Date _____   Time _____   Setting _____
Behavior _____
_____
                          Observer _____

Date _____   Time _____   Setting _____
Behavior _____
_____
                          Observer _____

FIGURE 7.5
Anecdotal record form

To keep a behavior tally, list the setting, time, and behavior being observed; then place a mark beside the description each time the behavior occurs.

time. If, however, the behavior occurred while you were presenting a lecture in class, it would be necessary to wait until a break or a change in activity to make notes.

It is helpful to develop a form for recording anecdotal records. The form should include provisions for the date, time, activity, name of the observer or recorder, and a description of the student's behavior. A form like the one shown in Figure 7.5 may be developed to aid in the systematic collection of the desired information. You may wish to review the completed anecdotal record forms that appear in Figure 7.2.

A behavior tally or counting of problem behaviors sometimes provides the kind of data necessary to determine the extent of a problem. Some behaviors are classified as problems because they occur so frequently. For example, if a student is late for class only once or twice during a marking period there would be little cause for concern. But if the student were late thirty-five times then tardiness might be a problem. To keep a tally of behaviors, you list the setting, time, and behaviors, and then place a mark beside the description each time the behavior

Date *October 10* _____   Time *10:00 – 10:50* _____   Setting *Play time* _____
Mary refuses to share playthings with classmates.   *HHt /*

Date *November 11* _____   Time *1:00 – 2:00* _____   Setting *Government Class* _____
Ross interrupts lecture by talking out.   *HHt HHt /*

FIGURE 7.6
Behavior tally records

occurs. You should not rely on memory, as there is a possibility that some error will result. Figure 7.6 shows two examples.

A behavior tally is most helpful when you need to determine the number of times a behavior occurs. Even though a behavior may be particularly irritating, its frequency may be low. When this occurs, the behavior may not be as significant as first thought. The data resulting from behavior tallies can also be used to evaluate the effectiveness of a management program designed to affect the frequency of the behavior.

A third type of direct observation is a continuous recording of student behavior. In cases where the student exhibits a number of behaviors of concern or where the duration of a behavior needs to be measured, it may be necessary to maintain an ongoing log of all the student's activities as they occur.

When it is determined that a continuous recording is necessary to collect the necessary observational data on a student, the aid of a special educator, a school psychologist, or a teacher's aide may be enlisted. This person is trained to use a stopwatch or clock with a second hand to note the amount of time the student spends at all activities in which he or she engages during a specified period of time. In the short example that follows, the student's on-task (paying attention to assigned work) and off-task behaviors were recorded. In this case, the teacher was concerned that the student did not pay attention to learning tasks. By adding up the time on- and off-task, the teacher was provided with an objective measure of how much Joey paid attention during the lesson.

When any type of direct observation of a student's behavior is made, it is important to consider a number of different points. First, to provide an accurate representation of the student's behavior, the observations must be carried out over a period of time, usually one to two weeks. Second, when possible, more than one person should observe the behavior to verify that the data collected are accurate. Third, the collection of observational data should be unobtrusive; the student should not be aware

Student ____Joey Black____ Time __10:00–10:10__ Observer __Miss Roy__

Setting Reading lesson. Teacher is presenting new words in the basal reader. All students in group are seated at their desks. Students are expected to remain seated, look at the words as they are presented, and say the words orally when directed by the teacher.

Time	Behavior
10:00–10:02	Off task, looking in desk
10:02–10:03	On task, paying attention to teacher
10:03–10:05	Off task, playing with toy airplane
10:05–10:08	On task, teacher directed him to pay attention
10:08–10:10	Off task, out of seat, sharpening pencil. End of lesson, still off task

Summary: on task – 4 minutes   off task – 6 minutes

FIGURE 7.7
Continuous record

that he or she is being observed. This knowledge may provide the student with the incentive to change his or her behavior temporarily, resulting in inaccurate data and a delay in the development of a program designed to increase more appropriate behavior.

Using Behavior Rating Scales   Behavior rating scales were presented earlier in this chapter as a source of norm-referenced data on students who may have behavior problems. One reason for using behavior rating scales is to help you be objective. Often your own emotions or unique standards of behavior for your students will make it difficult to determine whether or not a particular student's behaviors represent a significant problem. The score obtained on the rating scale can help you look at your own objectivity. If the scale differs from your assessment of the student you may seek outside assistance to insure that the student's needs are being met in your classroom. When rating scores are used in conjunction with observable data you can develop a greater understanding of the student's behavior problems.

Behavior rating scales may also be used to identify specific behavior problems by analyzing the individual items marked for a particular student. For example, if the student had been rated as frequently poking, tormenting, or teasing classmates, you can pinpoint these as specific concerns and use these behaviors as the focal point in an observation program. This approach may be helpful in identifying behaviors of con-

TABLE 7.1
When to use different recording methods

Data	When to select
Anecdotal record	To obtain a general picture of the student's performance in a specific setting.
Behavior tally	To document the number of times a particular behavior occurs.
Continuous record	To assess the duration of a behavior and note every behavior that occurs in a given time.
Behavior rating scale	To obtain a general picture of the student's performance in a specific setting.

cern, which can then be verified through observation of the student's behavior.

Selecting Appropriate Data Sources   A behavior assessment plan begins with pinpointing the precise behavior that presents a problem in the classroom. It is then necessary to determine the type of data to collect that will most effectively document the behavior. You might use the guide in Table 7.1 to make that decision.

The actual data collection should occur over a period of one to two weeks to allow the establishment of a baseline performance (the actual occurrence of typical behavior prior to intervention). These data are then evaluated and used to plan programs to increase appropriate student behavior in school.

THEORY INTO PRACTICE

Data Collection and Assessment

Mr. Clift, the principal, and Mr. Smith, a tenth-grade teacher, were having a spirited discussion. Mr. Smith was feeling a bit irritated. "I can't be expected to teach and spend half my time punishing misbehavior! Patrick simply will not respond to anything else. I've tried everything I know! It's either him or me. He goes or I go. I can't go back and face all that frustration even one more day! That kid is worse than any kid I've ever had. . . ."

"I can see you're upset. I've heard other comments, but I don't think we should transfer him out of your class. I don't think that would solve the problem; let's try having the resource teacher look into the situation."

The conversation continued on for over half an hour, and finally it was agreed that the resource teacher would see if anything could be done to solve the problem. Mr. Smith completed a referral and the Pupil Evaluation Team held an emergency meeting to consider the referral. Patrick's parents attended the meeting and readily agreed to a behavioral evaluation. They, too, had some problems with Patrick's behavior at home. The Pupil Evaluation Team devised an assessment plan as follows:

1. Mr. Smith agreed to collect anecdotal records for eight class days. He was to record all behaviors that disrupted the class or interfered with the class routine. The resource teacher provided him with an anecdotal record form.

2. Patrick's other academic instructors were also asked to keep a similar anecdotal record.

3. The resource teacher would spend two twenty-minute periods on different days conducting an ongoing record of classroom behaviors. He would carry out the observation so that Patrick would not be aware that he was the student being observed.

4. The resource teacher would interview the teachers and parents to determine whether they might have any clues regarding the nature of his behavior.

5. The teachers at the meeting also filled out behavior rating scales, which were to be scored and interpreted before the next meeting.

After the data had been collected and analyzed the following trends were noted:

1. Patrick spoke out inappropriately an average of seven times each class period in Mr. Smith's class and three times in other classes.

2. Patrick had been rated one to two standard deviations above the mean on the Devereux Behavior Rating Scales in needing approval, in dependency, and in poor emotional control.

3. Patrick's in-class behavior included numerous incidents in which he drew others off-task and disrupted the class routine by telling jokes, drawing cartoons, and changing the topic.

4. The direct observation showed that Patrick seemed to respond to teacher attention by exhibiting increased appropriate behavior.

5. For his four academic classes an average of twenty negative instances were reported each day. Over the course of the eight-day observation period 170 problem behavior incidents were described.

Faced with this mountain of data, the team concluded that the problem was significant. Patrick was disruptive in a variety of settings, and his behaviors were upsetting to both teachers and students. Patrick's needs were described by Mr. Smith: "I know what his needs are; he needs to learn how to behave better." The resource teacher said that he agreed, but a more precise statement would be that "Patrick needs to pay attention to the teacher, decrease his interfering with peers, and respond productively to discipline." The Pupil Evaluation Team also agreed and formulated goals for all of these areas. The team felt that the problem was serious enough to warrant classification as Emotionally Disturbed. This allowed the special education resource teacher to provide ongoing assistance to help develop a mangement program for Patrick.

It is frequently not difficult for the Pupil Evaluation Team to agree that a particular student has a significant behavior problem. Some students like Patrick are very conspicuous throughout the school. The most difficult task is to decide what steps to take to improve behavior. While there are many options to consider in designing effective behavior management programs, the first step is to determine appropriate objectives that describe how we *want* the student to behave. Then we can proceed to the next step of the problem-solving model to decide *how* to effect the desired changes. The selection of goals and objectives will be covered in the next chapter. In the meantime, analyze the data gathering assessment process for Lorrie, a kindergarten student who exhibits some behavior problems.

THEORY INTO PRACTICE

Data Assessment and Application

Last year, when Lorrie was tested prior to entering kindergarten, concern was voiced about her fine motor skills, physical maturity, and emotional development. Lorrie's parents had enrolled her in the kindergarten program against the advice of the pupil personnel director. Now it was April and the kindergarten teacher, Mr. Lawrence, had convinced Lorrie's parents to consent to a complete assessment of her behavior. He had, on occasion, described Lorrie as being "quite a handful."

Mr. Lawrence used existing observation data to identify specific problem behaviors. He then constructed a behavior tally record, which he used to record the frequency of problem behaviors. One week of observation revealed the following information:

- Lorrie, when given the choice during free play time, chose parallel play rather than engaging in shared play ten of ten times.

■   When given coloring tasks Lorrie did not finish seven out of eight times.

■   Lorrie began crying when her requests were not allowed five out of nine times. The time spent crying each time was approximately four, eleven, eight, twenty, and ten minutes respectively.

The school psychologist also worked with Lorrie. He began by interviewing Mr. Lawrence to obtain information on his specific concerns. He then observed Lorrie in the classroom on three different occasions. He was able to corroborate the classroom observation Mr. Lawrence had made. The psychologist also interviewed Lorrie once he had completed the classroom observations. As a result of his informal observations, the psychologist was able to document that Lorrie was a significant behavior problem in the classroom.

The data collected by Mr. Lawrence and the school psychologist were used both to document the specific types of problems that Lorrie exhibited and to develop some approaches for mediating the problems. As a result of these new ideas and the subsequent changes made in her instructional program, Lorrie was able to demonstrate more appropriate behaviors in the kindergarten classroom the remainder of the year.

Summary

Behavior problems frequently accompany leaning problems. There is little doubt that a major concern of teachers is determining how to improve the problem behavior of exceptional students in the classroom. In this chapter, we have presented several techniques for assessing student behavior, including behavior rating scales and observational techniques. By observing, recording, and measuring student behaviors, you have the information needed to determine the type and degree of behavior deficits. The results of behavior assessments can be used to formulate instructional goals and objectives, thereby completing the first two steps of the problem-solving model.

When carrying out a behavioral assessment it is important to consider the following points:

1. Data sources commonly available to teachers for behavioral assessment include specialist reports, anecdotal records, and behavior rating scales.

2. Direct observation of student behavior allows the teacher to collect valid, reliable data, which can supplement other data sources.

3. When using outside specialists the information obtained should be evaluated in light of what is already known about the student's behavior.

4. In order to be useful, anecdotal data needs to be descriptive and factual. No anecdotal record is complete without a record of who observed the behavior, the date, and description of the setting in which the behavior occurred.

5. Behavior rating scales provide a norm-referenced assessment of many different traits. While there is some apparent overlap, each scale measures different behavior problems.

6. There are several kinds of behavior that warrant careful evaluation. These include acts of violence, destruction of property, attention-getting, withdrawal, and behaviors that interfere directly with learning, such as daydreaming, inattention, wandering about the room, and so on.

Activities

1. Have the students in your class each compile a list of problem behaviors they have observed in classroom settings. Compare the lists and discuss their similarities and differences.

2. Obtain a behavior rating scale. Fill it out on a problem student you have known. Analyze and interpret the student's score.

3. Conduct an interview with a specialist. Determine how he/she identifies and evaluates problem behavior.

4. Practice devising good anecdotal records for behaviors you have observed in the classroom.

Study Questions

1. When should the classroom teacher consult with specialists to assist with the assessment of behavior problems?

2. List the necessary information that must be included in an anecdotal record.

3. Why is it necessary that anecdotal records be descriptive and not evaluative?

4. In what way are behavior rating scales and norm-referenced achievement tests similar?

5. What kinds of misbehaviors should concern the teacher?

6. When should behavior tally records be used?

7. Describe the observation known as continuous recording.

8. How are appropriate objectives selected once the behavior problems have been measured?

Questions for Further Thought

1. Why do you suppose that learning and behavior problems often coexist?

2. Would you expect any differences in the behavior problems of ED, LD, and MR students?

3. All students vary in their personality and behavior. At what point should these differences be of concern to the classroom teacher?

4. What problem behaviors are of greatest concern to you personally? Can you determine how you will assess these behaviors in your classroom?

Additional Resources

BOOKS

Boehm, A., and Weinberg, R. A. *The classroom observer: A guide for developing observation skills.* New York: Teachers College Press, 1977.

Buckley, N. K., and Walker, H. M. *Modifying classroom behavior.* Champaign, Illinois: Research Press Company, 1978.

Cooper, J. O. *Measurement and analysis of behavioral techniques.* Columbus, Ohio: Charles E. Merrill, 1974.

Cooper, J. O. *Measuring behavior.* Columbus, Ohio: Charles E. Merrill, 1974.

PROFESSIONAL JOURNALS

Journal of Applied Behavior Analysis

Psychology in the Schools

Chapter 8

Developing Goals and Objectives

Educational goals and objectives may be said to "mirror" weaknesses or deficits identified through the assessment process. For every significant problem, a goal or series of goals and objectives can be devised that, if mastered, will result in an improvement in skills and behaviors.

A frequently asked question is, "Why write goals and objectives; do they really help?" Some teachers might say, "I teach the same whether I have goals or not, so why take the time?" It is important to develop an understanding of why you should write goals and objectives, before you can develop a commitment towards using them with students. Some reasons for devising goals and objectives are:

1. *Goals and objectives clearly identify what to teach.* By keeping in mind what skills and behaviors the student is to demonstrate, you can plan activities that lead to the desired outcomes. Vague expectations may lead to vague lessons.

2. *Specific objectives enable the teacher to be aware of the student's progress.* By measuring growth towards mastery, you have a more objective view of the student's skills and behaviors.

3. *Goals and objectives help insure accountability.* As they are derived from deficits and problems and reflect our expectations, they provide a standard by which you and others teaching can judge the effectiveness of your teaching.

Designating goals and objectives is not, of course, the universal solution answer to all educational problems. The selection of appropriate goals and objectives is only one part of the process of designing effective programs. Goals and objectives provide the teacher with the opportunity to take the next step in the problem-solving process, which is to determine the teaching methods and materials that are to be used to help the student attain performance at the mastery level.

Goals and objectives based on the assessment process reflect needs. A major responsibility of the Pupil Evaluation Team is to ascertain that goals are realistic and necessary. Since it may not be possible to remediate every instructional deficit a student demonstrates during the development of a particular Individualized Education Program, it is important to select goals that are most necessary for the particular student's success.

Once goals and objectives have been established, it may be necessary to modify them if you find that a student is unsuccessful in mastering the designated skills and behavior changes. In some cases, although adequate assessment data were collected, the student's initial skill level (or entry skills) may have been below that shown in the data. This can occur when a student makes correct responses through guessing or is required only to use rote memory processes on tasks that may also require application. In other cases, the objectives may be appropriate for the student's skill level; the student, however, may be unable to achieve the objective because of the interaction of emotional or attitudinal problems. In these cases, the complexity of the student's responses must be evaluated and modified to increase the likelihood of student success. Goals and objectives, then, serve not only as a planning tool in establishing the direction for instruction, but also as a basis for instructional change when students are unsuccessful at some learning tasks.

Writing Long-Term Goals and Short-Term Objectives

Long-range goals and short-term objectives are similar in that they both identify what the student should learn. Short-term objectives serve as a starting point for immediate instruction of the student, while long-term goals provide a direction for future instruction. In this way, goals and objectives lend direction and continuity to instructional programs. Long-term goals and short-term objectives differ in that goals specify broad, general needs, while objectives detail the steps necessary to move the student from present levels of functioning to the goal. In both cases, they should be stated precisely and in observable and measurable terms to lend clarity and a means for evaluation of the instructional program.

LONG-RANGE GOALS

Long-range goals are statements of anticipated gains to be made by a student. The goals are based on an estimate of what the student may be able to attain during the period of time the goal covers, often the remainder of the school year. In this way, goals establish a direction for instruction.

Because goals are used to establish a direction for instruction, they are stated in broad terms. The following are examples of long-range goals:

1. Mary will master basic punctuation skills at a 90% accuracy level, as measured by a teacher-made test, by June 1.

2. John will read at the 4.5 grade level by the end of the year.

3. Cathleen will pass the driver's training course by the end of the term.

4. Kelly will participate in all science experiments conducted in laboratory classes during the fall semester.

As you can see, these goals are all broad statements of anticipated student progress. To write such a goal, first evaluate your student's strengths and weaknesses. Then, select an area in which your student must improve to be successful in school. This will become the focus for the goal. Based upon documented strengths and weaknesses and your knowledge of the student, estimate a performance level the student might reach by the end of the goal period. This period will usually be for the length of a semester or school year. Then write a statement that notes (1) the behavior expected of the student, (2) the level of performance to be attained, and (3) the time frame or deadline for reaching the goal.

Since goals are broad statements that do not address specific skill deficits, it becomes apparent that you must rely on more specific statements to develop lessons that will lead to success in meeting the goals. For each goal stated for a student, then, it is necessary to develop short-term objectives.

SHORT-TERM OBJECTIVES

Short-term objectives are specific statements that identify individual components of skills or social behavior a student must perform to be successful in the eventual mastery of stated goals. Since students who experience failure in school are often lacking in many basic skills, a series of sequential objectives should be developed for each goal stated. These objectives become the steps the student takes to move from the current skill level to mastery of the goal. You will find that short-term objectives are sometimes called behavioral objectives or instructional objectives.

These are general terms; they are usually interchangeable, and they do not refer to behavior problems and academic problems respectively. "Behavioral" simply means that the objective must relate to observable behavior on the part of the student.

Instructional objectives, whether they refer to academic or behavior concerns, should be stated in such a way that they are clear and convey the same message to different readers. The objectives should also serve as the basis for an evaluation plan. That is, the objectives should clearly specify how well the student is expected to perform on the task. A well-stated objective has the following components: (1) a clear *behavior* (a word describing action — something that can be measured for success), (2) *conditions* (a description of the setting, type of material used, activity in which the student should engage), and (3) a *measurable standard of success* (the criterion or criteria a student must meet for success). Attention to these components results in an objective that can be used as a basis for teaching and evaluating instruction.

Let's return to the long-range goals that were stated in the preceding section and develop objectives for some of them.

MARY

Goal
Mary will master basic punctuation skills at a 90% accuracy level, as measured by a teacher-made test, by June 1.

Objectives

1. When asked by the teacher, Mary will state three rules for using commas in written work.

2. Mary will correctly place commas in 20 sentences containing appositives, with 100% accuracy, within ten minutes.

3. After selecting a topic of interest, Mary will write a paragraph, using commas with 95% accuracy.

4. Mary will write a 250-word theme, using commas with 95% accuracy on the first draft and 100% accuracy on the revision.

These sample objectives provide a basis for instruction on commas. Mary has other skill deficits in punctuation in the areas of capitalization and the use of semicolons. Specific objectives for these problems will also be written.

KELLY

Goal
Kelly will participate in all science experiments conducted in laboratory classes during the fall semester.

Objectives

1. Kelly will take all required materials for each experiment to her work station when requested by the science teacher within three minutes of the request.

2. Kelly will follow the verbal directions of the teacher, setting her experiment up correctly.

3. Kelly will work with a partner when required by the experiment by sharing equipment and supplies, taking turns on steps in the experiment, and stating some of the observations.

4. Kelly will return all materials to their storage area within ten minutes of the conclusion of the experiment.

5. Kelly will submit in writing the results of her experiment within one day of the class. The results will be stated correctly (as Kelly found them) and the paper will be structured in the way required by the teacher.

These objectives were written for a student who had a behavior problem during science class. The objectives gave the teacher specific directions and could be used to let the student know the teacher's expectations.

When writing goals and objectives, it is important to keep the three components (behavior, conditions, and standards) in mind. The behavior stated in the objective should be in the form of an action verb. Words such as *print, write, draw, label, read,* and *point* describe the actual behavior the student is to exhibit. Such words do not leave room for misinterpretation or misunderstanding of the intent of the objective. In many cases, the behavior the student is to exhibit should occur in a particular setting or time of day. These conditions should be noted in the objective. Conditions may also reflect a particular material or the manner in which a student is to respond. Finally, the desired standard of performance should be stated. This allows for evaluation of the success of the student in meeting the specified objective.

Well-written objectives can be broken into the three components, as shown in the following examples.

1. Given a list of single-syllable CVC words, John will correctly read aloud at least 95% of the words at a rate of one per second.
   Behavior: read aloud
   Condition: single syllable CVC words
   Standard: 95% correct at one per second

2. During social studies John will raise his hand before speaking in class 100% of the time.
   Behavior: raising his hand
   Condition: during social studies class
   Standard: 100% of the time

3. Upon being directed by the teacher, Sally will come to the reading table and be in her seat within one minute.
   Behavior: coming to the reading table and being seated
   Condition: when directed by the teacher
   Standard: within one minute

By including each of the components in your goals and instructional objectives you will be able to facilitate clear communication. Anyone reading well-written goals and objectives will be able to understand what the student is to learn and use the objective as a basis for instructional planning. Clear instructional objectives allow you to take global problems, such as poor reading, negativism, and emotional disturbance, and describe them in more concrete terms, which leads to a better understanding of what can be done to help the student.

DERIVING GOALS AND OBJECTIVES FROM ASSESSMENT DATA

Assessment should always extend beyond the identification of weaknesses or deficits; it should also provide you with a logical set of teachable objectives based on needs revealed by the earlier stages of the assessment process. In most instances, the assessment of educational needs is carried out in these stages.

1. Analyze the task to be learned, developing a list of measurable skills students should demonstrate.

2. Select appropriate measures and determine a mastery level for each skill (accuracy, rate, and/or time limit).

3. Choose or develop appropriate testing materials.

FIGURE 8.1
Converting deficits to goals and objectives

Deficit
Laurie Kimball, a kindergarten student, cannot write her last name.

Goal
By the end of the second term, Laurie will be able to legibly write her name.

Objectives
1. When given a verbal request, Laurie will be able to recite her last name without a visual cue at 100% accuracy within 30 seconds.
2. When requested to do so, Laurie will correctly write her last name on a piece of primary writing paper.
3. Laurie will correctly write her name with letters of the correct shape, size and placement (100% as judged by the kindergarten standards).

Deficit
Ken, an emotionally disturbed high-school student, does not write correct paragraphs 50% of the time in his research papers.

Goal
Ken will improve his ability to write correct paragraphs by the end of the school year.

Objectives
1. Ken will write 10 paragraphs containing clear topic sentences with 90% accuracy within one class period.
2. Ken will write 10 paragraphs containing a single idea at 90% accuracy within one class period.
3. Ken will write 10 paragraphs each containing at least three logical supporting sentences.

4. Measure and record data on the student's performance in each skill or behavior.

5. Devise appropriate goals and objectives based on the student's measured deficits.

Once the student's current level of performance has been compared to what you would like the student to be able to perform, the learning needs can be stated as goals and objectives. Figure 8.1 shows some deficits and possible goals and objectives for several subject areas. Goals and objectives reflect the educational and behavioral needs of each student. Goals and objectives also reflect the student's age, intellectual capacity, cultural experience, type and degree of handicap, and emotional status. This means

Deficit
Mary Flynt, a gifted student with a behavior problem, does not follow the instructions in her chemistry lab book.

Goal
Mary will follow established routines during chemistry lab every day.

Objectives
1. Mary will write the required responses in her lab book 100% of the time on all assigned lab work.
2. Mary will carry out each step of the assigned experiments at the 100% accuracy level within each class period.

Deficit
Karl Schultz, a tenth-grader, pays attention in class an average of 58% of the time and interrupts the class an average of seven times per class period during lectures.

Goal
Karl will improve his in-class behavior by the end of the 3rd marking period.

Objectives
1. Karl will remain on-task an average of 85% of the time for two consecutive weeks.
2. Karl will interrupt class not more than three times per week in each class.

that the selection of goals and objectives is a complex process that takes into account a number of variables. In the following theory note how the teacher selected appropriate goals and objectives which she will later use as a basis for determining appropriate teaching activities.

THEORY INTO PRACTICE

Goals and Objectives

Mrs. Waverly became concerned about Joanna, an emotionally disturbed handicapped child in her class. She conducted an assessment by collecting data on her work samples and on her behavior during her English class. She came up with the following data:

   1. Joanna paid attention to class lectures less than half the time.

2. Joanna completed and submitted 60% of her homework assignments.

3. Although she could write sentences and paragraphs, Joanna did not write unified themes.

4. Joanna was unable to outline from oral lectures or from printed material.

Since she knew that Joanna was intelligent and had a low tolerance for frustrating experiences and could not deal with too many expectations, Mrs. Waverly wrote only a few objectives and did not establish overly stringent mastery criteria. The goals and objectives were, however, based on Joanna's measured strengths and deficits.

Goal 1

Joanna will exhibit appropriate participation during English class for the rest of the semester.

Objectives

1. Joanna will attend to class lectures at least 80% of the time. Attention is defined as looking at the instructor or the blackboard, or taking notes.

2. Joanna will complete and submit at least 90% of her homework assignments as they are assigned.

3. Joanna will write a paper from her outline, maintaining a central theme and using correct grammar, spelling, and punctuation.

Goal 2

Joanna will write a three-paragraph theme correctly by the end of the term.

Objectives

1. Joanna will select a topic for a paper when it is assigned.

2. Joanna will write an outline for the paper containing at least three main ideas and two supporting ideas (for each main idea), using the correct form and maintaining a central theme for the paper.

3. Joanna will write a paper from her outline, maintaining a central theme and using correct grammar, spelling, and punctuation.

When she stopped to analyze the specific objectives developed for Joanna on the basis of her assessment data, Mrs. Waverly found that she had clarified her own expectations of Joanna. She also found that she was ready to take the next step to structure learning experiences in the classroom to better meet Joanna's instructional and personal needs. In Chapters 9, 10, and 11 we will discuss how the teacher can help the student meet goals and objectives.

Selecting Appropriate Goals

Selecting goals and objectives might, on the surface, appear to be an easy task. Once assessment data are collected, goals and objectives can immediately be developed for the student. On occasion, though, a student may have so many instructional deficits that it becomes necessary to consider which of the student's needs are most pressing and develop goals and objectives for the most critical needs first. This, of course, involves the use of collective professional judgment on the part of the Pupil Evaluation Team. In another case, we may find that a student is unable to meet an objective due to the nature of the handicap. In these and similar cases, it is important to develop a rationale for the selection of goals and objectives for individual students.

DETERMINING THE APPROPRIATENESS OF GOALS AND OBJECTIVES

The logical starting point in teaching for mastery is the selection of clear and reasonable goals for those individuals who are experiencing learning and behavior difficulties. From the definition of mastery learning, you already know that goals must be clearly stated in such a way that mastery criteria are spelled out. However, the appropriateness of these goals for exceptional students, particularly those with actual learning difficulties, must be considered.

How can goals be judged as appropriate and reasonable for exceptional students? Admittedly, determining what is appropriate and reasonable is a matter of judgment. While there is no precise formula to use, there are several factors that warrant consideration. The first factor is the student's current level of performance as determined through the assessment process. If, for example, you know that a particular fourth-grader reads at a second-grade level, you can be certain that expecting the student to read at a fourth-grade level right away is an unreasonable goal. The same consideration must be given to the fifth-grade student who can accurately add only double-digit numbers without renaming, the seventh grade science student who reads at a fourth-grade level and therefore cannot efficiently obtain content from the science text, and the ninth-grade English student who cannot yet write a paragraph with a main idea and supporting details.

In each of the above-mentioned cases, even the most sophisticated teaching methods will fail if the instructional goals and tasks are too far beyond the current abilities of the student. Reasonable goals for these students would indicate that the fourth-grader should begin reading instruction at the second-grade level, the fifth-grader should begin math instruction that focuses on the addition of double-digit numbers that require renaming, and the English student should have instruction that first focuses on main ideas. The seventh-grade science student presents a double problem. Reading level must be improved, of course. But in the meantime, a way must be found to impart science content, with working through the science text or somehow circumventing it.

SETTING REASONABLE EXPECTATIONS

Knowing a student's current level performance, then, can help you to begin instruction commensurate with the student's abilities. However, an important question remains to be considered: How much can you expect the student to accomplish over a given unit of time, such as a marking period? If you are to begin instruction at the student's current level of performance, and the performance is significantly lower than most or all of the other students, then a decision has to be made about selecting different goals or different mastery criteria for the student in question. In short, how many new words, concepts, skills, and so on, should the student be expected to master in a given period of time?

The answer to the above-mentioned question requires judgment. Several strategies can help you make a good determination. One strategy is to determine the student's current level of accuracy. If, for example, a placement test suggests that a student can do spelling at a particular difficulty level (Level C) in a spelling series, you may assess the student's level of accuracy in that designated level in the series. Let us say that the student is expected to master twenty new words a week, but, even with some extra help, obtains a score of nine and ten on two successive weeks. You can use this current performance level to establish mastery criteria such as the following: Using Level C spelling words, the student will correctly spell at least twelve new words per week on a weekly test. This criterion level represents an attempt to stretch the student's accuracy level by a small, but seemingly reasonable, degree. The same procedure can be applied to learning addition facts and other specific skills such as vocabulary development and reading rate.

Another strategy to help identify reasonable learning goals is to identify several students who are performing at an acceptable level and use their performance to establish criterion level performance. You could, for example, determine the rate at which these students read words by taking an average and then establishing the obtained mean score as the target or mastery level for the student who is reading too slow. Let's say that Jack, our student in question, reads from a second-grade reading text at a rate of 75 correct words per minute. Next, we select three students who are judged to be making acceptable progress in a second-grade-level reading text and have each orally read from the text. Our findings were as follows:

- Tom: 105 correct words per minute
- Anna: 107 correct words per minute
- George: 115 correct words per minute

The average oral reading rate of this group of three is 109 correct words per minute, which might be a reasonable mastery criterion for Jack, who reads at 75 words per minute. By the way, when you use this technique to set minimum standards in your classroom, it is a good idea to determine the average for eight or ten students, to ensure a representative standard. And if you were conducting a thorough analysis of reading skills, you would test the students' understanding of the material they read.

It is a bit more difficult to identify the amounts of content that students are to master in areas such as science, social studies, literature, and the like, but it can be done. The first step is to define the mastery level for all students, as discussed in the last section. Then, based on the exceptional student's initial level of performance, some mastery goals can be modified to be more in keeping with the student's ability. For example, one ninth-grade literature teacher altered the mastery criteria for two students who had great difficulty with any type of comprehension beyond recall of main ideas and events. These students are quite concrete in their thinking and could not yet draw inferences or analyze motives. Rather than subject these individuals to frustration and almost certain failure, mastery criteria for a series of short novels focused only on vocabulary development and recall of selected main ideas. Inferential thinking was temporarily suspended as a learning goal for these students until they had mastered more basic skills.

Another consideration in selecting goals for exceptional students is limitations due to specific handicaps the students may have. You would not expect a student with a fluency or articulation disorder to read orally as fast or as accurately as others. Nor would you expect students with motor problems, such as cerebral palsy, to type or write as fast or accurately as others. Similarly, students with low intellectual potential will probably not be able to learn as rapidly as others and will surely have difficulty mastering abstract concepts. The presence of specific handicaps should alert you to the possible need to modify some objectives.

Modifying Goals and Objectives

Goals and objectives need to reflect a realistic appraisal of the exceptional student's abilities. For some students, the ultimate level of competence in math might be simple computation, while others might master advanced calculus. Goals and objectives should be reachable. As the student gains in proficiency, new goals and objectives can be written that reflect increased competency. A careful and thorough assessment of the basic skills usually provides enough information so that the goals and objectives selected are appropriate for the individual student. Occasionally a student has such severe skill deficiencies that, even with a thorough assessment of the student and carefully written goals and objectives, the student may not be able to master goals for a specific course or unit. In this case, it is necessary to make some type of modification in the objectives to increase student success. Modification can come in the types of behaviors stated in objectives, the level at which the first objectives are written, and the complexity of the response required of the student. Although modifications in this area may lead to curriculum changes, these changes are likely necessary for student success.

ESTABLISH THE ENTRY LEVEL

A thorough assessment of student needs should give an indication of the skills a student has acquired. It is possible, though, that an assessment may be general enough that it does not identify the student's entry level in all areas. If a student is failing, it is important to reassess the content area to determine the student's precise instructional level. Once the student's entry level (or current level of performance) has been established, goals and objectives can be modified to better meet the student's needs. Criterion-referenced techniques suggested in Chapter 5 can be used to assess the student's needs, and, in fact, should be used prior to developing any instructional program.

If the student is unable to perform skills needed for the current content being taught, the curriculum must be adjusted. In this case, instruction should begin at a level commensurate with the student's current performance, with the ultimate goal being entry into the regular curriculum. These goals result in a change in the curriculum for the student. The following examples illustrate the concept of entry level and its implications for curriculum adaptations.

CAROL

Carol was having difficulty completing her fourth-grade math assignments. Mrs. Edwards was concerned about Carol's progress and began to collect samples of her work. She found that Carol seemed to have trouble on assignments requiring carrying and borrowing. To further pinpoint the specific problems, Mrs. Edwards gave Carol a series of problems in addition, beginning with addition facts, working up to two three-digit numbers with carrying. Carol was successful with all addition until carrying was introduced. Mrs. Edwards observed that Carol sometimes computed problems from left to right and became quite nervous with the more difficult problems. She used a similar informal procedure to assess subtraction, and was able to describe precisely Carol's deficits. These statements were translated into instructional objectives. The curriculum for Carol was changed to accommodate these new objectives.

LISA

Lisa, on the other hand, was a freshman in high school who was having difficulty with English. Her teacher, Mr. Cohen, observed that while she frequently contributed to class discussions, raising relevant points and answering questions posed by the teacher, Lisa received failing marks on many of her written assignments. After assessing Lisa's skills, Mr. Cohen found that she could write simple declarative sentences, but had not learned to write interrogative, compound, or complex sentences. Based on this information, Mr. Cohen designed an instructional program for Lisa that focused on developing her sentence-writing skills. He used her entry level to determine a temporary change in the curriculum for Lisa. She continued to complete the class assignments, but focused on sentence development and structure rather than outlining the writing themes.

In both examples, the classroom teacher used informal assessment techniques to determine the entry level of their students. Mrs. Edwards used a task analysis of addition and subtraction as a basis for her assessment of Carol's daily work to note problem areas. Mr. Cohen used daily work assignments as a starting point, too. His assessment relied heavily on these and succeeding assignments.

CLARIFY STUDENT GOALS AND OBJECTIVES

Most teachers use goals and objectives as a basis for instruction in the classroom. The objectives, though, often relate to the direction of the entire class and may be derived from the curriculum or textbook series used in the school. While these are important in planning instruction for the class, some students require further refinement and clarification of objectives. These objectives would be used in addition to those already established for the class.

CAROL

In an earlier example, Mrs. Edwards assessed the entry level of one of her students, Carol. The data she collected enabled her to clarify her objectives for Carol in the following way. Mrs. Edwards already had several objectives for her students in arithmetic, including (1) increasing student proficiency in addition and subtraction; (2) introducing multiplication facts, multiplication problems, and division facts; and (3) increasing skills in math related areas such as money, measurement, and geometry. She maintained these overall objectives for Carol. In addition, she has written four more objectives for Carol, as follows:

1. Carol will write the answers to ten addition problems (two- and three-digit numbers) with carrying, with 90% accuracy.

2. Carol will write the answers to ten three-digit plus three-digit problems with carrying, with 90% accuracy.

3. Carol will write the answers to ten two-digit minus two-digit problems without regrouping, with 90% accuracy.

4. Carol will write the answers to ten two-digit minus two-digit problems with regrouping, with 90% accuracy.

These objectives help clarify Carol's curriculum needs and form the basis for her instructional program.

There are several advantages to clarifying objectives for some students. First, the objectives help focus on the student's specific needs. You become aware of the needs of the student, and the student knows the specific skills that must be mastered. Second, the objectives can form the basis for instructional programming and decision making. Since the objectives are clearly spelled out for the teacher, materials and methods can be selected that best aid in teaching the skill to the student. Well-stated objectives that contain criteria set a standard of performance for the student and you. Measurement of the objectives enables you to account for student progress and to make program changes based upon the collected data. Last, the objectives give you and the student an immediate goal. The focus is on immediate progress and knowledge, rather than skills that will be acquired at some point in the future. The student is able to receive frequent feedback on progress towards goals and objectives.

In some cases, the student continues to be unable to meet goals and objectives, even when alternatives have been defined and used. In those cases, it may be important to reevaluate the objectives, making further revisions. If the student continues to show little progress, you should assess the relevance of the goals and objectives for the student and possibly consider referring the student to the Pupil Evaluation Team.

CHANGE THE COMPLEXITY OF GOALS AND OBJECTIVES

Some students are unable to respond in the manner that is usually expected in the classroom. For example, a physically handicapped student may be unable to write well enough to complete some class work. For this student, it may be appropriate to change the type of response required on tests and certain assignments.

In addition to adaptations in the type of response, adaptations in the complexity of the response may need to be made. Some students are unable to cope with the amount of work required during a regular class period. This might be evidenced by incomplete assignments, progressively poorer performance on worksheets, and a lack of attention to the task on hand. For some students, facing an entire worksheet or a long assignment can produce feelings of anxiety, fear, or frustration. Others may be able to give part of a response or give the response in an alternative form to that required by the text or assignment.

The following are adaptations that may lead to a change in the type of response required and/or in the level of complexity of the response.

1. Worksheets can be cut into strips, giving the student one strip to complete at a time.

2. The student may respond orally to tests, rather than answering in writing on the test form.

3. Projects involving art and other creative expressions can be substituted for oral and written responses.

4. Selected problems from texts can be assigned, rather than expecting the student to complete every problem.

5. Oral reading can be shaped by requiring sentence-by-sentence reading, gradually increasing to paragraphs, pages, and stories as the student's confidence grows.

6. Role play and simulation activities can be substituted for situations that require the demonstration of a skill or recital of a sequence of information.

7. Use of a tape recorder can be allowed for listening to recorded stories and assignments.

These types of adaptations can lead to increased success for some students in the classroom. A student who is faced with fewer examples to complete at one time may be more willing to attempt the assigned task. Alternative methods for demonstrating competence may allow some students, who might otherwise have failed previously, to demonstrate their knowledge and proceed to new instructional material. Reducing the complexity of tasks may assist some students in focusing on critical skills, learning those skills more quickly, and using those skills to make the response required for the original task. In nearly all cases, tasks can be gradually made more difficult as the student experiences success.

Summary

Goals and objectives are at the heart of good instructional programs for exceptional children. By using them you can have a clear understanding of what knowledge and behavior changes you are trying to bring about.

Knowing what to teach will help you to go to the next step in the problem-solving model, which is to determine *how* to teach.

In this chapter the following major points were presented:

1. Long-term goals are broad statements that may cover general skill and behavior changes. Long-term goals establish a general direction for the instructional program.

2. Short-term objectives are specific statements that identify the specific skills or behaviors the student must learn in order to master the broader long-term goal.

3. Objectives should contain a clear behavior, conditions, and a measurable standard for determining mastery.

4. Goals and objectives are based on specific student needs which are identified through the assessment process. The specificity and form of the goals and objectives may vary for each student.

5. The selection of goals and objectives should represent reasonable expectations for the student. Goals should not be too difficult nor too easy.

6. The behavior specified in the objectives may change in type and complexity according to the needs of the student.

Activities

1. Identify a personal skill or behavior deficit. Write a long-term goal and short-term objective that represent mastery. By specifically identifying what you must do to be successful you are ready to select the methods for improving your performance.

2. Select a student with learning problems. Write appropriate goals and objectives for this student in your academic area.

3. Write a unit of instruction based on goals and objectives. Use your knowledge of assessment, goals, and objectives to teach something to a student. Share your experience with others in your class.

Study Questions

1. What is meant by the statement that goals and objectives "mirror" deficits?

2. Why is it useful to devise goals and objectives?

3. When might objectives need to be modified or changed?

4. How do long-term goals differ from short-term objectives?

5. Identify and define each of the three necessary components of a short-term objective.

6. How do we insure that the goals devised for a student are appropriate?

7. How do we establish entry level?

8. How is the complexity of the objectives changed?

Questions for Further Thought

1. You have probably experienced a class in which the goals and objectives were not clearly identified. What problems, if any, did you experience when trying to guess what the instructor wanted you to learn?

2. Although a strong case can be made for using specific goals and objectives, are they always necessary? Can you identify a teaching situation in which they are not helpful?

3. Is it possible to write objectives for such areas as honesty, appreciation for nature, or kindness?

Additional Resources

BOOKS

Mager, R. F. *Goal analysis.* Belmont, California: Lear Siegler, 1972.

Mager, R. F. *Preparing instructional objectives.* Belmont, California: Fearon Publishers, 1962.

Thompson, D. G. *Writing long term and short term objectives.* Champaign, Illinois: Research Press Company, 1977.

PART IV
TEACHING EXCEPTIONAL STUDENTS

You will have completed the first two steps of the problem-solving model when the assessment of behaviors and academic skills has been carried out and you have identified long-range goals and short-term objectives. Some of these goals and objectives will likely be developed by special education personnel who may be assisting you or working directly with students in your classroom. In any case, completion of these two steps of the problem-solving process leads to a clear idea as to what students need to learn and what you need to emphasize in your day-to-day teaching.

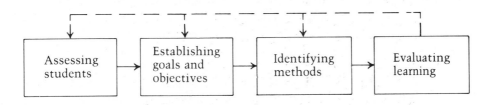

In this section, Steps 3 and 4 of the problem-solving model will be examined. Here, the broad question, "How can I teach and motivate exceptional students and also help them become more accepted members of the class?" will be explored. The four chapters contained in this section introduce a variety of teaching methods related to this question. When we speak of teaching methods we generally refer to the behaviors a teacher exhibits while interacting with students, the materials selected to meet the learning needs of specific students, the techniques selected to motivate students to learn skills and appropriate behavior, and the steps taken to promote acceptance and participation of exceptional students.

Many exceptional students have learning problems that require carefully executed teaching techniques. In Chapter 9, we will examine a variety of good teaching practices to enhance student learning. In Chapter 10, we will explore how teaching methods and materials that are commonly used in the regular classroom can be modified to ensure success for exceptional students. Taken together, these two chapters will provide you with a core of important methods to help nearly all students learn effectively and efficiently.

Some exceptional students demonstrate high levels of problem behavior. Others, or these same students, may be ignored or rejected by their classmates. In Chapter 11, we will examine methods to help students behave in more acceptable ways. Finally, in Chapter 12, strategies to promote acceptance and participation of exceptional students will be introduced.

Many of the methods contained in these chapters relate directly to students who are mentally retarded, emotionally disturbed, and learning disabled. The methods are also applicable to other exceptional students who may demonstrate problems in the area of learning, behavior, or social acceptance. While the methods have specific merit for exceptional learners, they are equally applicable to all students; we believe that good teaching methods are appropriate no matter who the students are. As you learn to select methods that result in improved performance of exceptional learners, your effectiveness with all students will probably be increased.

Evaluation is the final step of the problem-solving process. Some people believe that evaluation is something to be done when teaching is finished. We take a different position and assert that evaluation should be an ongoing process. We think that you need to watch closely to determine whether the methods you have selected are accomplishing important goals and objectives. In this light, evaluation is a good teaching practice. Thus, rather than devote a separate chapter, procedures for evaluation are contained in Chapter 9.

A final word about problem-solving needs to be mentioned. Our problem-solving model differs from other more conventional approaches to teaching in several ways. First, it is based on mastery learning: the idea that all students can achieve success in important skills and behaviors. Second, the model requires ongoing evaluation and adjustment. You cannot always expect methods that you select to be successful. Rather, you must stand ready to scrutinize the effects of your methods and change or modify them if they are not achieving desired objectives. This readiness to modify contrasts with other approaches, in which it is assumed that a certain number of students will be below average or will fail to learn the subject matter presented. The last distinguishing aspect of the problem-solving approach is that it views you, the teacher, as a decision maker who must be ready to assess goals, select teaching methods, and evaluate the impact of specific teaching methods on student performance. The material contained in the next four chapters is selected to lead to effective decision making for the benefit of exceptional and all other students in your classes.

Chapter 9

Using

Good Teaching

Practices

The success of a mastery approach to teaching depends on careful planning and implementation of instruction. Identification of student needs through assessment and the formulation of goals and objectives from the assessment data lead to clearly identified student needs, which in turn become the focus for instruction.

Even when student needs and objectives are clearly defined, however, it is incumbent upon the teacher to select instructional strategies that will increase the likelihood of student success during lessons. Careful planning is a key to instructional success; the application of good teaching practices during instruction is another. Such practices as modeling (the demonstration of desired behaviors), providing immediate feedback to responses, and using concrete materials to present ideas are essential techniques when teaching exceptional students.

While these techniques are presented as they apply to exceptional students, they are practices that are common throughout the educational system. All effective teachers utilize some of the practices in their everyday teaching. While there are no magic formulas used in teaching exceptional students, the precise application of these principles can streamline the instructional process for the teacher and students. It is important to review these common teaching practices as they apply to the education of exceptional students.

Plan for Small Increments of Change

Teachers can at times be impatient, expecting students with learning or behavior problems to make great changes all at once. Such expectations may make it difficult for students to experience success and, therefore, can frustrate both the teacher and the students. To eliminate or minimize failure and ensure mastery learning, it is important for you to plan for small steps or increments of change. Such planning is especially important for students who are experiencing learning difficulties.

The most logical way to plan for small increments of change is to break large goals into small steps, with each step becoming a goal or objective in itself. Consider the following objectives and notice how they are broken into smaller steps.

1. Count change in any amount up to a dollar with 95% accuracy.
   1.1 Identify all coins by name.
   1.2 Count up to twenty-five pennies.
   1.3 Count change using pennies and nickels (e.g., three nickels plus two pennies).
   1.4 Count change using pennies, nickels and dimes.
   1.5 Count change using pennies, nickels, dimes and quarters.

2. Spell twenty new grade-level words a week at 90% accuracy.
   2.1 Spell ten new grade level words a week with 90% accuracy for three successive weeks.
   2.2 Spell twelve new words at 90% accuracy for three successive weeks.
   2.3 Spell fourteen new words, etc., until the original goal is reached.

3. Write a 100-word theme that presents a main idea and provides supporting details.
   3.1 Given ten written paragraphs, the student correctly identifies the main ideas with at least 90% accuracy.
   3.2 Given ten written paragraphs, the student correctly identifies supporting ideas for each main idea with at least 90% accuracy.

As you can see, planning for small increments of change involves the use of task analysis. When you work with exceptional students, you will often find that the steps listed in a task analysis are still too complex for the student. When this occurs, you can use the task analysis process to delineate further the teaching steps within each previously defined step of the original task analysis.

These smaller goals, then, become objectives for daily or weekly instruction. Teaching towards these objectives provides a great sense of clarity and direction for both you and the student. By having smaller amounts to be learned, by learning one part at a time, and by building systematically towards a larger goal, the student is assured increased opportunities for mastery of objectives.

In thinking about small increments of change, it is possible to go overboard and break objectives into too many parts. Since this type of planning requires some time and consideration, a good rule of thumb to follow is to develop only as many steps as are needed to ensure success. Generally, those students who learn rapidly require fewer steps than slow learners or those with an inadequate background. Students who have considerable learning deficits may require tasks to be broken into many small steps.

Use Modeling, Prompting, and Shaping

The techniques of modeling, prompting, and shaping are used to help students make their initial correct response in a teaching-learning situation. *Modeling* is teaching by demonstrating the skill or behavior in such a way that the student may observe and imitate what the teacher or a peer does. In some cases the student is able to exhibit the desired response if the teacher provides clues or partial answers; this is known as *prompting*. *Shaping* involves the teaching of behaviors in a sequential step-by-step fashion until instructional techniques enable the student to learn new skills and behaviors efficiently and with maximum success (Payne, Polloway, Smith, and Payne, 1981). The delivery of instruction for each child or group of children should be based on your understanding of modeling, prompting, and shaping. Such techniques are particularly important for exceptional students who experience difficulty learning new skills.

Modeling, if properly used, is a powerful teaching tool. Modeling is based on the principle that students learn new skills and ways of behaving by observing others (Charles, 1981). In order to maximize the effectiveness of modeling, it is essential to be familiar with several important principles.

1. The student is more likely to engage in the model's behavior when the model is an important person. If the individual demonstrating the behavior is not viewed in a positive light, the student will be less likely to try to imitate the behavior.

2. The student must attend to and retain the skills or behaviors demonstrated by the model. The student's attention should be directed to the model, and the important elements of the model's behavior should be highlighted. The student should then have the opportunity to practice the behavior.

3. When the model is seen to be rewarded or to show pleasure while engaging in the behavior, the student is more likely to want to engage in the same activity. Making any behavior appear to be fun or to result in positive consequences will result in the student's wanting to imitate the behavior.

The power of modeling to educate and persuade has long been recognized. Television advertisers educate children to consume or use their products by showing sports figures and beauty queens using the product while obviously enjoying themselves or being happy. Others, including some parents in our culture, seem to be unaware of the power of modeling when they eat improper foods, have temper tantrums, or display other behaviors in which they do not want their children to engage.

In school, the implications of modeling are clear; if you want your students to learn something, you should arrange for them to see someone successfully demonstrating the skill you wish to teach. Several examples of modeling in a school situation are presented below:

MR. MASON

Mr. Mason had experienced some frustrations trying to teach his high school math students to follow a step-by-step procedure in solving problems. On a number of occasions during the past several years he noticed that some students attacked problems in a haphazard, almost impulsive manner. Many of these students became discouraged and felt incapable of succeeding. Mr. Mason finally decided to try another approach, since he was determined to teach his students to improve their skills as well as their attitudes. Before class started the second semester, he recruited several students who seemed to be respected by their peers. After teaching each student how to model problem-solving techniques, he started his class by having these students demonstrate a step-by-step procedure for solving problems to a small group of mainstreamed peers. Mr. Mason circulated through the class, constantly praising the tutors, mainstreamed students, and other students who were demonstrating the problem-solving techniques. As the mainstreamed students grasped the content, he singled them out and had them model their problem-solving techniques.

The success and attention they received proved to provide incentive for them, and led others to imitate them. All students, including the exceptional students, improved their problem-solving skills. In addition to peer modeling, Mr. Mason was careful to be a good model himself; this led to widespread success and a positive attitude shift in the entire class.

MRS. HUNT

Mrs. Hunt was a kindergarten teacher who had learned the value of beginning each new activity with a demonstration. When it was time to learn coloring, she sat among the children and colored. She always appeared to be having so much fun that the students were eager to do what the teacher was doing. Mrs. Hunt carefully selected her "work partners." When the emotionally disturbed student was having a particularly difficult day, she would sit next to her, modeling the skill being presented. At other times, Mrs. Hunt chose to sit next to and demonstrate skills to the mildly retarded student in the class. Since this student required several presentations, the repeated demonstrations Mrs. Hunt gave other students assisted this student in acquiring the skill.

During reading lessons, Mrs. Hunt demonstrated correct responses by pointing to each letter, saying the correct sound, and pointing to the letter as the class repeated the sound. She knew that without the model, her two exceptional students and many of her slower children would not make the correct response. Mrs. Hunt was always careful to demonstrate skills and behavior and to point out children in the classroom who were setting a good example.

Telling students how to do something is not, in most cases, as effective as showing them. It is an important responsibility of the teacher to be a good model, as inappropriate behavior can be learned as easily as appropriate behavior. By carefully modeling behaviors and being a consistent, positive role model, the teacher is likely to experience more success in teaching new behaviors and academic skills than teaching strictly by verbal methods.

Prompting is another technique that has as its major purpose helping the learner to make a correct response. Prompting means giving the student a clue that will help to ensure that the student is able to provide the appropriate response. For example, you might give a verbal prompt by describing the first step in a response to be learned. A math teacher might say, "Multiply this number by this number" while pointing to a complex problem. An example of a less direct clue is illustrated by the following language teacher's statement during a language arts lesson: "Remember, we're looking for action words; words that tell what people do." When the teacher provides verbal prompts, the student is better able to carry out the desired behavior.

There are other kinds of clues that you can provide. Gestures may be used in which you pantomime what the student is supposed to do. If the student is to write the letter *b* on a sheet of paper, you might draw an imaginary *b* in the air. The home economics teacher might show how to begin feeding fabric into a sewing machine by pantomime. Other similar prompts might be to orient the student physically to face the desired direction, point to the page where the student is to begin writing, or use hand movements to signal when the student is to respond. The use of prompts should be limited to instances in which the students are unable to respond without them. Prompts should be viewed as a means to enable the student to make a correct response; all prompts should be removed as soon as the student learns to perform without them (Becker, Engelmann, and Thomas, 1975). Usually prompts are removed gradually. Here are several examples:

MISS SEARS

Miss Sears, the typing teacher, had been teaching her students to type different styles of letters. After several weeks of intensive instruction, she observed her students with learning problems using the incorrect style or leaving important parts out of their letters. After pondering on the problem for awhile, she decided to make a bulletin board display with a proper example for each letter placed in full view of the class. During the three-week unit, she gradually removed part of each example until all prompts had been removed from the board. Initially, the students were successful but relied on the bulletin board display to come up with correct letters. As the prompts were removed, the students were forced to rely more on what they had learned until each student mastered the skill.

MR. HEATH

Mr. Heath was concerned about several handicapped students who could not write or read the letter *b* without mixing it up with *d*. He decided to construct some special clues that would enable the student to make the correct discrimination. First, he associated the letter *b* with a color by constructing flash cards where all *b*'s were copied in the color blue. He then taught his students that if the letter was blue it was a *b*. Then he used a blue marker to underline each *b* in the students' reading materials. When a student was writing something, the card with the blue *b* could be used to check that the *b*'s and *d*'s faced the proper direction. With the blue underlining, the students began to make the correct response. Over a period of time, the clues were systematically discontinued as the handicapped students were able to rely less and less on such prompts. Again, the clues were withdrawn totally when they were not needed.

Because teaching does not always lead to learning, even well-planned and executed teaching procedures may not be enough for some students. Without prompts, some students will make repeated incorrect responses, thereby practicing errors. When an error is repeated several times, the result may be that the student learns an incorrect response. When this occurs the student not only has to learn the correct response but to unlearn the incorrect one. The use of prompts is really a way of augmenting or changing well-planned teaching to meet the instructional needs of some students.

Shaping is a teaching procedure that is used to ensure success one step at a time. A common error made by teachers is to expect too much change all at once. Some students are not able to make large changes in their behavior. For example, you might be concerned about teaching a student to attend to your demonstrations. The final desired behavior might be sitting in an upright position, looking directly at you while you are speaking during at least 95% of the class period. The initial behavior expected, however, during shaping may be to have the student remain in his or her seat for ten consecutive minutes. As the student learned to stay seated, the time required would be increased. The next step would be to have the student remain seated and look at you for increasingly longer periods of time. Finally, the original goal behavior would be exhibited by the student. When systematically working towards a final goal by requiring closer successive approximations of the desired behavior, you are able to ensure greater success with some students. Shaping can be used to teach a variety of skills for which you can identify a series of logical steps that lead to mastery of a more complex goal.

Modeling, prompting, and shaping are techniques that, when used with students with learning and behavior problems, can be used to teach skills and behaviors to students. The demonstrations, clues, and changes in expectations can provide the student with examples of appropriate responses necessary to ensure learning. These techniques are especially helpful when teaching new academic skills to mildly retarded students and promoting appropriate classroom behavior with students exhibiting behavior problems in the classroom.

Provide for Practice, Review, and Generalization

Once you have been successful in causing the student to exhibit the desired behavior or skill, steps must be taken to have the students *practice* until they achieve mastery. Without some repetition, new skills and behaviors will soon be forgotten. This is particularly true for mentally retarded students, who require extensive drill and repetition to learn and retain new skills. The amount of practice varies greatly, depending on what is being taught. The student might learn not to touch a hot burner with a single incident, but most academic skills and behavior patterns require practice that might extend over several weeks.

When a student demonstrates mastery of a new skill, it is time to identify the next learning objective and to begin teaching this new skill. Skills mastered in the past need to be practiced on an occasional basis or the student will likely forget what has been learned. This periodic *review* ensures that the student will retain what has been taught in the past.

In addition to practice and review, the student needs to learn to generalize what has been learned. *Generalization* of skills means that students can exhibit what has been learned in situations outside the classroom and can use their knowledge in a variety of ways. For example, you would expect students who have mastered subtraction facts in school to be able to solve subtraction facts in other classrooms or at home. You would also be pleased if they were able to use their newfound skills to solve word problems or to make proper change in a store. Generalization is an important concern, for without it learning would be of little use to the student.

In order to maximize learning, students should practice skills correctly and not make repeated errors. If students practice the multiplication tables by consistently providing correct answers to each problem during practice time, it is likely they will continue to make correct responses in the future. Students who make many errors while practicing will likely continue to make mistakes. As far as possible, then, you should ensure that students do not practice errors. In those instances in which you are aware that a child has a learning problem, it is a good practice to structure the lessons so the student does not practice errors, as in the following vignette.

MRS. ROSS

Mrs. Ross, a third-grade teacher, had three learning disabled students who frequently made incorrect responses in class. During large group phonics practice, the children were supposed to say the letter sounds when she pointed to the letter printed on a wall

Students who practice errors will continue to make errors. Students should have the opportunity to practice consistent correct responses. Individualized instruction or small group practice with a teacher's aide can make this possible.

chart. During these daily lessons, she noted that one student rarely responded at all. Another seemed to respond but was pretending to respond by moving her lips without saying anything. The third student frequently gave the wrong response. It was impossible for Mrs. Ross to change the lesson format, so, rather than continue the inappropriate practice, she enlisted the help of a teacher's aide to work with the three children during the group practice period. The aide provided a different lesson in which each student was able to practice consistent correct responses. The aide took the three children aside and worked with them as a small group. She made a set of flash cards containing each new letter sound for each of the learning disabled students. She asked the students to respond individually to the letter sounds as she presented them. She would then make a game of seeing who could give the correct sound for the letters presented. By the end of the aide's five-minute mini-lesson, each student had said the sound for the letters at least twenty-five times; the students then rejoined the class for the remainder of the lesson. In addition to the lessons provided by the aide, Mrs. Ross made additional changes in other content areas to minimize the practice of incorrect responses. She tried to keep practice sessions short, finding that a small amount of appropriate practice was more beneficial to the student than long periods in which practice sessions were filled with errors.

How much practice should be provided? There is no clear, easy answer to that question. Enough repetitions of a behavior or skill need to be provided to result in mastery of an objective, but too much practice may result in the student's becoming bored with the routine. For efficiency, it is a good idea to provide the students with consistent practice on newly acquired skills and spend less time practicing old skills already mastered. There is no optimum number of repetitions for all students; some require many repetitions and others require only a few. This means that you must carefully observe each student to determine when the student has had enough — but not too much — practice. The following vignette illustrates this point.

JOE

Joe was a ninth-grader who was diagnosed as mildly retarded. For many years, school had been a frustrating place for him. In his weakest area, math, he was performing on about a third-grade level. His inability to master long division had resulted in his developing a mental block against math. Even though he had the capability to learn division, no one had been able to overcome his intense negative feelings. Now that he was mainstreamed into a regular classroom, his math teacher was determined that he master division skills. Joe's intense dislike for math made it difficult for the teacher to require practice. Through some very creative instruction using overhead transparencies, the teacher was able to have Joe do the first step in a single problem; but Joe made it clear that he hated it and would not work on any problems in the book. Rather than force Joe to repeat his performance many times, the teacher said to him, "Do just the first step correctly for two problems, and that's all the division you have to do." Two simple procedures didn't seem too daunting, so Joe consented and soon was doing the first step for two problems in less than one minute. After several days, the teacher added another step. After several weeks Joe was computing two problems correctly. His success led him to request more problems. Soon he was able to complete an entire page. In a short time, Joe had been taught an important skill by using only a few examples. If the teacher had begun by insisting on making him solve a large number of problems, Joe would probably have failed to learn division. In this case, mastery was achieved by providing appropriate practice in small doses.

When practice sessions result in boredom or tension, you should consider reducing the number of responses required. In those instances in which many repetitions are deemed appropriate, it is better to divide the longer practice time into two or more shorter periods. Students often seem to benefit more from doing two half pages at separate times than a whole page of work in one sitting.

The need for practice changes over time. When the student is first learning a skill, it may be necessary to provide many opportunities for practice. Once the skill is acquired, however, the need for practice lessens. With most students, an occasional review of the skill will assist in the retention of previously learned material. Good teaching, then, includes practicing new skills and reviewing objectives mastered in the past. By including review work in the curriculum, you will often find that while the majority of students are working independently on review work, you can provide individual instruction to students with learning and behavior problems.

Generalization of learning is an important educational task (Payne, Polloway, Smith, and Payne, 1981). Education should be of value outside the classroom setting if it is to be of any worth to the student. The student who understands addition and subtraction but fails to balance a checkbook reliably cannot generalize beyond the instructional setting. Similarly, the student who learns proper behavior in the classroom but does not learn to behave in public meeting places and at home has missed an important part of what education should offer.

Many teachers are chagrined at the seeming inability of their students to generalize skills they have been taught. Students who learn safe driving techniques in driver's training class may be observed driving dangerously. Students who can name the colors of their crayons may fail to identify correctly the colors of clothing or objects outside the school setting. Others who learn to write acceptable essays in language arts class might write incoherent term papers in history. Students who typically use correct speech in school may be observed using poor grammar in other settings. Much of this inability of students to show consistently what they have learned is because of the failure to teach for generalization. The generalization of learning from one situation to another usually requires that some special arrangements be made by the teacher. Simply stated, generalization is enhanced when you have the student practice the skill in a wide variety of settings using a variety of materials. Listed below are several typical generalization problems and solutions.

MS. SEWARD

After several weeks of teaching and intensive practice, Ms. Seward was overheard saying to a colleague, "The students in my class, including my mainstreamed students, know their single-digit addition facts, and it took less than one month for all students to achieve mastery." Several months later on the achievement tests, a significant number of the students with learning problems failed to achieve grade-level scores. Examination of the tests revealed that these students had failed to add correctly. The problem was that students had practiced with problems like this:

$$\begin{array}{r} 2 \\ +3 \\ \hline 5 \end{array}$$

The test printed them like this:

$$2 + 3 = \square, \quad 2 + \square = 5 \text{ and } \square + 3 = 5$$

Ms. Seward remedied this by using a variety of examples. In practice sessions the students were able to master single-digit addition problems quickly when presented in several forms. Ms. Seward had ensured that all students could apply their knowledge of addition facts beyond the classroom environment by using a variety of materials.

MARA

Mara was always regarded as a shy child. She was usually able to keep up with the class by handing in written work, even though she refused to speak in front of a group. As time passed, her lack of social participation was viewed as a significant problem that required special education intervention. It was feared that although she rarely bothered anyone, she would experience significant problems later in school. She was placed in a therapy group where, after six months, she had apparently learned to interact effectively with other students. When the therapist asked for a progress report from the teacher, he was shocked to hear Mara described as being more withdrawn than before. It was clear that Mara had learned some valuable skills but was not generalizing them to the school situation. Several strategies, which included having some of Mara's classmates attend the therapy group and training the teacher to facilitate social interaction, finally led to some improvement in Mara's level of social interaction. By making sure that Mara displayed appropriate social behavior in a variety of settings, her teacher and therapist enabled her to begin to apply what she had learned to other areas of her life.

_____

Some provision for generalization should be made for those students who receive part of their instruction outside of the regular class. Students should practice the skills in both the special and regular class setting. Regular communication among teachers and effective planning can ensure that generalization occurs. Varying materials and settings will also help the student to generalize outside of school. Where appropriate, skills should be practiced in and outside of various school settings. When this is not possible, role plays, simulations, and similar activities should be utilized to ensure that learning has some carry-over to behavior outside of school. Learning behaviors and skills that can be displayed only in limited environments are of little use when your goal is to teach skills that will have a positive impact on your students' lives. Indeed, you should accept teaching for generalization as an important responsibility, especially when given the task of helping students with learning and behavior problems.

Use Concrete Materials

In school you teach students about many things that they do not have the opportunity to experience firsthand. You may be asked to teach geography and want your students to develop an understanding and appreciation of natural landforms like the Grand Canyon, Mount Everest, or the Sahara Desert. You might be teaching your students about the value of democracy. Although you may be extremely skillful in your use of descriptive language, many students, particularly those with learning problems, would not gain true understanding of the material. Language is simply too abstract to convey some content; words can augment but rarely substitute for direct experiences.

Teachers have long recognized the fact that mere lecture does not meet the needs of some students; consequently, they often augment their teaching with pictures, charts, diagrams, role plays, and models. Similar additions to your instruction will allow students to gain more direct experience with the subject matter in a variety of ways. Your teaching results in success for more students because they are able to relate to, and thereby understand, what is being taught.

Fortunately, you can teach many skills in school through direct experience. Many students who have learning and behavior problems are able to learn by doing. Here are some ways to augment verbal presentations in the examples just cited: Rather than describing sandstone formations, you might supplement your teaching with instructional aids

TABLE 9.1
Student abilities and teaching

Student characteristics	Level of concreteness necessary to promote learning	Examples
Much difficulty learning	Concrete	Learning by doing; actual experience
Moderate difficulty in learning	Abstract with concrete aids	Instructional aids; simulations and role play
Learns all things easily	Abstract	Lectures; reading; vicarious learning

such as photographs and sandstone samples, and let direct experience promote the desired learning. In teaching the meaning of democracy, you might set up a school government based on democratic principles or set up a role play of situations in which democracy is not practiced. By providing more concrete experiences, you will be able to impart a greater understanding of many important curriculum goals.

Your success as a teacher is ultimately determined by what your students learn. It is, therefore, an important responsibility to select teaching activities that are appropriate for each student. By being aware that lessons can be relatively concrete or abstract, you will be in a better position to select learning activities for all students. Teaching activities that are removed from actual experience are usually not as appropriate for students with learning and behavior problems as actual experience. Table 9.1 illustrates the concrete-abstract continuum and how it relates to individual learning abilities.

As a general rule, the more abstract the learning experiences, the less students with special needs will be able to experience success. The student who has no learning problems will be able to benefit from all types of teaching. The more concrete techniques are beneficial to all students, but are particularly helpful for mentally retarded and learning disabled students. The teacher who uses less abstract methods will experience more success than the one who conducts lessons at the more abstract level.

Following are some examples of this principle in action.

MRS. JONES

Let's look in on Mrs. Jones, who is teaching her class about national parks. Many of her students had not had the opportunity to travel much, so she was concerned that they would not be able to learn from the instruction. Her solution to the problem was to provide the opportunity for more concrete experiences for those who needed them. When she taught about the Grand Canyon, she obtained a film that showed summer adventurers running the Colorado River rapids in rubber rafts. She showed slides and posters depicting the various scenes. She was able to obtain a relief map depicting the rugged terrain of northern Arizona. By selecting these and other instructional aids, Mrs. Jones was able to make sure that students with learning problems were provided with concrete learning experiences.

MR. HENRY

Mr. Henry, the high-school social studies teacher, had been given the responsibility for drug education in his school. Many of the students he hoped to reach had previously been exposed to horror stories on the legal and medical problems that might result from the abuse of certain drugs, even though they had little understanding of the stories they heard. He had tried lectures and had assigned readings. He had the feeling that the learning disabled students were unable to grasp the significance of what he had to say because they were unable to read the material and form the concepts presented in the text. He decided to try to identify some educational experiences that would lead to a greater understanding of medical and legal problems that might result from the misuse of drugs. He conducted some carefully planned tours of correctional facilities and institutions. He followed these actual experiences with discussion and lectures, which now seemed to have more meaning for some students. The actual experiences and firsthand look at the problems related to drug use enabled the students to understand the more abstract lessons.

An important point to remember is that the term "abstract," when applied to educational experiences, is a relative concept. A seemingly concrete teaching example may appear very abstract to a student who lacks experience and prerequisite skills. Moving towards the concrete learning experiences will result in more students with learning problems being able to learn successfully in the regular classroom.

Provide Feedback and Reinforcement

One of the most important roles a teacher plays is providing feedback and reinforcement to students who are learning new skills and practicing old ones (Mercer and Mercer, 1981). During the acquisition of new skills, the teacher guides the student by providing ongoing information regarding the correctness of what the student is doing. The teacher provides reinforcement by demonstrating to the student that there are positive consequences for desired behavior. Feedback and reinforcement, properly applied, can enhance your ability to teach skills and behaviors.

In order for the act of teaching to be complete it must contain some elements of feedback. The teaching act can be divided into three steps, as follows:

1. The teacher selects appropriate goals and objectives that reflect the needs of the student. Direct observation or criterion-referenced assessment is used to identify what the student needs to learn.

2. The teacher then provides appropriate instruction, conditions, and materials that will cause the student to display the desired skills and behaviors.

3. Once the student has responded to teaching, the teacher provides feedback that lets the student know how well his or her performance measured up to the goal and objectives.

Feedback allows the student to know what to change or to identify unwanted behaviors. Without feedback, students are likely to repeat errors or remain unsure of themselves. Imagine if you attempted to teach theme writing without any provision for feedback. The students might be exposed to good teaching techniques and be inspired to write many themes; if you did not critique the papers and provide feedback, it is likely that learning would be impaired. Feedback provided soon after the response is made increases the likelihood that students will profit from your instruction and learn the desired skills.

Providing feedback for classroom behavior is no less important. The student who is learning to improve social interaction can learn by having you point out the specific strengths and weaknesses in the student's attempt to display appropriate behavior.

There are several important guidelines regarding feedback. First, feedback should be specific. You should evaluate each aspect of the student's behavior and not label a complex act as entirely below par. Usually at least part of any behavior can be considered acceptable. When you provide specific feedback, then, you should pay attention to details. If a student had come up with the wrong answer to a math problem, you might say something like, "You have completed the first three steps correctly. On the fourth step you misplaced the decimal. Try that step again." A teacher who did not provide specific feedback might have responded to the same error by stating, "The problem is wrong; please do it over." Some students regard such general feedback statements as a form of punishment and are not motivated to risk another failure by trying again. If you limit corrective feedback to the specific behavior deficits, the student is given some

TABLE 9.2
General and specific feedback

General feedback	Specific feedback
You've been a good boy today, John.	John, you haven't had an angry episode for two days!
Mary, that letter *i* is not very well written.	Mary, the letter *i* is on the line, but it has a loop in it.
Do you call this a book report? It's worth a D grade!	This book report has some important points missing: there's no mention of the author, and the report is 80 words, which is below the 250-word minimum.
Mike, you're getting along better in class.	Mike, you did a good job sharing your experiences with your group twice. You looked at others when they spoke every time; that's much better!

direction and is immediately aware of strengths and areas needing improvement.

The second important guideline is to provide measurable feedback whenever possible. By labeling many student behaviors using words like "good" or "great" or "not so good," you are likely to be misunderstood by some students. Many who have developed negative attitudes towards themselves will shrug off such comments and will not believe you. For some students who have severe deficits in learning or behavior, a major improvement might still leave the child well below what can rationally be considered as "good." If you provide the student with a response like "good job," it may appear that you lack good judgment. Most important, however, feedback in measurable terms allows the student to be aware of small gains in performance. If the objective for a student is to improve oral reading ability, you can select accuracy and rate to give the student daily feedback. "John, your accuracy was 85% today and your rate is up to 68! You've gone up three percentage points on accuracy and your rate is up by two words per minute!" By reporting the performance in objective, measurable terms, you avoid saying things like, "That's good; I think you read better than yesterday"; or "Good reading!", which the student may not believe. Such vague statements are not helpful in making a student aware of specific strengths and weaknesses. Listed in Table 9.2 are some examples of general and specific types of feedback. It is obvious that specific, measurable feedback requires you to develop specific, measurable objectives. It is often difficult to identify subtle changes in behavior without measurable objectives. Without constant measurable feedback, the student cannot identify areas to improve. Students who receive no corrective feedback will frequently practice incorrect responses, which will interfere with later instruction.

Corrective feedback should be given during instruction. Since you cannot see the work of twenty to thirty students at one time, it may be important for you to focus attention on the students with learning problems during instruction and supervised seatwork periods. You should develop a nonthreatening process to teach students who make incorrect responses. This process, or *correction procedure*, can be applied in a variety of instructional settings (Anderson and Faust, 1973; Becker, Engelmann, and Thomas, 1975).

Let's observe an English teacher, Miss Michaels, instructing a learning disabled student on parts of speech. She has already explained the role verbs play in a sentence. They are currently working on identifying past-tense verbs.

Miss Michaels (pointing to the sentence, *John rode his bike to the store.*): What is the verb in this sentence?

Jenny: I don't know.

Miss Michaels: The verb is *rode.* What is the verb?

Jenny: Rode.

Miss Michaels: Good, the verb is *rode.* Underline the verb with your pencil. (Pause.) Good, you underlined the verb in the sentence. Now look at the next sentence. What is the verb?

Jenny (looking at the sentence, *Mary came home from school at 3:30.*): From?

Miss Michaels: No, the verb is *came. Came* tells us Mary's action. Point to *came.* What is the verb in this sentence?

Jenny: Came.

Miss Michaels: Yes, *came* is the verb. Look at the third sentence. What is the verb in *Cathy went to the movies last night?*

Jenny: Went.

Miss Michaels: Great! *Went* is the verb. Try the next example.

The lesson continued until Jenny was able to recognize the verb on three successive trials. Miss Michaels then had Jenny work two examples on her own and gave her feedback when they were completed. Since they were both correct, Miss Michaels had her complete the remainder of the assignment.

When Jenny responded that she did not know the answer to the first example, Miss Michaels supplied it rather than having Jenny guess. This part of her correction procedure set up a situation in which Jenny could easily make a correct response to the example, even though she did not know the answer at first. She could not guess and, therefore, could not make a mistake or feel frustration. When she did provide the correct answer, even though it followed a prompt from the teacher, Jenny was praised for her attempt. Jenny chose an incorrect word as the verb in the second sentence. Miss Michaels immediately corrected her choice and told her the correct word. Jenny was again praised when she found the correct word. When Jenny selected the correct word on the third example, Miss Michaels again praised her. This combination of correction procedures and reinforcement of correct responses enabled Jenny to practice choosing verbs rather than words that were not verbs, and to learn the material more quickly.

Feedback can also be provided through reinforcement of correct responses. Reinforcement can be broadly defined as any event following a response that causes the frequency of the response to increase. Teachers often use reinforcers to increase the likelihood that students will behave in a desired manner. When you say, "If everyone finishes the assignment we'll have five extra minutes at recess," you are using extra time at recess as a reinforcer. By posting good work on a bulletin board you can provide a positive consequence that will make students want to complete their work well. By saying "good," "great," "nice work," and so on after a student has displayed a desired behavior, you insure that the behavior will occur again in the future. A detailed discussion on reinforcement techniques as they are used to increase learning and improve behavior is presented in Chapter 11.

Systematic feedback is an important component of instruction and should be used with students who have difficulty learning in the classroom. While you may not always have the time to provide direct supervision of all students as they learn new skills, it may be helpful to use these techniques when you observe and assist students who have learning problems.

Communicate Effectively

Good communication between teacher and student lies at the heart of a positive learning climate. If a student feels understood, then possibilities for growth emerge. On the other hand, ineffective communication is likely to alienate students and render the teacher's skills useless. How, then, can communication be enhanced?

Thomas Gordon (1970), a student of interpersonal communication, offers a number of concrete suggestions to enhance teacher-student communication. Gordon warns that when adults and students discuss issues that relate to behavior, attitudes, and expectations, adult responses often cause students to feel anger, frustration, and hostility. Gordon notes a number of communication patterns that are particularly provocative. These include:

1. Ordering, directing, commanding.

2. Warning, admonishing, threatening.

3. Exhorting, moralizing, preaching.

4. Advising, giving ready-made solutions.

5. Judging, criticizing, blaming.

6. Name calling, ridiculing, shaming.

The following dialogue between Tim, a seventh grader, and Mr. Jones, his math teacher, illustrates the debilitating effects of some of these provocative communication patterns:

Mr. Jones: All right, class, let's begin our independent work. Each of you has a math card to complete. Those of you who don't begin right away will receive a minus grade. (Admonishing.)

Tim (feeling fearful of his math abilities): I hate this stuff. I can't see why we have to work alone.

Mr. Jones: Tim, why do you always have to be the complainer? (Criticizing/name calling.)

Tim: Who's complaining! I just think working alone is dumb.

Mr. Jones (a little angered): Tim, get to work now! If you don't, you'll be doing the work after school in detention. (Ordering/threatening.)

Tim (angrily): Good! I love detention and you can bet I won't do your lousy work there.

Mr. Jones (loudly): Tim, it's too bad things had to go like this again. Again, your temper got the best of you. (Blaming.) Please go down to the office and finish your work there.

From this brief dialogue you may note that Mr. Jones used a variety of techniques that not only blocked communication, but actually created a cycle of stress. The real issue of Tim's feelings of inadequacy was never considered, and Mr. Jones never got the opportunity to use his skills and experience to help Tim with his math. To minimize such fruitless and frustrating encounters, Gordon suggests that teachers use more positive techniques, such as the following:

1. *Listening carefully.* Demonstrate a genuine concern about the student's ideas, opinions, and feelings. Maintain eye contact with the

student and provide nonverbal cues that you are giving full attention (e.g., head nodding to show understanding).

2. *Reflecting feelings and ideas.* Paraphrase, summarize, and/or offer opinions. By taking time to restate the student's concerns, you not only show your interest, but also demonstrate your understanding of the student's point of view. Such techniques help to build acceptance and understanding and encourage the student to continue sharing thoughts and feelings in a constructive manner.

3. *Using "I-messages."* "I-messages" tell students how you are feeling or reacting to what they are saying or doing, without trying to establish blame. For example, you might say, "I feel frustrated when you say you can't do the work, because I know you can." Such messages describe your own feelings and are less likely to promote the stress cycle than "you-messages," which blame or criticize ("You make me angry," "Your attitude is unconstructive," "You are lazy.")

4. *Encouraging problem solving.* Ask students to identify ways they can solve particular problems instead of telling them what to do (e.g., "What can you do when you get frustrated and need help?") By asking students to help solve their own problems, you can sometimes serve as a helper or guide and minimize power confrontations.

In addition to adopting the communication techniques suggested by Gordon, it is important to recognize the effect of nonverbal communication on students. Eye contact, for instance, can convey a message of acceptance and caring; it can also serve as a means of telling a student that the behavior being demonstrated is inappropriate. A hand on a shoulder can communicate attention and awareness of a student's personal difficulties. Physical proximity, or your moving towards a student about to create a disturbance, can be used to prevent potentially disruptive classroom situations. Nonverbal communication can be used effectively to convey positive messages to students; when nonverbal communication is combined with communication techniques like those suggested by Gordon, the student receives a consistent, helpful message from you.

Let's look back for a moment at Tim and Mr. Jones and examine how some of these skills might be applied to promote positive communication.

Mr. Jones: All right class, it's time to begin independent work. Each of you has your math card to complete. Raise your hand if you need help getting started. (Instead of issuing a threat, Mr. Jones offers his assistance.)

Tim (feeling fearful of his math abilities): I hate this stuff. I can't see why we have to work alone.

Mr. Jones (recognizing that Tim's fear of failure causes stress): Tim, can I help you get going?

Tim: I hate this kind of work. Do I have to do it?

Mr. Jones (speaking privately): Tim, I guess you are a little worried about whether you can do this. (Reflecting feelings.)

Tim (looking sheepish): Yeah.

Mr. Jones: Remember how you got over the same hurdle last week? (Problem solving.)

Tim: Oh, yeah. I took it one problem at a time. When I got stuck on one I asked you for help.

Mr. Jones: Beautiful! Even though you were frustrated, you didn't let your feelings get the best of you. (Careful listening; reflecting feelings.) I think you can do it again. How about it? (I-message.)

While not all dialogues end in such a positive manner, the advantages of Gordon's effective communication skills are clear. Listening carefully demonstrates a regard for the student as a unique individual with legitimate concerns, feelings, and perceptions. Reflecting feelings can help clarify what may be causing the student's discomfort. It can also help to avert or defuse a potentially explosive confrontation by providing students a chance to drain off feelings of frustration, fear, or anger. Involving the student in the process of solving problems gives the student some leeway, indicates that the student should take some responsibility, and reduces the potential battle of the wills. In short, these communication techniques help to establish a tone of "teachers with students" rather than "teachers against students." Even if a particular problem is not immediately resolved, the door will be kept open for constructive dialogue at a later time.

Evaluate Instruction

Student progress is the primary measure of instructional success. The type of students for whom the adaptations discussed in this chapter are appropriate and necessary are, by definition, students who have failed in school or who are experiencing some sort of difficulty with academic tasks. The purpose of adapting instruction to meet the needs of these students is to increase their school performance. It follows, then, that the effectiveness of any instructional adaptation can be measured through student performance.

The evaluation of student progress should be based upon actual student performance. Although it is possible to analyze subjectively student performance, such analyses do not provide precise data on the effectiveness of instruction. The evaluation of instruction should include a measurement of the student's beginning level of performance, the collection of data during the altered program, and an analysis of student progress as a result of the program. Such data, when collected daily, can be used to modify and expand instructional programs to increase their effectiveness. The data can be used to support ongoing programs that assist students in improving their skills. Coincidentally, such information can also be used to document student progress towards objectives listed on Individualized Education Programs for students with identified special education needs.

The collected data may be present in several different forms. Graphs and charts kept on student performance, including those used to motivate students, are one way of collecting evaluation information. Grades on daily assignments may become a basis for measuring student performance on assigned work in the classroom. Anecdotal records may provide a comparison of several days' behavior. In all the mentioned cases, the data can be used to assess trends in student performance and make instructional decisions.

Student performance usually follows one of three general trends: (1) a trend towards improvement or an increase in the desired behavior, (2) maintenance of behavior at a certain level, showing little gain or loss, and (3) a decrease in performance or loss of skills being taught. In most cases, the student's performance does not follow just one trend; rather, the student may show gains over a period of time with some periods of maintenance, or a somewhat erratic performance with gains and decreases appearing in a seemingly unexplainable pattern. When a student is making good progress, the instructional program is probably effective and should be continued. When a student is maintaining a performance level when he or she should be progressing, or is not learning the material expected, the performance data would suggest a need for a change in the student's instructional program. The data collected on performance and observations of the student during instruction should assist you in determining the type of modification that may be helpful for the student.

Since the use of evaluation information in the modification of instruction is based upon the specific behavior and needs of individual students, it is necessary to illustrate the principles in actual cases. While each case is certainly individual in nature, the steps and procedures you use to make decisions based on data generalize from case to case.

RAYMOND

Raymond consistently had difficulty learning information that required memorization, such as beginning reading sounds and arithmetic facts. When his teacher, Ms. Gamez, recognized this learning disability, she began to collect data on Raymond's performance in basic math facts in division. When she noted no

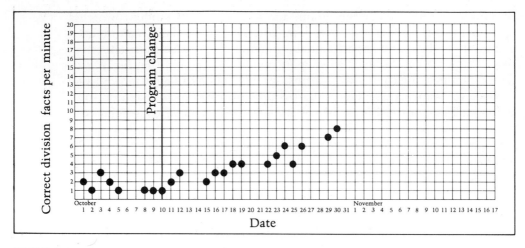

FIGURE 9.1
Evaluation of performance data

progress under normal classroom instruction, she instituted an instructional program for Raymond that included math fact games, a variety of worksheets, and a programmed instructional series. Ms. Gamez continued to collect data on Raymond's performance. The information she collected is presented in Figure 9.1.

At the beginning of October, Raymond usually averaged about two division facts per minute. After the instructional program was modified, he gradually began to increase his performance. Approximately three weeks later he was able to answer six to seven division facts per minute. Ms. Gamez decided that the modifications had helped increase Raymond's mastery of the division facts. As long as his performance improved, she continued to use all of the techniques. It should be noted, however, that some students may progress much faster than Raymond. In such cases, the teacher may not be satisfied with an instructional modification that yields results similar to these.

THEORY INTO PRACTICE

Good Teaching Practices

Billy, the learning disabled high school student introduced in Chapter 5, is enrolled in sophomore English. At the Pupil Evaluation Team meeting, a number of his teachers commented that his writing is unintelligible. He can express ideas verbally, but is unable to convey information in writing. Since he is required to submit most of his assignments in the form of at least paragraph-length responses or themes, he is experiencing difficulty in English as well as other content classes.

When the members of the Pupil Evaluation Team developed Billy's Individualized Education Program, they listed the following strengths and weaknesses related to written expression:

Strengths	*Weaknesses*
1. Billy has legible penmanship.	1. Billy is unable to write complete sentences.
2. He can identify a topic sentence in a given paragraph.	2. He uses sentence patterns that are difficult to follow.
3. He can use descriptive phrases.	3. He is unable to identify parts of speech.

Based on these strengths and weaknesses, goals and objectives were developed for Billy in the area of written expression. The goal and objectives follow:

Goal

Billy will be able to express his thoughts in paragraph-length responses by the end of the semester.

Objectives

1. Upon teacher request, Billy will write complete sentences with 100% accuracy.

2. When responding to end-of-chapter textbook questions, Billy will answer the questions using complete sentences 100% of the time.

3. Billy will write a paragraph containing at least four sentences, using correct sentence structure, upon teacher request.

4. Billy will submit a three-paragraph theme using correct sentence structure.

These objectives were designed to be met in all content areas.

Since the stated objectives applied most directly to Billy's performance in English, Mr. Jones, the English teacher, met with the special education teacher to outline instructional approaches that might be effective with Billy. They came up with several ideas.

1. *Plan for small increments of change.* Mr. Jones expected Billy to demonstrate skill development rapidly. Upon discussion, though, the teachers

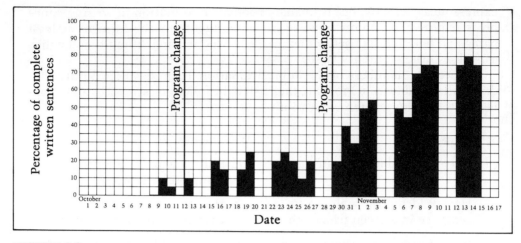

FIGURE 9.2
Data for Billy

felt that each level of performance should be outlined and Billy should be reinforced for each step he makes towards the stated objectives.

2. *Provide Billy with models of appropriate writing.* Since Billy did not see much value in writing, the teachers decided to provide learning activities in the classroom that encouraged written expression. Mr. Jones began by sharing some of his own writing. He also took time to work with Billy individually, showing Billy how to complete each step in the process of meeting the stated goals and objectives.

3. *Provide practice.* Mr. Jones had noticed over the years that most students who wrote well, wrote often. He gave Billy the opportunity to write frequently, providing positive feedback for all changes in his skill level and corrective feedback when Billy erred.

While he was teaching, Mr. Jones continued to keep data on Billy's performance. He had collected information on the number of complete sentences Billy wrote at the time of the Pupil Evaluation Team meeting. He continued to collect the information as he specifically applied the teaching practices to Billy's instruction. Mr. Jones recorded Billy's performance on a bar graph (Figure 9.2).

Billy's other teachers used similar techniques as they reinforced Billy's writing skills. Since all of the teachers were working towards the same goal, and reinforced all improvements, Billy's written expression skills improved dramatically; they found the same type of progress noted by Mr. Jones.

Summary

The use of good teaching practices with exceptional students can increase the likelihood that they will learn the skills expected of them in various educational settings. Because these students have specific learning needs, it is important to select teaching techniques that will be effective in meeting those needs. The consistent application of techniques can increase student success and reduce teacher anxiety and frustration. The major points covered in Chapter 9 are as follows:

1. When planning instruction for exceptional students, it may be necessary to break objectives into several smaller steps.

2. Modeling, prompting, and shaping are useful techniques to use with students who learn best from demonstrations and cues.

3. Exceptional students require repetition of skills through practice during skill acquisition and occasional review during maintenance of skills.

4. As exceptional students acquire skills, they should be taught the application of those skills in a variety of settings to increase generalization.

5. Concrete materials should be used to teach concepts to exceptional students.

6. Exceptional students benefit from reinforcement of educational success and feedback on responses.

7. The utilization of effective communication skills in the classroom can lead to increased interaction between the teacher and the student. The effective use of verbal and nonverbal communication can prevent problem behaviors from occurring.

8. Instruction should be evaluated to determine whether it is meeting the needs of exceptional students. Instructional changes should be made on the basis of student progress.

Activities

1. Select a task or skill you think you might teach students. List the steps you would follow when teaching the skill. Then break those steps into smaller increments that could be used with a handicapped student, if necessary.

2. Develop a lesson plan in your content area. Note on the plan the following elements:

   a) opportunities to provide models or prompts for students;

   b) practice activities selected to reinforce the skills being taught;

   c) concrete materials that could be substituted for abstract concepts;

   d) the method for evaluating the effectiveness of the lesson in reaching stated objectives.

   If possible, use your plan in a teaching situation. Note any modifications you would make in the lesson plan.

3. Correction procedures are helpful for providing feedback to students. Develop two correction procedures you could use. Try both of them in a teaching situation. Determine the correction procedure that provides the most positive feedback to the student.

Study Questions

1. In what way is planning for small increments of change similar to task analysis?

2. Briefly define the terms modeling, prompting, and shaping. Give an example of how each might be applied in a teaching situation.

3. How do carefully selected practice and review activities increase the likelihood that the student will generalize newly acquired skills?

4. When should a classroom teacher use concrete examples in teaching?

5. Explain the purpose of corrective feedback and when such feedback should be given to students.

6. Effective communication is an important key to successful learning. List three communication strategies a teacher can use to increase positive interactions between teachers and students.

7. Why should evaluation information be collected on student performance and how can such information be used in a teaching situation?

Questions for Further Thought

1. Many people suggest that because exceptional students' educational needs are unique, they require specialized instruction. Compare the teaching practices identified in this chapter with those presented in content methods courses. Note any similarities and differences you find.

2. Some people have suggested that the same teaching practices are utilized with all students; they are selected and utilized more systematically with exceptional learners. Evaluate this statement.

Additional Resources

BOOKS

Gardner, W. I. *Children with learning and behavior problems: A behavior management approach* (2nd ed.). Boston: Allyn and Bacon, 1978.

Joyce, B., and Weil, M. *Models of teaching.* Englewood Cliffs, New Jersey: Prentice-Hall, 1972.

Chapter 10
Modifying
Teaching Methods

Once you determine the curriculum for a student (or decide what to teach), it is necessary to decide how to present the instruction. Since most classroom instruction is presented to small or large groups of students, the needs of the mildly handicapped students may not be met through traditional methods and materials. It may be necessary to adapt or modify the presentation of lessons.

There are several ways of making instructional adaptations. In some cases, consideration should be given to the delivery of instruction. With some mildly handicapped students, simply modifying the technique used to teach a concept or idea may increase student success. In other cases, it may be necessary to change the person who actually teaches the student. Some students may learn more effectively from peers, or they may require instruction from a teaching aide on a one-to-one basis. Finally, some students benefit from adaptations in the timing of instruction. They may be much more successful at reading when it occurs early in the day. Other students may be more successful when the instructional setting changes, such as a change in seating arrangement or the elimination of classroom distractions.

Some of the curriculum adaptations presented in the goals and objective section of Chapter 8 may result in modifications of teaching methods. It may be equally important in other cases to modify the teaching method while keeping the goals and objectives of instruction constant. These types of adaptations can increase the likelihood of success for the mildly handicapped student in the classroom. Several possible variations in methods and techniques used in instruction are presented in this chapter.

Change How Instruction is Delivered

Instruction is presented in the classroom in a variety of ways, including large group instruction, small group instruction, the use of films and other media, experiments, and independent research. The textbook often serves as the primary source of information, and many class activities may be built around such books and their teacher's guides. Many students are able to learn quite successfully from such an approach. Some students, though, do not learn well under these conditions and need methodological adaptations to acquire the skills expected of them in the classroom setting.

MEDIA PRESENTATIONS

As a result of advanced technology in education, teachers have a number of media resources available for classroom use. Many of these resources, including films, filmstrips, slides, and tape recordings, have been used for a number of years as adjuncts to regular classroom materials. In more recent years, these same materials have been used as alternative modes of instruction for students with special needs. For instance, books are recorded for use by students who are unable to read the assigned text. Filmstrips with captions can provide content for low-level readers, as well as those students who seem to benefit more from visual presentations. These and numerous other adaptations can assist handicapped learners in developing skills and participating in the total classroom program.

In addition to these more traditional techniques, new devices have been developed for classroom use. Mini-computers and their programs have been designed to teach skills to students. These are used for initial instruction and presentation of information as well as providing a mechanism for repeated practice of a skill. A sophisticated computer program, for instance, can offer instruction in basic math facts in addition, and then allow for drill and practice of the skill by randomly calling up facts the student is learning. In some cases, these programs can also play instructional games with the student.

In addition to computers, teaching machines like the Language Master™, Little Professor™, and Speak and Spell™ have instructional programs or can be programmed by the teacher to provide instruction in specific skills.

There are advantages and disadvantages to using media presentations in the classroom. Such materials can provide variety and create novel learning opportunities. They may help the student focus attention on both the topic at hand and the presentation itself. When the skill being taught is one that has been presented a number of times, media can provide an outlet for the teacher and an impersonal means for presenting information that may, by now, be "old" for the teacher and the student. On the other hand, it is sometimes difficult to acquire all of the equipment needed for media presentations and keep that equipment in the classroom for extended periods of time. Equipment may break down in the middle of an important presentation, resulting in a disruption in the flow of material. Some media presentations are brief and may not provide an opportunity for repetition and review of the information. Despite these problems, media presentations are helpful for some students, particularly those who learn well from multisensory experiences.

Let's look into a classroom where the teacher is using media presentations during her phonics lesson with second-grade students.

MRS. SIMPKINS

Mrs. Simpkins is reviewing word families (words that have similar endings) with her class. She has chosen three techniques — wall charts, word slides, and overhead transparencies — to use in her review of the word families. Wall charts are used with each reading

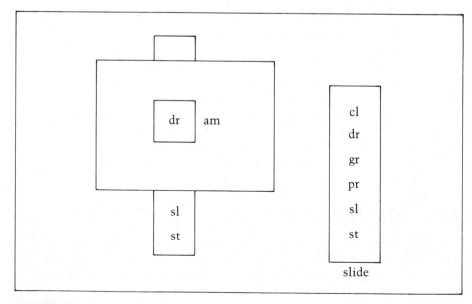

FIGURE 10.1
Word slide

group. The chart is large and contains four word families, ___ am, ___ ap, ___ it, and ___ up. The word families vary, depending upon the needs of each reading group. Consonant blends are added to the beginning of each "family"; students read the words orally as the teacher points to them. Each child is then given a word slide that has a word family printed next to a small window as shown in Figure 10.1. A slide containing consonant blends is inserted behind the window and slowly pulled through as the student reads the words formed by the blend and word ending.

The two students who are mainstreamed into Mrs. Simpkins's class have been placed in her lowest reading group. This group is currently practicing the ___ am word family with the consonant blends shown in Figure 10.1. Mrs. Simpkins has also developed a series of transparencies that contain word endings. Mrs. Simpkins fills in blends for each word ending, calling upon individual students in the reading group who have reviewed that word family to say the constructed word. Students may also fill in the blends, playing "teacher" to their classmates. When students have successfully completed these activities, they may practice blends by listening to a tape containing blends. The students then independently complete worksheets that correspond to the taped presentations.

LEARNING CENTERS

A learning center is a small area in the classroom emphasizing instruction and learning in a specific content area. A learning center may be used as the primary means of instruction for the content or for supplementary activities providing an opportunity for application and enrichment. The learning center can also be an area where students find practice activities designed to reinforce newly acquired skills. Instructional materials are coordinated and brought together to provide the student with a self-directed, independent learning experience, rather than a teacher-directed experience (Charles, 1976).

The components of a learning center will vary from topic to topic and from teacher to teacher. Most learning centers, though, have some consistent components. *Objectives* should be clearly stated and serve as the basis for the activities developed for the learning center. Specific *directions* should be stated for the students in language they can under-stand. These directions might include such information as what to do, how to go about it, how and where to obtain materials, where to put completed work, and the evaluation procedure to be used. In some cases, *samples* of the work the student is to complete can serve as motivators and additional sources of information and directions. *Media* may be used to provide some of the instruction. This may include resource materials, audio tapes, manipulative materials, or games. Once the learning center is developed and ready for use, a *schedule* should be developed for the students. The schedule should specify the number of students who may use the learning center at one time and the specific time(s) allocated for each student. Finally, some form of *record keeping* should be present. This system should enable you to keep track of who has used the learning center and the performance of each student on the learning tasks.

In addition to developing a learning center around the above-mentioned components, you must be prepared to monitor the use of the learning center and student progress towards the stated objectives. Each learning center should be introduced to the entire class at one time. The introduction should include an overview of the center and its instructional purpose, general directions on its use, and a plan for scheduling use of the center. Once students begin using the learning center, it is important to monitor both the effectiveness of the center in meeting the specified objectives and student usage of the learning center. Finally, you will need a systematic plan for monitoring student progress in the material covered in the learning center. This may be through student products and/or some form of written or oral evaluation. This is particularly critical if the learning center is the primary mode of instruction for the particular skill.

THEORY INTO PRACTICE

Learning Centers

Mr. Alexander has a spelling book that is assigned for the grade he teaches. He uses the word lists from the book for most of his students. He has some students with learning problems who read at a much lower level than the rest of the class and are not successful with the grade-level words. He uses alternative word lists for these students. Mr. Alexander had explained this difference to curious students by suggesting that it would be impractical for them to learn words they already know.

Mr. Alexander experimented with several techniques for teaching spelling to his class. He finally decided to set up a permanent learning center for spelling. When he first began using the learning center, he found that many students had difficulty completing the assigned tasks. After several weeks of refinement and instruction to the class and individual students, Mr. Alexander found a system that worked for all of his students.

The spelling center is located along one wall of the classroom. It consists of a table with four chairs, a tape recorder, the week's word lists for the students, dictionaries, headsets, and learning activities. Each student has a manila folder that contains the week's words, a sheet with directions for the week, and activities that are cued for specific students. Up to four students may work at the center at one time. Since the work is largely individualized, the only structured class time Mr. Alexander devotes to spelling is administering spelling tests each day. Once a student receives a 100% on a spelling test, he or she no longer takes that spelling test.

There are, however, other activities that must also be completed. At a minimum, each student must define orally or in writing each word on the spelling list and be able to use the word appropriately in a sentence. These three requirements, tests, definitions, and use of the words in sentences, remain constant each week. The activities students complete for the week vary. For example, the learning activities last week consisted of a puzzle containing all the words; the student had to find the words, vertically, horizontally, and diagonally. The words to be located and the complexity of the puzzle varied, depending on student skill. Tapes were produced with the words on them for practice spelling tests. Fill-in sheets were used to facilitate learning of word usage. In addition, students could make their own flash cards for home and school use. (Materials for the latter are always available to the students.) This week, the students have tapes with sentences. The student listens to the tape and provides the correct word for the blank in the sentence. Word usage is tied in with language arts where the class is studying alliteration. Students use their words to make up sentences that contain as many words as possible with the same first letter. The student places completed worksheets in a folder for the teacher to correct.

Mr. Alexander is able to monitor student progress through the work the students submit for correction and through their progress on the daily spelling tests. As mentioned previously, he is able to provide different word lists for students who are unable to master the grade level words.

Monica, who is mildly retarded, is one such student. Monica is reading three grades below her age peers. Her spelling lists come from a speller at her reading grade level. Mr. Alexander prepares her word lists and places them in her folder just as he does for every other student. She is expected to learn as many words each week, at her level, as her classmates. She receives the same type of worksheets each week as classmates, but they are specially designed to contain words from her list. There are several dictionaries at the learning center. Mr. Alexander has shown her the one written at her reading level. When preparing audio tapes, Mr. Alexander records similar activities for each word list he has prepared. The student's folder directs him or her to the appropriate tape.

Monica works independently on assigned tasks while Mr. Alexander gives the spelling tests until he gives the list she is learning. She then puts aside her other work to take the test. If she gets 100% correct, she need not take the test again. If she is unable to get 100% before the end of the week, she receives a grade based upon her score on Friday. Mr. Alexander provides students who are unable to get at least 80% on the Friday test with the opportunity to take a make-up test on Monday of the following week. The best score (Friday's or Monday's) is recorded.

As with any other approach to instruction, a learning center has advantages and disadvantages. Learning centers are impersonal in the sense that tasks can be presented to all students in an objective manner. The learning center does not know how often a student repeats a task prior to mastery of a skill and does not become frustrated as a teacher might. The student can learn independently of peers, reducing possible feelings of competition. It can assist a student in acquiring independent learning skills. A student can focus on one specific skill or task as specified in the instructional objective, rather than learning about a broad area in one sitting.

Learning centers, though, may be difficult to design for students who are having problems. These may be the very students who are unable to learn without direct teacher supervision and feedback. They may not have the self-direction to initiate and complete learning activities independently. In addition, most learning centers are designed for students who have at least minimal reading competence. Students who might benefit from a learning center as an alternative mode of instruction may be unable to utilize it effectively as a result of their instructional deficits. They will need to be taught the skills necessary for successful use of the center. In some cases, the learning center may benefit the handicapped student indirectly. That is, the learning center might free the teacher to provide more individual instruction for the student who has difficulty.

PROGRAMMED INSTRUCTION

Some exceptional students need instruction broken into very small steps with a great deal of repetition. Programmed instruction is a technique that can be used to provide instruction in small, repetitive steps to students. Material is presented to students in small learning units arranged in a logical sequence. The student responds to questions or statements in the text, checks the answer, and uses the immediate feedback to either reinforce correct responses or correct incorrect responses. This self-correcting feature is important in reducing failure, providing for practice and repetition, and increasing attention to tasks (Mercer and Mercer, 1981).

There are two major types of programmed learning. A *linear* program consists of a series of structured statements and questions that require a response of the student. The student reads the material, makes a response, and checks it. If the answer was correct, he or she moves ahead; if it was incorrect, the student repeats that particular portion of the instruction. The student must respond correctly to the material before moving on to new segments. The student proceeds in the step-by-step fashion through the instructional sequence. A *branched* program is similar to a linear program in that the student responds to presented material and progresses through it when making correct responses. When the stu-

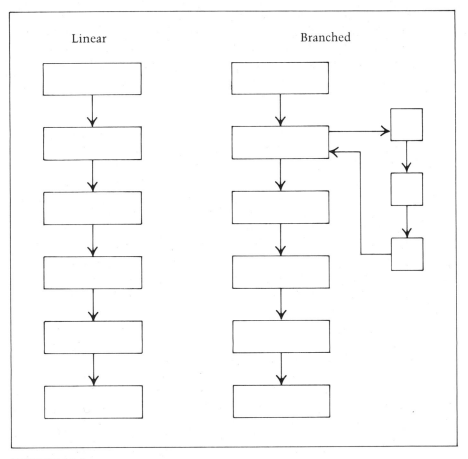

FIGURE 10.2
Programmed instruction sequences

dent makes an incorrect response, however, he or she is referred to another page or unit for further instruction on the skill before returning to the text. The student again receives immediate feedback on responses. Figure 10.2 shows a schematic of each approach.

There are some commercial programmed instructional materials available to teachers. Programmed materials exist for reading, arithmetic, English, and other subjects. It is also possible for the classroom teacher to develop programmed instructional sequences for students in the classroom. This can be done by specifying the content to be covered, breaking it down into a series of small steps, and writing instructional frames for the students to read and respond to. An example of a teacher-made pro-

	A noun is the name of a person, place, or thing. *Cat, refrigerator, New Jersey,* and *Bill* are examples of nouns.
	A _____ is the name of a person, place or thing.
Noun	*Karen, banana, school,* and *handkerchief* are more examples of nouns. *Karen* is the name of a person. *Banana* and *handkerchief* are words representing things. *School* is the name of a place. *Textbook, marketplace,* and *Abraham Lincoln* are examples of _____.
Nouns	Which of the following are examples of nouns? 1. jumped 4. fabric 2. battery 5. screamed 3. examination 6. wrench
2, 3, 4, & 6	Some nouns are called *proper nouns.* Names of people, streets, states, months, and days of the week are examples of proper nouns.

FIGURE 10.3
Programmed English grammar

grammed sequence appears in Figure 10.3. The program was designed for a group of seventh-grade students who are having great difficulty understanding parts of speech. Each box is called a frame. The student covers the page so that only one frame shows. After reading that frame, the student slides the cover down to expose the next frame, continuing in this manner until the entire page has been read.

Programmed instructional materials, including teaching devices such as the Little Professor™ and Data Man™ and printed texts, have been used effectively with students who have learning problems. The students must be taught how to use the material and how to work independently. They must also be given material at their instructional level in the content area to ensure success. When the teacher has taken these variables into consideration, programmed instruction can be used successfully with exceptional students.

As with all other alternative techniques, there are advantages and disadvantages in using programmed instructional material with exceptional students. The student does not have to wait for teacher feedback on responses. The material is presented in small instructional steps with repetition. It serves as an appropriate alternative for content that is concrete and requires little abstraction.

One disadvantage is that programmed materials have not been used to teach comprehension skills or higher level thinking skills. This is due, in part, to the difficulty in programming material that does not necessarily have one correct response. Another disadvantage is that some students copy the answers in the text rather than making responses and using the text to check their work. Also, programmed instruction does not consider individual student needs. All students must go through the same instructional program, although the speed at which they cover the material will vary as well as the number of branched programs they must complete. Programmed materials can become monotonous when used on a day-to-day basis with no other material or activities available for the learner. Finally, the skill being taught must be integrated into other curricular materials for maximum generalization.

ALTERNATIVE MATERIALS

Many students who experience difficulty in the classroom are unable to read the texts and other materials typically available in the classroom. Their reading level is often two or more grades below level; some texts are written a year or more above the grade level for which they are sold. These students are able to acquire the concepts presented but could learn them more effectively if provided with alternative materials covering the same content. This approach requires that you seek out other materials and texts that cover the same content at a lower reading level, such as library books, worksheets, filmstrips, and films. These might be available through the school library, public libraries, or teacher libraries. You should use a readability formula (a procedure for estimating reading level of printed material) to determine the actual reading level of alternative materials. (See Dale and Chall, 1948; Spache, 1953; Fry, 1968.) The student who reads at a lower level can still receive the input, participate in class discussions and activities, and use materials similar to those of his or her peers. Once the books and other materials are located, this approach does not require a great deal of your time.

EXPERIENTIAL APPROACHES

"Learn by doing" is a phrase that is often used in reference to learning and acquiring new skills. This is particularly true of students who have learning and behavior problems. In Chapter 9, it was suggested that, while many students are able to grasp and apply abstract concepts, others need concrete examples and experiences to learn the content or skill and to generalize the skill to other settings. For example, you may be able to introduce orally the idea that five plus two equals seven, and then assign a series of problems using this and other known facts to the class for completion. Two or three students, however, may need to work the problem using manipulatives (counters, chips, or other concrete materials), even though the concept of numerical value has already been taught. In another example, you may be about to introduce the concept of governmental structure to a group of junior high school students. Rather than lecture on the topic, you set up a series of activities in which students role play the various functions of governmental agencies and observe the interaction of these groups.

There are a variety of experiential approaches you may use. Role playing involves the assignment of a specific role to a student. The student then participates in a situation in which he or she acts as the character would act. A simulation activity is similar in that students act out various roles. For example, the class might reenact a slave auction or a historical debate. Solving problems is another experiential approach, particularly when the problems represent real-life situations for the students. This technique provides the student with an opportunity to apply skills and knowledge directly and observe the resulting solutions. Both are effective techniques, particularly when they are carefully organized and all students participate in some way (Schuncke, 1978). An example of the use of each technique in a classroom setting appears below.

MR. WEST

Mr. West was involved in an instructional unit on federal government with junior-high-school students. He decided to use several techniques to provide concrete learning experiences for his students in this area. He began by dividing his students into three groups. In each group, he assigned the following roles: president, vice president, two representatives, one senator, and selected cabinet officers. He explained the job description of each of these people and provided directions of how to accomplish some of the tasks related to that role. He then had students in each group simulate the legislative process in which a specific bill was introduced, discussed, and then voted upon. This was followed by a class discussion of the roles, problems inherent in each role, and the processes that facilitated group communication and productive decision making.

Mr. West was somewhat selective when assigning roles. He chose students who would be able to perform the role comfortably. That is, students who were confident in leadership became president and vice president. Students who were not as well versed were senators and representatives. Jane, a mildly disturbed seventh-grade student who was quite articulate and well-spoken, was assigned the role of president.

To assist in developing their own communication skills, Mr. West used a series of role play activities. He introduced each activity by stating its purpose and giving examples of the skills the student was to develop as a result of participating in the activity. Skills developed were active listening, group processes, and questioning techniques. Each role was put on tape; there were enough listening centers for the number of roles being used. The students who were unable to read the material could then receive their directions from the tapes.

Mr. West selectively paired students who had complementary strengths. Jane was paired with Jessie, a quiet student who seldom volunteered opinions in class.

Once the roles were assigned, students were given about ten minutes to act the role. They were then asked to evaluate the performance of their partner and their effectiveness in playing the role. The role play activities focused on leadership skills, questioning skills, listening skills, and identifying legislative problems. Although Jane frequently disregarded the opinions and feelings of others, she was able to complete successfully the skill activities in this setting.

Once the class had participated in the simulation activity and had developed the skills presented in the role play situations, Mr. West divided them into teams of six. Each team was assigned a specific legislative problem to solve, utilizing the communication skills previously learned. Mr. West found that all students participated in the problem-solving situations to some degree and demonstrated the desired skills. The average and above-average students developed some new problem-solving skills; the students who had difficulty in the classroom were able to grasp the processes used in government enough to participate in class discussions on local governmental issues. Because of her verbal skills and knowledge, Jane was able to utilize the role play skills in the simulation and help lead her group to a solution.

PARALLEL ALTERNATIVE CURRICULUM

The preceding examples have illustrated alternative approaches within the structure of the existing curriculum. Some students do not have the necessary reading skills to participate in the classroom curriculum without major changes because of their learning and behavior problems. A parallel curriculum may be an effective way of helping students acquire information in English, social studies, science, and other content areas despite their inability to read grade-level material (Swart, 1979).

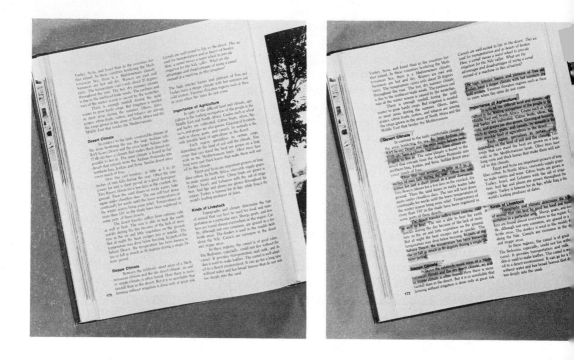

A parallel curriculum is one in which the student learns the same skills as classmates, but uses different materials and learning experiences to acquire the skills and knowledge. For instance, a student who has a low reading ability may utilize condensed versions of some books in literature classes. Another student may use tapes of books to learn the content. Still another student may have access to alternative books and materials in conjunction with the condensed books. In some cases, a specialist might present the content to the student in a special class setting. While a parallel curriculum might be used in basic skill areas, it is also very useful in developing learning experiences in content areas such as social studies, health, driver's training, and science.

There are a number of alternatives that, used separately or in combination, may result in a parallel curriculum. Some examples of these techniques are discussed below:

1. By yourself or in conjunction with a resource teacher, you may take time to adapt the text used in the class. You may highlight or underscore important content for the student who has difficulty reading the material. You may find that condensed versions of books are available commercially, particularly in the area of literature. Finally, you may rewrite critical portions of the text, using language the student can understand. In all of these cases, you must spend a considerable amount of time completing the adaptations. The products can be used by later stu-

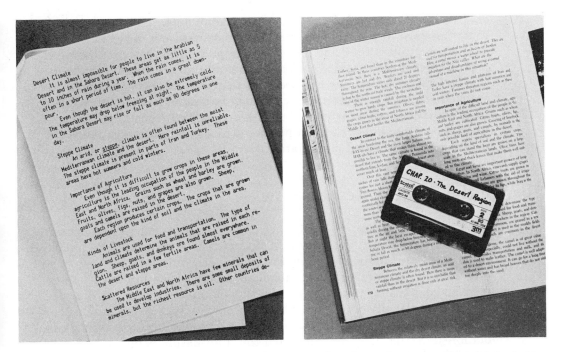

There are several ways to prepare a parallel curriculum from a basic text (far left), including (left to right) highlighting and glossing important or difficult passages; condensing and rewriting in language your student can understand; and taping written material for students who have difficulty reading.

dents, however. It is also difficult sometimes to rewrite text material and maintain the content that is presented to the student. This task is often done by a resource teacher or a curriculum specialist.

2. It is possible to tape the written material used in classes for students who have difficulty reading. Tapes are an effective way of disseminating the content to the student. It takes a considerable amount of time to tape material, but the task can be done by anyone who is a fluent reader, including other students and community volunteers. It should be recognized that it takes longer to listen to a tape than it does for a competent reader to read the material in a text. You may want to make some allowances for this when planning the material to be taped, eliminating some portions of a book or assignment.

3. As mentioned previously, it is possible to locate books that convey the same content, but are written at a lower grade level than the required text for the course. These books might be utilized in a parallel curriculum approach.

4. In some cases, publishers have developed materials that teach the same skills as those required for a particular grade level, but utilize a different approach than that of the textbook series. It may be possible to

adopt such a program for two or three students in the classroom if such materials exist in your content area. This may involve some restructuring of the use of class time and an additional preparation on your part, but it should result in increased performance from the participating students.

5. Oral presentations may be used in place of written material for some students. The written material may be available, but summarized by the teacher or other students in class discussions. This same material may also be presented through pertinent films and filmstrips, with the narrator giving the oral presentation.

Change the Student Response

Even when you adapt your instructional materials and techniques for exceptional students, you may still find that some students are unable to be successful in the classroom environment. Some students may benefit from the traditional instructional approaches used in the classroom or from adaptations you provide, but may be unable to provide the type of response usually required for the content or skills being taught. For these students, it is important to adapt the response required so they can demonstrate that they have acquired the information being taught.

When students first enter school, many responses to instruction are oral or involve fine motor skills such as coloring, drawing, or writing. As students progress through the school grades, written responses become more prevalent. For students who are mildly retarded, learning disabled, or physically handicapped, it may be difficult or impossible to use writing as an effective means of communication. It becomes necessary to adopt alternative response modes to enable these students to demonstrate the acquisition of skills.

There are several ways in which you can alter the response the student makes in the classroom. You might take advantage of oral responses. The student may be able to communicate in an alternate, written form such as typing. Prompts may be added to worksheets the student completes. Here are some of the techniques that can be used to provide exceptional students with the opportunity to respond to instruction in the classroom.

1. *Tape answers.* Some students are able to organize their thoughts clearly, but have problems with their penmanship or written expression. These students may benefit from the opportunity to tape their responses. The student is provided with a tape recorder and a quiet area in which to complete responses. The tape is then submitted to you for evaluation. These students may be expected to complete the same work as their classmates, but to provide the answers orally. In other cases, the student's

work may be different from that assigned to classmates. In either case, you can evaluate the student's response at some time later in the day and provide feedback to the student.

2. *Dictate answers.* There are times in the course of instruction when the teacher needs a written copy of the work of a student. Again, for those students who have difficulty expressing themselves in writing, it may be possible to dictate information to someone else who acts as a recorder. The recorder may put answers to questions, essays, and stories down on paper as the student dictates them. The teacher then has a written copy of the student's work for evaluation. A peer tutor or parent volunteer may be an excellent resource in this adaptation.

3. *Type answers.* There are many mildly handicapped students who have such poor penmanship that their writing is illegible. Mildly retarded students with fine motor coordination problems, learning disabled students who are unable to form letters, and blind or physically handicapped students may be unable to write clearly. These students may benefit from instruction in typing. Their response rate and their legibility in written work may increase significantly. It may also be helpful to allow students to use manuscript alphabet in their written work rather than require cursive writing. This single change can increase the written output of many exceptional students.

4. *Do projects.* In some situations, students may be able to demonstrate competence by giving an oral report or completing a project. Debates, speeches, oral reports, and panel discussions are techniques that can be used to determine student knowledge without requiring written responses. Projects such as dioramas, relief maps, and wall murals may also be alternative means for students to demonstrate knowledge of concepts, events, and historical relationships.

5. *Use graph paper to align work.* Some students have great difficulty organizing their work on paper. These students may benefit from the use of aids like graph paper, which help them organize their work and keep it orderly on the page. This technique can easily be applied in arithmetic. The student can use graph paper for written arithmetic work to help maintain the place value relationships in computation problems.

6. *Limit the type of response required on a single page.* Worksheets designed for exceptional students should require a single type of response. This alleviates student confusion and increases the likelihood that the student will be successful on the page.

7. *Use a consistent format.* Some exceptional students are unable to respond to a variety of stimuli. You may be able to reduce confusion for these students by developing certain formats for certain types of assignments. The student can then recognize the skill required by the format of the assignment sheet, thereby reducing one possible source of error for the student.

Adaptations in student responses can increase success in the classroom. It is important that you carefully select any adaptations used in the classroom. The instructional needs of the student, the student's skill level, and the nature of the content must be taken into consideration when making these types of changes in classroom procedures. It is also important to note that other students in the classroom may also benefit from similar adaptations; they may be used to introduce novelty and alternative choices for all students.

Change Who Delivers Instruction

The classroom teacher is typically the individual responsible for delivering instruction to students. While this is an appropriate mechanism for the delivery of instruction, it is not always the most effective means of imparting information to students. In some cases, you simply do not have enough time in the school day to provide the necessary individual help to the students who need it. Some students learn more effectively from peers than from adults. Other students need a variety of presentations and personalities when learning new content. In these and other cases, it may be appropriate to consider changing who presents the information to the student.

There are several different people in the school and the community who may deliver instruction. Peer and cross-age tutoring is an important resource available in the school setting. Instructional aides and adult volunteers may be available to teach some skills to students who need additional help and attention. In some cases, teaching devices, such as Language Masters™, teaching machines, and puppets, are the most effective ways of presenting some information. Each of these is an important alternative to consider when planning instruction for mildly handicapped students.

TUTORS

Tutors can provide additional instructional time in the classroom. Peers, older students, and other adults in the school may serve as tutors to students who are having difficulty in school. While the principles of training and utilizing tutors are similar for students and adults, there are some issues that should be addressed for each group.

Peer and cross-age tutors may be readily available in the school setting. Other students in the same class may be able to teach certain skills to their peers. Students from other classes or schools may be available to provide the direct instruction in the classroom or during assigned study halls (McCarthy and Stodden, 1979). While these students are readily available, it is important to consider the effect of the lost instructional

Peer tutoring is an important resource available in the school setting.

time for them also. The student who is providing the tutoring may miss some classroom time and must be able to make up the work at a later time in the day. It is also important to select and supervise carefully the students who become peer tutors. Some students who are able to perform the skill cannot necessarily teach the skill to others. Others may use their knowledge of the student's skill level to tease or poke fun at the student on social occasions. This can destroy all progress the tutor has made with the student.

Adult aides are usually working in the school setting on a daily basis and are regularly available when their job description includes tutoring. You should establish a regular schedule for the tutor and for the individual who supervises the tutor so the time the aide spends in direct instruction is not disrupted. Adult volunteers may come into the school simply for the tutoring time. It is important that these volunteers view themselves as being an integral part of the ongoing instructional process. In most cases, careful scheduling of aides and the involvement of volunteer tutors can be worked out to the mutual satisfaction of all parties involved.

Whether a tutoring program is based upon the use of other students or adults, you should keep certain factors in mind. First, the tutor must possess the skills the student needs to learn, although it is important to note that the tutor will likely acquire new skills during the tutoring process (Dineen, Clar, and Risley, 1977). After it has been determined that the prospective tutor does, indeed, have those skills, the teacher should check to see that the tutor can teach those skills to another person. Knowledge of the skill cannot be equated with ability and interest in teaching. In some cases, even an adult tutor will need to review a skill since it may be something that adults no longer use on a regular basis.

Second, the tutor should be trained in the instructional sequence and in the procedures to be followed in teaching the skill to the student. If the tutor is involved in the instruction of a specific skill or skill sequence, you should describe the entire sequence to the tutor. This allows the tutor to understand how the instruction fits into a larger framework. If the tutor is involved in an activity such as listening to students read, this may not be as important. You should also train the tutor in teaching procedures. This includes how to teach (skills such as modeling, verbal cues, and providing practice) and reinforcement and evaluation procedures.

Finally, you should establish a record keeping procedure for the tutor to report student progress on a daily basis. You need to know how the student is progressing and may not be able to confer with the tutor following each instructional session. Student progress can be noted through charts, graphs, completed assignments, and anecdotal records kept by the tutor. A reporting system should be established as well as a system for you to convey information to the tutor on a regular basis. You should, by all means, be involved in planning, implementing, and evaluating student performance, but must rely on the reports from the tutor regarding the effectiveness of lessons.

In addition to the training and monitoring procedures mentioned above, you should be aware of the needs of the tutor for recognition. Since the tutor is providing an important service for both you and the exceptional student, it is important that you plan time on a regular basis to meet with the tutor, providing positive, supportive feedback for the assistance rendered. In many situations, student tutors acquire an enhanced classroom status as a result of their role (Bowermaster, 1978). This status can be shared by affording all students the opportunity to tutor when possible (Rosen, Powell, and Rollins, 1978).

Following are some examples of successful tutor relationships.

JOHN

John is a sixth-grade student who is reading at a 3.2 grade level. He receives remedial instruction in reading. On Tuesday and Thursday mornings, John goes to the second-grade classroom and listens to Derek and another mildly retarded student read orally for ten minutes each. The teacher pretested John to be sure he had mastered the second-grade vocabulary, gave him instructions on how to provide corrective and reinforcing feedback, and a means for reporting back to her on the children's oral reading. She observes John once every two weeks to monitor his program.

CARL

Carl is a fourth-grader who is gifted in arithmetic as well as verbal communication. When other students in class have difficulty with assigned seatwork, Carl serves as a resource person for assistance.

MRS. MERRILL

Mrs. Merrill has had either a parent volunteer or a college practicum student in her classroom every semester for two years. When volunteers first enter her class, she provides them with a written description of her program and trains them in daily classroom procedures. She then assigns them to work with small groups of students with learning problems who need individualized attention, more immediate feedback, and instruction as they complete work assigned by the teacher. The volunteer corrects all papers and reports back to the teacher in writing after each session.

In all three examples, the tutor was assisting students and the classroom teacher. While the tutor works with some students, the teacher is free to give attention to other students in the classroom. The tutor can give direct instructional assistance to those students who need more individualized contact to successfully learn the material presented in the classroom.

TEACHING DEVICES

Some students do not respond well to adults or peers. These students may have experienced a great deal of failure in instructional settings and find it difficult to listen to and respond to the adults who are now trying to teach them. Other students have developed inappropriate ways of relating to the people in their environment. For instance, they may be very manipulative, trying to keep the teacher from presenting the desired lesson. And still other students are unable to work with the distractions that other people and noises in the environment provide. In these cases, teaching machines or indirect contact with teachers through role play and puppets may be effective techniques to develop academic skills and teach the student appropriate skills for relating to the instructional environment.

Teaching machines are devices that present material to students for a response. Some examples of these are Language Master,™ Little Professor,™ and Speak and Spell.™ The instructional sequence presented on the teaching machine is usually programmed, either commercially or by the teacher. The student receives immediate feedback on responses and is able to correct mistakes. The student does not need to come into direct contact with the teacher. Such programs may provide the student with the opportunity to learn basic skills, but will generally be unsatisfactory as a total program due to the limitations discussed in the section on programmed instruction.

IAN

Ian, the fourth grade learning disabled student, has difficulty in arithmetic. Since he receives instruction in basic arithmetic processes from the resource room teacher and practices some of his arithmetic skills in the classroom, the two teachers have worked together to design appropriate practice activities for Ian. One part of the instructional program involves the use of teaching machines.

The resource teacher found that Ian could compute basic addition, subtraction, and multiplication facts. However, because of his elaborate finger counting system, he was unable to use his facts to complete more difficult problems efficiently. Both teachers wanted to provide Ian with additional practice in number facts. A Little Professor™ calculator was placed in Ian's classroom. When Ian had free time or was assigned to practice his number facts, he would take the Little Professor™ to his desk. Ian would select the type of combination he wanted (addition, subtraction, or multiplication), watch for the problems to be presented, and answer them. Ian enjoyed this type of practice.

When Ian began to make correct responses consistently, he was given a Data Man™ to use. Since Data Man™ indicates the amount of time used to answer the problems as well as the number of correct responses, Ian was able to compete with himself to try to improve his performance. Ian found this motivating, enjoying the practice sessions immensely.

Not all teaching devices need to be mechanical. When a student is not responding to teachers in the school setting, the use of puppets or other roles may be a technique to consider. Many younger students will talk to puppets or to people when they are playing defined roles not associated with the school setting. In these cases, the puppet or the role character allows the student to express ideas in a more neutral setting. This technique may be used as a step in the process of developing interpersonal communication skills for some students. While this strategy is often employed by specialists, it may also be of use in the classroom.

Change the Conditions of Instruction

Some students respond well to the classroom curriculum and to the teaching methods typically used by the classroom teacher. They are unable, however, to participate in the large group setting or work effectively in other groupings in the classroom. For these students, it is important to consider such variables as when and where the instruction occurs and the group size used for teaching. Manipulation of these seemingly simple variables can result in improved performance for some students.

WHERE INSTRUCTION OCCURS

Most instruction takes place in the classroom. In many content areas, the instruction is delivered to all students in the class. This type of setting, while appropriate for many students, may be ineffective for some. Some students feel lost in a large group. They are unable to maintain a positive identification and interaction with their peers. Other students are easily distracted by irrelevant stimuli. Some students need to identify with a particular place or person or need more personal space to work effectively. For these students, an adaptation in the setting can make a significant difference in performance.

There are many relatively easy changes you can make to adapt the "where" of instruction. Many of the adaptations suggested earlier (learning centers, experiential approaches, and mediated presentations) result in a change in the location of instruction. Hence, a change in delivery may result in a change of location. For students who seem to feel lost in a large group, you can make a designated working space on the perimeter of the group, where the student can be close to you while instruction is delivered.

Some students need consistency in both their work location and assigned space. For these students, a consistent seating arrangement in which this student retains his or her original seat when changes are made can be helpful. Assigned work spaces can also help students establish their own working space, allowing them to utilize as much space as necessary for their particular needs. While these may seem like commonsense suggestions, they should not be overlooked as possible aids to instruction.

Some students need more structure and differentiation in their work space. The student who is easily distractable may benefit from a work space that limits visual contact with other stimuli in the classroom. A study carrel is one way of confining the work space so that the student's vision is blocked on three sides, thus helping the student focus on the learning task. Study carrels are available commercially, can be built from lumber scrap, or can be simulated by arranging classroom furniture to make individual, private work spaces. For some students, using these spaces may be mandatory when completing assigned seat work. The students may be able gradually to return to working in the group setting when they are able to complete assignments without becoming distracted. Other students may wish to make occasional use of such settings when completing work in the classroom.

You may wish to establish several special areas in the classroom for activities such as free reading, browsing, or academic games. Rules can be established for each area, indicating to the student the expectations and providing guidelines for behavior. This provides flexibility for the student and allows for different types of behavior in the classroom without disrupting the structure of the class. You may also wish to arrange student seating carefully to maximize potential modeling of appropriate behavior and to minimize the opportunity to distract other learners. Since teacher proximity can be an influence on increasing appropriate behaviors, some students should be seated where you can reach them quickly and frequently during the course of the day.

WHEN INSTRUCTION OCCURS

Every student has an optimal learning time. For many young children, the morning or the first couple hours they are at school is the best time to provide instruction. As students grow older, stamina and length of time from the beginning of school until the time of instruction appear to be not so strong a factor. Most students, though, have a preference for work time. With some students who experience difficulty in school, it is sometimes critical to make maximum use of such preferences.

The morning is usually considered the best time to provide instruction in basic skill areas like reading, arithmetic, and language arts. Students are fresher and able to lend more concentration to the tasks at hand. Secondary level teachers may not be able to take advantage of this principle as easily because of scheduling factors. It may be important to provide instruction in these critical skill areas in the morning when possible.

Some students, though, bring their home problems to school and may be unable to participate effectively in instruction early in the school day. They may need some time to acclimate themselves to the school setting and to get some distance from events that may have occurred in the home. These students will likely profit more from instruction later in the morning or in the afternoon.

You should observe the behavior, interest level, and attention span of students at various points during the day if an adaptation in this area seems warranted. Such observations can provide data on optimal times for instruction for particular students and may result in schedule changes.

Many students need variety in their schedule. As an adult, you may find it difficult to sit in one place for an extended period of time without a break or moving around. Yet students are often expected to do just that. When developing a schedule for the day, assess the types of activities and the order in which students encounter them. It will help many students, particularly those who are in self-contained elementary classes, to have a less structured activity involving physical movement follow a more structured learning experience. A two-minute stretch time can also provide a release for the student who is active and needs a break from the structure of learning tasks. This variety in scheduling can prevent many "behavior problems" from occurring in the classroom.

In addition to scheduling instruction for optimal learning times and incorporating variety into the student's schedule for physical activity, you should observe when large group, small group, and individual instruction occur during the day. If the bulk of the morning time is small group instruction and assigned seatwork and the afternoon is devoted to large group activities, it may be helpful to distribute the grouping differently during the school day. The coordination of large and small group and individual instruction during the day can assist some students in monitoring their own performance and provide variety in the type of interaction required of students throughout the school day.

GROUP SIZE

Group size is an important variable to consider when evaluating the conditions of instruction. Instruction frequently involves groups of twenty to thirty students, groups of four to six students, and individual instruction. Students vary a great deal in their response to the size of the group being taught. Some students, as mentioned earlier, are lost in a group of twenty or thirty students, while others are able to participate and concentrate on what is being taught. Other students profit from one-to-one instruction with a teacher or tutor. The effect of group size varies from student to student, so it is necessary for you to observe carefully its effect on each student.

Many teachers have been told that students who are not making progress need personalized instruction. This is not always the case. Some students do make maximum progress when they work by themselves with a teacher. Direct feedback and interaction with the teacher may be reinforcing and may serve to motivate the student to learn the material being presented. Some students, though, learn more quickly when they have a sense of competition with their classmates. While we do not suggest introducing competition into learning, the progress of other students can be a motivating factor for some students. Finally, some students are uncomfortable with the immediate, direct attention of the teacher in small group and one-to-one instruction. This discomfort can lead to less progress than the student might make in a large group setting. It should be noted that some skills, like socialization, discussion, questioning, and interactive skills, cannot be taught effectively in one-to-one settings. So in addition to considering learning preferences of the student, you should consider the effect of grouping on the content to be taught.

Group size, then, is a variable that should be considered when structuring a program for a student who is having difficulty in the classroom. Since it is impractical to provide individual attention for all students, one-to-one instruction and small group instruction should be used with students who are unable to learn effectively in the large group classroom setting.

THEORY INTO PRACTICE

Methods Adaptations

John, an eighth-grade learning disabled student, reads at a 5.6 grade level. The resource teacher has put the eighth-grade social studies book on audio tape. John listens to the tape in the school library during his study hall.

Because John is easily distracted, his math teacher has set aside an individual work space for John and other students who need to work by themselves.

Mrs. Smith, the literature teacher, has provided John with a condensed version of the classic being read during class. John participates in all class activities and discussions.

Since health concepts are important for daily survival, the teacher has paired several students who study major concepts together. John's partner is a good reader who can easily discuss what she has read on both concrete and abstract levels.

Choose Appropriate Adaptations

A number of adaptations have been suggested in the area of methods and techniques. It is important to use a systematic approach in determining the adaptation(s) most appropriate for any one student. Following are some guidelines that may be used when considering adaptations for students with learning and/or behavior problems:

1. Review the assessment data collected on the student, particularly observations of the student's performance in the classroom and preferred learning styles.

2. Establish the learning goal(s) and objectives for the student.

3. Review the content to be taught, noting the methods to be used with the class as a whole.

4. Select the adaptation that varies the least from the typical method used for the content to be presented.

5. Evaluate the adaptation, based upon the student's needs. If it seems appropriate, try it. If not, select the next adaptation and evaluate its potential for success. Continue this process until an adaptation is selected that meets the student's needs.

The steps in this process are designed to enable you to make the least amount of change necessary to ensure student success in the classroom. Adaptations that are similar to the typical classroom methodology decrease the amount of extra teacher preparation and probably increase the participation of handicapped students. It should be noted that one adaptation should be tried at a time, using the one closest to the usual classroom methodology that best seems to meet the student's needs. Data should be collected on the student's performance on a regular basis to document the effectiveness of instruction. Further changes should be made if the student does not seem to make progress with the adaptation. It is also possible that changes are necessary in the curriculum or with the motivational approaches used with the student.

Summary

When exceptional students are placed in the classroom for some portion of their school day, it is usually necessary for you to adapt your instructional approach to accommodate the students' specific needs. The adaptations you select will depend upon the students' limitations and the approaches that seem to work best for each student. Since the primary purpose of instruction is to assist the student in meeting stated goals and objectives, careful attention to teaching methods is important. The main points covered in this chapter are as follows:

1. You can adapt instruction by changing how the instruction is delivered. The use of media presentations, learning centers, programmed instruction, alternative materials, experiential approaches, and a parallel alternative curriculum can increase the success of exceptional students on educational tasks.

2. Students may be able to acquire the information and skills being taught in the classroom, but be unable to provide the expected response because of learning handicaps. Taping, dictating, and typing answers; the use of projects, debates, and panel discussions; and changing the response format of assignments can be valuable adaptations for some exceptional students.

3. In some cases, a change in the person who presents information to the student can be helpful. Peer and adult tutors, computer assisted instruction, and teaching devices can be used to present content and provide for practice and review.

4. Group size, the time of day, and the location in the classroom are additional instructional variables that can be modified to increase student success.

5. When adapting instruction for exceptional students, the goals and objectives written for the student and the student's learning style should be of prime importance. One relatively minor change may suffice for one student; three or four adaptations may be necessary for another. No one plan will meet the needs of all exceptional students.

6. Once instructional adaptations for exceptional students are implemented, data should be collected and the effectiveness of the adaptation should be evaluated.

Activities

1. Select a topic area you will teach students. Develop a learning center to accompany your unit of instruction using the steps described in the chapter. Collect and develop all materials needed. If possible, set up the learning center in a classroom and evaluate its effectiveness.

2. Locate and review several programmed instructional sequences. Try completing one of the sequences yourself. Note your reactions to this instructional approach. Now try to write a programmed sequence that you might use with students when teaching. Keep in mind your own reactions to programmed material and the drawbacks to such instruction as you write your sequence.

3. Locate a basal text you might use at your grade level. Select a lesson from the text, carefully reading the suggestions for presentation of the lesson. Then adapt the lesson for a student with a learning problem. If possible, try your adapted lesson with a student in a regular classroom.

4. Identify an assignment you would make to students in the grade level you wish to teach. List at least three types of responses students could make that would demonstrate their mastery of the content or skill.

5. List three ways in which you could use tutors in your classroom. Note in each case whether it would be best to use peer or cross-age tutors and why.

Study Questions

1. List four changes a teacher can make in teaching methods/techniques to accommodate exceptional students. Note two advantages and two disadvantages for each.

2. What is a parallel alternative curriculum? How can it be used effectively in the classroom to provide appropriate instruction?

3. Mr. Johnson has assigned an essay on the causes of the Civil War. Some of his students are unable to provide an essay-type response. List three alternative types of responses these students could make, noting how each response must demonstrate the same knowledge required of other students.

4. Describe the components of a peer-tutoring program, including training, teaching, and feedback.

5. What is the effect of classroom environment on student learning? Give one example of a change in environment that may lead to increased student performance.

6. What factors should a teacher consider when determining group size for instruction?

Questions for Further Thought

1. When instruction is adapted for students with learning problems, these students complete objectives and assigned work in a much different manner than their peers. Should this difference be reflected in the evaluation and grading process? If so, how?

2. To what extent should the classroom teacher be expected to accommodate exceptional students in the instructional process? What resources may be necessary for successful mainstreaming?

Additional Resources

BOOKS

Hammill, D. D., and Bartel, N. R. *Teaching children with learning and behavior problems* (2nd ed.). Boston: Allyn and Bacon, 1978.

Charles, C. M. *Individualizing instruction* (2nd ed.). St. Louis: C. V. Mosby, 1980.

Mercer, D. C., and Mercer, A. R. *Teaching students with learning problems.* Columbus, Ohio: Charles E. Merrill, 1981.

Piercey, D. *Reading activities in content areas: An idea book for middle and secondary schools.* Boston: Allyn and Bacon, 1976.

PROFESSIONAL JOURNALS AND MAGAZINES

Learning

Instructor

Grade Teacher

Professional Journals in Specific Content Areas

Chapter 11

Promoting

Positive Behavior

No doubt many of you have been in classrooms that were marked by a continual struggle between teachers and students. Lessons in such classrooms are often interrupted by minor misbehaviors, such as talking out of turn or walking aimlessly about the room. Assigned work is rarely completed and teachers devote far too much time to criticizing students for misbehaving.

What can you do to avoid this type of scenario and motivate students to learn and behave appropriately? Certainly, modifying instructional goals and techniques and increasing chances for success are important considerations. You can also show enthusiasm for what you are teaching and demonstrate a personal interest in your students. But there is more. In this chapter we will examine several systematic approaches to motivating students. These include providing structure, developing effective student management skills, reinforcing positive behavior, and providing consequences for persistent misbehavior. These approaches are applicable to all students but are particularly useful for those who are labeled mentally retarded, emotionally disturbed, or learning disabled.

Provide Structure

Central to any effort to help exceptional students is the establishment of adequate levels of structure. Many exceptional students, particularly those with learning and behavior problems, can perform better when expectations are spelled out in a simple, direct manner and when a daily routine is observed (Hewett and Taylor, 1980).

DEVELOP CLEAR EXPECTATIONS

To many problem students, general reminders such as "be good," "be a helpful student," or threats to take away privileges or reduce grades are vague or meaningless and should be avoided. Instead, rules and expectations should be spelled out in a positive manner that provides a reachable goal to work towards. Consider the following expectations, each of which provides a clear and reasonable goal:

- Accurately complete at least ten math problems by 9:30.

- Raise your hand before talking.

- Volunteer at least one answer during today's class discussion.

- Line up without hitting or pushing anyone.

- Do not get out of your seat more than twice during the work period.

- Begin your assigned work within two minutes.

- If you get frustrated or stuck on your work, raise your hand for help.

One way to present expectations to individual students is to place them on a personal checklist such as the one presented in Figure 11.1. Such checklists contain important behaviors the student is to demonstrate and may be kept at your desk or the student's desk. You and the student review the important behaviors to practice each day. Either you or the student may enter check marks at the end of each activity period. Check marks indicate whether the student met the stated objective.

Since most students with behavioral difficulties have a history of failure in academics as well as in coping with rules, routines, and stress, it is important to develop expectations that are clear and easily achievable. To help students achieve success, think in terms of small, daily steps of improvement rather than dramatic, global changes. Daily accomplishment of such objectives will help bolster self-confidence and develop a commitment to appropriate classroom behavior rather than inappropriate behavior to gain attention.

As students learn to accomplish each objective, further improvement can be outlined in subsequent objectives. For example, you may expect a particular student to complete ten math problems within fifteen minutes. As the student masters this expectation, you can increase the number of problems to be completed in the same period. Likewise, for the

<table>
<tr><td colspan="3">Name Scott _____ Date _____</td></tr>
</table>

Important behaviors to remember.	Yes	No
1. Complete math seatwork with at least 80% correct.	X	
2. Stay in your seat during math. Do not get out without permission more than once.		X
3. Line up during recess without hitting, running, or pushing.	X	

FIGURE 11.1
Sample checklist

student who continually talks out of turn, your first objective might be
to have the student talk out no more than three times during a morning.
As the student learns to meet this objective, you can set a new objective
of talking out no more than twice, and so on, until the problem behavior
is eliminated or reduced to an acceptable level.

DEVELOP CONSISTENT RULES AND ROUTINES

Some students with behavior problems have not learned how to follow
a daily schedule of activities or work at one task with sustained attention.
These students appear to be impulsive. They act before considering the
consequences of their actions and have difficulty observing rules. A few
of these students may come from chaotic backgrounds in which meal-
time, bedtime, and other routines are virtually nonexistent. Others may
have impulsive models at home or simply have not yet developed good
learning habits. These students need a consistent, carefully established
set of procedures to help them become less impulsive. Some guidelines
for developing rules and routines for these students are listed below.

■   Develop and follow a daily schedule of class activities. Post the
    schedule in view of the students.

■   To help students become aware of a sense of routine, review the
    schedule from time to time each day. You might say, for example,
    "We are just finishing math. Now we are going to get ready for
    reading."

Develop a few simple but clear rules, and review the rules before beginning each new activity.

- Develop a few simple but clear rules for behavior for each class activity. Rules such as "Work quietly," and "Raise your hand before talking," are more effective than general rules, such as "Be a good citizen."

- Review the rules prior to beginning each new activity.

- To help students prepare for transitions from one activity to another, provide a reminder that one activity is going to end in a few minutes. Such reminders will help students finish their work or their thoughts and begin to get ready for the next activity.

- To help students start each new activity with a feeling of success, begin with several verbal or written problems that the students can solve with ease.

- When students follow rules or comply with expectations, recognize their positive efforts right away. Recognition can come in many forms: a smile, a thank-you, a pat on the back, or a positive note to the student.

- From time to time conduct discussions about classroom behavior and rules. Ask students to identify which of the class rules they are observing well and how it affects the class. Ask students to identify areas in need of improvement.

■ If a student has difficulty with a particular behavior, such as talking out of turn, ask the student to identify a target goal to work towards (e.g., not talking out more than twice during each activity). Then ask the student to suggest ways to accomplish the goal. Help the student identify several ways to keep track of progress, such as making a check mark on a personal chart each time he or she talks out of turn.

Develop Effective Management Skills

The establishment of reasonable learning objectives and clear rules and routines can reduce but not completely eliminate student misbehavior. Momentary upsets and disruptions are likely to occur, and some form of teacher response will be necessary. You will want to learn to respond to these disruptions in such a way that you do not inflame the situation or create what Long and Dufner (1980) call a stress cycle of misbehavior.

THE STRESS CYCLE

Stress is a subjective reaction to specific events and generally causes the individual both psychological and physiological discomfort. Long and Dufner assert that many students with learning and behavior problems are victims of an escalating stress cycle having four interrelated components, each described below.

1. *Stressful incident.* The stress cycle begins with a painful incident, such as being called a name, feeling incompetent as a result of not knowing how to do an assignment, being reprimanded for misbehavior, or being criticized by a parent or other authority figure.

2. *Feelings.* Stressful incidents, by definition, cause a variety of feelings, such as anger, hatred, revenge, guilt, jealousy, powerlessness, sadness, isolation, and rejection. Although it is entirely normal to experience these feelings, many students with learning and behavior problems experience overwhelming degrees of these emotions, which lead to overt behaviors.

3. *Overt behavior.* Students with persistent behavior problems often lack self-control and vent stress-induced feelings through inappropriate behaviors, such as shouting, arguing, swearing, hitting, withdrawing, teasing, tearing up papers, or becoming sullen.

4. *Teacher reactions.* How you react to the overt behavior is the final component of the stress cycle. If, for example, you overreact to certain misbehaviors, additional stress is likely to result, and the stress cycle begins again on a more intense level. Thus, inappropriate teacher reactions to misbehavior may only serve to further fuel the stress cycle

and intensify student feelings, behavior, and teacher reactions to the behavior. The cycle may continue until a shouting match or other type of confrontation occurs, in which case both the teacher and the student are likely to experience anger, frustration, or guilt.

AVOIDING THE STRESS CYCLE

How can the stress cycle be avoided? Instead of becoming personally offended or threatened when a student becomes upset, you should remember that the student is probably experiencing strong emotions that need to be reduced. One way to respond is to use some of Gordon's communication skills presented in Chapter 9. If you recall, Mr. Jones was able to help Tim cope with his frustration by listening carefully, reflecting Tim's feelings, and engaging Tim in problem solving. By using these techniques in a calm, accepting manner, Tim was able to begin his work and Mr. Jones was able to carry on with his lesson.

Not every instance of student misbehavior requires such an involved response as that made by Mr. Jones. A group of techniques designed to help you respond constructively to momentary student misbehaviors were developed by Redl and Wineman (1951) in their work with aggressive students. They have been further refined by Long and Newman (1980). The significance of these techniques is that they offer concrete steps for minimizing misbehavior during ongoing learning activities. The first three techniques are the easiest to implement in that they can be used without stopping the lesson and do not give undue attention to the misbehaving student. The remaining five techniques require more direct efforts.

1. *Planned ignoring.* Certain students misbehave in an effort to gain attention or "get the teacher's goat." Some minor misbehaviors such as talking or whispering, complaining about an assignment, or making inappropriate noises may best be ignored if past experience suggests that the misbehavior will not spread to others and will cease after several moments if not confronted. Ignoring such behaviors has at least two advantages. No attention is paid to the misbehavior, and arguments or confrontations are avoided over relatively minor misbehaviors. These misbehaviors, however, may also be a cue that the student is frustrated and needs help. In such cases, the misbehavior should be ignored but help should be provided as soon as possible.

The value of ignoring misbehavior is sometimes confused and overstated. Clearly, some misbehaviors may cause harm to others, disrupt the lesson, or set off a chain reaction of similar misbehaviors from other students. These should definitely not be ignored. On the other hand, experimentation with this technique may lead to the understanding that some minor misbehaviors have a natural and quick death if left unrecognized.

2. *Signal interference.* Some misbehaviors can be quietly stopped through a variety of nonverbal signals conveyed to the student. These signals may include eye contact, gestures such as signalling for quiet, facial expressions, and acts such as turning off the lights. These signals can be particularly effective if the student is just beginning a minor misbehavior (pencil tapping, talking to others) and if the student is responsive to your attention.

3. *Proximity control.* Standing near some students can help them maintain composure, keep task oriented, and feel supported. Circulating about the room and offering help or checking work is one example of proximity control. Other examples include placing the student's desk close to your primary work area, sitting near the student during group activities, or sitting or standing next to the student as signs of fatigue, stress, or frustration are noticed.

4. *Tension decontamination through humor.* Humor can occasionally be used to defuse a tense situation and get students back to work. Consider the following example provided by Long and Newman (1980, pp. 237–238).

> I walked into my room after lunch period to find several pictures on the chalk board with "teacher" written under each one. I went to the board and picked up a piece of chalk, first looking at the pictures and then at the class. You could have heard a pin drop! Then I walked over to one of the pictures and said that this one looked the most like me but needed some more hair, which I added. Then I went to the next one and said that they had forgotten my glasses so I added them, on the next one I suggested adding a big nose, and on the last one a longer neck. By this time the class was almost in hysterics. Then, seeing that the children were having such a good time and that I could not get them settled easily, I passed out drawing paper and suggested that they draw a picture of the funniest person they could make. It is amazing how original these pictures were.

Note that the teacher had to feel self-assured to use this technique. Some teachers take things personally and are quick to levy punishment on the entire class or demand a confession from the guilty student. Though tempting, such tactics usually only serve to increase tension and conflict and may result in overly harsh punishment. Use of humor need not be construed as tacit approval of the misbehavior. You can remind students that certain behaviors are inappropriate after the tension has been reduced. Of course, other techniques can be used if the misbehavior persists.

5. *Hurdle help.* For some students, momentary frustration with academic tasks can begin a cycle of stress. Not knowing how to begin a task, becoming stuck on a difficult problem, or being faced with a long series of problems can be a genuine source of anxiety. Knowing in advance how a particular student is likely to react under these conditions, you can take effective steps to help overcome the hurdle and prevent more

Hurdle help can reduce frustration.

serious outbursts. Helping the student do the first few problems, assisting the student with difficult problems, or carefully explaining directions to the student are all examples of this technique.

6. *Restructuring the activity.* While it is true that structure and routine are important, occasionally it is helpful to vary an activity in response to the mood or general tone of the classroom. Again, an example may help (Long and Newman, 1980, p. 238):

> The children were just returning to the room after the recess period. Most of them were flushed and hot from exercise, and were a little irritable. They were complaining of the heat in the room, and many of them asked permission to get a drink of water as soon as the final recess bell rang. I felt it would be useless to begin our history study as scheduled. So I told all of the children to lay their heads upon their desks. I asked them to be very silent for one minute and to think of the coolest thing they could imagine during that time. Each child then told the class what he had been thinking. The whole procedure lasted roughly ten minutes, and I felt that it was time well spent. The history period afterward went smoothly, the atmosphere within the room relaxed, and the children were receptive.

Note that in this case the orderly transition from one type of activity to another was threatened. Rather than attempting to force the students to comply with the original activity, a slight variation in the structure was used. Another example is switching from a discussion activity to a seatwork activity or vice versa if the activity seems to be provoking confusion or frustration.

7. *Direct appeal.* Direct appeals or requests can be made for students to correct their own behavior. One way to issue an appeal is to simply ask the student to stop the misbehavior ("Please sit down now."). At times your appeals can have greater impact if you provide a basis for the appeal. For example, you can make an appeal on the basis of reality consequences ("If you continue to talk you won't get your work done, and then you won't have time to read your magazine."). This type of appeal reminds the student, in a nonthreatening way, of the consequences of continued misbehavior. You can also make appeals on the basis of peer reactions ("How do you think other students will feel about you if you continue to interrupt them while they are talking?"), preestablished rules ("We have a rule that says only two people at a time can be at the listening center"), or a personal relationship ("All that noise is giving me a headache. Please tone it down."). The basis on which you make an appeal should have meaning to the student. For example, appealing to peer reactions would have little impact on the student who was unaware of or unconcerned with peer reactions.

8. *Physical restraint.* On very rare occasions, a student may become so upset that all self-control is lost. The student may hit himself or herself, throw objects, or begin running about the room with every indication that the misbehavior will continue to accelerate. Firm restraint should be used to prevent the student from doing serious harm to himself and others. A supportive, nonpunitive form of restraint can be used by standing behind the student, crossing his or her arms around the sides and firmly holding onto the wrists. During this episode, sincere concern should be expressed. You should reassure the student that as soon as he or she regains composure, the student will be released. Long and Newman (1980) suggest that many students go through a cycle from initial anger and rage, to crying and sobbing, to silence, at which point that student may ask to be let go. If you believe that the student has regained sufficient self-control, the student may be released. Obviously, your own physical stature may be a factor. With older students, you may need to call the building principal or other teachers for additional help.

Needless to say, the use of physical restraint is a dramatic and exhausting tactic. It may even have legal consequences. As a rule, advantages and disadvantages of restraint for particular students should be considered at Pupil Evaluation Team meetings. If such a technique is believed to be necessary for a particular student, decisions should be made beforehand as to whether you or other persons will do the actual restraining and whether it will occur in the classroom, hallway, or a quiet office.

The behavior management techniques just reviewed will not be equally effective for all students. Some students, for example, will be quite amenable to proximity control. Others will become embarrassed by such closeness. Hurdle help may prove quite useful for students who need immediate assistance. Other students can be ignored with the knowledge that their misbehavior will not influence other students and will quickly subside. Indeed, part of the challenge of building a repertoire of constructive behavior management techniques is to identify which techniques work best for you and which techniques work best for specific students.

Reward Positive Behavior

Some students, particularly those who have been labeled emotionally disturbed, mentally retarded, or learning disabled, need to learn that it is more rewarding to complete academic tasks and behave appropriately than it is to misbehave. Although most students are rewarded by the satisfaction of completing a task or by the anticipation of a good grade, those who have experienced failure are not inwardly motivated to achieve. These students need additional incentives or rewards to help them accomplish daily objectives before they will be motivated by success alone.

WHAT TYPES OF REWARDS ARE AVAILABLE?

What incentives can elementary and secondary teachers use to promote positive behavior? Many rewards are effective, including praise and teacher attention, feedback, privileges, and tangible rewards.

Praise and Attention   Your attention is an often overlooked and underestimated reward. In fact, the careful application of praise, proximity, and approving smiles and gestures can serve as a powerful, yet subtle reward. To make sure students know why they are being praised, you should identify the behavior you are rewarding, as indicated in the following examples:

- George, I'm glad you are in your seat on time!
- Al, you used the correct verb tense in just about every sentence in your theme; nice going!
- Sara, thank you for raising your hand before talking.
- Great going, Scott! You got your work done on time!

Naturally, once students understand why they are being praised, these elaborate statements can be replaced by shorter phrases, smiles, and other nonverbal gestures. As a rule, praise should be administered as soon as the desired behavior is demonstrated.

Feedback   Closely related to praise is the use of feedback. Feedback, or knowledge of results, can be highly motivating. Grades are one form of feedback. Knowing how one performed in relation to a standard or a goal is another form. For example, many students are interested in knowing how many words they spelled correctly, how many math problems they completed in a fixed time period, or how many times they remembered to raise their hand before talking. Indeed, feedback is a mechanism for keeping track of how well one did toward meeting a particular objective. Once students realize that some form of scorekeeping is being used by themselves or by others, they may automatically try to improve their behavior.

Privileges   In some cases, praise and feedback may not be powerful enough to change misbehavior. More substantial incentives, such as privileges or activities that students may earn for accomplishing predetermined objectives, may need to be instituted. The following list represents only a few of the many privileges or activities typically available to elementary and secondary students:

- feed or water animal
- pass out papers
- play a game
- library pass
- listen to a record
- play a game with a friend
- extra recess
- work on a special project
- have a class party
- TV time at home
- read magazines
- class outing or field trip
- give the class spelling test
- read a story to a lower grade
- no homework

Making these privileges available as a reward for appropriate behavior represents an application of what is sometimes called "Grandma's Law." This time-honored principle reminds us that dessert should be served only after meat and vegetables have been eaten. In an educational context, enjoyable activities should occur after completion of more difficult tasks, as in the case of the following students.

ANNA

Anna, a second-grader, enjoys coloring. But she has a difficult time completing her independent reading work, which begins at 9:30 each morning. The teacher arranges things so that Anna may color from 10:00 to 10:15 if her seatwork is completed correctly by 10:00. The brief reward, plus a moment of hurdle help at the beginning of the seatwork period, provided ample incentives to help Anna complete her work nearly every day.

ALEX AND JACK

Alex and Jack are ninth-graders who often talk out of turn and banter in a loud manner. Their classwork is rarely completed. The science teacher feels he spends too much time reminding these two and some other students to do their work. Threats of detention hold little, if any, influence over these students. Rather than continually attending to their misbehavior, the teacher allowed these students ten minutes of free time at the end of class period if they each answered at least one discussion question, completed their work with at least 80% accuracy, and did not have to be reprimanded more than once.

Privileges or special activities should not be given in a haphazard fashion. Instead, they can be used to reward responsible student behavior according to a carefully worked-out plan. You first identify specific behaviors for the student to demonstrate and then privately review the behaviors with the student. Privileges or activities that appear desirable are selected by you and the student, and a clear agreement is reached as to what the student must do to earn the privilege.

As a general rule, privileges should be offered as soon after the desired behavior occurs as possible. This usually means at the end of an assignment or class period. In some cases, however, substantial privileges, such as attending a special event, may occur at the end of a week or longer. In these cases, care must be taken to reward the student with praise or attention on a more frequent basis. Indeed, the use of privileges does not negate the use of praise. Praise should always accompany the administration of privileges ("Jack, you did a great job getting your work done on time. Now you have earned ten minutes of free time.").

Tangible Rewards   Tangible rewards represent a more costly form of reinforcement and should be used only when the previous rewards are insufficient motivators. Such rewards usually involve actual items the student may keep, including fancy stickers, good behavior certificates, posters, pencils, used paperbacks or comics, model planes and cars, home allowance, cookies, and similar items. As in the case of privileges, the rewards are earned for meeting objectives set by you and the student.

DESIGNING SYSTEMATIC REWARD PROGRAMS

The use of a variety of informal rewards can be incorporated into your teaching repertoire. For example, praising good efforts and providing feedback should become a natural way of responding to all students. Organizing class schedules so that brief periods of fun or relaxing activities follow intensive work sessions is an easy way to put "Grandma's Law" into action. Offering occasional letters of merit or achievement is another way of rewarding students for their efforts.

Some exceptional students, particularly those with learning and behavior problems, need more carefully designed reward programs than those mentioned in the preceding paragraph. To develop such programs, several steps should be followed. First, clear expectations must be developed. Then a reward meaningful to the student must be selected. As a rule of thumb, the least costly rewards should be tried first. Praise in combination with feedback is a good starting point. If these rewards prove insufficient, more powerful rewards, such as privileges or certain tangible rewards, can be added. Finally, rewards must be offered at frequent intervals, particularly at the onset of a program. Requiring a student to wait for several days until the reward is earned may only lead to discouragement. Students should generally be able to earn rewards on a daily basis. Younger students may need them even more frequently. Examples of a variety of systematic reward programs appear on the following pages.

GOOD BEHAVIOR CHARTS

A useful system for providing students with systematic feedback, praise, and, if needed, privileges or tangible rewards is the good behavior chart. The variety of charts that can be developed is almost limitless. Good behavior charts list the specific behaviors the student is to demonstrate and then provide space for the teacher to indicate how well the student performed along each listed behavior. An example of such a chart appears

Student _____   Date _____

	Mon.	Tue.	Wed.	Thur.	Fri.
1. Reading seat work completed by 10:15.					
2. Stayed in seat during seatwork time (9:30–10:15).					
3. Lined up for recess without pushing, running or hitting.					
4. Raised hand before talking during social studies or science class (11:00–11:40).					

☺   Excellent — All tasks or behaviors completed.

2   OK — Most tasks or behaviors completed

1   Needs Improvement — Some tasks or behaviors completed.

FIGURE 11.2
Good behavior chart

in Figure 11.2. This chart is a variation of charts developed for Sara and Bob, emotionally disturbed students introduced in Chapters 1 and 4. Both Sara and Bob needed the clear expectations and ongoing feedback provided by these charts.

Good behavior charts can be kept either at your desk or on a bulletin board. You and the student briefly review the chart each morning to remember the behaviors that need to be improved. At logical periods, such as the end of the seatwork period, after recess, and after a particular class, you may spend a moment with the student to enter the appropriate code onto the chart. Enthusiastic praise is provided along with the marks that are entered onto the chart. Lower ratings are entered in a matter-of-fact way with encouragement to improve during the next activity. Additional reinforcers, such as special activities or privileges, can be earned. For example, if the student receives at least two "excellents" and no "needs improvement," then a reward can be earned at the end of the morning or school day.

Good behavior charts can be adapted for use with secondary-level students. For these students the chart should be reviewed privately at the end of each class period. When the student goes to several different classes each day, a checklist that focuses on the same behaviors across different classes can be developed. Here, teachers must agree upon common objectives for the student. An example of such a checklist appears in Figure 11.3. The use of such checklists involves a fixed routine. For example, the student may bring the checklist to you at the beginning of each class. You complete the checklist at the end of the class period. A teacher, counselor, or administrator reviews the checklist with the student at the end of the day and may provide additional rewards.

Both elementary and secondary students can take increasing responsibility in completing the chart as their skill and reliability improve. At the beginning of the charting program, you may complete all ratings to insure continuous attention and consistency. As behavior improves, the student may take increasing amounts of responsibility until, finally, the

Name *Jack* _____ Date _____

	Math	English	Social Studies	Shop
1. In class on time.	3 L.L.	3 R.A.		
2. Completed assigned work.	3 L.L.	2 R.A.		
3. Accepted teacher help without sarcasm or anger.	2 L.L.	3 R.A.		

Code: Enter a **3** if the student did excellent work, a **2** if the student met all requirements but needed several reminders or warnings and a **0** if the student failed to meet the requirement. Please initial each entry.

FIGURE 11.3
Checklist involving several teachers

Good behavior-gram

To: *Mrs. Smith*

From: *Ms. Dodge*

This note is to recognize outstanding effort by your child in the following areas:

1. *Mike has completed all of his math and reading work this week!*

2. *Mike has avoided fighting all week.*

Anne Dodge
Signed

FIGURE 11.4
Home-school note

student rates his or her own behavior with you endorsing the student's self-rating. Such a procedure fosters the development of responsibility and self-control.

Home-School Notes   Good behavior charts can be easily adopted for use as home-school notes, which often have a positive effect on student behavior (Imber, Imber, and Rothstein, 1979). To initiate a home-school note program, a phone call or personal conference between parent, teacher, and student should be conducted to determine whether the parent is interested in this type of program. If so, procedures must be clarified, such as how often the note is to be taken home, what happens if the note is lost or destroyed, what types of ratings or points the student must earn to receive a reward, and what types of rewards will be used. Parents should be reminded to provide the reward only when earned and not to punish the student for poor performance.

Other, less formal, home-school notes such as the one presented in Figure 11.4 can be used to bring outstanding achievements or efforts to the attention of parents. Such notes have a distinct advantage in that they emphasize positive student behavior. Notes are generally issued somewhat less frequently than daily performance charts and are used to single out and reward outstanding behavior, attitudes, or good academic progress.

Academic Performance Charts   Directly related to the use of good behavior charts is the recording of academic progress. Some students are
unaware of their progress. When they see graphically that they are performing at a higher level each day, they become motivated to learn more
and improve their performance. The use of these individual charts or
graphs can be a powerful reinforcer for many students.

There are several steps to follow when setting up an academic chart
or graph for a student. First, the behavior to be recorded should be clearly
defined. It might be the number of correct spelling words on each test,
the new words acquired in each reading session, or the percent of homework assignments completed each day. Once this has been determined,
decide the best way to measure the behavior. If the number of spelling
words given each week is constant, for example, simply recording the
number correct is appropriate. If the number of words is not constant, it
may be necessary to convert the score into a percentage figure when
recording the performance. Next, establish a time each day when the
desired behavior can be practiced, assessed, and entered onto the chart.
Finally, once the response has been measured (data collected from the
assessment of student performance), record it on the chart or graph in
front of the student.

It is possible to teach most students to chart or graph their own
performance. Many students find this to be a reward because they are
developing the charting skill and they can immediately see their own
progress. These charts and graphs can also be used by you to assess the
effectiveness of the instruction the student is receiving. Two examples
of charts and graphs used to record student performance appear in Figure
11.5.

Good Behavior Games   Good behavior games can be used for a group or
an entire classroom and are especially effective for reducing disturbing
behaviors such as talking out of turn, interrupting, and getting out of
one's seat. Points for the entire class are earned for appropriate behaviors,
with a special activity or privilege occurring if the group reaches a specified number of points. The game procedure is illustrated in the following
case study involving an entire classroom.

DAVE WARREN

Many of the twenty-six students in Dave Warren's sixth-grade
social studies class were anxious to receive his attention and
recognition. Their enthusiasm, however, led to frequent
misbehaviors, such as talking out of turn, getting out of one's seat,
and interrupting the teacher. Dave found himself responding to

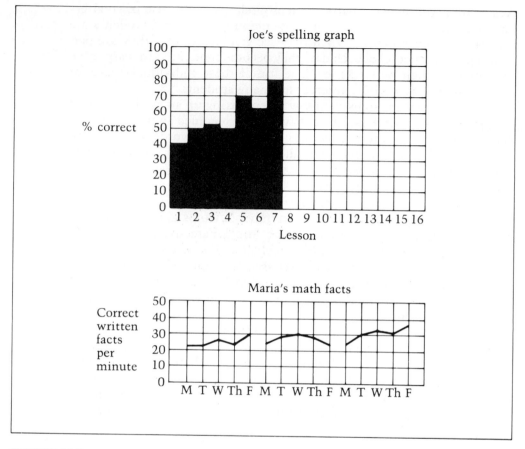

FIGURE 11.5
Sample graph and chart

most of these behaviors by continually reminding students to sit down or raise their hands before talking. However, his frequent warnings did little to improve behavior, consumed valuable teaching time, and made it difficult to carry out lesson plans. To begin working out of this cycle of misbehavior, Dave selected two behaviors for students to focus on during daily social studies classes. He wanted students to decrease talking and whispering while he was teaching and to raise their hands and wait until called upon before talking. To promote these behaviors, Dave developed a Good Behavior Chart and put it on the chalkboard in full view of the class. Since his social studies period was 40 minutes long and he wished to give students frequent feedback regarding their performance on the two behaviors, he divided the

11:15–11:20	11:20–11:25	11:25–11:30	11:30–11:35
2	3	3	2

11:35–11:40	11:40–11:45	11:45–11:50	11:50–11:55
1	3	3	3

FIGURE 11.6
Good behavior chart

chart into eight five-minute blocks. Dave then developed a system
in which points were entered into a time block at the end of each
five minute period. The class earned three points if no more than
one or two students talked or interrupted him, two points if three
or four students talked or interrupted and only one point if more
than four students talked or interrupted. Dave selected an activity
reinforcer that he knew the entire class enjoyed and made this
activity contingent upon good behavior. That is, if the class earned
twenty points, they would be able to play an outdoor game such as
soccer for twenty minutes that afternoon. As student behavior
improved, the game procedure was modified. Time blocks were
expanded to ten minutes, which reduced the number of times
Dave had to stop the lesson and report scores. New behaviors for
the class to improve were gradually added. After about a month
the game was no longer needed.

Some variations on the game structure can be introduced. It is possible to introduce a competitive factor and divide the entire class or the
disruptive students into two teams, with each team trying to earn the
highest number of points. However, to avoid frustration, each team should
be able to earn a reward if it reaches the required number of points.

Contracts   A contract is a written agreement between the teacher and
student that specifies (1) academic and/or classroom behaviors to be demonstrated; (2) rewards to be earned upon completion of tasks; and
(3) consequences for noncompletion. Contracts may be used to accom-

---

Good behavior contract

Activity *Library story hour*

Rules 1. *Find a seat quickly.*
2. *Listen to the story.*
3. *Stay in seat during story.*

Agreement
You may participate in the activity as long as you follow the rules. If you have to be reminded more than two times, you must return to your classroom.

Student _____

Teacher _____

FIGURE 11.7
A good behavior contract

plish a single task or behavior or a cluster of tasks and behaviors. They may be developed for a single class period or activity, or an entire day, week, or marking period.

A relatively simple "good behavior" contract such as the one presented in Figure 11.7 can be developed to help improve performance

---

Task
1. *Complete daily social studies assignment.*
2. *Participate in discussions without interrupting others.*
3. *Raise hand and wait until recognized by the teacher before talking.*

Reward
1. *Five points for completing each daily assignment. You will also receive a two-point bonus for neatness.*
2. *One point for each time you raise your hand and are recognized by the teacher before you contribute to the discussion.*
3. *Each point earns one minute of free time.*

Conditions
1. *Social studies can be done with a partner as long as you work quietly.*
2. *You must remain seated during the group discussion.*
3. *Points may be cashed in at 2:30 or at a later time for an agreed-upon activity.*

Signed _____ (student)

_____ (teacher)

FIGURE 11.8
Sample contract

I _____ hereby agree to work my hardest
    student
to do the following:

_____

_____

_____

_____

I _____ agree to provide the follow rewards
    teacher
or privileges for completion of the above.

_____

_____

_____

This contract shall be in effect for the week of

_____ Date _____

                                   Student _____

                                   Teacher _____

FIGURE 11.9
Form for a general contract

during specific activities or class periods. Good behavior contracts clarify ground rules and expectations for specific activities that may be enjoyable yet troublesome for the student. You review the contract with the student, who, upon agreeing with stated expectations, also signs the contract. The reward is implicit in that the student is allowed to engage in the activity. You may also place check marks or stars to indicate successful compliance with each behavior.

Slightly more elaborate contracts, such as the one in Figure 11.8, can involve both academic and behavioral expectations for an entire class period. Here, academic tasks and class behaviors are stated clearly. Agreed-upon options for rewards are listed. Conditions, or additional constraints, qualifications, and student options may also be spelled out.

A more general contract, such as the one presented in Figure 11.9, can be drawn up and used for a variety of purposes. Such a form provides categories that must be completed by you and the student.

Guidelines for Developing Reward Programs   When developing systematic reward programs, these guidelines may prove useful.

1. *Involve the student.* If the student is at all amenable to discussion, efforts should be made to discuss and agree upon desired behaviors and tasks to improve, as well as rewards and consequences. Such a strategy helps many students assume responsibility and gradually develop a commitment towards improving their academic performance and classroom behavior.

2. *Keep contracts and charts simple.* Young students or those whose behavior is quite disorganized or disruptive should have simple contracts or charts that encompass brief tasks. For such students, behaviors may need to be spelled out for each activity period. This procedure helps to insure success. The complexity of the contract can gradually increase as student skills develop.

3. *Be consistent.* As in any behavior change technique, consistency is a hallmark. Remind the student of the contract or chart each day. Complete the chart or contract and provide rewards at agreed-upon times. If a student fails to complete a task, do not back down or acquiesce to pleas to be allowed to receive the reward. Remember, students must learn that they will earn rewards for appropriate behavior, not for pleading, crying, or other inappropriate behavior.

4. *Involve parents and other teachers.* If the student works with a resource or special class teacher, efforts should be made to coordinate reward programs. These teachers are often in a good position to administer earned rewards. Similarly, parents can play a crucial role in a reward program by providing home reinforcers such as allowance, TV time and special treats.

5. *Don't neglect well-behaved students.* One criticism of systematic reward programs is that they discriminate against the well-behaved students by concentrating teacher efforts on the not-so-well-behaved. This need not happen! Well-behaved students should receive praise and encouragement for their efforts.

Provide Consequences for Persistent Misbehavior

Successful behavior change programs place far greater emphasis on rewarding appropriate student behavior than on paying attention to misbehavior. However, some misbehaviors cannot be completely ignored, particularly if they disrupt classroom learning. In these cases, consequences for inappropriate behavior must be spelled out and applied in a consistent manner.

Consequences may vary in degree and complexity. Simple consequences for misbehavior involve the failure to earn part or all of the agreed-upon reward or privilege. For example, a consequence for not completing assigned work would be the failure to earn the specified reward. More serious misbehavior may require additional consequences, such as a note or phone call to the student's parents describing the misbehavior, exclusion from class for a short time, or being removed from school for the day. Since some consequences may be relatively drastic, they should first be worked out with the student, building principal, and parents. The following techniques are sometimes used by teachers and administrators.

TIME-OUT

Time-out is a flexible procedure in which the student is removed from a desirable activity for brief periods of time (Gast and Nelson, 1977). The most simple application which may be quite useful for younger students is to require the student to place his or her head down and rest for two or three minutes. More elaborate procedures may involve moving the student to an isolated area of the room for a specific period or moving the student to the principal's office or similar location. The central purpose behind the use of time-out is to present an immediate consequence, removal from the group or the learning activity, for persistent misbehavior. The assumption is that such a brief period of removal will help the student learn what behaviors cannot be tolerated and will also help the student regain composure so as to be able to participate in the remainder of the learning activity.

PLANNED SUSPENSION

In some schools a more drastic consequence for persistent misbehavior is to send the student home for the remainder of the school day if misbehavior continues to exceed limits. This procedure cannot be arbitrarily applied. Rather, careful planning between the parents and building principal needs to be developed. Specific misbehaviors that require suspension need to be listed. These behaviors are generally ones that threaten the safety of the student or others (fighting, throwing desks or chairs, hitting others, and so on). Procedures for notifying parents need to be established, including who will call home and who will take the student home. Also, parents should be encouraged not to levy severe punishment at home in addition to the suspension, which by itself is a relatively drastic punishment. Loss of some privileges for the remainder of the day may, however, be applied. An example of the effectiveness of planned suspension is illustrated in the case of Bob Jones, an emotionally disturbed student introduced in Chapter 4.

BOB

Bob Jones spent half-days in a regular third-grade classroom and a self-contained class for emotionally disturbed children. The use of good behavior charts and privileges helped him to complete assigned work on time and without talking out of turn. However, on several occasions, Bob entered the regular classroom after recess in a rage, throwing chairs and flipping over several students who were already seated at their desks. On each of these occasions, the special education teacher was summoned to restrain Bob. These outbursts continued and his parents were consulted over the telephone. A plan was worked out that involved Bob's removal from school for the remainder of the school day if he demonstrated chair or desk throwing or attacked any student. The special education teacher was to remove Bob from the classroom and then call the parents, who were to come to school and take him home for the day. These consequences were discussed with Bob who indicated his understanding of the limits. On the very next school day, Bob again threw several chairs upon entering his classroom at the end of recess. The special education teacher removed him and called his parents. Bob became very anxious and promised not to throw chairs again if he could stay in school. Despite Bob's apologies, the consequences were carried out in as calm a manner as possible. The special class teacher emphasized that Bob knew the limits and consequences. As a result of this suspension, Bob did not throw chairs, desks, or any other objects for the remainder of the school year.

A related form of planned suspension is in-school suspension. Here, the student may be sent to a particular room that is designated for such a purpose and monitored by a teacher, administrator, aide, or secretary. The student is afforded little opportunity to interact with other students or adults, the message being that time to think about appropriate behavior and consequences for misbehavior is needed. This procedure lies between time-out and removal from school for the entire day. The procedure may be a useful compromise if parents are unable or unwilling to participate in a planned suspension program.

Several points about the use of consequences for persistent misbehavior need to be stressed. First, consequences should not be used in the absence of incentives for positive behavior. Remember, an important goal is to help students learn that appropriate behavior is more likely to receive attention and recognition than inappropriate behavior. Second, consequences should be clearly spelled out to the student at the beginning of a systematic behavior change program. The student should not only know what behaviors he or she is expected to demonstrate and what rewards there will be, but also what consequences will be applied for serious misbehaviors. Third, a system in which the student receives one or two warnings or reminders before applying the consequences may be instituted, except in cases of harmful behavior. However, keep in mind that too many reminders may result in too much attention being paid to misbehavior. Finally, if the student exceeds the limit and the consequence must be applied, do not accept pleas, promises, or requests for another chance. Giving in may inadvertently teach students that they are not responsible for their own actions.

Summary

In this chapter we have reviewed a variety of techniques to increase student motivation to complete academic tasks and improve classroom behavior. These techniques are applicable to all students but are particularly useful for students who are mentally retarded, emotionally disturbed, or learning disabled. Major ideas that were considered are listed below.

1. Many exceptional students need to have expectations presented in a clear, simple manner.

2. Consistent routines are useful for many students.

3. A range of techniques exists to help avoid the stress cycle.

4. Appropriate learning and classroom behavior should be reinforced.

5. Behavior charts, academic performance charts, home-school notes, good behavior games, and contracts are examples of systematic reward programs.

6. Students, parents, and other teachers can be involved in the development of some reward programs.

7. Consequences for persistent misbehavior should be spelled out and applied consistently.

Activities

1. Observe a classroom teacher to determine the types of techniques (e.g., active listening, hurdle help, planned ignoring, etc.) used in response to minor student misbehaviors. Describe the student misbehaviors, techniques used by teachers, and apparent outcomes.

2. If you are working in a practicum, develop a good behavior chart with one or more students. Implement the program over a two-week period and keep a daily record to determine whether the objectives are met.

3. Consider the following questions in analyzing a lesson that you teach: How clear were your expectations for appropriate behavior? How often did you use feedback and praise? What techniques to reduce the stress cycle did you use?

Study Questions

1. Why are clear expectations and consistent routines so important for students with behavior problems?

2. What is the stress cycle of misbehavior?

3. List and describe several of Long and Newman's techniques to avoid the stress cycle.

4. Define and provide examples of three types of rewards available to classroom teachers.

5. What ingredients should be contained in a good behavior chart?

6. How are contracts, home-school notes, and good behavior charts alike? How are they different?

7. List several guidelines for developing reward programs.

Questions for Further Thought

1. Think of your own experience as a student or a teacher. Can you recall stress cycles that caused feelings of frustration or anger to intensify? What was said during these episodes?

2. List some ways you could provide structure for students with behavior problems.

3. Some teachers argue that using rewards such as stickers or special activities is a form of bribery. What do you think of this argument?

Additional Resources

BOOKS

Blackham, G., and Silberman, A. *Modification of child and adolescents behavior* (3rd ed.). Belmont, California: Wadsworth, 1980.

Charles, C. M. *Building classroom discipline.* New York: Longman, 1981.

Kaplan, P., Kohfeldt, J., and Sturla, K. *It's positively fun—techniques in managing learning environments.* Denver, Colorado: Love, 1975.

Jones, V., and Jones, L. *Responsible classroom discipline.* Boston: Allyn & Bacon, 1981.

Chapter 12

Improving Interaction Between Exceptional and Nonexceptional Students

As you now may understand, teachers can take specific steps to help exceptional students improve their academic performance and classroom behavior. In this chapter our attention will turn to another important area regarding the placement of exceptional students in regular classrooms: how we can promote positive interaction among exceptional and nonexceptional students. In the first part of the chapter we will focus on ways to help students develop basic problem-solving skills. Such skills are necessary if exceptional students are to learn how to work effectively with others. Then, the focus will broaden to include all students as we examine strategies to promote acceptance and understanding of exceptional students.

Developing Self-Control and Problem-Solving Skills

Students with learning and behavior problems often use inappropriate strategies to solve conflicts and cope with frustration. The need to share materials; wait to take one's turn; work cooperatively with others; and solve everyday conflicts, such as deciding who can play what game, can cause stress. A few students react to this stress by becoming discouraged or relying on the teacher to solve the problem. Others channel their frustration into aggressive acts. While the behavior change programs discussed in Chapter 11 can help students improve specific behaviors, other measures can be taken to help students develop skill in solving problems and using self-control. Several of these measures are presented in this section. The techniques to be discussed can be used with all students but have particular value for those who are experiencing problems in the area of self-control.

TEACHING CONFLICT RESOLUTION SKILLS

Students can be taught specific techniques for solving some interpersonal conflicts that revolve around everyday problems, such as sharing ma-

---

Ways to solve conflicts

	Constructive ways: Try these.
Sharing	Try to agree to use the same item or game at the same time.
Taking turns	If you can't use the same item at the same time, try taking turns. One person can have the item for a while, and then the other person can have it.
Apologizing	If you accidentally hurt someone's feelings or do something that bothers that person, say you are sorry in a polite way.
Chance	Sometimes you can flip a coin to decide the outcome of a conflict.
Negotiating	Try to explain your feelings and work out some type of compromise. When you compromise, each person gives in a little bit.
Giving in	Sometimes you can let someone else have his or her way if you decide it is not important to you. You can find something else to do.
Getting help	Sometimes you need help to solve a conflict if you don't think it can be solved. A teacher or another adult might be able to help.
	Unconstructive ways: Avoid these.
Fighting	Letting yourself get so angry that you start hitting, screaming, or shouting.
Bullying	Trying to win a conflict by forcing someone else to give in.
Name calling	Getting upset and calling the other person a name.
Tattling	Telling on someone without first trying to solve the conflict.

FIGURE 12.1
Conflict resolution techniques

Source: Adapted from Palamores, U. and Logan, B., *A Curriculum on Conflict Management*, San Diego, California: Human Development Training Institute, Inc., 1975.

terials, taking turns, using games and other items, and avoiding arguments and fights due to basic misunderstandings. One program developed by Palamores and Logan (1975) helps students become aware of a variety of positive and negative conflict resolution techniques people often use. Through discussion, students are introduced to different ways to solve conflicts. Positive ways include sharing, taking turns, apologizing, explaining one's behavior and motives, getting help, and flipping a coin. Less constructive ways include fighting, tattling, name calling, and withdrawal. These techniques can be listed on a poster or bulletin board similar to the one in Figure 12.1.

Equipped with a basic awareness of conflict resolution techniques, students can be introduced to activities in which they have to suggest constructive ways to solve specific conflicts. For example, situations such as the following can be presented to students and then discussed.

TOM AND MARY

Tom and Mary both get to the last swing at the same time. Each one begins shouting, "I got here first, it's mine." After a lot of shouting, Tom feels as though he'll never get the swing so he pushes Mary away, calls her a baby and gets on the swing.

1. What happened to Tom and Mary?

2. What conflict techniques did they use?

3. If a teacher were watching Tom, what do you think would happen to him?

4. How do you think Mary may be feeling about Tom?

5. What are some positive conflict techniques that Tom and Mary could use to avoid a fight?

JOHN AND JERRY

John walks to the front of the room and accidentally knocks a book and several papers from Jerry's desk. Jerry stands up and says to John, "You did that on purpose, you rat." John then says, "I did not, you big baby." Jerry then pushes John and a fight begins.

1. What is apt to happen next to John and Jerry?

2. What conflict technique did John use when Jerry accidentally knocked a book from his desk?

3. What technique did John use when Jerry called him a rat?

4. What are some positive techniques each of these boys could have used to avoid angry feelings?

BOB AND FRANK

Bob and Frank are playing checkers. George is afraid of being left out, so he keeps telling each player where to move next. Both Bob and Frank are getting frustrated and angry with George and call him names.

1. What is apt to happen if Bob, Frank, and George continue their behavior? How might they feel about each other?

2. What conflict technique is George using?

3. What conflict technique are Bob and Frank using?

4. What are some positive techniques Bob and Frank could use?

5. What are some positive techniques George could use?

Practice in the use of specific conflict resolution techniques can be accomplished through role playing. As students identify constructive techniques to use in situations presented to them, they can be asked to demonstrate the technique through role playing. Many students with behavior problems need the extra practice that comes from observing another student demonstrating the appropriate behavior and then getting a chance to practice the behavior themselves.

A variety of conflict situations can be developed quite easily by observing common problems encountered by students and by modifying conflicts that appear in various stories. In developing a conflict situation, care should be taken to select conflicts that are capable of being resolved by using one or more of the conflict management techniques in Figure 12.1. Also, the situation must be described in enough detail to provide meaning to the students.

You can help students apply conflict resolution techniques to their own lives by encouraging them to practice good techniques in and out of school and by praising good efforts. For example, when several students are seen discussing how to solve a conflict rather than arguing or fighting, they should be praised for their efforts. Occasional class discussions can be held in which students are asked to describe examples of conflicts they faced and techniques they used to resolve or cope with the conflict. Although not every conflict will or can be resolved in a constructive manner, students should be encouraged to use positive techniques whenever possible.

CONDUCTING GROUP DISCUSSIONS

Regular group discussions are another means for helping students develop problem-solving skills. In these meetings students discuss specific problem behaviors they or others are trying to improve, specific ways they have used conflict resolution techniques, and other social or behavioral topics. One successful example of the benefits of such group discussions is described by Elias (1979). He had groups of emotionally disturbed boys ranging from seven to fifteen years old view and then discuss selections from the "Inside/Out" series. This educational television series presents a number of videotapes that depict various conflict situations and show children working through common problem situations, such as dealing with peer pressure, name calling, and coping with strong emotions. Follow-up discussion activities are developed for each videotape. Elias showed the videotapes and conducted follow-up discussions twice a week for a five-week period. Classroom teachers noted improvements in the behavior of students who viewed the videotapes and took part in the discussions.

Another group discussion technique to improve self-control is the "Pow Wow" (Kerr and Raglund, 1979). The Pow Wow is a brief discussion conducted daily for up to fifteen students at a time. The goal of the Pow Wow is to improve social and emotional behavior through group goal setting and peer feedback on the behavior of individuals in the group. The teacher initiates the procedures by listing one goal for improvement for each student. Goals focus on items such as "finishing work on time," "avoiding fights on the playground," "not hitting or pushing others" and "avoiding yelling at others." The actual Pow Wow is convened by the teacher at a set time each day. The teacher begins the session by selecting a student, reading his goal and then letting the student know whether or not he met his goal and why (e.g., "John, I think you met your goal; you finished your work on time," "Frank, I don't think you met your goal of avoiding a fight; you were fighting with someone on the playground"). Then, every other student is encouraged to give feedback to the student regarding whether or not the goal was met. After each student has given feedback, a vote is taken and if it is determined by the majority that the student's goal for the day has been met, a round of applause is given. Other than the negative peer feedback received, there are no consequences for failure to reach a goal.

When students begin to show interest in their daily performance as well as a basic understanding of areas in which they need to improve, they can be asked to establish daily performance goals for themselves. These goals do not supplant your own goals, but rather serve as a personal

My goals for today

Name _____ Date _____

Today I want to accomplish the following:
1. *All of my work;*
2. *Playing checkers or another game and not loose my temper.*
3.

Stephen
Signed (student)

FIGURE 12.2
Personal contract

commitment the student makes each day or week. An example of a completed daily contract appears in Figure 12.2. Daily contracts can be established each morning. You can help the student formulate reasonably clear goals. At the end of the day you can ask the student to evaluate his or her own performance.

Your role is critical in group meetings like the Pow Wow. It is important to keep the tone positive and constructive and to help students cope with the feelings of disappointment and possible anger when goals are not reached or when students receive negative feedback from peers. Kerr and Raglund (1979) offer several important suggestions to help maintain a constructive tone. (1) Develop a few basic rules for group discussion, such as having only one person talk at a time and listening carefully to each other. (2) Encourage students not to get angry or stop listening when told by others that they missed their goal. Here the student can be reminded that each group member is entitled to his or her opinion and that it is important to listen to everyone. (3) Remind students to provide feedback that relates only to the individual's goal. Pointing out other misbehaviors the student may have displayed is discouraged by a simple reminder to focus only on the student's goal. (4) Remove students from the group for the remainder of the session if they become disruptive and indicate an unwillingness to listen to others or provide honest feedback. The authors suggest that temporary removal from the group (time-out) is an effective tool for dealing with disruptive behavior.

BEHAVIORAL IMPROVEMENT PROJECTS

Closely related to the Pow Wow is the development of behavioral improvement projects. This technique is particularly useful for students who have a desire to improve aspects of their behavior. Each member of the class, including the teacher, identifies one behavior in need of improvement. Students select their own behaviors to change. You may help each student make his or her goal specific, such as "not yelling more than once a day," "finishing my math on time," "avoiding a fight," or "saying a positive thing to another student." Once goals are identified, students develop a written or verbal plan as to how they intend to accomplish their goal. Then each student keeps a personal check list each day that indicates whether his or her goal was met. You can review the check list with some students on a regular basis. From time to time class discussions can be conducted in which you and the students give progress reports regarding their behavioral improvement projects.

CRISIS MEETINGS

Despite your efforts to develop a positive, success-oriented classroom, disruptions in the way of fights, serious arguments, misunderstandings, and angry feelings occur from time to time. What can you do to help students (and yourself) cope with these situations? Crisis meetings are impromptu meetings to help students understand and resolve serious conflicts (Redl, 1971). These meetings, which involve only those students who were actually involved in the problem situation, can take place in the classroom, lunchroom, or on the playground. To conduct a crisis meeting, the following steps are usually taken:

1. *Cooling off.* Students should be given a few minutes to "cool off" if they are very upset and not ready to engage in thoughtful discussion. If necessary, students can be sent to their desks, a quiet area, or the principal's office.

2. *Rules.* You initiate the meeting, speaking in a calm manner. Ground rules for the discussion are set. These may include avoiding arguing and listening to what each person has to say.

3. *Active listening.* Here, you ask one student to describe the incident, what led up to the incident, and how he or she feels. You listen carefully and, where appropriate, rephrase what the student says to show understanding. You may ask other students to summarize or repeat what the first student said. Then you ask the other students to give their recollection of the incident. During the active listening phase, the main goal is to obtain a clarification of what happened and how the participants are feeling. Helping students clarify their feelings may also serve to drain off some of the anger or frustration the students may have.

4. *Problem exploration.* In this step, a discussion of the problem is considered in length. Questions such as how could the problem have been avoided, what can be done next time such a problem begins, and what consequences should occur this time for the students can be pursued.

Crisis meetings provide opportunities to help students develop self-awareness and learn new, more constructive ways to cope with problems. To help them reach these goals, you must be willing to take the time to hold these brief meetings and must also be careful to keep the tone as constructive as possible.

Promoting Acceptance of Exceptional Students

As we mentioned at the beginning of this book, simply placing exceptional students in a regular classroom is no guarantee that they will do well academically, behaviorally, or socially. Just as positive steps need to be taken to insure academic and behavioral growth, so too must you take direct measures to promote the active participation and acceptance of exceptional students. As Jones and his colleagues so aptly state ". . . often it is the understanding, support, and help received from non-handicapped classmates that are the critical variables for handicapped children's success in general education classes" (Jones, Sowell, Jones, and Butler, 1981). In this section we will examine specific techniques to increase such understanding, support, and help.

PLANNED PEER INTERACTION ACTIVITIES

Simply stated, planned peer interaction tasks are any activities or games that require students to work in a cooperative manner. By carefully placing exceptional and nonexceptional students in small work groups, you can help each to experience sharing, helping one another, and working together towards a common goal. An interesting body of research suggests, quite strongly, that such activities lead to more positive interactions between exceptional and nonexceptional students (Jones, Sowell, Jones and Butler, 1981; Leyser and Góttlieb, 1980) and create more positive attitudes towards exceptional and minority group students (Martino and Johnson, 1979; Aronson, 1975). The following activities are just a sample of the wide variety of tasks that can be developed to promote positive peer interaction.

1. *Pantomime.* In pantomime, students act out an event without props or words. Pairs of students can be given specific events to depict, such as playing catch, consoling a hurt friend, playing table tennis, or setting a table. As students gain skill in working cooperatively, skits that require increased cooperation can be developed. For example, groups of

four to six students can be assigned topics, such as playing a slow motion volleyball game, setting up a tent, or being at a surprise birthday party.

2. *Peer helping tasks.* Peer helping tasks require one student to demonstrate helping behaviors towards another student. For example, one member of a pair of students can be blindfolded and the sighted member given instructions to guide the partner in a safe, caring manner. A variety of tasks may be used, such as walking about the room, guiding the blindfolded student through a maze or series of obstacles using only verbal directions, and helping the blindfolded student acquire written information. Roles should be reversed during each of these activities to ensure that each member of the pair experiences the opportunity to be dependent and to provide help. Follow-up discussions can focus on what it was like to be blind or to be a helper and on good ways of providing help.

3. *Cooperative academic tasks and games.* In cooperative academic tasks and games, pairs or small groups of students work together to reach a common goal. At a basic level, two students with comparable academic skills may be given one page of twenty math problems. One student is instructed to complete the odd-numbered problems and the other to complete the even-numbered ones. Students are to help each other to produce accurate and neat responses, with the same grade earned by each student. As cooperative skills improve, more complex tasks can be assigned. One example of a complex cooperative task is jigsaw learning (Aronson, 1975). In jigsaw learning, each member of a small group is given one part of a lesson to study. Group members do not have access to each other's information. Rather, each student must present his or her information to the other group members in an informal lesson. The entire group is tested on all of the information, so students must rely on each other to pass the test or complete the assignment. You serve as a facilitator when necessary, helping groups to develop such cooperative skills as listening carefully to one another.

4. *Interview tasks.* Interview tasks require pairs of students to obtain information from each other using a predetermined set of questions you have selected. Questions can focus on academic or social areas. In the academic realm, students can quiz each other on important academic goals and thus help each other review important concepts. Interview questions can also focus on the application of knowledge (e.g., "describe two or three ways you can use your knowledge of levers and pulleys to help around your home") and on questions of value (e.g., "Who was your favorite character in the story we just read, and why?"). Pairs of students can also interview each other regarding personal, social, and contemporary topics. Questions such as the following can stimulate sharing and lively interaction:

- What would you do if you had a million dollars?

- If you were a king or queen, what are five laws you would establish?

- If you could control how others treat you, how would you have them act towards you?

- What do you hope to be doing when you are twenty-one years old?

- What are several important qualities of a good friend?

- Who is the most important person in your life?

- What are some important qualities of a good parent?

- When were you born, and what are your favorite foods, hobbies, TV programs, and books?

After devoting five or ten minutes to a question, interviewers switch roles and ask each other the same or a similar question. Then, volunteers can be asked to share their interview findings with the entire class.

5. *Skill sharing.* In skill sharing, pairs or small groups of students are formed with the purpose of sharing skills, hobbies, or interests. One student may take one or more activity periods to display products or actually teach specific skills to other interested students. Thus, exceptional students have an opportunity to be viewed as competent individuals with interesting skills to demonstrate or teach.

As in any group interaction task, the activity must be planned carefully and with sensitivity to all involved students. Pairs should be selected with caution. You should not hesitate to match the pairs or small groups yourself, making sure that exceptional students work with the more accepting, concerned students. As all students gain experience with these tasks, matching can be used to make sure that a variety of students work with each other. To reduce confusion and ensure that students practice constructive behaviors, appropriate behaviors should be reviewed at the beginning of each new task and then discussed at the end of the session (e.g., "What were some examples of helpful behaviors during today's blind walk activity?"). Thus, each positive peer interaction activity should be introduced by a brief statement of the goals of the activity, the helping behaviors to practice and then concluded with a follow-up discussion focusing on what the students experienced. Finally, to prevent saturating students, peer interaction tasks should be used sparingly, perhaps for a brief period each day or several times a week.

TEACHING STUDENTS ABOUT EXCEPTIONAL INDIVIDUALS

In addition to increasing the quantity and quality of interaction and participation of handicapped learners, direct steps can be taken to help all students acquire greater understanding and insight regarding the social and emotional needs of all individuals, exceptional and nonexceptional. Such understanding can serve as an important social learning objective in itself. In addition, increased sensitivity regarding the nature of various handicaps may help nonexceptional students respond to their handicapped peers in a more constructive manner. Several teaching approaches to promote understanding of and acceptance of individual needs can be used.

Magic Circle Discussions   A variety of commercial programs have been developed to help improve human relations and foster self-awareness and self-esteem. One program, The Human Development Program (Bessell, 1972), can be used to help all students become more accepting of themselves and others. The program is based on the magic circle, a special time for sharing and listening carefully to one another's feelings and ideas. The program contains a series of carefully sequenced discussion topics and activities centered around three interrelated goals: Awareness, Mastery, and Social Interaction.

Awareness activities focus on helping students clarify their own feelings and thoughts and become more understanding towards others. Typical discussion topics include these:

- Good feelings that we have
- What I like and dislike about school
- What is real and what is fantasy
- Real and exaggerated fears

Mastery concerns help students gain a greater appreciation of their own strengths and weaknesses. Discussion topics include the following:

- What is self-control
- Something I'm very proud of that I can do
- Something I want to do for myself but don't know how

Social interaction topics focus on improving interaction with peers and adults using discussion topics such as these:

- A way in which I was able to help someone when he or she needed help
- Something I did that was appreciated by another person
- A time when somebody made me do something I didn't want to do
- How I included somebody in an activity

Magic circle discussions can be held daily or several times a week. Discussion periods typically last for twenty to thirty minutes.

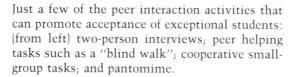

Just a few of the peer interaction activities that can promote acceptance of exceptional students: (from left) two-person interviews; peer helping tasks such as a "blind walk"; cooperative small-group tasks; and pantomime.

You usually initiate the discussion by reviewing simple ground rules and then introducing the topic. For example, you might say: "Today our topic is including people in activities. Let's each think of a time when we included someone in an activity. See if you can describe what you did and then tell how you might have made that person feel and how you felt. Who would like to go first?" The effective communication skills suggested by Gordon, particularly listening carefully and reflecting feelings, are practiced. You should be careful not to turn these into amateur therapy sessions that probe into home or family matters or place students in the hot seat. Instead, emphasis should be placed on creating a climate of sharing, mutual respect, and problem solving. Each student should have an opportunity to respond without being forced to.

Case Analysis Situations   Case analysis situations are brief written descriptions of human problems and dilemmas that are presented to stu-

dents for discussion. After presenting the problem, students are asked to discuss how the characters may be feeling, why they may have behaved as they did, and what other ways the problem could be solved. The major purpose of these techniques is to help students become more sensitive to the needs of others and develop constructive problem solving skills.

Case analysis situations can be taken from novels, history, or current events, as well as from actual problems experienced by students in the classroom. Sample topics include:

SALLY

Sally is a pretty lonely third-grader. Nobody in class gives her any attention. Some kids even make fun of her because she comes to school in old, dirty clothes. Sally is also not very good in reading or math. Some kids call her dumb, ugly, or stupid. Sally sometimes goes home and cries by herself because she is unhappy. Suppose Sally were in your class.

Questions to ask:

1. Have you ever felt lonely? What made you feel that way?

2. How do you feel when people make fun of you or criticize things you can't change?

3. What could the other class members do to help Sally feel better?

4. What things about a person should we consider other than his or her clothes and other material things?

5. What are some needs people have regardless of their wealth?

THE YOUNG SOLDIER

In *The Red Badge of Courage*, the young soldier found it impossible to fight when he first entered the battle. He loved life and resented destroying it. He was afraid and sought personal safety. Eventually he felt guilty for withdrawing from his military duty. In time, he was stimulated to make a commitment.

Questions to ask:

1. What might have led to his change in behavior?

2. Do people necessarily have to change their feelings and attitudes in order to change their own overt behavior? Explain.

3. How would you describe the feelings of the young soldier?

4. How would you feel if you were in such a situation as the young soldier?

5. What would you do?

TOM

Tom usually does poor school work and doesn't have any close friends. He talks in class when others are trying to study, and he frequently gets into trouble with the teacher and with other students because he is so aggressive.

Questions to ask:

1. What might have been some of Tom's needs?

2. What might be some acceptable ways that Tom could get attention from other students and the teacher?

3. How might he get approval and affection?

As in the case of magic circles and other discussions, you should use effective communication skills and avoid excessive probing of individual students. If a case analysis situation is based on an actual problem experienced by one or more students, care should be taken to avoid embarrassing the individuals. If necessary, names can be changed and situations modified slightly to remove attention from the actual students.

Simulation Simulation is a form of role playing in which individuals experience what it is like to be in a real situation. Since it is very difficult for people without handicaps to actually feel what it is like to have a disability, you can create activities to help students experience what it is like to be blind, deaf, learning disabled, emotionally disturbed, a slow learner, or physically handicapped. Oftentimes, these activities lead to increased understanding and acceptance of exceptional individuals. Typical simulation activities include the following:

1. Blindfold students and have them experience a number of different tasks and activities, such as walking about the classroom or school, eating lunch, participating in recess, "watching" a film, and participating in a class lesson. Teams of students can be formed with one member serving as a guide and the other as the blind student. After a designated period of time students can switch roles.

2. Simulate deafness by having students wear ear plugs and try to participate in a class discussion. Have students listen to a movie with the sound at a barely audible level.

3. Have students try walking on crutches, using only one limb, or wearing a leg brace to simulate specific physical disabilities.

4. Help students experience coordination and fine motor difficulties by wearing gloves or mittens and trying to tie shoelaces, button shirts, and cut with scissors.

5. Have students discover what it is like to have a severe reading problem or learning disability by giving them a paragraph to read out loud

with selected words presented in mirror images and other words improperly spaced, as in the following example:

John went ot eJH store ot uby
a an annivezary card Forzid mother.

6. Have students experience being a slow learner by giving them rapid and complicated directions to a difficult task. Such tasks may also be used to simulate feelings of frustration and failure experienced by some emotionally disturbed children.

7. Help students to understand rejection, being ignored, or being overly protected because of a handicap. For example, a brief role playing situation may be created in which a sighted person does far too much for a blind or retarded individual, or a student is left out of a game and told to wait on the sidelines. After the role play, students can discuss what happened and then identify more constructive responses.

Simulation activities need to be introduced carefully to make sure that students understand what they are to do. Prior to beginning each activity, the purpose should be stated and ground rules for participation should be clarified. After students have had an opportunity to participate, a follow-up discussion should be conducted in which students are encouraged to share feelings they experienced while simulating a particular handicap. Typical questions for discussion include the following: What feelings did you experience? What did your partner do to help you? What did you learn about the handicap? How would your life be different if you had this kind of handicap? What would be some useful ways of helping people with this handicap?

Aids and Appliances   In addition to participating in simulation activities, students can explore the types of aids handicapped people sometimes use. Learning to finger spell and use basic signs, exploring hearing aids, Braille-writers, crutches, braces, wheelchairs, and other equipment can help develop a realistic understanding of the needs of many handicapped individuals. Developing such an understanding will go a long way towards helping students react in an accepting way to people who require such devices.

Reverse Mainstreaming   In reverse mainstreaming nonexceptional students do volunteer work in special education settings for younger or less capable exceptional students. The nature of the volunteer work can vary. A student may be a tutor, a playground assistant, or an assistant physical education instructor (Folio and Norman, 1981). One program entitled "Project Special Friend" (Poorman, 1980) had older elementary aged volunteers work with younger, moderately retarded students who were placed in a full-time special class. After an orientation period, which focused on the needs of retarded children, the volunteers worked with individuals in a variety of activities, such as putting puzzles together; playing ball; gross motor skills, such as jumping and hopping; self-help skills such as dressing, eating, and drinking; and other activities. Half of the volunteers worked for thirty minutes every Monday and Wednesday morning and the other half worked for the same time on Tuesday and Thursday morning. Ongoing supervision was provided by the special classroom teacher.

The benefits of reverse mainstreaming are clear for all students. Exceptional learners receive individualized and often very skillful help from their older volunteers. The attitudes of nonexceptional children often change for the better. As Poorman (1980) notes, "The attitude change throughout the school was remarkable after the volunteer program was underway. A positive attitude definitely evolved as a result of the new project and the opportunities for direct interaction with the special children. The elementary teachers found that the students' reactions toward each other had changed for the better also. The students seemed to be more aware of their classmates' problems, and a willingness to help, or at least to understand the feelings of others, was more evident."

LITERATURE AND COMMERCIAL KITS

Young people's literature represents a rich source of material to help students become aware of the unique needs, feelings, and experiences of exceptional children and adults. Stories can be read to children or made available for older students to select for themselves. For example, Behavioral Publications, Inc., has developed a series of psychologically relevant children's books. One book, *Please Don't Say Hello*, by Phyllis Gold, explains autism to seven- to thirteen-year-olds through a moving story in which Eddie, a nine-year-old autistic boy, and his brother arrive in a new neighborhood and are faced with making friends and winning understanding. Another title, *One Little Girl*, by Joan Fassler, reveals the feelings of a slow learner and her growing awareness of her own unique strengths. A bibliography of selected young people's books appears at the end of various chapters in this text.

Commercial kits represent another source of information to help increase students' understanding of exceptional individuals. Kits often

TABLE 12.1
Commercial kits to promote understanding of exceptional individuals

Be My Friend. Canadian Council on Children and Youth, 323 Chapel, Ottawa, Ontario KIN 722.

Disabilities: Physically handicapped, hearing impaired, speech impaired, visually impaired, mentally retarded.

Stories, games, and illustrations are included in this coloring book for grades 2-3.

Everybody Counts! A Workshop Manual to Increase Awareness of Handicapped People. J. M. Ward, R. N. Arkell, H. G. Dahl, and J. H. Wise. The Council for Exceptional Children, 1920 Association Dr., Reston, Virginia 22091.

Disabilities: Covers all disabilities

This workshop is designed as an initial experiential learning strategy to assist groups toward a fuller understanding of the needs and desires of disabled individuals. It includes a discussion guide for twenty-five simulation activities that allow participants to feel what it is like to be disabled. Included are an eighty-page manual and a tape cassette.

Kids Come in Special Flavors. The Kids Come in Special Flavors Co., P. O. Box 562, Dayton, Ohio 45405.

Disabilities: Learning disabled, hearing impaired, mentally retarded, visually impaired, cerebral palsy, spina bifida.

This kit, which is suitable for grades K-12, contains a book of simulation activities, a cassette, and materials for simulation activities.

My New Friend Series. Eye Gate Media, Jamaica, NY 11435.

Disabilities: Hearing impaired, visually impaired, physically handicapped, mentally retarded.

This kit contains four filmstrips and cassettes.

What Is a Handicap? BFA Educational Media, 2211 Michigan Ave., Santa Monica, CA 90404.

Disabilities: Orthopedically handicapped, communication disordered, hearing impaired, emotionally disturbed, multiply handicapped.

This kit, suitable for grades 4-6, contains six duplicating masters, four cassette tapes, and four filmstrips.

What If You Couldn't? Selective Educational Equipment, Inc., 3 Bridge St., Newton, MA 02195.

Disabilities: Visual impairments, hearing impairments, mental retardation, learning disabilities, emotional problems, orthopedic handicaps.

This series contains a teacher's guide for each of the above-mentioned disabilities. Included are sample lessons, simulation activities, and follow-up readings for children and adults. The program is geared to elementary-aged children.

contain filmstrips and audio tapes that introduce people with various handicaps. In addition, many kits contain follow-up discussion and simulation activities. A listing of some available kits appears in Table 12.1.

Summary

We have examined a variety of techniques to improve interaction between exceptional and nonexceptional students. Two broad themes were introduced: improving self-control and problem-solving skills of exceptional students and promoting acceptance of exceptional students. Major ideas that were introduced include the following:

1. Direct steps can be taken to improve interaction and acceptance of exceptional learners.

2. Some students with learning and behavior problems need to learn self-control and problem-solving skills to help them interact successfully with their peers.

3. A variety of strategies can be used to improve self-control and develop problem-solving skills. Included are conflict resolution training, group discussion activities, and crisis meetings.

4. Planned peer interaction activities can be used to promote interaction between exceptional and nonexceptional students.

5. Peer interaction activities should be planned carefully. Care should be devoted to the matching of students.

6. A number of approaches can be used to increase understanding of exceptional individuals. These include magic circle discussions, case analysis situations, simulation activities, experimentation with aids and appliances, reverse mainstreaming, and literature and commercial kits.

Activities

1. Conduct a lesson with school-age children on conflict resolution techniques using the procedures outlined in this chapter.

2. Develop, conduct, and evaluate several activities to foster peer interaction.

3. Read several children's books that focus on handicaps. Begin an annotated bibliography of books that can be used in your teaching.

Study Questions

1. Describe a general procedure by which students can be taught conflict resolution skills.

2. Why might role playing appropriate conflict resolution skills benefit students with behavior problems?

3. Describe the purpose and procedures involved in the Pow Wow.

4. List the steps involved in a crisis meeting.

5. Describe four types of peer interaction activities.

6. How can case analysis techniques help students become more sensitive to others?

7. Discuss how simulation can be used to increase sensitivity to exceptional students.

8. What steps can teachers take to avoid confusion when using planned peer interaction and simulation activities?

Questions for Further Thought

1. Why is it crucial to use good communication skills when conducting crisis meetings, group discussions, and similar activities?

2. How much time can be devoted legitimately to activities to improve interaction and foster self-control? Will the use of such activities occur at the expense of academic goals?

Additional Resources

BOOKS

Fagan, S., Long, N., and Stevens, N. *Teaching children self-control.* Columbus, Ohio: Charles E. Merrill, 1975.

Barnes, E., Berrigan, C., and Bicklen, D. *What's the difference? Teaching positive attitudes toward people with disabilities.* Syracuse, New York: Human Policy Press, 1978.

PART V
COMMUNICATION, SENSORY, AND PHYSICAL PROBLEMS

As you have seen earlier in this text, students enter the classroom with a wide range of abilities and behaviors. In the past, students who deviated significantly from the norm in learning and/or behavior characteristics could be excluded from public school programs. Recently, however, litigation and legislation have mandated public education services for handicapped students.

Mental retardation, emotional disturbance, and learning disabilities are not the only handicapping conditions present in the classroom. Speech and language, hearing and vision, and physical and health problems may also be present in the classroom environment and have an impact on the provision of instruction. Educational programs for students with these problems may include specialized compensatory approaches to help them overcome their particular disabilities. In addition, students who have communication, sensory, and physical problems may present learning and behavior problems just as other exceptional students do in the classroom. The educational plans for these students will include specialized training and materials as well as program prescriptions resulting from the problem-solving model.

Communication problems — speech and language disabilities — are present in many classroom settings. Some students are unable to form and pronounce words correctly. Others are unable to convey ideas orally in a meaningful fashion. The development of speech and language is traced in Chapter 13, as well as the problems encountered in each area.

This is accompanied by a discussion of the educational needs of students with speech and language problems, and a description of the role of the classroom teacher and the specialist in providing services for students with communication disorders.

Many students in school have hearing or vision problems. Relatively few of these students, however, have such severe hearing or vision problems that they require specialized training or curriculum modifications. The types of problems encountered by these students, areas of specialized training, and suggestions for the classroom teacher are presented in Chapter 14.

In Chapter 15, we present information on some of the more common physical and health problems present in school. Various neurological, medical, and terminal problems are discussed. Specific forms of treatment are presented when appropriate. You are alerted to the roles of several professionals who work in this area, and you are presented with general information on assisting the student in the classroom.

While these students may have some unique educational needs as a result of their disabilities, these can often be met in the classroom with proper training, stimulation, and educational experiences. When the student also has learning and behavior problems, you should draw upon the process and techniques presented in Chapters 6 through 12.

Chapter 13
Speech and Language Disorders

One of the unique characteristics of human beings is their facility for speech and language. Although thoughts and ideas can be conveyed through drawings, paintings, gestures, and written material, the use of speech is taken for granted in daily living. Speech is an accepted and efficient means of communicating with others, expressing concerns, and developing human relationships.

Some students in school have difficulty in the area of speech and language. They may be unable to formulate and say words in an accepted manner. Other students may be unable to select and phrase the words necessary to convey their thoughts to listeners. Students with speech and language disorders require specialized programs to assist them in the development of oral communication.

The Acquisition of Speech and Language

Speech and language are terms that are often used synonymously, but actually describe two separate parts of oral communication. Speech refers to the actual sounds and words a person produces. Language refers to the expression of ideas. Learning to speak and to express ideas in a meaningful way is a complex process requiring coordination of the speech mechanisms (tongue, mouth, and jaw) to form words and the cognitive development necessary to understand and produce language.

TABLE 13.1
Development of speech

Stage	Approximate age	Description
birth cry	infancy	The first inhalation of air and resulting sound; crying; cooing.
babbling	two months	Random vocal play (infant makes noises).
lallation	five to six months	Repetition of heard sounds (child repeats sounds he makes).
echolalia	nine months	Imitation of heard speech (model produces sound; child repeats same sound).
true speech	twelve months	Association of word meaning with word.

The acquisition of speech and language is a learned process that begins with the birth cry and is continually refined throughout the lifetime of the individual (Van Riper, 1972). The early vocal experiences of a child, including cooing, whimpering, and crying, set the course for later speech. The stages of speech development are presented in Table 13.1.

Most children acquire speech in the pattern presented in Table 13.1. They progress from random vocal play (testing and experimenting with new sounds) to speech (words associated with meaning). When any of the stages is interfered with, the development of speech may be interrupted or delayed. Children who are deaf or hard of hearing utter a birth cry and babble up to approximately six months of age, but do not progress beyond the stages where imitation is required for further speech development; they are unable to hear their own voice or that of other models.

The acquisition of speech in young children can be promoted in many ways. Children should be allowed to play and experiment with sounds both in private and in the company of others. Adults and older children who interact with the child should model appropriate speech; that is, they should use speech sounds correctly and speak normally rather than using "baby talk" as the child develops speech. The child should be able to complete sentences without interruption. The child should be stimulated to speak in his or her environment through a wide variety of experiences and activities accompanied by adult speech (Weiss and Lillywhite, 1976).

Language develops concurrently with speech. The two, speech and language, become intermingled as the child progresses beyond true speech into the development of vocabulary and language or patterns used to express ideas. There are three types of language: receptive, inner, and expressive language; the three are interrelated so the absence of or deficiency in any one area diminishes the ability to utilize effectively oral and written forms of communication.

Receptive language refers to the comprehension of stimuli in the environment as they are paired with spoken language. Since the receiving and understanding of spoken language precedes the development of spoken language, it is important to help students develop a large receptive language vocabulary.

Inner language involves the internal process of associating stimuli with meaning (Weiss and Lillywhite, 1976). As a result of previous stimulation, this capacity for translating stimuli into usable information continually expands the student's level of receptive and expressive language. Some students seem to have good receptive language or comprehension of spoken words but experience difficulty in using words. This difficulty may result from deficits in the internal processing of information, limiting the student's utilization of language. Of the three areas of language, inner language is the least well understood and the most difficult to assess.

Expressive language is the utilization of words to convey thoughts and ideas to others. The selection of words and the order in which the words appear in sentences can enhance or detract from the message sent to the listener. Expressive language can further be subdivided into the areas of semantics, syntax, and phonology. Expressive language disorders are discussed in the next section.

The acquisition of language can be promoted in many ways. Children should be bombarded with the names of objects and actions when they are young. Language should be associated with objects and activities to increase the child's receptive vocabulary and to give the child the words to use for expression at a later time. When the child engages in an activity, parents or other models should describe the activity and materials to the child. This form of stimulation should occur with young children in all situations. It may also assist older students in the internalization of new vocabulary and concepts. Parents and teachers should be realistic in their expectations of language development. Until a child internalizes a word, for example, he or she does not use the word in his vocabulary. Children should be given enough opportunities to hear and practice language so that they can begin to use it effectively themselves. The development of language is outlined in Table 13.2.

Speech and language, then, usually develop in a somewhat orderly fashion in children. Although children do not learn the same words in the same order, they do progress through a series of stages when acquiring speech and language skills. Alert parents and teachers can enhance the development of these skills in young children and in students in school as they learn new vocabulary and concepts in different content areas.

TABLE 13.2
Development of language

Approximate age	Description
8–10 months	Attaches meaning to words, associating phrases with experiences.
10–12 months	Comprehends what people say through environmental cues. Produces first words.
12–18 months	Generalizes words to classes of objects. Uses single words.
2 years	Combines words into two-word phrases.
2 1/2–3 years	Uses three-word combinations. Adds noncrucial words to speech. Begins to use simple, grammatically correct sentences.
5–6 years	Produces grammatically correct sentences.

They can also be alert to any lack of development and obtain the services of a specialist as soon as trouble is detected.

Defining Speech and Language Disorders

Students in school may have speech problems, language problems, or a combination of the two. It is important to recognize the types of problems the student may have in each area and the characteristics of these students. Since speech and language are two distinct, although interrelated, areas the two types of problems will be handled separately.

SPEECH DISORDERS

Speech is the means for expressing language. It is the physical act of forming and saying words. Speech is considered defective ". . . when it deviates so far from the speech of other people that it calls attention to itself, interferes with communication, or causes its possessor to be maladjusted" (Van Riper, 1972). Speech should be of concern to the classroom teacher, then, when it affects negatively the communication or emotional wellbeing of a student. There are three types of speech problems that are of concern to the classroom teacher: articulation disorders (which are the most prevalent), voice disorders, and fluency problems.

Articulation Disorders   Articulation refers to the actual formation of speech sounds. An articulation disorder is present when the student cannot form speech sounds correctly or does not use the speech sounds correctly in words. Articulation problems can be further subdivided into four areas: omissions, substitutions, distortions, and additions.

An omission occurs when a sound or sounds are not pronounced during speech. Rather than "I see the sky," the student might say, "I ee the ky." Here, the student has omitted the /s/ sound. A substitution is the replacement of one sound for another, such as "The wabbit wan up the woad" (substitution of /w/ for /r/). A distortion is the inaccurate formation of a sound. For example, the student might make a sound in the back of his throat in place of the correct sound for the letter "g." Additions occur when students say sounds that are irrelevant to a particular word. For example, the student may say, "axtel" for "axel."

Let's look in on a second grade teacher who is questioning a student about a passage from a story. See if you can identify any articulation errors.

Dan: Well, he wan down the woad, yooking for a cat. He found the cat and ave it back to the man.

Mrs. Brown: Good, Dan, that's exactly what Carl did. He ran to find the cat and gave it back to the owner. Now tell me this: Do you think Carl was glad he found the cat?

Dan: Yes. He yiked the owner and was sad when the cat wan away. He felt ood hyeping someone else.

Mrs. Brown: That's right. Carl liked to help people. Let's read the next paragraph now.

As you can see, Dan does make some articulation errors. If you noted that he substituted /w/ for /r/ and /y/ for /l/, you were correct. Dan also omitted the sound /g/ altogether. Although Mrs. Brown did not specifically correct Dan's errors, she did model the correct way of saying most of the words Dan mispronounced.

Many preschool children have articulation that is not fully developed. Some speech sounds may not appear in some children's speaking repertoire until later years. Preschool and primary grade teachers should be aware of the development of speech sounds and structure the learning environment to reinforce the acquisition of these sounds. A speech improvement program in primary grade classes is an important component of the curriculum. The student who displays serious articulation errors from approximately the third grade forward should be referred for a speech evaluation.

Voice Disorders   A second type of speech problem is a voice disorder. Voice refers to the characteristics of loudness, pitch, and quality, which make each person sound unique. Disturbances in any of these areas can result in speech problems that interfere with communication and that may cause some emotional problems. Several types of voice problems are described below.

1. *Pitch.* Pitch is the highness or lowness of the voice. A person with an exceptionally high- or low-pitched voice would have a voice problem.

2. *Loudness.* Loudness refers to the strength or weakness of the voice. A person who always speaks in a whisper or who talks in a voice so loud that it is uncomfortable for the listener may need help in learning to speak at a more desirable level.

3. *Flexibility.* Flexibility is the variability in one's voice. A monotone voice is an example of limited flexibility.

4. *Quality.* The quality of a voice refers to the characteristics that make each voice unique. A very nasal voice, non-nasal voice, raspy voice, or thin voice may all be considered voice quality disturbances.

5. *Duration.* Duration refers to the length of time a sound is held. Some people speak so quickly that individual sounds run together and make the speech unintelligible to the listener. Some people extend single sounds to such a degree that it is difficult to understand their speech. These are examples of problems in duration.

Voice disorders are not as common as articulation problems. A voice disorder may be the result of a physiological disorder, such as nodules on the vocal folds, swollen adenoids, cleft palate, or disturbances in the soft palate. Voice problems may also be the result of psychological conditions. Students with disorders in this area should be referred to a specialist for diagnosis and treatment.

Fluency Problems   Some people experience difficulty in the fluency of their speech. They may have extended hesitations as they talk or they may repeat sounds when trying to communicate with others. A common problem in speech fluency is stuttering. Stuttering occurs when there are prolonged hesitations in the speech and a repetition of some sounds, syllables, and/or words during speech. A student who stutters may speak like this: "D-d-d-d-d-d-did you s-s-s-s-see the cat?" Since stuttering may lead to intense frustration and anxiety over speech, care should be taken to minimize situations that are threatening to the student. Students who stutter should be referred to the speech and language pathologist for diagnosis and treatment.

LANGUAGE DISORDERS

Language is the reception and expression of ideas. While much attention has been given to speech disorders, the area of language is a relatively new field of study. Research is being conducted in the area of language (receptive, inner, and expressive) and its relationship to other thought processes. Many of the language and academic problems students experience in school are a result of the inappropriate use of words (semantic problems) or simplistic or inappropriate word order in sentences (syntax).

Students may have language difficulties as a result of deprivation, developmental delays, or learning disabilities. A child who is deprived of physical nourishment and intellectual stimulation will not acquire language skills, as other children do. This child may enter school with little language and may not have acquired the foundations upon which language can be built. By the same token, those students who have developmental delays as a result of retardation or physical and health problems may exhibit delayed language development. Finally, you may have some students who come from home environments where language stimulation has been provided and who seem to be progressing normally in all areas but language-related skills. These students may have a learning problem that is impeding the development of appropriate language skills.

Semantics   The term semantics refers to the meanings of words and the relationship of these words to other words in sentences. Since words often have more than one meaning and since several words may describe a single characteristic, it is easy to see why some students in school have difficulty in this area. Students who come from homes where language is used in a simple form (limited vocabularies with little verbal interaction) or whose environments do not allow for the exploration of new ideas and concepts will have more limited vocabularies than students from homes where such stimulation occurs on a regular basis. The language problems these students present in school may include limited vocabularies, inappropriate use of terms, or slow acquisition of new terms. Because semantics refers to the meaning and relationship of words, there can be a wide variety of errors that students make in this area.

The acquisition of language is a developmental process. Experiences, actual usage, and the expansion of conceptual knowledge increase the language skills a student possesses. Most young children may make semantic errors as they learn and test new words and meanings. These types of errors should not be of concern unless they persist beyond the time appropriate for development of such word usage in age peers. On the other hand, young children who have very limited vocabularies and are unfamiliar with word usage may need attention at a relatively early age. Since the acquisition and use of semantics is a developmental process, it is important to assess whether the student is demonstrating skills appropriate for his or her age level and, if not, to consult with a specialist in this area.

Syntax   Syntax is the order in which the parts of speech can occur and the relationship among the parts of speech in a sentence. Syntax corresponds to grammar: the rules people use for combining words into phrases and sentences. The development of syntax begins with the first words spoken by a child and continues through the acquisition and use of rules governing complete sentences.

Many children come to school with appropriate language patterns as a result of experiences and modeling in the home. Some children, though, have not learned standard syntax or have used a different set of rules governing language. They are unable to express ideas in sentences using correct syntax, or they use sentence structures that do not conform to our notions of "standard English."

As with the development of semantics, syntax develops systematically. Children begin very early to use one- and two-word sentences to communicate ideas, wants, and needs. From these relatively short utterances, they progress to complete sentences. Following this, older children acquire the rules allowing them to expand their language patterns to complex sentences. Through instruction, observation, practice, and maturation, most students become proficient in the use of the language.

It should be noted here that not all children acquire syntactic rules in the same order. It is also important to note that some dialects use different word patterns and sentence structures. Appropriate syntax, then, may vary from region to region in a country or among different races or ethnic groups in a particular area. This should be kept in mind when developing language programs and referring students for assistance from speech and language pathologists.

The following is a case study of a student who has experienced speech and language problems in school:

CANDY

Candy entered school with some speech and language problems. She was able to communicate her needs to the teacher through a system of speech and gestures. She had entered kindergarten with many of the skills necessary for instruction in reading and had recently indicated an interest in learning to read. Her teacher, Miss Philips, was concerned that, while Candy had the prerequisite skills for reading, her speech problems were so severe that it would be difficult to determine her performance on oral reading tasks. Miss Philips began to record the specific problems she felt Candy presented.

Miss Philips began her observations of Candy during free play activities. She found that Candy did not say many of the sounds needed for speech. She was not saying these sounds at all: /s/, /y/, /l/, and /t/. In addition, she distorted the sounds /k/ and /g/ when they occurred at the end of a word. In order to make her needs known, Candy had developed a system of substituting sounds for the ones she did not say, causing many of her vocal utterances to be totally undecipherable to all but her parents and closest friends. For example, she would substitute /b/ for /v/ when /v/ appeared in the initial position in words and /w/ for /v/ in all other positions in words.

Miss Philips recorded all of her observations of Candy's speech and referred Candy to the Pupil Evaluation Team for a speech evaluation. The speech and language pathologist was able to utilize the observations of Miss Philips to plan his assessment program.

CHARACTERISTICS

Students who have speech problems usually do not differ significantly from the norm in academic and social areas, although they may experience some frustration when attempting to communicate with others if their speech problem is so severe that it interferes with successful communication. This frustration may result in some emotional or behavior conflicts that should be resolved along with the remediation of the speech deficit. In some cases, students with speech disorders may be hearing impaired; the lack of hearing results in the inability to produce speech sounds.

Students who have language problems, on the other hand, may differ from the normal student in several areas. Some language problems occur as a result of low intelligence. The acquisition and use of language is associated with intellectual development. Therefore, many retarded students may have language deficits. Deaf and hard-of-hearing students may also perform at a lower level than age peers on tasks that rely on language skills. These students may score at such a low level on tests of intelligence and have such severe deficits in reading comprehension, written language, and oral communication that they may even be misdiagnosed as mentally retarded.

Severe language problems may interfere with the development of social and emotional skills. Many students will shy away from peers who have not developed appropriate language skills or who use language in a manner different from that of others. If academic, emotional, and social problems exist as a result of impaired language, the educational program designed for the student should include goals and objectives in these areas.

PREVALENCE

Approximately 5% of the school population is classified as having speech and/or language deficits (Kirk and Gallagher, 1979). Since services in the past have focused on the remediation of articulation problems, most of the students served have had speech problems. Recently, however, the proportion of students with language problems who are being served is increasing because of increased emphasis on language development. This shift could change the estimates of students receiving services in this area in the future.

Identification of Speech and Language Disorders

Speech and language problems can be identified through formal tests, informal tests, and observations of the student's receptive and expressive language. You can provide important information on the occurrence of problems in the classroom setting by sharing observations and anecdotal records made on students about whom you are concerned. The speech and language pathologist may use informal techniques much like those of the classroom teacher, as well as formal tests, to assist in the diagnosis of specific speech and language problems.

FORMAL TESTS

Formal tests have been developed to enable speech and language pathologists to assess the student's articulation, receptive language, and expressive language. These tests are usually administered individually. The tests can be used diagnostically to identify specific speech and language deficits. Since there are a number of tests available in each area, representative tests have been selected for discussion.

Articulation   Articulation tests assess the student's ability to produce various speech sounds. The clinician asks the student to produce speech sounds in isolation, in words, and in sentences. The Goldman-Fristoe Test of Articulation (Goldman and Fristoe, 1969) is an example of a test used to assess articulation skills. The student is expected to name pictures or answer questions about pictures to provide the examiner with the opportunity to assess consonant sounds in the beginning, medial (middle), and end positions in words. The examiner also reads short selections to the student, provides the student with pictures related to the selections, and asks the student to recount the details of the selections. In this way, the examiner is able to assess the production of the sounds in various positions in words as well as in more complex oral communication settings.

Receptive Language   Receptive language, or the understanding of what is heard, can be assessed using formal diagnostic instruments. The Peabody Picture Vocabulary Test (Dunn, 1980) and the Boehm Test of Basic

Concepts (Boehm, 1971) may be used to determine the extent that students understand vocabulary and the conceptual knowledge of words respectively. The student is asked to look at pictures and select the example that illustrates the word given by the examiner. The information derived from tests like these can assist the examiner in determining the receptive language level of the student in relationship to peers and plan remedial programs to increase language comprehension if necessary.

Expressive Language   Expressive language can also be measured through the use of formal diagnostic tests administered by a speech and language pathologist. The Developmental Sentence Analysis (Lee, 1974) can be used to assess syntax in spontaneous speech. The Test of Language Development (TOLD) (Newcomer and Hammill, 1977) may be used to assess vocabulary and syntax. This particular test not only provides information on expressive language, but also gives a measure of the student's receptive language and articulation. Because of the range of speech and language areas covered in the TOLD, it is often used by personnel in school districts to identify student strengths and weaknesses in speech and language.

Another test of language frequently administered by speech and language pathologists is the Illinois Test of Psycholinguistic Abilities (Kirk, McCarthy, and Kirk, 1968). This test was designed to measure the child's ability to understand, process, and produce verbal and nonverbal language. It provides the specialist with information on a variety of language skills.

INFORMAL ASSESSMENT

A number of specialists and nonspecialists within a school system might contribute to the assessment of speech and language in a student through the use of informal observation techniques and through structured informal assessments. Observations might be made by the classroom teacher, the school principal, and any others who notice that a student is having difficulty with speech or language. The speech and language pathologist might also provide some informal assessment techniques to determine specific speech and language deficits.

Observation   The classroom teacher is in the unique position of being able to listen to students during the school day. You often have the most direct contact with the students and can notice differences in student performance. You may make note of sounds the student consistently mispronounces, substitutes, or distorts. You may notice unusual, undeveloped, or faulty language patterns used by a student, the development of the student's vocabulary, and the student's understanding of the language used in the classroom. When you notice that a student is having difficulty in one or more of the areas mentioned, you should refer the student to the Pupil Evaluation Team for evaluation. The speech and language pathologist will then thoroughly assess the student's speech and language skills.

These observations are not limited to the classroom teacher by any means. Any person who comes into contact with a student who has speech and/or language problems may make similar observations of the student and refer the student for additional evaluation and, if appropriate, remediation. In addition, the speech and language pathologist may also utilize informal observations in school settings to complete an evaluation of student performance.

Assessment   When assessing students who may have speech and language problems, the speech and language pathologist will utilize a variety of techniques to identify the specific problem the student has. An example of an informal assessment technique a speech and language pathologist uses is a speech survey. This technique consists of conducting a personal interview with the student, asking questions designed to elicit various speech sounds, and asking the student to repeat certain sentences containing various speech sounds. In addition to listening for the specific speech sounds the student uses, the specialist is able to evaluate the student's language skills. Conversation structured in this manner of casual interchanges can provide the specialist with information on the student's use of speech and language outside a test situation.

The Classroom Teacher and the Specialist

The classroom teacher and the speech and language pathologist are the two professionals in the school setting who spend the greatest amount of time with students who have speech and/or language deficits. Since the speech and language pathologist is usually an itinerant teacher (that is, serves more than one school) and sees students on a limited basis, it is important to understand the role of the specialist and of the teacher when educating children with problems in this area.

THE CLASSROOM TEACHER

Most classroom teachers are not trained in the direct remediation of speech and language problems. However, you will see students with such problems for a significant portion of the school day, so you are in a unique position to encourage the development and use of appropriate speech and language on a daily basis. This can be incorporated into existing lessons and into the daily communication you have with the individual students. As a classroom teacher, you can encourage the development of speech and language through the following techniques:

1. Model appropriate speech and language. Students tend to imitate the classroom teacher and other adults who are important to them. If you

model appropriate speech and language, students will frequently imitate your behavior.

2. Reinforce newly learned speech and language skills. Students at all ages are acquiring language skills. When a student learns a new skill, recognize the growth on the part of the student. If a student is receiving help from a speech and language pathologist, find out the skills being taught. When the student exhibits those skills in your classroom, reinforce the student. Not only does this help the student learn appropriate skills, it also helps the student generalize the skills outside the remedial setting.

3. Name objects and events for your students. Since we *learn* speech and language, it is important for the teacher to provide the opportunity for students to enrich their language and improve their speech. By using frequent oral communication and applying names and labels to objects and activities, you can increase a student's receptive language and expressive language. This is particularly important when new concepts are being developed at both the elementary and secondary levels.

4. Provide the opportunity for students to speak. As with the learning of all skills, speech and language must be practiced to be maintained. Plan learning activities that encourage speech in the classroom. This need not mean public speaking activities, but may include informal speaking experiences in small groups.

5. Provide the motivation to enlarge the speaking vocabulary and skills. Oral communications should be positive. You can structure the classroom environment so students become excited about the acquisition of new language skills.

6. Promote the use of speech with students who stutter. While listening to a person who stutters can be very frustrating, that individual needs the opportunity to speak. You can assist students who stutter by accepting their speech (and communicating acceptance of them), reducing stressful speaking situations for them, and providing an open, caring atmosphere for oral communication.

The classroom teacher, then, can play an important role in the development of speech and language in the school setting. By carefully structuring the learning environment to promote speech and language, you can establish a pattern of active learning for students. Close work with speech and language pathologists can provide you with teaching ideas as well as information on how to assist specific students who are receiving therapy in speech and/or language.

THE SPEECH AND LANGUAGE PATHOLOGIST

The speech and language pathologist is trained in the evaluation and remediation of speech and language disorders. One of the most important roles of the speech and language pathologist is to provide direct services

A speech pathologist may give one-to-one remedial help, as above, or may provide in-service training for classroom teachers to deal with speech and language problems.

to students. When a referral is made to the Pupil Evaluation Team, the speech and language pathologist may be assigned to assess the student's skills to see if there is a need for special education services. In this capacity, the specialist may observe the student in the classroom and other school settings to determine the student's use of speech and language on a daily basis. The speech and language pathologist will also use formal and informal testing procedures to evaluate speech and language skills. He or she may evaluate the student's hearing or refer the student for outside evaluation, since some speech and language problems are associated with hearing losses. Following the collection of data, the Pupil Evaluation Team, with input from the specialist, will develop a program for direct remediation of the speech and/or language deficits to be carried out by a trained speech and language pathologist.

In addition to direct remediation, the specialist can play an important in-service training role in the school. For example, the speech and language pathologist may plan and implement a formal in-service training program for classroom teachers. Such training might include general awareness of speech and language problems, approaches for enhancing the use of speech and language in the classroom, the use of cued speech, and the integration of hearing impaired students into school settings. The specialist may provide in-service training on a one-to-one basis with classroom teachers who have students being seen for speech or language problems. In this case, the speech and language pathologist may suggest techniques for encouraging and reinforcing newly acquired skills and speech and language in the classroom.

Most speech and language pathologists also have an administrative role in school settings. Since speech and language problems are considered handicapping conditions under PL 94-142, the speech and language pathologist is involved in the Pupil Evaluation Team meetings that result in the development of Individualized Education Programs for the students he or she serves. The pathologist may also be responsible for scheduling students, reporting on the progress of students, and reporting on the effectiveness of the remedial program.

There is some controversy at the present time over the role of the speech and language pathologist and the learning disabilities specialist in serving the needs of students who are language impaired. Few specialists have been prepared to meet the needs of this population. Some university training programs have begun to emphasize the evaluation and remediation of language disorders in their preparation programs for speech and language pathologists. Others have placed heavy emphasis on language in the preparation of learning disability specialists. It is important to determine which of these specialists is trained to work with language disorders in your school and seek appropriate services for students through the Pupil Evaluation Team.

Many school personnel, then, may be involved in the process of identifying and remediating speech and language problems. The case study presented below illustrates coordination between school personnel and parents in providing a speech and language program for Joel.

JOEL

Joel is a third-grader. When he entered school as a kindergartner, he had such severe speech problems that the teacher could not understand him. Joel could make some of his needs known through gestures and pointing; although he did speak, the speech was of little use in communicating needs and ideas. Since verbal communication is such an important skill and since Joel's speech represented problems beyond normal maturational delays in the acquisition of some sounds, the kindergarten teacher referred him to the Pupil Evaluation Team for evaluation of his speech.

After receiving parental approval for an evaluation, the Pupil Evaluation Team requested that the speech and language pathologist conduct a thorough evaluation. After ruling out hearing problems, he found that Joel had some articulation problems, primarily substitutions and omissions of sounds. He also found that Joel had not developed appropriate language skills for his age. While Joel could form simple sentences and did attempt to communicate his needs, he had some lags in this area due partially to his speech problems. When Joel tried to talk, he was asked to repeat what he said several times and eventually limited his verbal expressions as a result of the frustration he was feeling. The speech and language pathologist brought his findings to the Pupil Evaluation Team, which recommended an instructional program for Joel, to be implemented as soon as possible. The speech and language pathologist was able to work Joel into his case load the following week. The program developed for Joel included an emphasis on improving his articulation skills and increasing his use of language. The latter part of the program focused on both semantics (vocabulary development and associating names with concepts) and syntax (learning alternative sentence patterns and structures). The speech and language pathologist worked with Joel for forty-five minutes, three days a week.

In addition to the remediation provided by the specialist, Joel's classroom teacher and parents were involved in a program that focused on encouraging and reinforcing the development and use of more appropriate speech. By the end of kindergarten, Joel could make most of his needs known through oral communication. Since he still had some articulation problems and needed additional work in language, it was recommended that Joel continue to receive services from the speech and language pathologist.

Joel worked with the speech and language pathologist during first grade. By midyear, he was using language skills appropriate for a first-grader. This part of his program was discontinued, and the amount of time he spent with the specialist was decreased. He continued to meet with the speech and language pathologist for two half-hour sessions a week. This program was continued through the middle of second grade. At this time, Joel was able to speak, using appropriate speech sounds most of the time.

Summary

Speech and language are important survival tools, both in daily communication and in the instructional process used in schools. Students who have speech and language problems are unable to participate fully in the classroom experience. In order to make the maximum use of classroom instruction and the students' own capabilities, it is important for you to understand the nature of speech and language and the types of deficits these students may have. The major points covered in this chapter are as follows:

1. Speech and language are acquired through exposure to a variety of experiences.

2. Speech and language develop in an orderly fashion. Children do not learn words and sounds in the same order, but they progress through similar stages of development.

3. There are three major types of speech problems: articulation disorders, voice disorders, and fluency problems. Of these, articulation disorders are the most prevalent.

4. Language disorders may be present when the student has difficulty with semantics and syntax in the expression of ideas.

5. The speech and language pathologist may use any one of several formal tests to diagnose speech and language problems.

6. You and the speech and language pathologist may use classroom observation, speech surveys, and interviews to document precise speech and/or language problems the student may have.

7. Through good teaching and attention to appropriate speech and language in the classroom, you can assist students in developing good speech and language habits.

8. The speech and language pathologist may provide direct remediation for the speech and/or language impaired student as well as consulting and in-service training to the classroom teacher.

9. Students with language problems may be seen by either a speech and language pathologist or a learning disability specialist depending upon the needs of the student and the background and training of the specialists in your particular school district.

Activities

1. Interview a speech-language pathologist. Focus on the types of services the individual provides, the ages of the students in the program, and the services provided for classroom teachers.

2. Observe an individual or a small group of students in a speech therapy session. Note the techniques and materials used by the speech-language pathologist as well as the skills being taught during the session.

3. Some speech and language problems are not problems at all; they are examples of patterns peculiar to a geographical area. See if you can identify any speech sounds or language patterns that are used more frequently in your part of the country than in other areas.

Study Questions

1. Define speech and language. What is the difference between the two terms?

2. What are receptive language, inner language, and expressive language? What is the relationship between the three areas?

3. List three types of speech disorders and give an example of each.

4. Briefly define semantics and syntax. Give one example of a problem in each area.

5. What are two informal techniques a classroom teacher can use to screen for speech and/or language problems in the classroom?

6. List at least four techniques the classroom teacher can use to develop and reinforce appropriate speech and language in the classroom.

7. Name at least two services the speech-language pathologist can provide for the classroom teacher.

Questions for Further Thought

1. Psychological and educational examiners often find a relationship between intelligence test scores and a student's level of language functioning. Why does such a relationship exist and what might it tell teachers about educational programs for mildly handicapped students?

2. What are some potential effects of the home environment on the development of speech and language in children during the preschool years? Can the classroom teacher have a significant impact on the growth of language once the child enters school?

3. Is it the role of the classroom teacher to try to change speech that is understandable, but incorrect grammatically or socially?

Additional Resources

BOOKS

Lloyd, L. L. (Ed.). *Communication assessment and intervention strategies.* Baltimore: University Park Press, 1976.

Travis, L. E. (Ed.). *Handbook of speech pathology and audiology.* New York: Appleton-Century-Crofts, 1971.

Van Riper, C. *Speech correction: Principles and methods* (6th ed.). Englewood Cliffs, New Jersey: Prentice-Hall, 1978.

Weiss, C. E., and Lillywhite, H. S. *Communicative disorders: A handbook for prevention and early intervention.* St. Louis: C. V. Mosby, 1976.

PROFESSIONAL JOURNALS

Journal of Speech and Hearing Disorders

Language, Speech and Hearing Services in the Schools

Journal of Speech and Hearing Research

ASHA

PROFESSIONAL ORGANIZATIONS

American Speech and Hearing Association (ASHA), 10801 Rockville Pike, Rockville, Maryland 20852

CHILDREN'S LITERATURE

Hunter, E. *Child of the silent night.* New York: Dell, 1971.

Kelley, S. *Trouble with explosives.* New York: Bradbury Press, 1976.

Lee, M. *The skating rink.* New York: The Seabury Press, 1969.

Chapter 14

Hearing and
Vision Impairments

Many of us take vision and hearing for granted in our day-to-day functioning. We unconsciously use our hearing to assist us in oral communication, warn of approaching danger (sirens, cars, trains), and acquire information from our environment. We rely on vision in much the same way. Our eyes help us determine the message others are sending us; they let us read signs, books, and advertisements; and they increase our travel mobility. Although relatively few people have vision or hearing impairments, it is important for you to be aware of their problems and to be able to make appropriate educational adaptations.

If you look around, you will notice a few people who have impaired hearing to the extent that they must wear a hearing aid to improve their hearing or engage in alternative forms of communication such as sign language and finger spelling to talk with others. In most social settings in which several people are gathered, some will be wearing glasses or contact lenses to improve their vision. When vision can be corrected to normal, the individual will likely have no exceptional learning needs. The small number of students and adults who have hearing or vision impairments to the degree that they are unable to learn in the same manner as others may require some modifications in their learning situations.

Since hearing impaired and visually impaired students are enrolled in the classroom for most or all of their school day, it is important that
you be aware of the unique instructional needs of these students. The

focus of this chapter is on the identification of these students, your role in providing instruction for them, and the specific educational and environmental adaptations that may be necessary for these students to participate fully in the classroom. The role of specialists and other ancillary personnel is also discussed, particularly in relationship to the services these professionals can provide you and the mainstreamed student.

Hearing Impairments

Have you ever had occasion to talk to an older relative who was losing his or her hearing? Have you watched children play, observing that one was wearing a hearing aid? Have you ever been in a small sandwich shop with a group of people who were using sign language to communicate with one another? If so, you have come into contact with a small portion of our population who share one thing in common. These people are all hearing impaired. Their impairment may prevent them from communicating with others who are speaking in normal tones, resulting in a need for special adaptations in school and social settings. Begin your exploration by observing a teacher who is concerned about one of her students.

ANDY

Andy was a typical third-grader. He seemed to enjoy school and actively participated in activities, particularly in outdoor group sports. Andy was very friendly, responding to adults and fellow students alike. Academically, Andy had always been an average student, not seeming to excel in any particular area in school.

At the beginning of third grade, Andy's teacher, Mrs. Anderson, presented material that was a review for the students in arithmetic and reading. Andy was successful in completing this work. As the work became more difficult, however, Andy began to slip behind the class. His teacher noticed that he seemed to make sporadic progress; some material he seemed to pick up very quickly, while at other times he seemed not to grasp the simplest concepts. After noting this trend in Andy's performance, Mrs. Anderson began to observe his behavior more closely in preparation to referring him to the Pupil Evaluation Team. These observations proved to be most helpful in identifying Andy's needs.

Mrs. Anderson began by tracing Andy's academic performance. While he performed within the average range in the classroom, he had difficulty with some kinds of tasks, particularly those that required careful listening. Once provided with an example of the expected response, Andy could make the response and maintain it in his repertoire. It seemed that he did not hear some of the stimuli presented in day-to-day instruction. This increased Mrs. Anderson's awareness of possible explanations for Andy's sporadic performance.

Mrs. Anderson then began to observe Andy during different tasks assigned in the classroom. She noted that he seemed to perform well when he received instruction individually, either from the teacher or from another student. During large group activities, he seldom completed the assigned task. It seemed as though he was not paying attention to directions and instruction from the teacher. Mrs. Anderson also noted that Andy relied on cues from students sitting around him. He usually accomplished an assigned task if the students around him were working on the task, so he could model their behavior.

In addition to these observations, Mrs. Anderson noticed that Andy tried to focus on classroom activities, but had difficulty doing so. He would often turn his head slightly to the right while listening to others. Occasionally, he would move closer to the speaker or source of sound in the classroom. Mrs. Anderson noted that Andy had occasional difficulties interacting with peers on the playground. He would seem to ignore their requests during games, causing his team to lose points or possession of the ball. During critical plays, this lack of response on Andy's part brought a great deal of anger from his playmates.

Based upon her observations, Mrs. Anderson referred Andy to the Pupil Evaluation Team. Upon their recommendation, Andy was evaluated by the speech and language pathologist and an otologist, a physician who specializes in disorders of the ear. Because Andy did have a mild hearing loss, which interfered with successful school performance and could be corrected with the use of a hearing aid, he was referred to a specialist who fitted him with one. The specialist also trained Andy to use the hearing aid to his best advantage, gave the speech and language pathologist information on Andy's hearing aid, and provided the classroom teacher with a number of suggestions designed to enhance Andy's participation in the classroom.

DEFINITION

Hearing impairments can be defined in a number of ways. In some cases the degree of loss serves as a basis for defining hearing problems. The impact of the loss upon language development is often considered. Both of these will be discussed here as well as types of hearing losses.

Hearing is measured in decibels (dB) and hertz (Hz). Decibels refer to the intensity of loudness of sound. The smallest unit, zero dB, represents the smallest sound a person can perceive; the larger numbers represent increasingly louder sounds. The frequency or pitch of sound is measured in hertz. This tells the cycles per second of sound. Very low pitched sounds have few cycles per second, while high sounds have a higher number of cycles per second. Both decibels and hertz are used when measuring the degree of loss and classifying the hearing loss. These classifications are presented in Table 14.1.

TABLE 14.1
Classifications of hearing loss

Hearing level	Classification	Effect on understanding speech and language
27–40 dB	slight	May have difficulty hearing faint or distant speech.
		Will not usually have difficulty in school.
41–55 dB	mild	Understands conversational speech at a distance of 3 to 5 feet.
		May miss as much as half of class discussion if voices are faint or not in line of vision.
		May have limited vocabulary or speech anomalies.
56–70 dB	marked	Conversation must be loud to be understood.
		Will have increasing difficulty with school group discussions.
		Is likely to have defective speech.
		Is likely to be deficient in language use and comprehension.
		Will have limited vocabulary.
71–90 dB	severe	May hear loud voices about one foot from the ear.
		May be able to identify environmental sounds.
		May be able to discriminate vowels but not all consonants.
		Speech and language defective and likely to deteriorate.
		Speech and language will not develop spontaneously if loss is present before one year of age.

(continued)

Table 14.1 continued

Hearing level	Classification	Effect on understanding speech and language
91 dB or more	profound	May hear some loud sounds but is aware of vibrations rather than tonal patterns.
		Relies on vision rather than hearing as primary avenue for communication.
		Speech and language defective and likely to deteriorate.
		Speech and language will not develop spontaneously if loss is present before one year of age.

Source: Based on International Standard Organizations (ISO)

Audiometers are used to assess an individual's hearing. As an examination is being conducted, the audiologist prepares an audiogram, which graphically displays the individual's level of hearing at various frequencies. An example of an audiogram appears in Figure 14.1. This audiogram depicts the degree of hearing loss evidenced by Andy, the student in the case study. To read the audiogram, first look at the code. The "o" indicates the level of hearing in Andy's right ear; the "x" is used to indicate the hearing in the left ear. A person with normal hearing would have plots on the audiogram between 0 and 10 dB from 125 to 8,000 Hz. As you can see, Andy hears at about 40 dB in each ear. Consequently, Andy has what might be called a mild loss in both ears at all frequencies.

While the system previously mentioned provides a general frame of reference for hearing losses and may assist specialists in determining the most suitable mode of treatment for the loss, it does not assist the classroom teacher in planning adaptations for a particular student in the classroom. Dunn (1973) suggests that a definition that takes into account the effect of the hearing loss upon the development of speech and language is more relevant to those involved in the education of the hearing impaired. Such a definition might read as follows:

- *Deaf:* A hearing loss so severe at birth and in the prelingual period that it precludes the development of normal speech.

- *Hard of hearing:* A loss of hearing in the prelingual period that does not preclude the development of some spoken language; or a loss of hearing occurring later in life.

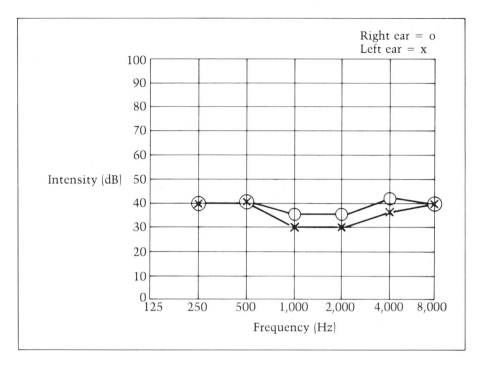

FIGURE 14.1
An audiogram

An important characteristic of these definitions is the reference to the age of onset of the hearing loss. A child who loses his or her hearing very early (at birth or in the first few months of life) will likely not acquire spoken language spontaneously. Since speech is learned through imitation of sound, these children have limited or no opportunity to develop oral communication. Children and adults who lose their hearing after having acquired spoken language are likely to retain speech.

TYPES OF HEARING LOSS

There are three major types of hearing loss. A *conductive* hearing loss involves the middle and outer ear. This part of the ear conducts sound waves to the nerve for processing; when the passage of these sound waves is obstructed, sound is not conducted to the nerve. A *sensori-neural* loss is the result of damage to the cochlea or the auditory nerve in the inner ear. A person suffering from this type of loss may be able to hear sound, but the message that is transmitted is distorted or garbled. In some cases, a *mixed* loss may be present. An individual with this type of loss has

TABLE 14.2
Types and causes of hearing loss

Types of loss	Causes
Conductive	Excessive ear wax Missing outer ear or ear canal Insertion of objects into ear Adenoid infections Bacterial and virus infections Cysts Perforation of the eardrum Eustachian tube blockage Aging
Sensori-neural	Environmental noise Premature birth Some antibiotics Mumps and measles Rh incompatibility

both a conductive and a sensori-neural loss. The types of losses and potential causes of each are presented in Table 14.2.

CHARACTERISTICS

Students who are hearing impaired may not differ significantly from the population in general. With intervention, they have the same potential for intellectual and academic development as their age peers and the ability to cope with everyday living situations. Although hearing impaired students begin at levels similar to age peers, their hearing impairment can affect their intellectual, emotional, and adaptive living skills. Since hearing impairments can affect the development of speech and language, these students may perform well below grade level academically, score low in IQ tests, and encounter some social or emotional problems as they mature.

Academic work and social interaction in a public school setting are based upon verbal and written communication to a large degree. Hearing impaired students are unable to relate totally to the verbal communication that serves as a basis for the development of language skills in the home and the school. The hearing impaired student often lags behind peers in the development of language and in the concepts acquired through language. This can directly affect performance in academic subjects such as reading, language arts, and social studies. The ability to use written language may also be limited, since the hearing impaired student is not practicing language and language patterns the way hearing students can.

To increase the student's language and academic skills, it is important for the classroom teacher to focus on language development, providing examples of new terms and concepts. It is also important to assist the student in understanding how language is used, including idioms and expressions that are peculiar to an area.

Students who are hearing impaired have the ability to make normal social and emotional growth. However, the hearing impaired student may experience rejection and isolation as a result of inability to hear well. It is difficult to communicate with someone who is unable to hear. Many hearing individuals are uncomfortable socializing with those who are hearing impaired and therefore avoid social contact with them. In these cases, the nature of the physical handicap interferes with successful social interaction, particularly as the student grows older. Such isolation can lead to emotional difficulties.

IDENTIFICATION

School personnel may use a variety of techniques to identify students who have hearing problems. Teachers may observe certain behaviors that lead them to suspect that a student may have a hearing problem. Instruments, such as a pure tone audiometer, and informal tests, such as speech audiometry, may be used by specialists to further assess hearing disorders. Finally, medical specialists should diagnose and treat any specific medical problems presented by the child.

You are often in the best position to observe a student on a day-to-day basis and to make some comparisons of normal behavior between students. When you are concerned about a student's performance and suspect that he or she may have a hearing loss, you might follow an observation program very similar to that of Mrs. Anderson in the case study. You might look for cues such as the student cupping a hand behind the ear, turning the head towards the speaker, moving closer to the source of the sound, and asking frequently for oral communications to be repeated. The student may have frequent colds and earaches, recurring tonsilitis, and fluid in the ear. The student may not follow directions. The student may rely on cues from other children to successfully complete tasks. The student may not pay attention, particularly during group instruction. There may be evidence of a speech problem. When one or more of these behaviors or medical conditions (summed up in Figure 14.2) exist, you should refer the student to specialists who can give thorough medical and audiological examinations.

Specialists have several tools available for assessment of a student's hearing. An audiologist may administer a hearing test using a pure tone audiometer. Tones at which speech occurs can be assessed by setting the frequency and intensity of sound at those levels. The student's ears are covered with earphones while the examiner plays selected tones. The

Behaviors

Confuses or has difficulty following directions.

Cups hand behind ear.

Turns head toward source of sound.

Asks for repetitions of oral statements and directions.

Has some speech problems.

Depends on classmates for instructional cues.

Displays lack of attention.

Physical symptoms

Frequent earaches

Excessive ear wax

Frequent colds and sore throats

Tonsillitis

FIGURE 14.2
Hearing problems checklist

resulting profile, such as the one presented for Andy in Figure 14.1, provides a record of those tones the child hears. The specialist may also assess the child's hearing by interviewing the child, noting the sounds, if any, the child does not produce or produces incorrectly.

If an audiologist determines that a hearing problem exists, a referral should be made to a medically trained person requesting a thorough examination. A physician who specializes in disorders of the ear is an otologist. The medical specialist will further diagnose and treat disorders that are identified through examination. If the student has a conductive hearing loss and can benefit from a hearing aid, such a recommendation will be made. Both the specialists and the physician may make recommendations to the classroom teachers to increase the participation of the student in the educational program.

PREVALENCE

Although estimates vary somewhat, approximately 0.6% of the school population are hearing impaired to the degree that they require special education services to be successful in school (Bureau of Education for the Handicapped, 1979). It is estimated that another 4.5% of the school population have hearing losses that do not require assistance from special education personnel. These students, however, may still have special needs that must be met by the classroom teacher.

The Hearing Impaired Student in the Classroom

Hearing impaired students can usually benefit from specialized training and adaptations in the classroom environment. The training aspects of the students' program range from better utilization of residual hearing (use of the hearing the student does possess) to various communication techniques. To increase classroom participation for the student, you must be knowledgeable about both specialized training and classroom adaptations. It is also important to be aware of the specialists that may be working with the student and the services they may be providing.

SPECIALIZED TRAINING

A number of techniques are used to increase the hearing impaired student's participation in educational and social experiences. These techniques relate to the student's ability to use cues in the environment and to communicate effectively with others. Successful experiences in these areas can lead to increased awareness of the environment and increased success in school.

Auditory Training   Few people are totally deaf. It is important to train the hearing impaired to use what hearing they do have to the maximum extent possible. The hearing impaired student is taught to use and care for his or her hearing aid, to use environmental cues when conversing with others, and to become aware of sounds and their meanings. While a specialist may do the actual training, you are often in the best position to reinforce use of these skills on a regular basis and perhaps to structure activities that increase the use of hearing in the school day. For example, you might develop a learning center where students listen individually to taped material and respond by completing a worksheet.

Speech   Many hearing impaired students also have speech problems. These students will require speech therapy to improve and maintain intelligible speech. Since speech is the primary vehicle for communication, particularly in social settings, it is important for the hearing impaired to develop this skill to the maximum extent possible.

Communication Systems   Students with severe hearing problems often do not develop intelligible speech. Some specialists believe that these students should be taught through an *oral* approach. When trained with

Cued speech, a relatively new technique, involves the use of speech reading. The speaker supplements his or her spoken words with hand signs near the face to interpret words that appear the same, such as *bat* and *pat*.

this approach, the student is taught to use amplification, auditory training, speech reading (lip reading), and speech to communicate with others. Another approach used to educate severely hearing impaired students is *manual* communication. With this particular approach, the student uses sign language (gestures and signs that represent words), finger spelling (hand positions for individual letters of the alphabet), or a combination of the two. Finally, some specialists rely on a total communication system utilizing techniques from both the oral and the manual approaches. The total communication system assists the student in developing as much oral communication as possible, while providing the student with skills in manual communication.

A relatively new technique, *cued speech*, is being used with some hearing impaired students. This involves the use of speech reading supplemented by hand signs near the face to tell the hearing impaired individual how to interpret words that appear the same, such as *bat* and *pat* or *son* and *sun*.

While these techniques may seem complex at first, it is possible for classroom teachers and students to learn to use some of them in the classroom setting. In fact, the use of such techniques can be a valuable learning experience for students in the classroom, who will gain an additional communication system for themselves.

ELECTRONIC AND OTHER DEVICES

In addition to knowing the types of training that hearing impaired students may require, it is important for school personnel to be aware of devices that can be used to improve the ability of the student to acquire information in the classroom. Hearing aids and advancements in educational technology can provide the student with increased involvement in the learning environment.

Hearing Aids A hearing aid may assist a student who has a conductive hearing loss. Although a student may wear a hearing aid in the classroom, it is important to note that, while the student's hearing may be improved through use of the aid, it may not be within the normal hearing range. Consequently, the student may require adaptations in the classroom similar to those of other hearing impaired students.

When a student enters the classroom with a hearing aid, you and the specialists who work with the student should consult with the student or the student's parents to determine if there are any special instructions for care of the hearing aid. Students with hearing aids may change the volume control during school activities. It may be important for the student to maintain good hearing with the aid during instructional sessions in the classroom. It may be to the student's benefit, however, to turn the volume down on the aid when working independently. Since the hearing aid amplifies all sounds, the noise level in the classroom, as amplified, may be uncomfortable for the student; by lowering the volume, the student may have better concentration on assigned work.

Educational Technology Classroom teachers have frequently utilized media presentations in the classroom. Films, filmstrips, and slide programs that are captioned increase the message the hearing impaired student receives from the material. You should also keep abreast of new technological developments that may be available for classroom use. For example, teletypewriter (TTY) systems may have some educational applications as they are developed. These systems allow deaf people to send and receive typewritten messages over telephone lines. Close-captioned television programs provide printed subtitles for an increasing number and variety of programs. A special television or adapter is necessary to receive the captions.

CLASSROOM ADAPTATIONS

You can play an important role in the education of hearing impaired students. Since the students spend a great portion of their school day with you, it is important that you feel at ease with the student and make use of various ways to assist the student in the classroom. Some suggestions for classroom adaptations are listed below.

1. Observe students in the classroom. You may be the first person to observe and recognize that a student is hearing impaired. Mild hearing losses that often go undetected may interfere with the student's ability to perform successfully in school. When you suspect a hearing loss, refer the student for a thorough evaluation.

2. The hearing impaired student should be seated near the source of sound, whether it be a person or a piece of equipment. This may require some flexibility in the use of the room arrangement to allow the hearing impaired student to choose the place in the classroom in closest proximity to the sound source.

3. Seat the student so he or she has good visual contact with your face. The hearing impaired student will rely on cues from facial expressions and on speech reading. Be sure that the student is seated in such a way that you are always visible. In addition, the student's seating should be flexible so he or she can move about the classroom as necessary to benefit from oral communication. Try to arrange group discussions in such a way that the student can see each face.

4. Use well-lighted areas when teaching. Take care to avoid shadows in the classroom when presenting information to the students; avoid standing in front of windows that create glare behind you. If necessary, request that additional lighting be installed in the classroom.

5. Supplement verbal instructions with printed material. Provide hearing impaired students with as much material as possible in print. When giving a lecture in class, develop a printed outline of the material to be covered or list major points on an overhead transparency or chalkboard, taking care to refrain from talking while writing on the chalkboard. When assigning work, make sure all directions are on the worksheet or write them on the chalkboard.

6. Learn the mechanics of the communication system used by the student. Although it may seem very complex, the communication systems used by the student can be learned by classroom teachers and students. The student's success in school will increase if the school can adapt to the student's needs. Such learning expands the communication vehicles open to other students as well.

7. Since you are not always immediately available for assistance, it may be helpful to set up a buddy system, by which other students in the classroom provide directions and help to the hearing impaired student when needed. These students should be trained to speak with the hearing impaired student, using the form of communication used by the student.

THE SPECIALIST

Your work with hearing impaired students is supported by other professionals. The hearing impaired student is frequently seen by such specialists as the speech and language pathologist, audiologist, and otologist.

In some school systems, a teacher of the hearing impaired may be available to work directly with the student and to consult with the classroom teacher; in many districts, though, this becomes the responsibility of the speech and language pathologist. Since the role of the speech and language pathologist was discussed in detail in Chapter 13, it will not be covered in this section.

Teacher of the Hearing Impaired   Some school districts provide the services of teachers who are trained to instruct hearing impaired students. These teachers may serve several functions in the school setting. First, the teacher of the hearing impaired may be responsible for direct instruction for hearing impaired students. He or she may teach the student basic skills and communication techniques for some portion of the school day. Second, the teacher of the hearing impaired may serve as a resource teacher, providing instruction supplemental to that of the regular classroom to increase student success in the curriculum offered there. Third, the teacher of the hearing impaired may serve as a consultant for the classroom teacher. In this role, the specialist might bring you information, provide you with techniques to use in the instruction of the student, and provide or develop instructional materials that may help the student in the classroom setting. Finally, the teacher of the hearing impaired may serve as a liaison between the school and other specialists who are working with the hearing impaired student.

The Audiologist   An audiologist is a specialist who is trained to assess hearing. This person is able to screen students for hearing problems and administer individual hearing tests when screenings of students result in specific referrals for help. In addition, a classroom teacher who suspects that a student is suffering from a hearing loss may refer the student to an audiologist for examination. If a hearing loss is present, the audiologist may refer the student to an otologist for further examination.

The Otologist   The otologist is a physician who specializes in disorders of the ear. The otologist can determine the exact nature of the hearing loss and whether medical treatment is necessary for the student. If treatment is necessary, including the use of a hearing aid, the otologist will prescribe a plan for the student to follow.

Vision Impairments

Vision impairments have an effect similar to that of hearing impairments in that the student must learn to function in a world where others are able to use a sense organ that he or she cannot. Imagine for a moment what it would be like to see everything as a gray shadow with some movement in it. Or imagine how it would feel to be left out of social activities because others felt you would not be able to participate since you could not see. Think of the frustration you might feel if you could not see the events that someone else was pointing out to you. Students who are visually impaired feel some of these frustrations. Since they are unable to perceive their environment the same way others do, it is necessary to make accommodations for them in the instructional setting. The case history for this chapter is Mary Ellen, a visually impaired student. She has been enrolled in a school system that has been willing to accommodate her special educational needs as she has progressed through school.

MARY ELLEN

Mary Ellen is currently enrolled as a junior in the public high school. When Mary Ellen was two years old, she was diagnosed as partially sighted. Since she lived in an urban area, her family physician was able to refer her family to a center for the visually impaired. Professionals at that center provided Mary Ellen's family with activities they could use to help Mary Ellen develop the skills that sighted children learned at her age. She learned to utilize an adapted work area that had special lighting and magnification for close work like reading, coloring, and drawing. She was also put in a play group with other children, some of whom were also visually impaired, and began to develop social skills necessary for success in a classroom setting. By the time she entered kindergarten, she had the readiness and adaptive skills necessary for success at that level.

Mary Ellen's first big hurdle in school came when she was introduced to reading. Although she had the ability to read and had special equipment available (lighting and magnification), she was unable to participate in group instruction. She could not read the print in the text without her adaptive equipment, and the reading group did not meet in an area where she could use her equipment. As time went on, the reading skills she acquired at the beginning of reading instruction began to deteriorate, and Mary Ellen refused to read. At the suggestion of the resource teacher, the classroom teacher decided to provide Mary Ellen with individualized instruction in her reading area. This continued for the remainder of the year. By the end of the year, she was reading on grade level.

Mary Ellen had to overcome a second problem in the third grade. The school district had introduced a physical education program into the school beginning in the third grade. The physical education teacher had not previously worked with handicapped children and was afraid that Mary Ellen would be injured if she participated in active sports. As these sports were introduced Mary Ellen was forced to sit on the sidelines. When this came to the attention of the classroom teacher, she suggested that the physical education instructor observe Mary Ellen during recess on the playground. When he saw that Mary Ellen was as active as any other student and participating in several games each day, he decided to include her in all activities. The classroom teacher also asked the resource teacher to provide the physical education teacher with techniques for increasing Mary Ellen's participation.

The remainder of the elementary school years continued in much the same manner. After consulting with the resource teacher, each classroom teacher made adaptations for Mary Ellen consistent with his or her own style of teaching in some academic areas. Others moved Mary Ellen's equipment to the instructional area or made Mary Ellen's area the instructional setting. She was involved in all the activities in the classroom, whether academic or social. By the end of the sixth grade, it was impossible to differentiate Mary Ellen from her age peers either academically or socially.

Junior high school presented some logistical problems for Mary Ellen. In the past, she had been able to establish a work area in each classroom with adequate lighting and magnification of printed material. Now she was to move to six different classrooms. Since six different classes also used the same room, it was impossible to set aside a work area for her in each classroom. It was necessary to make her equipment portable. Several school personnel contributed suggestions, including the school custodian, industrial arts teacher, resource teacher, and principal. The result was a portable system that could be carried in a small case and set up in a short period of time between classes. The case included a light source and the magnification stand, which could be folded and stored compactly as a result of some minor modifications. Since Mary Ellen did not require any further special assistance for academic reasons, she was able to participate successfully in the entire range of curriculum offered in the junior high school.

Mary Ellen also found that she was the subject of some staring and snickering in school. Since she had attended a neighborhood elementary school, she had come to be well known and even protected by the children in her class. Now, however, she was meeting new students, many of whom did not understand her vision problems and used teasing and ridicule to express that lack of understanding. After some painful analysis of the situation,

Mary Ellen decided to try to overcome the situation. Since some of the students were in her classes, she made a point of greeting them each day. In two of her classes, she used reports and group discussion opportunities to relate information about vision to her peers. Even though this was effective with some students, others still treated her differently. Mary Ellen discovered that if she ignored the cracks these students made, they no longer felt a need to ridicule her. She also found that, as other students developed more sensitivity to individual differences, they would also ignore the teasers and not join in.

Now a junior in high school, Mary Ellen has the same academic program as her age peers. She has developed the social and emotional skills to participate in a community setting such as a school, and successfully adapt to the demands of that environment. She has also developed the necessary systems to assist her in academic pursuits through the various modifications made on her equipment. She is now looking forward to a college career, planning to major in her primary area of interest, American literature.

DEFINITION

The visually impaired have long been identified through the use of legal definitions. These definitions focus on how much central visual acuity the individual has as measured by an eye examination. A person is said to be *legally blind* when they have central visual acuity of 20/200 or less in the better eye with correction. A *partially sighted* individual has central visual acuity of 20/70 to 20/200 in the better eye with correction (Blake, 1981).

To better understand these definitions, let us look at the meaning of 20/200. Normal vision is considered 20/20. That is, a person sees at 20 feet what the normal eye sees at 20 feet. A person who is legally blind and sees at 20/200 actually sees at 20 feet what the normal eye can see at 200 feet. By the same token, visual acuity of 20/70 means that the person sees at 20 feet what a person with normal vision sees at 70 feet. It is important to note that these measures are taken with corrective lenses for visually impaired students. While this definition may be helpful in a legal sense, it does not necessarily classify children efficiently for educational purposes. Two people who have the same visual acuity may have very different needs with respect to printed material. For example, some students may be legally blind by definition, but able to read large-print books or regular-print books with magnification. Others, however, must rely on brailled as well as taped material for reading. The educational needs of these students would be quite different.

Concern over the educational relevance of the legal definitions of vision problems led to the development of educational definitions. The educational definitions of visually handicapped individuals follow:

- An *educationally blind* person is one who relies primarily on braille and other tactile materials.

- An *educationally partially sighted* person or one who has low vision can read large print or regular print under special conditions and may be educated like a sighted person. (Dunn, 1973; Heward and Orlansky, 1980)

From the perspective of the classroom teacher, this definition is much more helpful. Instead of focusing on the degree of loss, it suggests the types of accommodations that are necessary for the particular student in the classroom. Providing a student with materials in braille or tape recordings of printed materials is much different from providing a well-lit space for a visually impaired student who only requires that adaptation. Some students may require a combination of the two approaches. The educational definitions, then, can provide the classroom teacher with a basis for instructional planning for visually impaired students.

CHARACTERISTICS

Students who are visually handicapped have the potential to develop intellectually, academically, socially, and emotionally at a rate similar to that of their age peers. Their vision handicap, though, makes their development more challenging in many of these areas.

The development of concepts, language, and cognitive skills in any child depends upon the ability to receive stimuli (such as seeing objects, hearing words, manipulating objects) and translate them into something that can be comprehended. Most children are able to use all of their senses; when one or more sense cannot be used, the development of some concepts and skills can be slowed. In some cases, visually impaired students have not developed some conceptual and language skills that their age peers have attained. For example, they may be unable to name abstract concepts such as colors, and textures. As a result of this delayed development, these students tend to score below grade level on IQ tests and achievement tests. They can learn the skill, but need additional experience to be successful.

Physically, the visually impaired have the potential to develop like other children their age. However, the lack of adequate vision may affect mobility. Rather than explore in the home, the child may be limited in movement to protect him or her from injury. Such restrictions may lead to limited awareness of one's physical self, spatial relationships, and mobility. Thus, there may be a need for the educational program to address physical development and mobility.

Socially and emotionally, the visually impaired can show the same general development as anyone else. However, visually impaired students sometimes develop problems resulting from insensitive treatment by others. Since the population as a whole has not been taught about vision problems and how to treat people who are visually impaired, others may react in such a way as to lower the visually handicapped person's self-esteem. A cycle begins that can result in emotional problems for the handicapped individual.

Behavior

Rubs eyes excessively.

Shuts or covers one eye.

Has difficulty in reading and other close work.

Holds books close to eyes.

Is unable to see distant things clearly.

Squints or frowns frequently.

Appearance

Crossed eyes

Red-rimmed, encrusted, or swollen eyelids

Recurring styes

Complaints

Eyes itch, burn, or feel scratchy.

Cannot see well.

Dizziness, headaches, or nausea experienced following close eye work.

Blurred or double vision.

FIGURE 14.3
Vision problems checklist

Source: From *Teaching About Vision* by the Joint Study Committee of the American School Health Association and the National Society for the Prevention of Blindness, Inc., 1972, p. 9.

IDENTIFICATION

There are a number of ways of identifying students who have visual impairments. Although those with the most severe impairments will often be identified prior to entry in school, it is important to know about the tools available. Identification usually involves the use of one or more of the following: observation of the student in question, screening instruments, and examination by a specialist.

Some vision problems will come to your attention as a result of observation. You might notice that the student frequently rubs his or her eyes, complains that his or her eyes hurt, or squints when working. Some students may avoid close work, such as handwriting and reading, saying that it hurts them or that they have a bad headache. On occasion, a student may have difficulty copying and doing other fine motor tasks like drawing. While any one of these in and of itself may be the result of several possible conditions, they may indicate that the child has a vision problem. Figure 14.3 shows several symptoms that might indicate vision problems. If you notice any of them, you should refer the child for further screening to determine if a problem exists or to rule out vision as a problem.

Most public schools have vision screening programs and periodically screen all students for possible vision problems. Schools often use the Snellen Eye Chart as a screening measure. The procedure consists of placing a chart (like the one in Figure 14.4) containing *E*s of graded sizes and turned in different directions, or letters of the alphabet, also in graded sizes, 20 feet in front of the student. The student tells the examiner which direction the particular *E* is pointed or which letter is being shown. The child's score is then recorded. Since this is a screening tool, it does identify some children who have vision problems. There are students, however, who have visual problems that are not detectable by administration of the Snellen. For example, students with near vision problems or visual perception deficits may pass the Snellen screening, but have significant vision impairments.

It is important to realize the limitations of screening devices such as the Snellen. They are not a complete eye examination. Personnel who administer them (often parents or volunteers) are not usually qualified to diagnose vision problems. Screening devices can, however, assist you in referring children who may have vision problems to an appropriate specialist. If you suspect that a vision problem exists, even though it is not noted on an instrument such as the Snellen Eye Test, a referral to a specialist is still in order.

Students who have possible vision problems are referred to ophthalmologists or optometrists. An ophthalmologist is a physician who has completed medical school and specializes in diseases of the eye. An optometrist is a person who has specialized training in disorders of the eye

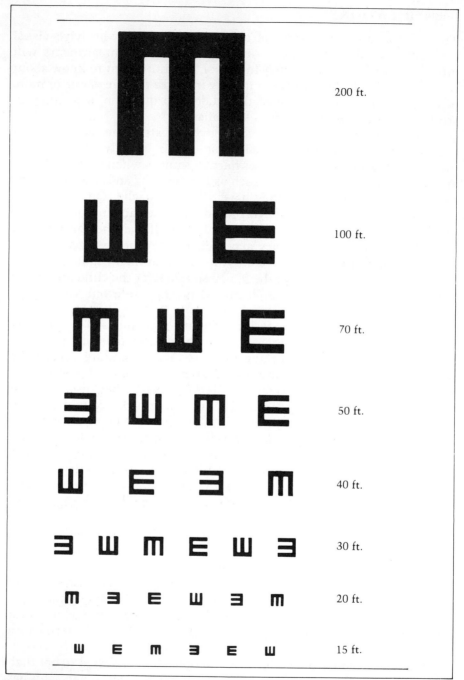

FIGURE 14.4
Snellen symbol chart

Source: From the National Society for the *Prevention* of Blindness, New York, by permission.

and can measure visual functioning. Both can prescribe and fit glasses. The specialist is the one who actually determines if the student has a vision problem and decides upon a form of treatment.

PREVALENCE

According to the Bureau of Education for the Handicapped (1979), approximately 0.1% of the school population is visually impaired to the degree that they need special education services. This, of course, does not include all students who wear prescription lenses, but only those whose needs require special education help. Many students with vision problems do not need any adaptations in the learning environment at all.

The Visually Impaired Student in the Classroom

The academic goals for visually impaired students are the same as those for other students. The delivery of instruction and the student's response to that instruction may need to be adapted, though, to best meet the student's educational needs. Several possible areas of training and educational adaptations are described below. These should be utilized depending upon the needs of a particular student; that is, not every visually impaired student will require the same adaptations and training for success in school.

SPECIALIZED TRAINING

Educational programs for visually impaired students are similar to those of the hearing impaired students in that the students require some forms of specialized training to function in a seeing world. The student must develop some skills at a much higher level than age peers and must be taught some skills that are taken for granted in a school setting. It is important to build the teaching and practice of these skills into the student's instructional program.

Sight Utilization   Visually impaired students should be trained to utilize what residual vision they have. Since this training may require some specialized skills, a physician or teaching specialist may provide the actual instruction in this area. You may be able to reinforce the training in day-to-day activities in the classroom.

Reading   Skills utilized for reading should be developed early in the student's program. There are several options available today to assist visually impaired students in learning to utilize printed material. For some students, reading is taught in the usual manner, allowing for adjustments

Some of the technology that gives visually impaired students access to printed materials: the Perkins Videoscope (above) projects enlarged images of printed matter on a television screen; the Perkins Brailler (right) allows for the preparation of original materials in braille; Optacon (facing page, left) converts print into tactile stimuli; and the Kurzweil Reading Machine (far right) reads books out loud in a synthesized voice.

in print size, lighting conditions, and special reading glasses or other magnification. Large-print books may be obtained from local and/or state lending libraries. Students who are unable to read print materials may need to rely on braille. While you will not likely learn braille, it is important to be familiar with the principles behind it and know when to supplement braille material with oral explanations. Some students will rely on taped materials for instruction. In these cases, the texts the students are using are recorded for the student. These may be available from state libraries; in some areas, state departments are providing services in this area for visually impaired students and adults.

Some recent technological advances are enabling visually impaired students to have greater access to printed materials. The Optacon is an electronic device that converts print into tactile stimuli. The reader feels the image of the letter itself with the finger and may learn to effectively use printed material for reading through training in the use of this system. The Kurzweil Reading Machine is a computer that reads books out loud using a synthesized voice. Its speed and tone can be controlled by the user, and it has the capability to spell words letter by letter. Advances such as these increase the flexibility of instructional programs for visually impaired students and provide greater access to printed materials.

Listening Skills   Since the visually impaired student must rely on cues other than visual cues in the classroom, it is important to make maximum use of the other senses. The visually impaired do not have naturally better hearing as a result of their vision problem; they can, however, be trained to make as much use as possible of their other senses. In addition to helping the student to develop listening skills, it may be important to assist the student by allowing class lectures to be put on audio tape. When using material on the chalkboard, it is important to read the information orally, so the visually impaired student can acquire the information. This procedure may include reading outlines written on the board, orally describing diagrams used on overhead transparencies, and describing illustrations in films and photographs.

Orientation and Mobility   Students who are visually impaired need to develop an orientation to their surroundings. This may involve an outside trainer touring the physical plant of a school, detailing the layout of the facilities and describing the relationship of pertinent areas on the campus. The student may also need training in skills such as cane travel, independent travel, and the use of public transportation. When in the classroom setting, it is important for you to notify the visually impaired student of changes in schedules requiring movement in the school, safety matters such as fire exiting procedures, and changes in the classroom arrangement. Planned changes in the classroom can assist the visually impaired student in increasing skills in travel and provide the opportunity to learn some independent travel and orientation skills.

Daily Living Skills   Many students who are visually impaired do not require training in this area. There may be an occasion, though, when a student needs training in skills such as dressing, eating, clothing selection, and personal hygiene. The direct instruction may be given by a specialist outside the classroom setting. You may be able to reinforce the use of these skills during the school day.

Adaptive Physical Education   Since many visually impaired students may have had limitations placed on their physical activity, it is important to include physical education training in their educational programs. PL 94-142 mandates the provision of adaptive physical education for those students who require the training; these services may be provided by a specialist in this area. When adaptive physical education training is provided for the student, the specialist should work closely with you or the physical education teacher to increase the amount of carry-over between the two physical education experiences.

Typing and Alternative Response Modes   It is important to develop efficient means for gathering responses from visually impaired students in order to enhance communication and performance. The acquisition of typing skills at an early age may be important in doing school work in such a fashion that you can evaluate it. There may be occasions when oral responses given directly or on a tape recorder may be helpful. In any case, you should allow for such adaptations when necessary to increase total communication. The specific needs of an individual student will dictate the adaptations necessary in the classroom for academic and social success.

CLASSROOM ADAPTATIONS

You have an important role in planning and providing instruction for visually impaired students. Careful planning on your part can create a positive learning environment in which the student can maximize skill development and participate successfully with peers. The types of accommodations the teachers made with Mary Ellen at the beginning of the chapter are examples of some of the adaptations classroom teachers can make in the classroom for visually impaired students. Some other suggestions follow:

1. Carefully observe students, noting when students seem to have vision problems. Among the general population, most mild vision prob-

lems can be corrected through the use of glasses or contact lenses and do not interfere with the normal activities presented in a school day. When the vision impairment is such that it does require educational modifications, these should be made by the resource teacher and you in conjunction with the advice of specialists.

2. Supplement printed materials with oral instructions. Even when the student is able to utilize printed material, it may be important for you to provide additional instruction to ensure that the student is able to learn effectively from the printed material.

3. Provide the student with learning options. You may need to consider alternative modes of instruction and responses for the visually impaired student. For example, it may be necessary to administer tests orally to the student. The student may need to bring a typewriter to class for in-class assignments. These alternatives can increase the successful integration of visually handicapped students into the classroom setting.

4. When appropriate, use concrete examples of new concepts. Visually impaired students may be unable to acquire concepts in the same manner as peers. To increase the likelihood of conceptual learning, increase the use of concrete models. A geography lesson on land forms, for example, might incorporate models of the land forms being discussed. These models could be handled by all students to help form the concept.

THE SPECIALIST

The roles of the specialists primarily involved in the treatment of vision problems have already been discussed. The ophthalmologist and the optometrist play important roles in the diagnosis and treatment of vision problems and diseases of the eye. Educators who specialize in the education of visually impaired students should serve as consultants to classroom teachers in program development and modification. Teachers of the visually impaired may play a role very similar to that of the teacher of the hearing impaired. That is, the teacher may provide direct instruction, resource help, consultation with the teacher, and act as a liaison with community resources. If teachers of the visually impaired are not available in your school district and you need their assistance, get in touch with your school administration requesting the assistance.

Summary

Some students enrolled in the school program have sensory handicaps that prevent them from learning in the same manner as their classmates. These students, the hearing impaired and the visually impaired, have unique characteristics which require attention for maximum success in the school environment. You can adapt the learning environment for these students, providing educational experiences that meet the needs of the students in the context of the classroom setting. A few of the major points related in this chapter are presented here.

1. Hearing impaired students are those who have a mild to severe hearing loss that will require that the student receive adapted instruction in the classroom setting.

2. A student may have a conductive, sensori-neural, or mixed hearing loss.

3. You may detect the existence of a hearing loss through careful observation of students in the classroom.

4. Any student with a suspected hearing loss should be referred to an audiologist and/or a physician specializing in diseases of the ear for thorough evaluation.

5. Hearing impaired students should be trained in the use of residual hearing, the use of hearing aids if appropriate, speech, communication systems, and the systems used in the classroom.

6. You should rely on specialists to determine the nature and treatment of the hearing loss and the types of adaptations that might be most effective for that student.

7. A visually impaired student is one who relies on braille or requires large print or special conditions such as lighting or magnification of regular print for reading.

8. Visually impaired students often function one or more grade levels below their age peers as a result of their vision impairment.

9. Visually impaired students may be identified through teacher observation and the use of screening devices like the Snellen Eye Chart. Any students with suspected vision problems should be referred to an optometrist or opthalmologist for evaluation.

10. Visually impaired students should be trained to use their residual vision; provided instruction in reading which meets their needs; and trained in orientation and mobility, daily living, and physical skills.

11. You and the specialist should work together to provide visually impaired students with the instructional modifications necessary for them to participate in the school program.

Activities

1. Simulate a vision or hearing handicap. Using a blindfold or ear plugs, spend one to two hours attempting to follow your normal routine. Attempt tasks like eating a meal, choosing clothing for the day, and

attending classes. Note the responses you get from your peers as you simulate the handicap.

2. Locate books containing the manual alphabet and sign for words and phrases. Practice using the signs to communicate with others.

3. Visit your campus library or the local public library. Ask if the libraries contain any large print or talking books. If they do, review the materials.

4. Take a tour of a school for the deaf or a school for the blind. Visit their educational and residential programs; discuss the needs of students from the school who may be placed in public school settings.

Study Questions

1. Hearing losses may be defined by degree of loss or through educational factors. What are the major characteristics of each definition?

2. How may hearing losses affect the intellectual, academic, and social-emotional growth of students in school?

3. List at least four signs or cues a teacher might use to screen for hearing problems in the classroom.

4. List three types of specialized training that may be used with hearing impaired students. Give one example of the use of the technique in the classroom.

5. What are some strategies the classroom teacher should use when presenting instruction to a class that contains a hearing impaired student?

6. What are the educational definitions of visually impaired students? What implications do these definitions have for classroom instruction?

7. How are the characteristics of visually impaired students compared with those of hearing impaired students?

8. What are some methods a teacher can use to screen for vision problems in the classroom?

9. How can the classroom teacher combine suggested teaching techniques with the specialized training a visually impaired student may need to be successful in the classroom?

Questions for Further Thought

1. Techniques used for communicating with hearing impaired students are quite different from those used in everyday communication.

Should a classroom teacher be expected to learn and use those techniques if a hearing impaired student is enrolled in the classroom?

2. Why is environmental stimulation so important in the early education of visually impaired students?

Additional Resources

BOOKS

Birch, J. W. *Hearing impaired children in the mainstream.* Reston, Virginia: Council for Exceptional Children, 1975.

Hanninen, K. A. *Teaching the visually handicapped.* Columbus, Ohio: Charles E. Merrill, 1975.

Martin, G. C., and Hoben, M. *Supporting visually impaired students in the mainstream.* Reston, Virginia: Council for Exceptional Children, 1977.

Nix, G. W. (Ed.). *Mainstream education for hearing impaired children and youth.* New York: Grune & Stratton, 1976.

PROFESSIONAL JOURNALS

American Annals of the Deaf

Education of the Visually Handicapped

Journal of Visual Impairment and Blindness

The Volta Review

CHILDREN'S LITERATURE

Brown, M., and Cane, R. *The silent storm.* Nashville, Tennessee: Abingdon Press, 1963.

Charlip, R., & Charlip, M. B. *Handtalk: An ABC of finger spelling and sign language.* New York: Parent's Magazine Press, 1974.

Head, B., & Sequin, J. *Who am I?.* Pittsburgh: Family Communications, 1975.

Wolf, B. *Anna's silent world.* New York: J. B. Lippincott, 1976.

Charles, R., and Mathis, S. *Ray Charles.* New York: Thomas Y. Crowell, 1973.

Heide, F. *Sound of sunshine, sound of rain.* New York: Parent's Magazine Press, 1973.

Little, J. *From Anna.* New York: Harper & Row, 1972.

Wolf, B. *Connie's new eyes.* New York: Lippincott, 1976.

PROFESSIONAL ORGANIZATIONS

American Foundation for the Blind, 15 West 16th Street, New York, New York 10011

National Association of the Deaf, 814 Thayer Avenue, Silver Spring, Maryland 20910

National Society for the *Prevention* of Blindness, 79 Madison Avenue, New York, New York 10016

Chapter 15

Physical and

Health Impairments

Students with physical and health impairments comprise a diverse and varied group. These students may have actual neurological disorders, such as cerebral palsy, or special health problems, such as asthma or diabetes. Consider, for example, Kathleen and Carlos, two students who are in the regular classroom and who have physical and health conditions that warrant special consideration.

KATHLEEN

Kathleen is a bright, alert ten-year-old who has spastic cerebral palsy. Kathleen has a great deal of difficulty controlling her muscles. Her movements are jerky and uncoordinated and she needs braces and crutches to help her walk. She can write but makes large, seemingly uncoordinated letters. Kathleen receives physical therapy each day to aid in muscle control. In addition, she receives speech therapy four days a week. Kathleen is happy that she does well in academics but feels a sense of loss at not being able to join her classmates in most of the playground games.

CARLOS

Carlos is a thirteen-year-old boy with epilepsy. For the most part, his disability is hidden, except on the few occasions when he has had grand mal seizures in school. Carlos takes medication each day that virtually eliminates seizure activity and allows Carlos to participate in all aspects of school. Several weeks ago Carlos had a seizure in his English class. Although his teacher and classmates were aware that Carlos had epilepsy and a few of the students had observed his seizures in the past, the episode proved too uncomfortable and frightening for most of them.

Students with physical and health impairments do not always have learning and behavior problems that require special teaching approaches. Instead, they may need certain modifications such as special chairs or devices to keep books and papers open and in place. They may also need physical and occupational therapy to help them use their muscles better and speech therapy to help them speak more clearly. In all cases, these students need caring, supportive classroom teachers who can challenge them to become all they are capable of being and help them develop realistic and positive attitudes about themselves.

A complete discussion of the physical and health conditions that may be present in a public school would fill a book rather than a chapter. Since there are so many conditions that may be present in schools, we have elected to discuss a few of the more prevalent ones. The topics to be addressed in this chapter include neurological dysfunction, health conditions requiring first aid care, and the impact of terminal illnesses in children. This discussion will be followed by a description of adaptations that may be helpful or necessary for those students and the role the classroom teacher can play in increasing the likelihood of successful integration of such students into the school program.

Prevalence of Physical and Health Impairments

Since there are so many different types and degrees of physical and health impairments, it is difficult to obtain a reliable incidence figure. Certainly vaccination programs over the years have had a profound effect on virtually eliminating polio and reducing birth defects resulting from German measles. On the other hand, the number of children who are disabled because of automobile accidents has increased considerably.

Current prevalence estimates suggest that ½ of 1% of the school aged population has physical and health impairments severe enough to warrant special education and related services. This means that one student out of every 200 is likely to be in need of special education assistance because of a physical impairment or a chronic health problem. The Bureau of Education for the Handicapped estimated that in 1978, over 229,000 students with physical and health impairments were receiving special education services. There are, of course, many more students with physical and/or health problems who do not require any special education assistance or classroom modifications.

Neurological Conditions

The notion of brain damage as a possible cause of learning difficulties was introduced in Chapter 5. As you may recall, it is almost impossible to tell if a student with learning disabilities is actually brain damaged as there are no overt signs of brain dysfunction. Rather, brain damage is inferred from certain overt behaviors such as short attention span, hyperactivity, irritability, clumsiness, language difficulties and specific problems in math, handwriting, or reading. There are cases, however, where actual neurological impairment can be documented and results in physical impairments that may affect classroom performance.

EPILEPSY

Epilepsy is a disorder marked by seizures of varying degrees of intensity and duration. A seizure is a spontaneous, uncontrolled firing of neurons in the brain resulting in one or more of the following: a loss of consciousness, muscular contractions, a trancelike state, or jerking of the limbs. A person who has epilepsy may be subject to sudden and uncontrollable movements as well as a loss of consciousness.

Types of Seizures   Although epilepsy is often associated with one particular type of seizure, there are several forms of epilepsy that students in school may have. The least obvious, a *petit mal* seizure, may go unnoticed by some teachers and even by the student having the seizure. A petit mal seizure is characterized by a momentary interruption of speech, reading, or other activity (Best, 1978). A temporary loss of consciousness occurs and the individual may nod his head, drop objects, stare into space, or engage in a series of rapid eye blinks. The lack of consciousness usually lasts only a few seconds and is of no particular danger to the student. The student may give the appearance of "tuning out" for a brief period of time followed by a resumption of activity. A student with a petit mal seizure may appear to be inattentive, clumsy, or a daydreamer; since it is not always easy for teachers to distinguish between the child who is having seizures and the child who is inattentive, you should consult with medical professionals if the characteristics are recurrent and you suspect that a medical problem may exist.

A *grand mal* seizure is the most common form of seizure and can be disturbing or frightening to teachers and students alike (Haslam and Valletutti, 1975). A grand mal seizure is characterized by a complete loss of consciousness, a stiffening of muscles, and violent shaking of the entire body as the large muscles alternately contract and relax. During the seizure, saliva may flow from the mouth, and the student may experience loss of bladder and bowel control. After a few moments, the contractions diminish and the person, who is often quite exhausted, may fall asleep or regain consciousness in a confused or drowsy state (Heward and Orlansky, 1980). In some cases, epileptics experience an *aura* just prior to the seizure. An aura is a sensation such as a particular sound, odor, color, or other sensation that consistently appears just prior to a seizure.

Psychomotor seizures are characterized by purposeless, inappropriate behavior. Lip smacking, walking around aimlessly, making rocking motions, tearing at clothing, or tremors that begin in one appendage and work their way through the entire body are among the behaviors that may be exhibited by individuals experiencing this type of seizure. Psychomotor seizures may be preceded by a warning of aura, and often last for several seconds to several minutes. The seizure activity may spread to the brain motor areas, progressing to a major motor convulsion (Haslam and Valletutti, 1975; Peterson and Cleveland, 1975). The person usually experiences some confusion following the seizure, but does not remember the seizure itself.

Seizures in the Classroom   You can play an important role in dealing with seizures that occur during the school day. Since seizures can be a frightening experience for all students, it is important that you understand how to treat seizures and potential implications for instruction when seizures do occur.

Most epileptic students are on medication designed to control seizure activity. Over half of seizure activity can be almost entirely eliminated through the use of drugs such as Dilantin and phenobarbital (Gadow, 1979). These drugs, while effective in controlling seizures, may cause side effects such as drowsiness and irritability. They may also affect the student's ability to complete school tasks. In some instances, the side effects of the medication may cause more problems than the actual seizure. Under such conditions, the use of medication may be reduced or eliminated.

What can you do when a student is experiencing a seizure? Your role in handling seizures that may occur in the classroom varies depending upon the type of seizure the student is having. For students who have petit mal seizures, there is little for you to do. The seizure is brief in duration and harmless. When such a seizure occurs, you should make note of it; you may want to repeat any instruction presented while the student was having the seizure. Psychomotor seizures, those that involve repetitive and purposeless movements, cannot be stopped and must run their course. You should not try to restrain the student unless he or she is in danger; dangerous objects should be moved so the student does not become injured. A few students may respond to spoken directions and can gently be steered to areas in the room where they are not likely to injure themselves. Again, you should make note of the seizure and repeat any instruction that occurred while the student was having the seizure.

The type of seizure that requires the most attention is the grand mal seizure. You should remain calm during the seizure, reminding students in the classroom that the student having the seizure is not feeling pain and that no one can "catch" epilepsy. You should provide the student the assistance outlined in the list below.

1. Allow the seizure to run its course; do not try to stop it or interfere with movements.

2. Ease the student to the floor and loosen any tight-fighting collar.

3. Remove sharp, hard, or other objects that may injure the student.

4. Do not force anything between the student's teeth. An outmoded form of treatment was to place a spoon or tongue depressor in the person's mouth to prevent biting or swallowing the tongue. This is not necessary. However, if the mouth is already open, you might place a soft object such as a handkerchief between the upper and lower teeth.

5. Place a pillow, blanket or soft piece of clothing under the student's head to prevent the student from banging his or her head on the floor.

6. Turn the student's head to one side to allow saliva to exit.

7. Allow the student to stay put and to sleep if he or she wishes; or assist the student to a quiet area of the room.

8. Record the date, time of the seizure, the duration of the seizure, and measures taken to assist the student. Notify the school nurse or principal, who will then notify the parents.

9. If the seizure continues or if the student passes from one seizure to another, call the nurse and doctor for instruction.

At the conclusion of the seizure and any rest period the student may require, it may be helpful for the student to return to the classroom so classmates can see that he or she is all right.

Since a seizure can be a frightening experience for you and the other students, it is important to help students understand how to react if one of their classmates has seizures (Epilepsy Foundation of America, 1974). This can be accomplished in a number of different ways. First, you can inform the class about the condition, or a physician or a school nurse may be invited to visit the class to provide general information. The epileptic student may wish to share general information with the class. In any case, it is important to be sensitive to the student's needs and feelings about participating in such an educational process. Secondly, class members should be taught appropriate care measures. The student may have a seizure outside the classroom and need assistance. One or more students should remain with the student to provide protection from injury and at least one student should get the classroom teacher, school nurse, or principal. Finally, you should set a model for the students to follow in treating anyone who has a seizure. Acting in a calm, supportive manner is essential.

CEREBRAL PALSY

Cerebral palsy is another neurological condition that may affect performance in school in a number of ways. Cerebral palsy is a condition in which motor function disturbances in one or more limbs, as well as in speech, exist as a result of damage to the brain or central nervous system. The condition is not progressive, nor is it contagious. Cerebral palsy usually occurs prior to, during, or shortly after birth. This is referred to as congenital cerebral palsy and is often caused by factors such as infections, lead or arsenic poisoning, and direct trauma to the brain.

Types of Cerebral Palsy   Cerebral palsy is classified by the type of motor impairment that results from the central nervous system injury. *Spasticity* is the most common form of cerebral palsy. It refers to contractures or shortening of the muscles, which produce jerky, uncontrolled movements. In more severe forms of this condition, the contractures may pull the limbs close to the body (similar to a fetal position), resulting in limited range of motion. In less severe cases, the student will exhibit fine and gross motor dysfunctions that impair physical functioning.

A student with *athetoid* cerebral palsy has large, irregular, and uncontrolled movements. An effort to turn the page of a book, pick up a pencil, or make a speech sound may result in uncontrollable flailing movements accompanied by facial grimaces. Tense, rigid muscles and difficulty with oral communication are usually present.

A form of cerebral palsy known as *ataxia* involves balance, coordination, and body position. Individuals with ataxia appear dizzy, jumpy, and unsteady; some of these people may fall easily.

Educational Implications   Since cerebral palsy is the result of damage to the central nervous system, it is often accompanied by a variety of related handicaps. Approximately 50-60% of cerebral palsy students are retarded and show deficits in perceptual and cognitive development; many of the remaining students have specific learning problems, either as a result of the brain damage or as a result of the physical limitations their condition imposes upon them (Haslam and Valletutti, 1975). Many cerebral palsied students require speech therapy to achieve greater control over the muscles used for speech and increase their ability to communicate orally. Occupational and physical therapy may be important components of the student's educational program, with a goal of increased fine and gross motor coordination and the development of physical skills necessary for independent living.

Although you will not provide many of these specialized programs, you may be asked to reinforce skill development in the classroom. You may need to adapt the physical environment to meet the mobility needs of students with cerebral palsy. Adaptive equipment, such as keyboard guards for typewriters and alternate communication systems (e.g., substituting typewritten for oral and/or written responses) may increase the opportunity for the student to participate in the classroom program. The student should be encouraged to be as independent as possible in the school setting. Finally, you should be sensitive to the rejection or isolation that students with cerebral palsy may experience. Classmates should be allowed to discuss their feelings and concerns regarding ways to understand, approach, and interact with cerebral palsied students just as they should with any individual who has a special problem.

OTHER NEUROLOGICAL CONDITIONS

There are other neurological conditions that may affect the participation of a student in the school environment. You may be confronted, for example, by students who have spina bifida and/or hydrocephalus. *Spina bifida* is a congenital defect that occurs when the bones of the spine fail to grow together. There is often a protrusion on the back where this occurs, and it can cause paralysis, loss of bowel and bladder control, and frequent kidney infections. Spina bifida occurs in approximately 3 out of every 1,000 live births (Myers, 1975). Students with spina bifida may be placed in regular classrooms when such placements meet their educational needs and when toileting and mobility problems can be adequately managed in that setting.

Hydrocephalus is a condition that exists when the circulation of cerebrospinal fluid in the brain is blocked. This blockage, when untreated, can result in brain damage and subsequent retardation. Retardation can be diminished and in some cases avoided altogether by the use of a shunt that drains the excess fluid into the atria of the heart or the abdominal cavity. Since the condition itself or the insertion of the shunt can cause some brain damage, students with hydrocephalus may require some special education. However, many of these students are able to participate in some or all of the classroom activities provided for their age peers. It is important to determine the extent of brain damage, if any, and accommodate the student's educational and physical needs when necessary.

When students who have neurological dysfunctions are enrolled in the classroom, it is important for you to consult with the students' parents, physician, and educational specialists to determine the types of educational and physical modifications that are necessary. Many of these students are able to participate successfully in the classroom setting with minimum adjustments.

Health Impairments

A variety of medical conditions that result in health impairments can affect student performance. Since there are a great many medical conditions, it is impossible to review all but the most common ones. A brief definition of each disorder as well as implications for the classroom teacher are discussed.

ASTHMA

Asthma is a chronic health condition that occurs more frequently in younger children. Symptoms such as labored breathing, wheezing, coughing, and increased respiration are present only during an attack. The attack may be brought on by a specific allergy or by emotional stress. The labored breathing may frighten the child, resulting in crying, gasping, and much anxiety, which may complicate the effects of the attack (Best, 1975). Some students have asthma attacks infrequently; these cause few school problems other than the need to make up missed work. For other students, the attacks occur more frequently, resulting in greater implications for the educational program.

What can you do for students who have frequent asthma attacks? First, efforts should be made to create a positive, nonthreatening learning environment for the student. This might include taking a moment to make sure the student understands difficult learning tasks, reassuring the student from time to time, and reducing emotional stress in the classroom. Since asthma attacks are used as a means of escape by some students, learning activities should have a purpose the student understands and should have a positive emphasis in the classroom. Second, supervision regarding the nature and amount of physical activity should be provided, as extreme physical activity can trigger an attack in some children. Third, efforts must be made to help the student learn critical academic skills that may be missed due to frequent absences. Finally, you should work closely with parents and medical personnel to develop consistent approaches to the student with an eye to reducing the asthma problem. It is important to understand that, even though asthma attacks may be brought on by emotional stress, it is a real condition that should be treated medically and educationally.

ALLERGIES

Some students have reactions to some foods and/or substances in the environment. The reactions may appear in the form of sneezing, coughing, rashes, or hives. When students have these types of reactions, it may be necessary to make a change in diet or in the classroom environment to eliminate the agent causing the reaction. In some cases, the allergic re-action can cause serious physical harm, so it is important to be aware of any first aid procedures that should be followed should such a reaction occur during the school day.

Some students may have a reaction to grasses and pollens that are in the air in the spring. In some cases, it may be helpful to close the windows in the classroom when the wind is blowing or the grass is being mowed. Other students have reactions to insect bites, particularly bee stings. A bee sting can be the cause of death for some, so it is important to know when students are allergic to insect bites. Some foods, additives, and dyes can cause allergic reactions. Whenever possible, these foods should be avoided in the student's diet. If a student has an allergy, then, make a note of the allergy, the reaction the student has, and any first aid care that should be rendered should a reaction occur during the school day.

CONGENITAL HEART DISORDERS

Children with congenital heart disease may show shortness of breath, limited exercise tolerance and a blue appearance of the skin due to poor oxygenation of the blood (Myers, 1975). With recent advances in medical technology, many heart defects can be surgically corrected, and the child can gradually engage in all normal activities. Other than missing school and having to make up critical skills, students with congenital heart disorders do not have learning problems. They may, however, have to monitor and/or limit physical activity if the heart defect has not been entirely corrected.

Heart disorders are often a cause for great concern on the part of parents and teachers alike. For the teacher, it is important to understand the status of the child's condition so that realistic limits and expectations can be established. According to Myers (1975), a child with complete surgical correction may be capable of engaging in all normal activities but may still be fearful and use many excuses to avoid full school par-ticipation. On the other hand, a child whose activity needs to be restricted may push himself or herself as a way of compensating for the disorder. Parents, the school nurse, and the child's doctor can help teachers to arrive at appropriate expectations and precautions for these children.

DIABETES

Diabetes is a metabolic disorder that exists when the pancreas does not produce enough insulin to enable the body to utilize sugar, resulting in a high level of blood glucose. A characteristic of juvenile diabetes mellitus, the form of diabetes found in school-age students, is the total lack of insulin. These students must be treated with injected insulin; oral medication and diet management are insufficient to balance the chemical needs of the body (Haslam and Valletutti, 1975).

Students who have diabetes may require some care during the course of the school year. If the student purchases school lunch, the dietitian should be aware of any dietary restrictions the student may have. When class parties are planned, it will be necessary to provide refreshments that the diabetic student can eat. The student may need to eat at scheduled times during the day to balance the insulin intake. This may include the opportunity for a snack during the school day or a scheduled time for lunch. You should adhere to any dietary or scheduling restrictions the student may have.

Diabetic students may have reactions to excessive or insufficient levels of insulin in their systems. An insulin reaction may occur when there is too much insulin in the student's system. This may be brought on by a lack of food, a delayed meal, or an unusually high level of activity. A diabetic coma, on the other hand, results from too little insulin in the

TABLE 15.1
Treatment of insulin reaction and diabetic coma

	Symptoms	Treatment
Insulin reaction	Sudden onset	Provide sugar or food containing sugar.
	Restlessness	
	Headache	Call a doctor.
	Hunger	Do not give insulin.
	Excessive sweating	
	Tired or weak feeling	
	Sudden change in behavior	
Diabetic coma	Develops slowly	Call a doctor at once.
	Loss of appetite	Keep child warm and in resting position.
	Increased thirst and urination	
	Sweet or fruity odor to breath	Give child fluid without sugar (only if child is conscious).
	Dry skin	

system. Emotional stress, deviation from the diet, or fever may cause a diabetic coma. Since either of these conditions may occur during the school year, you should be prepared with the appropriate first aid techniques for both conditions. Symptoms and treatment of insulin reaction and diabetic coma appear in Table 15.1.

AMPUTATIONS

Amputation is an orthopedic disability that refers to the absence at birth or the removal at a later time of a limb or limbs (Best, 1978). Amputations that occur at birth are due to congenital anomalies such as the failure of a limb to develop. Automobile accidents and other traumatic injuries are the cause of most amputations that occur after birth.

Many students with amputations can be fitted with prosthetic devices. Such devices are artificial parts designed to replace missing arms, legs, or hands. In some cases, the devices can help the individual regain some strength and movement while in other cases the prosthesis may serve only cosmetic purposes.

Students with amputations do not necessarily have learning or behavior problems and, therefore, are likely to be in regular classrooms. You need to be aware of physical problems, such as skin breakdown, which may be caused by improper wearing or use of the prosthesis, as well as mechanical breakdowns in the device itself. Of course, these should be reported immediately to the school nurse and parents. You should also take steps to make sure the student is included in as many aspects of the school program as possible.

Emotional problems are likely to occur for students who have recently lost a limb or suffered some form of disfigurement. Although it is not your role to counsel students, understanding is important. Students may experience frustration at not being able to do things readily that were once taken for granted. Pain caused by the use of prosthetic devices may also lead to frustration, anger, or discouragement. On the other hand, a few students may overcompensate for their disability by engaging in excessive risk taking. It is important to understand that these students are attempting to protect their self-esteem by assuring themselves and others that they are still capable individuals.

Terminal Conditions

Some students suffer from traumatic, fatal, or near-fatal conditions caused by accidents or diseases, such as leukemia or muscular dystrophy. These conditions cause great stress for the victims as well as their family, friends, classmates, and teachers. After describing leukemia and muscular dystrophy, two of the more common terminal conditions, we will discuss implications for the classroom teacher.

LEUKEMIA

Leukemia is a malignancy of the bone marrow in which there is massive overproduction of white blood cells (Myers, 1975). Treatment of leukemia through modern drugs (chemotherapy) has increased the survival time from six months to as much as five years or more. Children undergoing drug treatment may evidence side effects such as a puffy face (moon face), loss of hair, and obesity. Children who are absent from school a great deal will need assistance in being accepted as a member of the class as well as help in learning important skills.

MUSCULAR DYSTROPHY

Muscular dystrophy is a progressive and continuous weakening of the voluntary muscles. The first indications of the disease may begin as early as three years of age. Early characteristics involve a swayback appearance and increasing clumsiness in walking. Frequent falls may also occur. Facial, neck, hand, and chest muscles are the last of the muscle groups to be involved. An inability to walk at all often occurs by the time the child is ten to thirteen years old, thus confining the child to a wheelchair. Death due to cardiac arrest or upper respiratory infection may occur by the late teens or early twenties (Best, 1978).

EDUCATIONAL IMPLICATIONS

Your first concern is to make school a comfortable and rewarding place for the terminally ill student. Since it is likely that the student will miss school while undergoing medical treatment, it will be important to provide as much continuity as possible by keeping close track of the work the student has completed.

Efforts should also be made to include students in as many activities as possible, as it is likely that school may be the main source of social as well as academic opportunities. Other children in the class may seek an explanation of the student's illness. Rather than denying the illness, you should describe it and discuss it in an open manner. Slides, films, and other resources can be made available for students who wish to read about children and young adults who have serious illnesses.

Of particular interest is the growing emphasis on confronting death and dying (Kubler-Ross, 1969). Since death is a topic that rarely surfaces for discussion in our society, you may be faced with the task of helping students understand the conditions that led to the death of a classmate or parent and help explore their own feelings about that loss. Conducting such discussions requires that you first understand your own feelings in order to more successfully assist students in coping with their reactions. You may wish to plan some group activities relating to the loss of a class member and provide support systems within the class. In addition, you may be in a position to provide or recommend direct counseling to a student or students who need more personal assistance.

You may be assisted in this task by some resource people. Many colleges and universities are recognizing the need for training and awareness in the area of death and dying and offer courses for teachers and counselors. In addition, hospitals are recognizing the need for counseling to help family members cope with the needs and conflicts generated by the terminally ill. Many hospitals now have programs to deal with these issues and personnel who are trained to counsel others. These people may prove to be an invaluable aid to you in helping students cope effectively with the death of a classmate.

The Teacher and the Specialist: A Team Approach

Students with physical and health impairments constitute a diverse group of individuals with a variety of special needs. Providing a sound education program for these students requires the services of a number of specialists as well as specific classroom adaptations. Indeed, a coordinated, team effort is needed. In this section we will examine some of the services provided by specialists and then discuss implications for classroom teachers.

SPECIALISTS

Because students with physical impairments and chronic health problems have many needs, the services of a variety of ancillary personnel may be required. Medical professionals may assist with the actual treatment of any physical and health problems. Speech and language pathologists and physical and occupational therapists may assist the student in developing fine and gross motor coordination necessary for oral communication and school success. Teacher consultants and adaptive physical education specialists may help develop physical modifications in the enrironment and specific programs for the student.

Medical Specialists   Most students who have physical or health impairments are under the care of one or more physicians. These professionals can provide school personnel with reports on the student's physical condition. They can also provide you with specific suggestions for the student's care in the classroom if that is necessary. The school nurse can assist you in any required first aid techniques as well as serve as a consultant for in-service activities developed to explain specific physical and health problems to other students in the school.

Physical Therapists   Physical therapists use special knowledge of the muscle and skeletal systems to help individuals learn to develop and

improve useful fine and gross motor movements. Individuals with cerebral palsy, amputation, muscular dystrophy, or other impairments may
need the services of a physical therapist. The physical therapist usually
works under the direction of a physician. Special exercises, massage treatments, stretching, swimming, and hydrotherapy are some of the techniques used by physical therapists to help individuals achieve maximum
use of their bodies and keep muscles limber. The physical therapist also
serves as a consultant and may devise a treatment plan to be carried out
by parents, teachers, and aides.

Occupational Therapists   Occupational therapy is similar to physical
therapy except greater emphasis is placed on developing life adjustment
skills. These skills range from learning how to tie shoes, dress and feed
oneself to learning how to type, cook and use free time, as well as developing vocational skills. As in the case of physical therapy, the occupational therapist may develop a plan of activities to be carried out by
others who work with the students.

Speech and Language Therapists   The type of speech disorders children
with physical and health problems are likely to have are the same as
those identified in Chapter 13. These include articulation, voice, and
fluency problems, as well as developmental delays in language. Some
children with cerebral palsy have particular problems related to articulation and fluency. For these students, therapy is a vital part of the education program.

Educational Specialists   In some schools, *consulting teachers* are hired
to develop and maintain the adaptive equipment necessary for the integration of physically handicapped students in the classroom. While these
teachers do not provide direct instruction for the student, they serve as
consultants for classroom teachers who need assistance in modifying the
classroom and instructional activities to best meet the needs of the physically handicapped.
     Another educational specialist who can play an important role in the
development of physical skills in handicapped students is the *adaptive
physical education specialist.* In the past, physical education has not been
available for some physically handicapped and health impaired students.
If the student did participate, it was usually from the sidelines, keeping
score or cheering for friends. As a result of the mandates of PL 94-142,
there is an emphasis on providing physical education for these students
and structuring classroom physical education activities so these students
can be included. Adaptive physical educators may be physical education
teachers who have received additional training in providing physical education opportunities such as skiing, walking, hiking, indoor games, and
many other activities for children and adults with a variety of handicaps.

Adaptive physical education specialists develop and provide physical education activities for students with a variety of handicaps.

THE CLASSROOM TEACHER

It should be clear by now that you are part of an interdisciplinary team. A broad range of services needs to be developed and coordinated for many physically handicapped students. In addition to serving as a member of this team, you should consider the practices and adaptations that you may need to make.

Advance Preparation   When class assignments are made at the beginning of the year, you should review all student records, noting which students have unusual health problems. Should a health or physical impairment be evident, you should try to develop an understanding of the condition through reading or by consulting the school nurse or family physician. With the help of medical specialists, you should determine what, if any, first aid procedures may be necessary and how to carry them out in different school settings. Since some health and physical conditions require modification of the classroom environment and/or instructional procedures, you should prepare for these. You should consult with previous teachers of the student to find out what techniques have been used successfully with the student. Finally, you may wish to prepare some material for educating the class about various medical conditions, including the ones they will meet in the classroom. There are professional groups that can provide information on specific physical and health problems and that can serve as a basis for in-service training in the classroom.

Student Attitudes   Many children with physical and health impairments suffer from excessive pity, sympathy, and overprotection. Others may be excluded, rejected, and teased. It is important for you, the classroom teacher, to accept the handicapped student as a worthwhile, competent individual who has unique strengths, interests, and needs. Such children should never be allowed to do less than they are capable of. Instead, they should be encouraged to meet reasonable standards of performance and behavior and to develop a realistic view of themselves and their conditions (Heward and Orlansky, 1980).

If handicapped students are to develop a sense of self-esteem and acceptance, then the attitudes of their classmates must be considered. Classmates should be taught about the particular health problem, if it is an obvious one. Classmates can be helped to develop realistic attitudes and ways of interacting with their handicapped peers by engaging in some of the activities outlined in Chapter 12. Most important, however, is the establishment of a genuine attitude of acceptance.

Classroom Arrangement   Some physically handicapped students are in wheelchairs, have braces on their legs, or use crutches or walkers for mobility. While these students may need few, if any, adjustments in their academic program, assuring adequate mobility is essential. Bathroom facilities may need to be modified to accommodate a wheelchair. The classroom arrangement should allow for ease of movement to and from all important centers in the classroom. Desks and tables may need to be raised or lowered. The cafeteria, gymnasium, and other school facilities should be accessible to the student. Although you may not be in a position to effect most of these changes yourself, you may need to campaign for them with your school administration.

Time Schedules   Due to fatigue, handicapped or health impaired students may be unable to participate in the full schedule of school activities. The priority areas for instruction, such as reading, arithmetic, and language arts, should be scheduled while the student is in school. Tutoring in the home may also be considered. In some cases, provision should be made for rest during the school day for students who fatigue easily.

Adapted Equipment   Many physically handicapped students need equipment to help adapt to the learning environment. If the student is unable to hold a book, a book rest should be secured. A tape recorder may be necessary for note taking. A typewriter with a keyboard guard that permits the striking of only one key at a time may assist a cerebral palsied student

Braces and crutches (below) are not the only tools for integrating the physically handicapped into everyday life. Today you will also find specially adapted rest rooms and drinking fountains (left); wheelchair ramps on many public streets and buildings (bottom left); and certain parking and travel areas reserved for use by the handicapped (bottom right).

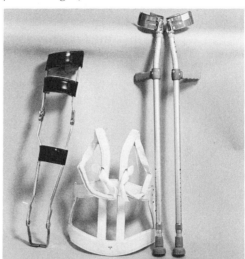

in making written responses. Such equipment could be purchased or produced to aid in the education of the physically handicapped.

Summary

Some students in public school programs have physical and/or health problems that may prevent them from fully participating in classroom activities or that may require some form of first aid in emergency situations. While these students may not have learning and behavior problems per se, they may require some forms of educational modification, either in the physical environment of the classroom or in the type of instruction presented and responded to in the educational process. The major points covered in this chapter are as follows:

1. A very small proportion of the population have physical and health problems. Of these people, not all require educational adaptations to be successful in school.

2. Epilepsy is a condition that results in seizures. You should know how to treat a seizure should a student have one during the school day.

3. Cerebral palsy is a neurological condition that may result in a need for services from speech and language pathologists, physical and occupational therapists, and special education personnel. Some students with cerebral palsy will be successful in the classroom with few, if any, adaptations.

4. Some students have physiological reactions to stress, environmental factors, and foods. Students with asthma and allergies should be provided with environments that are as free as possible of the agents that cause reactions.

5. Students with congenital heart problems may require some adaptations in the daily schedule to accommodate their physical limitations.

6. Teachers should be aware of the needs of diabetic students and the procedures to follow should a student have an insulin reaction or go into a diabetic coma.

7. Students who are amputees may be able to fully participate in the school program. Those who use prosthetic devices or require wheelchairs may need to have some adaptations in the arrangement of the classroom.

8. You should be prepared to assist students with death and dying when experiences in the home or school result in a need for

understanding and assistance in working through the feelings we all have related to death.

9. You and specialists should work closely together to provide an integrated, well-planned range of services to students who are physically or health impaired.

Activities

1. Develop a classroom in-service unit for students who may be encountering a peer with one of the physical or health problems noted in this chapter. Focusing on one specific problem, note all activities you might use to sensitize your students to the conditions: speakers, field trips, children's and adolescent's literature, and simulation activities.

2. Simulate a physical handicap for a portion of your day. This can be accomplished in a number of ways: wearing a mitten on your dominant hand, using a wheelchair, using crutches, and immobilizing one limb. Follow your normal routine while simulating the problem.

3. Interview a physically handicapped peer or other adult. In the interview you might discuss: a) the person's experience as a student in school; b) public attitudes towards them; c) the affect of their handicap on their personal, social, and academic growth; and, d) any suggestions they have for classroom teachers.

Study Questions

1. List the steps a teacher should follow if a student has a seizure in the classroom.

2. If a student has cerebral palsy, what educational accommodations might a classroom teacher need to make for successful integration of the student in the classroom?

3. Asthma and allergies are similar in that each is a reaction to some element in the environment. List three steps a classroom teacher can take to help reduce asthma and allergy attacks during the school day.

4. What is diabetes? How should the teacher treat an insulin attack and a diabetic coma?

5. Name three steps a classroom teacher can take to help students cope with death and dying.

6. What are two services specialists may provide for students with physical and health problems?

7. List three considerations a classroom teacher should keep in mind when planning for students with physical and health impairments.

Questions for Further Thought

1. Many people feel that those who are physically handicapped are also mentally retarded. Why do you suppose this attitude exists?

2. Physical and health problems, particularly those that result in premature death, are seldom discussed openly. Why do you think we avoid these topics in public discussions?

3. As noted throughout the text, there are a number of handicapping conditions. Do you think the public is more comfortable with academic and social-emotional problems or with sensory and physical problems? Why?

Additional Resources

BOOKS

Bigge, J. L., and O'Connell, P. A. *Teaching individuals with physical and multiple disabilities.* Columbus, Ohio: Charles E. Merrill, 1976.

Bleck, E., and Nagel, D. A. *Physically handicapped children: A medical atlas for teachers.* New York: Grune & Stratton, 1975.

Edgington, D. *The physically handicapped child in your classroom: A handbook for teachers.* Springfield, Illinois: Charles C. Thomas, 1976.

Haslam, R. H. A., & Valletutti, P. J. (Eds.). *Medical problems in the classroom: The teacher's role in diagnosis and management.* Baltimore: University Park Press, 1975.

PROFESSIONAL JOURNALS

Journal of Rehabilitation

Rehabilitation Literature

PROFESSIONAL ORGANIZATIONS

American Heart Association, 44 East 23rd Street, New York, New York 10011

Epilepsy Foundation of America, 1828 L Street, N.W., Washington, D.C. 20036

United Cerebral Palsy Association, 66 East 34th Street, New York, New York 10016

CHILDREN'S LITERATURE

Campanella, R. *It's good to be alive.* Boston: Little, Brown and Company, 1959.

Fassler, J. *My grandpa died today.* New York: Human Sciences Press, 1969.

Little, J. *Mine for keeps.* Boston: Little, Brown and Company, 1962.

Luis, E. *Wheels for Ginny's chariot.* New York: Dodd, Mead and Company, 1966.

Savits, H. *Fly, wheels, fly.* New York: John Day, 1970.

Shumsky, L., and Shumsky, Z. *Shutterbug.* New York: Funk and Wagnall, 1963.

Slote, A. *Hang tough, Paul Mather.* Philadelphia: Lippincott, 1973.

PART VI
EMERGING
DIRECTIONS

As you have seen in the first five sections of this text, there is much to learn about teaching exceptional children in the regular classroom. Let us now pause and reflect upon the major themes before going on to the last section of the book.

The focus of Part I was on the two dominant themes in the history of special education — the advance of knowledge and the evolution of humane treatment. In Part II we focused on learning more about students who may be labeled as mentally retarded, emotionally disturbed, or learning disabled. In Part III, the assessment of learning and behavior problems was presented as being an important concern of the classroom teacher. All teachers have the responsibility to become effective data gatherers and analyzers. Some suggestions on how to teach new skills within the regular classroom and understanding and working effectively with behavior problems were presented in Part IV. The purpose of Part V was to acquaint you with the specific issues in working with those students whose handicapping conditions result in specialized interventions beyond working with learning and behavior problems. You should now have been exposed to the major concepts and issues in the field of special education as they relate to you, the regular classroom teacher. There are, however, a few important points yet to be made in this last section.

The term "exceptional" refers to anyone who falls outside of the normal range on some important, measurable dimension. To many people, students who are gifted and talented should also be called exceptional and fall under the purview of the legal mandates. The argument that gifted and talented students deserve an appropriate educational program is a compelling one. If one believes that all students should have an appropriate education, then one must accept the idea that gifted and talented students be provided with educational services that meet their unique needs. Chapter 16 is devoted to furthering this idea.

A major theme of the text has been to present a process we call the problem-solving model. The last chapter describes how the problem-solving approach can be used to formulate an Individualized Education Program (IEP). We believe that all planning for individual students should be based on knowledge of exceptionality and data collected that reflect academic and behavioral needs.

While every student referred to the Pupil Evaluation Team (PET) presents a unique challenge, the elements in the process are the same. At each step the collective wisdom of the professionals on the Pupil Evaluation Team is used to find answers to such questions as these:

- What are this student's behavioral and educational needs?
- What should I teach this student?
- How should I teach this student?

As long as the Pupil Evaluation Team can keep in mind that it is in fact responsible for collecting and examining data to answer specific questions, then developing an appropriate educational plan can be an efficient process. By viewing each step of the process as a question to be answered, and by knowing what data can be used to find an appropriate answer, educators can use their collective wisdom to learn from each other and grow.

As you read the case study in Chapter 17, see if you can formulate how you might use your knowledge to devise an IEP for other exceptional children.

Chapter 16

Gifted and

Talented Students

The focus of this text has been on the unique educational problems of students who have learning, behavior, and sensory or motor difficulties in school. There is another population of students, the gifted and talented, who also have special learning needs that should be accommodated in public school programs. These students have been included in various legislative acts for exceptional students in the past. They are not, however, covered by PL 94-142 as it is currently written; therefore, special programs for these students are not mandated nationally as they are for other exceptional students.

Who are the gifted and talented students in our schools? What are they like? What impact do they have on a classroom or school program? Do they require special educational services to meet their potential? How might you prepare the learning environment to best meet the needs of gifted and talented students? These and other questions related to the education of the gifted and talented in our schools will be addressed in this chapter. But first, let's meet Ken, a gifted student.

KEN

Ken, an eighth-grader, is the first of three children. When he was very young, it was apparent that Ken was an exceptional child. He walked well before the normal age and acquired speech and language skills far in advance of his peers. By the time he was three years old, Ken had taught himself to read.

Ken lived in an atmosphere that always bustled with activity. His mother owned a small shop that she operated from the home. Customers frequently engaged in conversation with Ken, discussing a variety of topics. Ken was encouraged to interact with these people. Both of Ken's parents were involved in home and community projects, which brought many people into their home and provided stimulation and enrichment for Ken at an early age.

By the time he entered school, Ken had acquired many of the skills expected of students who were several years ahead of him in grade placement. He read books written on eighth- to tenth-grade levels. He could use basic arithmetic skills to compute problems he encountered as he pursued his areas of interest. He developed a keen interest in chemistry and community welfare, and began conducting experiments and recording data on local water supplies. These interests were fostered by his family through reading, discussion, and participation in projects and experiments.

When Ken was enrolled in school, he was given a school readiness test that indicated that he had the skills necessary for successful completion of kindergarten with the exception of some fine and gross motor skills. (These were skills that other children his age had also not yet developed.) He was placed directly into the first grade. The classroom was typical of most first grades, with an emphasis on beginning reading, arithmetic, handwriting, and basic concept development. Since Ken had already mastered many of these skills, he was given work more appropriate to his level in reading and arithmetic. He was expected to participate with the class in activities related to gross and fine motor skills; in content areas such as health, science, and social studies; and during play and social activities. Ken's interests in community welfare and chemistry were not addressed at school, but were still an important component of his time at home. At the end of the year, there was no question of promoting Ken to the second grade.

Ken's program in the second grade paralleled his first grade program. He was still given advanced level material in reading and arithmetic, but was expected to stay with the rest of the class in other content areas. He was included in all social and play activities with his age peers. As the year progressed, Ken was successful in all academic areas. It seemed, however, that the school program did not entirely meet his needs. He had mastered reading and arithmetic skills at such a superior level that there was little left for instruction in the elementary school setting, even with an enriched program. He became increasingly bored and restless during instructional periods that were not at an advanced level. Ken's parents continued their home enrichment program for him. By the end of second grade Ken began to question the value of some of the work he was required to do in school and was disruptive in the classroom. It became apparent that the instructional program, as it had been established, was not meeting Ken's needs.

When Ken entered third grade, he encountered an entirely new program. He was no longer given instruction in reading and arithmetic. Instead, he was presented with a structured program for the study of literature. Books were selected based upon his reading ability, his level of understanding, and his various personal interests. Ken did most of the reading and related assignments on his own. He would then confer with a sixth-grade teacher who was assigned to help plan, review, and discuss the material. In arithmetic, he was given more advanced work from a programmed text that was, for the most part, self-instructional. His classroom teacher monitored his progress and provided direct instruction when needed. Ken was still required to participate with the class in other content areas. He was, however, given the opportunity to explore each unit presented in some depth, selecting an area of interest, developing a model or project for class utilization, and presenting his work to the class when other students made their class presentations. Ken also worked on a regular basis with the school librarian, who helped him develop study and research skills. Again, Ken was required to participate with the class in social and play activities. The flexibility offered in the third grade proved to be stimulating and provided Ken with success in the school program. As he continued through the public school system, similar adaptations were made to accommodate his exceptional needs.

As an eighth-grader, Ken is enrolled in the local junior-high-school program. He participates in the grammar and literature components of the language arts program, but receives no instruction in reading and spelling. He is excused from the junior high school for two class periods each day to attend an advanced chemistry class and a calculus class at the high school. Ken then returns to the junior high school for lunch, physical education, social studies, and art. Ken is enrolled in regular class settings during the last three classes. He enjoys the activities in his physical education class and the social interaction with his peers. He has chosen, in consultation with his parents and the school guidance counselor, to remain in the traditional social studies program so he can acquire the general information presented in the class and focus his energies on his studies in chemisty and calculus. Ken's instructional program is tailored to meet his academic achievement level and his personal needs and interests.

Defining the Gifted and Talented

The gifted have long been recognized as a group in the school population that possesses exceptional qualities and learning characteristics. This group has often been identified by the level of intelligence they possess. In the past, a gifted individual was often defined as one who had an IQ of 130 or above and whose intelligence was reflected in academic achievement. As this group was studied, however, it was found that there were areas in which some students excelled besides intellectual and academic achievement. It was also noted that gifted and talented students seemed to share some common characteristics, many of them contradictory to beliefs held about the gifted.

DEFINITION

Because students excelled in areas other than intellectual and academic achievement, it became necessary to broaden the definition used to describe the gifted. Students with special talents in areas such as art and music, creativity, and leadership could contribute to the school community and often needed specialized programs to enhance and develop the abilities they possessed. Consequently, the most recent definitions of the gifted have been expanded to include talented individuals as well. The current definition appears in Public Law 95-561, The Gifted and Talented Children's Act of 1978:

> For the purposes of this part, the term gifted and talented children means children, and, whenever applicable, youth who are identified at the preschool, elementary, or secondary level as possessing demonstrated or potential abilities that give evidence of high performance capabilities in areas such as intellectual, creative, specific academic, or leadership ability, or in the performing and visual arts, and who by reason thereof, require services or activities not ordinarily provided by the school.

The above-mentioned definition bears careful review. A specific IQ score is not mandated; in fact, a talented individual may not have an extremely high IQ. Rather, he or she may excel in creative thought or physical prowess. Exceptional ability in several categories, including intellectual ability, are recognized in this definition, thus changing the potential scope and breadth of programs for the gifted and talented. A brief explanation of each element of the definition follows.

Intellectual Ability   Some students possess a high level of native intellectual ability, which enables them to learn quickly and at advanced levels. These students may be characterized by ". . . intellectual curiosity, exceptional powers of observation, ability to abstract, a questioning attitude, and associative thinking skills" (Tuttle and Becker, 1980). Intellectually gifted students often excel in several areas and may have a wealth of knowledge about their world.

A student with high intellectual ability will usually score at a very high level on an individual intelligence test, often receiving an IQ score of 130 or higher. These students can usually excel in most, if not all, of their academic courses. They acquire information and skills quickly and are able to think and understand what they are learning at an abstract level. Intellectually gifted students may have particular interest areas that they pursue vigorously; sometimes this interest may interfere with performance in other academic and social areas.

Creative Ability   Some students are able to use unique thought patterns to conceptualize and develop new processes and/or products. These students have an ability to break away from conventional approaches to situations and problems and utilize their talents to arrive at unique solutions. Although there is not total agreement on a definition of creativity, the following statement provides a basis for discussion.

> Creativity is a combination of the flexibility, originality, and sensitivity to ideas which enables the learner to break away from usual sequences of thought into different and productive sequences, the result of which gives satisfaction to himself and possibly to others. (Jones, 1972, p. 7)

A characteristic commonly attributed to creative students is *divergent thinking* (Gallagher, 1975; Guilford, 1979). Divergent thinking refers to an ability to study a problem and develop a number of solutions. This is an unusual skill in that most of the population tend to look at a problem and come up with one solution, one that many others would also present. The divergent thinker is not limited by the conventions imposed upon and accepted by most people.

Specific Academic Ability   Some students in the school system excel in academic work. They consistently achieve at a high level, performing well on tests, receiving high grades in their courses, and demonstrating an ability for a particular academic area. For example, a seventh-grade student may be working on advanced mathematics (trigonometry and calculus) while another student may have an interest and excel in the study of ancient history. These students may perform at an average level in other subject areas. Specific academic ability, then, relates to the student's ability to excel in one or more academic areas (Khatena, 1977).

Some students may have specific academic ability not related to the school curriculum. These students may excel much as the students mentioned in the preceding paragraph, but do not demonstrate their capabilities in the school setting. The academic excellence is nurtured in the home or other settings, allowing the student to pursue interests outside school. Examples might include model building, electronics, or short-wave radio.

Leadership Ability   "Leadership involves use of power, productive interactions with others, and self-control" (Tuttle and Becker, 1980). Students who are gifted in leadership generally exhibit personal characteristics that enable them to be responsible for their actions and effectively lead others. These students are not necessarily the popular students in a school. Rather, they are the students who demonstrate a unique talent for organizing and motivating others, accomplishing projects, or influencing opinions.

While we tend to think of leadership as a very positive attribute, it may be used both positively and negatively in a school setting. An academic leader in school may be a student who performs at a high academic level and seeks ways for other students to excel as well through organizing student talent and developing a support system. The student who, on the other hand, is a leader of a gang in the school or community also demonstrates a gift for leadership.

Performing and Visual Arts   The visual and performing arts refers to such areas as painting, sculpture, dancing, playing musical instruments, and performing in dramatic productions. Giftedness in these areas may not be apparent to the classroom teacher; the superior talents of some students are demonstrated outside the school setting. Some school programs support the development of specific talents in students; others do not provide the training or opportunity for the student to pursue the talent during school hours.

The definition of gifted and talented students suggests that these are students who need differentiated programming to meet their unique educational needs. Some students perform well in many of these areas, but do not need educational programs developed specifically to meet their needs. This definition excludes those students, but includes students who, as a result of their exceptional abilities, require instruction not usually available in the classroom to meet their unique needs and abilities.

It should be noted that the above categories are not mutually exclusive. An intellectually gifted student may also be very creative. A student who excels in musical performance may also be intellectually gifted. Some students will be gifted or talented in one area only; other students will show a multitude of talents.

Gifted and talented students, then, are those who have an exceptional ability or skill in one or more of the areas mentioned and who also require specialized programming to maximize their abilities and skills. They are individuals ". . . whose performance in any line of valuable activity is consistently or repeatedly remarkable" (Witty, 1972).

CHARACTERISTICS

Numerous studies have been conducted on the gifted and talented to determine what, if any, specific characteristics are present in this population. Before we begin a discussion of the characteristics of gifted and talented students, though, let's first look at the stereotypes some people have of gifted students.

There are many misconceptions about gifted and talented students. For instance, some people believe that gifted and talented students are eccentric, exhibiting many unusual behaviors. Others believe that gifted students are bookworms who rarely participate in social and physical activities and are often of delicate health. And still others feel that gifted and talented people live in a world of their own, unable to communicate with others of normal intelligence.

Contrary to the pictures some people have, gifted and talented students are average or above average in physical development and health. Additionally, gifted and talented individuals are usually emotionally healthy and stable. Although gifted students are sometimes stereotyped as emotionally disturbed, absentminded, or neurotic, actual observations do not bear this out. Most gifted and talented students are accepted by their peers; they are not social recluses or outcasts.

In reality, most gifted and talented students are much like other students in the school environment. These students often come from a home background that is better than average educationally and economically and from an average or above-average socioeconomic background. Being the firstborn child in a small family is associated with being gifted and talented (Pulvino and Lupton, 1978). It is important to realize that such a background is not a prerequisite to giftedness; however, these students are more frequently identified as gifted and talented than students from other backgrounds. It is necessary for schools to be aware of this potential bias and identify all students with exceptional abilities no matter what their background.

In general, then, the gifted and talented are much like their age peers in physical, emotional and social growth. There are, however, some differences. These students are often academically superior to their age peers. They more often utilize higher thought processes, such as analytical and divergent thinking. They often have a curiosity not present in others, which may lead them to inquire about and investigate new areas. They are usually persistent and motivated to do well in their areas of interest (Newland, 1976). The characteristics of gifted and talented students are summarized in the list below.

1. intellectually curious

2. persistent when pursuing tasks

3. large vocabulary

4. early reader with greater comprehension of language

5. able to sustain interest in an area over a long period of time

6. able to make abstractions

7. keen sense of humor

8. independent and responsible at an early age

9. able to see relationships between diverse ideas and draw generalizations

10. critical and analytical of self and others

11. able to generate many ideas for a specific problem (divergent thinking)

12. sensitive to injustice

13. highly verbal

14. able to learn easily

15. able to concentrate for long periods of time

16. creative

17. eager to assume leadership roles

18. eager to question and study to answer questions

19. widely read in one or more subject areas

Let's now return to our discussion of Ken and compare his abilities and characteristics with those covered in the definition and the preceding section.

KEN

Ken has been given three individual intelligence tests while in school. His IQ score on the last test administered was 147; his scores have all been above 140. He participates in the school testing program, taking the scheduled achievement tests every other year. The last tests were administered in seventh grade. At that time, Ken scored in the 99th percentile in all academic areas tested. When taking tests administered in school, Ken frequently scores 100%, sometimes finding teacher errors on exams.

Ken interacts well with his peers. He enjoys outdoor sports like soccer, baseball, and track, and can be competitive during physical education classes and in after-school games. He finds opportunities during the school day to socialize with his friends and frequently joins them in after-school activities. In the classroom, Ken shares his skills and information with the class. He is able to present what he has learned in a nonthreatening manner so all class members can understand what he is teaching.

While Ken is working on his personal projects and studying science and mathematics, he is demonstrating the ability to process and synthesize information. He works with the local water commissioner to solve some of the problems plaguing some parts of the community. Ken's work and theories have led to two solutions that were implemented in the water program. The ability to utilize information in other areas is also apparent; however, Ken focuses most of his energy in this area.

Ken is a gifted and talented student. He is intellectually gifted, as demonstrated by his performance on intelligence tests, his intellectual curiosity, and his ability to think on an abstract level. He also demonstrates a talent for creativity in his work on the chemical analysis of water problems. He uses divergent thinking to come up with solutions to problems that have been present for some time in the community. Based upon his performance in school activities, Ken is also gifted in his academic ability. He consistently performs at a high level and requires educational adaptations in the school program to meet his intellectual and educational needs.

PREVALENCE

Since the definition of gifted and talented has evolved to include categories in addition to the intellectually gifted, it is difficult to give a precise prevalence figure. One estimate is that approximately 3-5% of the population fall into this category (Lyons, 1981; Mitchell and Erickson, 1978). It should also be noted that since there are no exact criteria used to distinguish between those who are gifted and talented and those who are not, the percentage in any given school district may vary from the figure just cited.

Identifying the Gifted and Talented

Because the definition of gifted and talented student contains so many areas, a number of techniques have been utilized to identify the students. The type of gift or talent the student possesses will assist in the determination of the techniques used to document its existence. In initial screening programs, a variety of techniques will be employed to identify the students who are eligible and will benefit from specialized instruction in the program that will be established. These techniques include standardized tests; checklists; teacher, peer, or parent nomination; and past accomplishments.

TESTING

Group and individual intelligence tests are frequently used to identify students who are gifted and talented, particularly in intellectual and specific academic areas. While these tests may indicate high levels of intellectual functioning, they do not measure all skills associated with thinking and intellectual development. In particular, group IQ tests are a rough measure of intellectual ability at best because they do not measure unusually high ability very well. In addition, students who are exceptionally bright may make incorrect choices in test situations for very logical reasons. Information on how the student approaches an intellectual problem and arrives at an answer is lost in a group testing situation.

Achievement tests are also used to identify those students who are intellectually gifted and/or who demonstrate specific academic ability. Students who excel intellectually and academically tend to have high achievement levels. However, the same concerns are raised about the use of group achievement tests with the gifted student. The test will not necessarily identify gifted students, nor will all gifted students perform at high levels on achievement tests.

Specific tests have also been developed to measure creativity in gifted and talented students. These tests attempt to measure creative or divergent thinking in problem situations. The Torrance Tests of Creative Thinking (Torrance, 1966) measure divergent thinking through verbal and figural tests of creativity. The student is then scored on fluency, flexibility, originality, and elaboration (Callahan, 1978). There is some question about the use of these tests in identifying creative students; students seem to score more similarly to their intelligence test score than they do to other measures of creativity, and it is difficult to distinguish truly creative responses from responses that seem creative but have been learned as a result of broad experience.

While information from intelligence tests, achievement tests, and tests of creativity may assist in identifying gifted and talented students, it is important to assess the usefulness of the data collected. Test scores may not accurately represent the student's performance level. Additionally, they provide a profile of only one aspect of the gifted and talented student's abilities. Other measures should be used in conjunction with tests to identify the gifted and talented and their precise educational needs.

	Seldom to never	Occasionally	Frequently	Almost always
1. Is an avid reader.	————	————	————	————
2. Is uninhibited in expressing opinions.	————	————	————	————
3. Quickly grasps underlying principles.	————	————	————	————
4. Prefers to work independently.	————	————	————	————
5. Grasps relationships of individual steps to total process.	————	————	————	————

FIGURE 16.1
Sample checklist items

CHECKLISTS

There are a number of commercially prepared checklists that help in the identification process. Checklists like the Scales for Rating the Behavioral Characteristics of Superior Students (Renzulli and Smith, 1979) provide a list of behaviors characteristic of many gifted and talented students. The teacher is asked to observe the student(s) in the classroom and rate them on their characteristics. Figure 16.1 shows some typical checklist items. The results of the ratings may be compared to norms established for that population, and decisions may be made on appropriate educational programming for the student(s).

The results obtained from checklists should be used with some caution. First, every teacher brings some bias to an observation setting, using both his or her own interpretation of the statements used to observe student behavior and his or her personal perspective on what the particular student needs. In the establishment of a new program for gifted and talented students, you may be asked to rate a large number of students in a relatively short period of time. You should be aware of the possibility of rater bias and devote as much time as necessary to completing the survey accurately for each student rated (Callahan, 1978).

TEACHER NOMINATION

Teachers are often asked to identify students in their classrooms who are gifted and talented. This may be accomplished through observation and/

or the use of checklists or other guides. Teachers do not tend to be a reliable source of identification. In some cases, they under-refer (do not select students who are actually gifted); in other cases, they over-refer or include students who achieve at a high level, but who are not gifted (Tuttle, 1978). The problem of under-referral and over-referral decreases as classroom teachers are trained in the characteristics and identification of gifted and talented students.

PEER NOMINATION

Other students frequently know who their gifted and talented peers are, although they may not address this overtly in their daily interactions in school. Teachers can use sociometric techniques to determine which students their peers see as having exceptional abilities. The classroom teacher might prepare an informal inventory for the class to complete that contains hypothetical situations and asks the students whom they would most like to have help them. For example, the students could be told to imagine being trapped in a cave. They would be asked to identify one student they would particularly like present to help solve the problem of how to get out of the cave. In a series of situations, a few students' names will often emerge in most responses. This technique can be particularly useful in the identification of students with exceptional leadership abilities. Other abilities can also be addressed through careful selection and phrasing of the questions posed to students.

PARENT NOMINATION

Many people discount the value of parental input in the identification of gifted and talented students. Parents are in a position to observe their children over an extended period of time and are quick to realize when their child is developing much more rapidly than normal or has a particular talent. They are a particularly valuable source of information when children are first enrolled in school. When a parent believes that his or her child is gifted or talented, it is important to investigate the student's strengths and weaknesses and determine if the student requires additional programming to meet his or her educational needs.

PAST ACCOMPLISHMENTS

Students who are gifted and talented often demonstrate their abilities in school and at home over a long period of time. A record of actual demonstration of abilities can be very helpful in the identification process. This method of identification is particularly relevant for students who show leadership ability or talent in the visual and performing arts. A biographical inventory (Tuttle, 1978; Tuttle and Becker, 1980) can provide a summary of the student's accomplishments and interests in a concise report.

PROBLEMS IN IDENTIFYING THE GIFTED AND TALENTED

While there are several procedures for the identification of the gifted and talented, some students remain undetected. These students have many of the same characteristics and learning needs as other gifted and talented students, but do not appear as often in programs for the gifted and talented. For a variety of reasons, current screening and identification procedures sometimes fail to identify underachieving, minority, and handicapped gifted students.

The Underachieving Gifted Student   Some students seem to perform at very high levels on tests designed to measure intelligence and academic achievement (Laycock, 1979). These students, however, do not demonstrate the same level of ability in the school setting. In some classroom situations overachievement is not socially acceptable, and peer pressure is brought against those who exceed the norm. In some cases, students who are gifted or talented are singled out for attention, causing them to withdraw and, perhaps, decrease their performance in some areas. In other cases, the student simply has not had the opportunity to shine and needs the interest and encouragement of someone else to bring out the potential in the student. Finally, some students become bored with the lack of stimulation in the school. Ideally, all students should be provided with the opportunity to learn at their own rate with support and encouragement from everyone in the school setting. If you recognize a student who seems to have more potential than he or she is demonstrating, you may want to provide a positive opportunity for intellectual growth. The challenge may motivate the student to participate more in his or her own instruction.

The Minority Gifted Student   Another group of students often neglected in programs for the gifted and talented is the minority gifted. Because of cultural and experiential differences, these students may not perform well on the measures used to identify the gifted and talented. Witty (1978) and Chinn (1979) suggest that the minority student should be trained in test-taking skills, provided the motivation for performing well in school, and encouraged to develop a positive self-concept. You can foster these characteristics, be sensitive to the student's personal and cultural needs and help the student understand his or her own strengths. Any assessment of students from minority groups should be as culture-free as possible and focus on the student's knowledge and types of responses without examiner limitations.

The Handicapped Gifted Student   Some students who have learning, behavior, sensory, or physical handicaps are also gifted. For example, students with cerebral palsy can be intellectually gifted. Mentally retarded students can be talented in art (Morishima, 1974). These students may be particularly difficult to identify, since their handicapping condition may mask any particular gifts or talents the individual possesses. In addition, it may be impossible to measure adequately the individual's level of functioning due to the handicap. It is as important to observe the handicapped students, noting areas of exceptional or gifted achievement, as it is to observe students in the rest of the population.

Some Solutions   Although PL 94-142 does not provide provisions for the education of gifted and talented students, funds for establishing programs are available to states through the Gifted and Talented Children's Act of 1975. Many states, therefore, are developing identification procedures for the gifted and talented similar to those established for handicapped students. These include the use of more than one measure to determine classification, the establishment of criteria to be applied in the identification process, and the development of programs to meet identified needs. Most schools determine the type of program they wish to offer gifted and talented students (e.g., focus on intellectually gifted or focus on visual and performing arts), establish the criteria for entry into such programs, and then identify specific measures to determine which students are eligible and will benefit from the program. This type of process is important. The area of gifted and talented education is broadly defined, and most programs do not have the scope to meet the needs of all gifted and talented students residing in the service area.

Educating the Gifted and Talented

Many people have suggested in the past that the gifted and talented student would be able to succeed on his or her own without any special attention. It has been found, though, that quite the opposite is true. While some gifted and talented students continue to excel in the school environment, many do not, because of the lack of challenge and support (Tuttle, 1978). In fact, some school experiences actually reinforce performance at an average level. Gifted and talented students in such a setting tend to perform at the average level rather than excel and face criticism and ostracism from peers and teachers alike. It is important, then, to develop instructional programs and educational experiences that meet the needs of the gifted and talented students.

EDUCATIONAL AND SOCIAL NEEDS

Because of the breadth of the current definition of gifted and talented students, it is difficult to specify needs for this group as a whole. Each

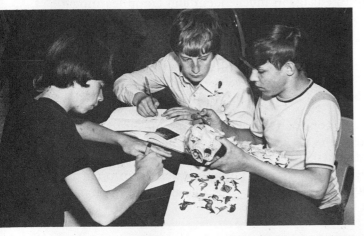

Gifted students may have superior talents in the performing arts, such as music (top left). Approaches to educating the gifted and talented include individual work in a shared area of interest with a mentor from the community (above); homogeneous groupings of students with similar interests and talents (left); and fully or partially accelerated programs (below).

student's particular area of giftedness or talent needs to be considered and should form the basis for specialized programming. Some general needs, however, can be specified. These include the following:

1. Fostering excellence and accelerated growth in particular areas of giftedness.

2. Promoting the development of all aspects of higher thought, such as analysis, synthesis, and evaluation.

3. Developing problem-solving skills, including hypothesis setting and research skills.

4. Fostering creative thinking abilities and the production of creative work.

5. Increasing knowledge and skills in academic areas of normal development.

6. Improving ability to engage in independent and group learning activities.

7. Promoting written and verbal communication in daily living.

8. When necessary, developing social skills and sensitivities to increase positive interaction with age peers, who may feel intimidated by the gifted and talented.

As with all categories of exceptionality, it is important to stress that these are general statements of needs. They do not necessarily reflect the needs of any one individual. It is important to observe, talk with, and carefully assess students who may be gifted or talented in order to establish their educational needs and the type of education program that might most enhance their development.

PROGRAM OPTIONS

Many gifted and talented students are educated in a regular classroom setting, receiving only the instructional modifications the teacher is able to make in that setting. In local districts and states that mandate services for gifted and talented students, though, three major types of program options exist: homogeneous grouping of gifted and talented students, acceleration, and enrichment.

Homogeneous Grouping   Segregated, self-contained special classes have served as a program option for gifted and talented students (Laycock, 1979; Tuttle, 1978). In these classes, gifted and talented students are grouped for instructional purposes. The students remain with the same teacher for all or part of their school day. In some cases, the grouping extends across the entire school program. Identified gifted students are enrolled together in one class. In other cases, gifted students are grouped for instruction in specific academic areas during the school day, remaining in a regular class setting for the remainder of their instruction.

There are advantages and disadvantages to the homogeneous grouping of the gifted and talented. Where programs are carefully conceptualized and students are selected for the program on the basis of their achievement and needs, grouping tends to produce higher levels of achievement than heterogeneous grouping. Successful programs are those in which grouping occurs across grade levels, the teacher is trained to provide for the unique educational needs of the students, and resources are available to the teacher and students. Schools must be careful to define the parameters of the program to be offered. Indiscriminate placement of students who are gifted and talented may result in frustration for the teacher and students. Since the definition of gifted and talented is so broad, no single program will be effective for all students.

Acceleration   Acceleration is a process of sending gifted and talented students through school faster. The student may skip one or more grades during his or her school career. In other settings, the student might remain in his or her chronological grade level, but work with materials several grades ahead of the current level. Finally, the student may have an accelerated program in one or more areas; that is, the student may remain with age peers during the bulk of the school day, while advancing to work at a higher level for one or more class periods. In the case study at the beginning of the chapter, Ken participated in a partially accelerated curriculum. He did not study those areas in which he had previously demonstrated his competence (reading and spelling), and he attended high-school classes while still a junior-high-school student.

One of the major concerns expressed regarding the acceleration of gifted and talented students is the effect of advanced placement upon their social and emotional development. In programs in which no attention is paid to this part of a student's development, acceleration may prove less useful to the student. Simply moving the student through content more quickly may not meet the needs of the gifted learner (Tuttle, 1978). Laycock (1979) and Tuttle (1978) summarize existing research on the efficacy of acceleration and report that rapid advancement through content combined with effective teaching and attention to the personal needs and interests of the students may stimulate and challenge gifted students, place them in institutions for advanced study earlier, and provide them with more productive years on the job market.

Enrichment   Enrichment is the provision of extra, supplemental materials for a student in order to increase the scope and breadth of the student's knowledge in a particular area. Enrichment usually requires that the student move beyond the acquisition of knowledge to the application of knowledge in evaluating, synthesizing, and conceptualizing new information (Tuttle, 1978). Effective enrichment programs provide students with the opportunity to explore areas in more depth or to pursue interests, expanding their own knowledge and expertise. Enrichment programs that merely offer more of the same — additional grammar worksheets when the assigned grammar activities are completed, for example — are not successful in providing appropriate educational experiences for the gifted and talented.

Enrichment programs have been established in many forms. In some situations, the student is allowed to complete his or her assigned work as quickly as possible. The student then utilizes the remaining instructional time to pursue the subject in an advanced area or to pursue areas of personal interest. A seventh grader, for example, might be given all the assignments for the current unit in mathematics at the beginning of the unit. When she has completed the work, she then explores the application of mathematical theory to music. In other situations, the student may be paired with a teacher in the school who has some expertise in the area of interest to the student. The teacher then guides the student's study and development in this area. The work may occur before or after school, during a study hall, or at another time of mutual convenience. A third variation of enrichment is the use of mentors. Individuals from the school and community are selected to work individually with gifted and talented students in areas of their interest. The mentor provides information on the field of study, an opportunity to observe, problems that need to be solved, and an interaction that challenges the student.

Enrichment programs may include several of the variations mentioned above. Renzulli (1977), for example, advocates a three-level enrichment program that includes encouraging students to explore areas of personal interest, developing thinking and feeling skills, and investigating in depth an area of choice. A variety of activities like these can increase the scope and depth of the program offered the student.

When selecting a progam option for a particular student, it is important to assess the student's entry level, motivation, and personal needs. The instructional program should then be developed, taking these variables into consideration. In all cases, the program should help the student extend his or her knowledge at an abstract level. The program should allow for active student participation with other students, interaction with materials and resources necessary to pursue the areas of interest, and an environment of positive challenge and stimulation.

THE GIFTED AND TALENTED STUDENT IN THE CLASSROOM

Many classroom teachers are uncomfortable about the presence of gifted and talented students in the classroom. Teachers ask some of the following questions: How can I teach a student who knows more than I do? What if I make a mistake and the student corrects me? How do I keep this student busy while I teach the rest of my class? What can I do to enhance the intellectual and personal growth of this student while he or she is enrolled in my classroom? While no single answer exists for any of these questions, there are some things you can do to capitalize on the unique opportunities a gifted student presents in the classroom.

1. Accept the gifted and talented student. While the student certainly has skills well beyond other students, the student is still a member of your class who needs support, guidance, and instruction.

2. Develop a program direction for the student. Gifted and talented students, like all other students, are progressing through a sequence of academic work. Develop goals and objectives for the student that will provide a basis for program directions.

3. Teach the student independent research skills. Since many gifted and talented students are self-motivated, they are able to work independently for long periods of time. The student can pursue areas of interest and participate in enrichment programs more efficiently when he or she can utilize library materials, use interview techniques, organize information, and develop independent thoughts and ideas in a coherent, precise way.

4. Be flexible. Gifted and talented students may respond in unexpected ways. If they are divergent thinkers, they may give answers and solutions that are unique. They may also need stimulation from you at unexpected times.

5. Serve as a catalyst for the student. Use instructional opportunities to encourage students to be creative and explore their environment. Structure your teaching to encourage curiosity, discovery, and imagination (Khatena, 1978). This can be beneficial for all students in the classroom.

6. Set a good model. Most students look up to you, the classroom teacher. If you demonstrate acceptance of intellectual and personal differences, your students usually will as well. If you are excited about learning and explore unknown areas in the presence of your students, they are likely to follow suit.

Summary

Gifted and talented students are enrolled in school programs across the country. In some states, programs for these students are mandated by state law. In others, students may receive supplemental or special instruction at the discretion of the local school district. In either case, gifted and talented students have unique educational needs that must be met by the school. Although people have not focused energy on the provision of programs in the classroom and through special services in the past, there is a growing demand for appropriate educational programs for these students. The needs of gifted and talented students, then, should be considered in all educational programming. The main points of this chapter are as follows:

1. Although "gifted" was first recognized and defined as intellectual ability, the current definition has been expanded to include students with intellectual, creative specific academic, leadership, and visual and performing arts abilities.

2. Physically, emotionally, and socially, most gifted and talented students are very much like their age peers in development.

3. Gifted and talented students are identified through the use of several types of measures. Intellectual and academic tests; tests of creativity; checklists of characteristics; teacher, parent, and peer nomination; and biographical sketches of past accomplishments are used to determine those students who are gifted and talented.

4. Some students who are gifted and talented are not identified for programs. The underachieving, minority, and handicapped gifted students may remain unrecognized as a result of academic, cultural, environmental, or physical limitations imposed upon the students.

5. Educational programs for gifted and talented students should focus on the development of the particular gifts and talents the student possesses.

6. There is a variety of program options available for gifted and talented students. Options should be selected that allow maximum growth for the student.

7. Homogeneous programs for the gifted and talented allow for grouping of students with similar abilities and educational needs. These students can then learn from and stimulate one another.

8. Acceleration, the advancement of the student in the content or skill area, can provide the gifted student with the challenge necessary for academic and intellectual growth.

9. Enrichment activities can be used to provide additional learning experiences for gifted and talented students in the classroom setting. The student is able to explore a topic at an advanced level while classmates are learning more basic or concrete skills.

Activities

1. Read the biography or autobiography of a person who has made an exceptional contribution as a result of his or her gifts or talents. This may include people like Leonardo da Vinci, Michelangelo, Albert Einstein, and Alexander Graham Bell.

2. Develop a unit in your content area that could be used for enrichment for a gifted and talented student. Note how the unit enhances critical thinking skills as well as expands upon the scope of content normally available for other students.

3. Survey two to four programs for gifted and talented students. Compare and contrast the types of programs offered in these schools.

4. Talk with peers who have participated in enriched or accelerated programs. Find out their impressions of the programs and the impact the programs had on their intellectual and social-emotional growth.

Study Questions

1. List and briefly explain the five major areas covered in the definition of gifted and talented students.

2. In what ways are gifted and talented students similar to and different from their age peers?

3. What are three techniques that may be used in public school settings to identify students who are gifted and talented? List at least one positive and one negative aspect in the use of each.

4. What are three types of experiences a classroom teacher can provide to enhance the skills a gifted and/or talented student may possess?

5. Compare and contrast homogeneous grouping, acceleration, and enrichment programs.

Questions for Further Thought

1. Some people feel that gifted and talented students should be trained in their specific areas of strength so they can make significant contributions to society. Do gifted and talented individuals owe society more than other people?

2. Many people view gifted and talented people as being eccentric. Why do you think this image exists?

3. In some cases resentment has been expressed towards special programs for gifted and talented individuals. Why do you suppose this attitude exists?

Additional Resources

BOOKS

Education USA Special Report. *The gifted and talented: Programs that work.* Arlington, Virginia: National School Public Relations Association, 1979.

Heimberger, M. J. *Teaching the gifted and talented in the elementary classroom.* Washington, D.C.: National Education Association, 1980.

Morgan, H. J., Tennant, C. G., and Gold, M. J. *Elementary and secondary level programs for the gifted and talented.* New York: Teachers College Press, Columbia University, 1980.

Tuttle, F. B., and Becker, L. *Characteristics and identification of gifted and talented students.* Washington, D.C.: National Education Association, 1980.

PROFESSIONAL LITERATURE

Gifted Child Quarterly

G/T/C

Journal for the Education of the Gifted

PROFESSIONAL ORGANIZATIONS

American Mensa, 1701 W. 3rd Street, Suite 1-R, Brooklyn, New York 11223

Association for the Gifted, Council for Exceptional Children, 1920 Association Drive, Reston, Virginia 22091

Chapter 17

Meeting The Challenge: The Problem-Solving Process

Success or failure in teaching depends to a great extent on your ability to bring about positive changes in your students. Knowing how to teach so that all students will learn new academic skills and appropriate behaviors is, therefore, an important responsibility. If you are able to understand each student's strengths and weaknesses, select appropriate teaching methods and materials and provide a positive learning climate for all students, you will experience a greater degree of success and happiness as a teacher. By learning how to understand and accommodate the needs of exceptional students, you are learning teaching skills that can be applied to the varying needs of nonhandicapped students as well.

The Problem-Solving Process: A Review

In the preceding chapters we have discussed an approach to teaching that we called the problem-solving model. We believe the steps in the process represent a systematic, logical procedure leading to an understanding of how to help the student who has special needs. Each step requires that decisions be made about the student's needs or program, and each decision provides the Pupil Evaluation Team (PET) with the means to make the next higher level decision. Finally, after the steps in the process have been completed, the student will have the best possible educational experience. As you will recall, the steps in the model are as follows:

1. assessing (gathering data to determine needs)

2. specifying goals and objectives (identifying what to teach)

3. identifying methods (determining how to teach)

4. evaluating learning (deciding if efforts have been successful)

The steps in the problem-solving process lead to the formulation of the Individualized Education Program (IEP) as required by PL 94-142. The IEP should contain the following elements:

1. A statement regarding the student's present level of functioning. This can be stated as strengths and weaknesses and may include a statement on the student's learning style.

2. A statement describing the student's annual goals. These may also be called long-term goals.

3. A listing of the short-term objectives, which represent the measurable steps between the present level of functioning and the mastery of annual goals.

4. A description of the educational program to be provided. This consists of a detailed description of all accommodations, methods, materials, and people needed to meet the student's needs, as well as time lines, plans for integration into the classroom, and those responsible for implementing the plan.

5. An evaluation plan describing how student progress will be determined. This tells who will evaluate progress and how they will do it.

Even though all plans contain these elements, each plan differs according to the unique needs and characteristics of the student for whom it is written. The wide differences among all students insures that no two IEPs will be exactly alike. In the following section note how the problem-solving process can be used to devise an appropriate IEP.

PRESENT LEVEL OF FUNCTIONING

The strengths and weaknesses of the student are determined by carrying out step 1 of the problem-solving model. Assessment results in your possessing data to understand the specific academic and behavioral needs of the student, which can be used as a basis for logical decisions.

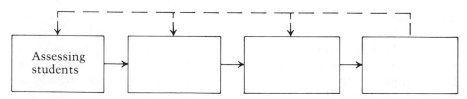

Step 1 of the problem-solving model

It is useful to view this part of an IEP as providing a broad, balanced view of the student. As the plan is in the initial stages of development, the listing of student strengths provides an initial view of the positive side of the student. Admittedly, it is sometimes difficult to come up with strengths for some students, but the section should not be overlooked. If necessary the team can select relative strengths by listing the characteristics of the student that represent higher level skills for that student. Generally, the list of strengths listed on the IEP includes consideration of attitudes, academic skills, social competence, and physical attributes or skills. Strengths and weaknesses are determined by reviewing the data obtained through formal and informal assessment as described in Chapters 6 and 7.

The weaknesses section serves as a signpost for identifying the student's deficits to be addressed by the remainder of the IEP. It is usually practical to list broad general areas. Long, detailed explanations of weaknesses are usually not helpful in this section. The following list illustrates how weaknesses might be listed:

Weaknesses

1. Reads four years below grade level.

2. Does not socialize well.

3. Disrupts class routines.

4. Is frequently absent.

5. Failed chemistry.

Without becoming too elaborate, a list such as this one allows the Pupil Evaluation Team (PET) to go on record as recognizing a problem in one area or another.

The strength and weakness section, then, insures that the PET will look at the student's overall abilities. By analyzing the data provided by team members, the team can agree on the general areas where the student does and does not need to improve. The IEP can begin to take shape. By comparing the present level of functioning with where they believe the student should be, the PET is able to identify pertinent goals. The next decision by the team is to look at the identified weaknesses and formulate long-term goals.

ANNUAL GOALS AND SHORT-TERM OBJECTIVES

Goals and objectives typically reflect student weaknesses or areas where the student needs to improve skills or behaviors. The formulation of goals and objectives is represented by step 2 of the problem-solving model.

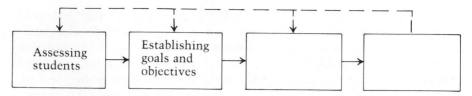

Step 2 of the problem-solving model

Annual goals are formulated as the team looks ahead to what the student can be expected to accomplish by the end of the school year. Some school districts choose to write long-term goals for each marking period. Local policies will dictate the time period to be accounted for in your school district.

There is no way to identify precisely how much behavior change should be expected in a long-term goal. Usually this depends on the degree to which the student is handicapped, the student's age, and other such considerations. You might teach one student all of the basic math skills in a half year. Another student might work four years to master the same material. When the team makes the decision about long-term goals, all pertinent factors need to be weighed and accounted for.

Some teachers are reluctant to choose overly optimistic goals. It is not crucial that the student master all long-term goals each year. Even though a goal is not reached, if the student has improved and made some progress, then the plan may be judged as appropriate. There is a psychological advantage to believing that significant gains are possible. Shooting for a dramatic gain may encourage teachers to try harder and to transmit these higher level expectations to the student. Goals that are too ambitious can always be rewritten or revised at a future time if necessary.

There is no set number of goals that may be written for each weakness listed in the first part of the IEP. This is determined by the Pupil Evaluation Team after reviewing the assessment information. The following example shows two of the many possible approaches to the selection of appropriate goals for one weakness.

Weakness

John reads four years below grade level.

Goals

1. John will master the sound-symbol relationships for each single letter of the alphabet by January 15, 1984.

2. John will accurately decode words in the first-grade reader by June 1, 1984.

Another Pupil Evaluation Team might look at the assessment data and formulate a different but still appropriate long-term goal for the same weakness.

Goals

1. John will read second grade material at the mastery level by May 1984.

In each instance, the writing of a goal served to identify, in general terms, what the student was to be doing at the end of the school year. In global terms, the team has identified the direction of its future efforts.

SHORT-TERM OBJECTIVES

Short-term objectives are precise, measurable learning and behavior objectives that represent the smaller components within a broader long-term goal. Ideally, when all of the short-term objectives in an area are met, the student has automatically mastered a long-term goal. By keeping track of the student's progress on the short-term objectives, the teacher can document daily or weekly progress towards overcoming the larger academic or behavioral weaknesses.

As in the case of long-term goals, short-term objectives can be written to have varying degrees of specificity. Larger skill areas can be broken down into many subgoals, or they can be broken down into a smaller number.

As you have seen earlier in Chapter Eight, all objectives should have a clear condition, a measurable response, and a specific mastery criterion. In the IEP the individual responsible for teaching the skill must also be identified. This can easily be done by writing the educator's name on the plan indicating which objectives are his or her responsibility.

By the time PET has selected appropriate objectives, the decision as to what the student is to learn has been determined. The next section of the IEP will require the PET to identify the elements of the educational program to be selected for the individual student.

DESCRIPTION OF THE EDUCATIONAL PROGRAM

The third step in the problem-solving model is concerned with how to teach the student. Programs, methods, and materials are selected with the student's strengths and weaknesses in mind.

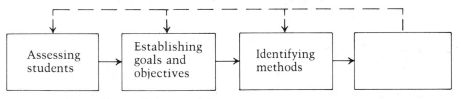

Step 3 in the problem-solving model

The program description section of the IEP essentially tells what is to happen to the student. Based on the severity of handicap, the PET has

the option of selecting the type of classroom, which can range from restrictive hospital or institutional settings to regular class placement with
special education consultation being provided. These options were discussed in detail in Chapter 1. By examining the data available, the PET
can select an appropriate option. In the majority of cases, students will
be placed in the regular class for most of their school day and will
receive part-time special education services. If a student has a relatively
minor handicap, or if the short-term objectives can be met in the regular
classroom, then direct contact with special education professionals will
be minimal. In any case, the team determines the daily schedule of the
student and puts it in writing on the plan. Such a description might look
like this:

> Steven will attend regular classes for the first four periods. Periods five
> and six will be spent in the resource room working on reading in the
> content areas.

> This program will be 5 days each week for the remainder of the school
> year.

In some cases, other professionals might be deemed a necessary part
of the proposed program. Counselors, social workers, psychologists, physicians and others may assist in the designing or carrying out of the IEP.
When the PET decides that other professionals are to be included in the
services provided, a written description of the planned services should be
included. The professional's role, and the frequency, time, and type of
service, should be described in some detail.

The IEP program description section should also contain a listing of
specialized equipment, materials, and methods to be used. Tape recorders,
typewriters, talking books, language kits, or any items that are separate
from the regular curriculum should be listed in the plan. As you have
seen in Chapters 10 and 11, there are many possible instructional accommodations to choose from.

Finally, any special transportation arrangements necessary to carry
out the plan should be described. Special transportation to school or
between schools may be required to take the student to the location
where the special service is being provided. In most cases, the transportation is considered a part of the special program and is paid for by the
schools.

EVALUATION PLAN

The final step in the problem-solving model is to make provisions for
evaluation of student progress. Evaluation results in the teacher knowing
whether or not the plans made for the student are working. Evaluation
is an ongoing process that enables you to make immediate adjustments
when they become necessary to ensure continued skill and behavior
development.

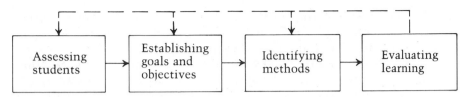

Step 4 in the problem-solving model

Evaluation, then, is a mechanism that can be used to refine the IEP by monitoring the student's progress towards mastery of goals and objectives. Say a student's short-term objective stated that she was to obtain a minimum of 90% on the weekly history quizzes for four weeks in a row. The PET might ask the history teacher to record the grades in the roll book until the four-in-a-row criterion was met and then to write the date of mastery on the IEP. If an objective for a student was to learn to write the answers to the six times tables in two minutes, the team might decide to have the math teacher or student keep a chart, such as in Figure 17.1.

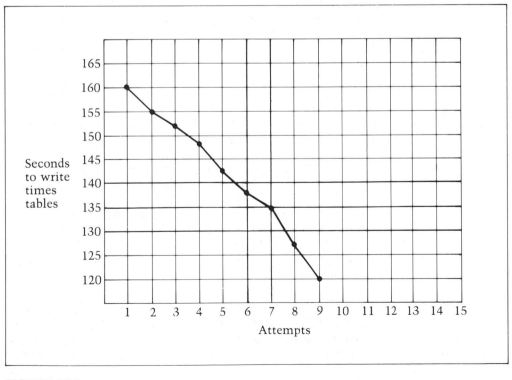

FIGURE 17.1
Student progress chart

As you can see, on the ninth test, the student mastered the objective. By using a simple graph the team can readily evaluate the student's progress at any time. The principles of evaluation of instruction as covered in Chapter 9 can be used to make sure the IEP is effective. In evaluation, a number of approaches may be used. In some cases, the evaluation plan may include giving special tests. For example, if the objective called for the student to master language concepts on grade level, then a test of language concepts might be scheduled. At a minimum, the evaluation plan focuses on the student's progress towards overcoming educational deficits. The plan should include a listing of who will collect and record what data. A precise plan allows the PET to monitor and evaluate student progress.

In some instances, changes should be made in earlier steps in the problem-solving model based on the evaluation of data collected on the student. For example, the student may need further assessment, new goals and objectives, or different teaching methods. The dotted lines on the model illustrate how evaluation may lead to changes in a student's educational program.

TABLE 17.1
Summary of IEP process

Problem-solving step	Element	Purpose	Outcomes of PET efforts
1. Assessing students	Present level of functioning	Gives a balanced view of the student and locates areas needing improvement.	A listing of strong points and weak points. Describes present level of functioning.
2. Establishing goals and objectives	Annual goals	Provides direction to the plan, tells what the student is to accomplish.	A broad description of what the student might accomplish.
	Short-term objectives	Identifies what will be taught.	Behavioral objectives that support the long-term goals.
3. Identifying methods	Program description	Tells who will teach what to the student and how it will be done.	Schedules, equipment, transportation, support personnel and services.
4. Evaluating learning	Evaluation plan	Describes how the success of the plan will be determined.	A listing of data to be collected, how they will be recorded and assessed.

THE IEP: A SUMMARY

The IEP developed using the problem-solving model is more than a plan to identify what will happen to an individual student. The IEP is a vehicle for a sequential planning process that helps educators find appropriate solutions to educational problems. A summary of the process is presented in Table 17.1.

As a classroom teacher you will not be required to carry out the steps of the process by yourself. You will, however, be a valuable part of the Pupil Evaluation Team and will help determine the effectiveness of the process in helping the exceptional student attain mastery of the goals and objectives in the IEP.

The Problem-Solving Model in Action

The following case study was selected to show how the problem-solving model was applied in one instance in which a student's IEP had evolved over several year's time:

RANDY

Several years had passed since the local school had begun developing IEPs for students who received the majority of their education in the regular classroom. Several teachers who had initially resisted being responsible for "special education" students were now enthusiastic supporters of appropriate programs. Mr. Oldroyd, a history teacher, was overhead saying, "When I first heard about this special education law I said to myself, not another responsibility! We are doing too much now. But I soon found that I was receiving help with the problem students I used to teach without any support. Now if a student has a real problem I can go through the Pupil Evaluation Team and in most cases get special equipment, support, or anything else the student needs. Now I'm not up against a stone wall; I have a way to help these students. It's true, I have to attend meetings, and I have participated in some in-service training, but I feel much better about my ability to help kids. That's what it's all about, isn't it? I mean, aren't we here to help kids?" Mrs. Evans, the Director of Special Education, had "accidentally" overheard that statement as she stood outside the conference room waiting for the rest of the Pupil Evaluation Team members to arrive. She smiled to herself. It had been quite a campaign to convert the teachers to believing in the rightful place of special education in the school. Although The

Education for all Handicapped Children (PL 94-142) act had been passed in 1975, no one had taken any progressive steps to implement the law in the school until it was literally forced on them by the state education department. It happened like this:

Randy Miner, then a fourth-grader, had moved into the school from a more affluent school district in a large metropolitan area. In his previous school, Randy had received special services to help him overcome an apparent severe learning and behavior problem. The only special education service available in his new school district was a classroom of fifteen students who were classified as mentally retarded. In the next county, thirty miles away, there was a self-contained class designed for the emotionally disturbed, but Randy's school had no special education services available appropriate for his needs. Furthermore, no teachers in the elementary school had received any training to deal with special needs children.

Soon after their arrival in town, Randy's parents had asked the school to provide the necessary services. When the school board rejected the proposed special program at the school, they immediately requested a due process hearing. Under the law, if the parents are not in agreement with the program or services provided, they have the right to have their case heard by an impartial hearing officer.

Before the hearing actually took place, the school district administration was made aware of its rights and responsibilities under the law and decided to petition the board for a change in its earlier decision. Upon a rehearing of the facts, the school board reversed its earlier decision and decided to pursue the installation of a comprehensive district-wide special education program. A special education director, Mrs. Evans, was hired, and the school district embarked on developing a full spectrum of special services for all exceptional children.

Now, four years later, Mrs. Evans mused, "Randy's parents really got the ball rolling. Special Education has become a lot more sophisticated these past few years." Today's PET was meeting to review Randy's IEP to evaluate his progress and to determine if any changes should be made in his program. Randy had made a lot of progress in these past four years. He had moved from a self-contained class in the school to the point that he now only attended a resource room program for one hour per day, and received tutorial help in his study hall period. He was maintaining a C or better average in all his academic subjects.

The Miners were now walking down the hall with Randy, coming to the meeting in which Randy would also play an important part. For the past two years he had attended and participated in the annual reviews of his case. By becoming

---

Special Services Agenda Form

Student *Randy Miner*   Grade *8*   Time *3:00 p.m.*

Purpose *Annual review*

Place *Mountain Junior High* Date *May 9*

The following persons are requested to attend the PET meeting and to bring materials pertinent to the agenda items listed below.

1. *Mr. Oldroyd: History*
2. *Miss Hardy: Principal*
3. *Mr. & Mrs. Miner: Parents*
4. *Mrs. Dunham: Resourse*
5. *Mr. Day: Reading*
6. *Mr. Levine: English*
7. *Mr. Laclare: Tutor*
8. _____
9. _____
10. _____

Agenda Items

1. **Review IEP for updating.** *Mrs. Dunham has expressed the opinion that Randy's plan is outdated and that each section needs to be made to reflect his current level of functioning. (His progress on the goals and objectives needs to be reviewed.)*

2. **Consideration of continual placement in special reading class.**

   Randy's latest reading test placed him on the 7th-grade level.

3. **Consideration of an alternative behavioral program.** *Mr. Oldroyd has stated that the behavioral contract is possibly no longer needed.*

FIGURE 17.2
Sample agenda

involved in the meetings he had come to feel, in part, responsible for what was happening to him in school. What a dramatic change this represented! Of course, having parents and students as participants in the PET meetings also had required a lot of careful planning and preparation. Home visits, letters, phone calls, the distribution of a parent's manual, plus a lot of public relations, had really paid off. It was the rare exception that at least one parent did not attend the meetings for their children.

Now that everyone was present — parents, an administrator, the special education teacher and several other of Randy's teachers — the meeting began. Mrs. Evans referred everyone to the agenda she had prepared (Figure 17.2). Listed on the agenda were major issues to be resolved at the meeting. As the agenda had been passed out several days in advance, each teacher present had been able to assemble the necessary data related to Randy's IEP and program.

Everyone had also had a chance to review the IEP, which had been available for review several days in advance. Now each section of the plan was quickly discussed and revised. During the past four years, Randy's plan had changed greatly. His first IEP reflected his severe needs at the time. The plan had been six typewritten pages. But as his learning and behavior problems had been effectively dealt with and his needs had become less severe, the plan became less complex. The first section of the plan was changed again at this meeting after only a few minutes' discussion. The changes that were made are shown in Figure 17.3.

Randy's earlier problems of being unprepared on his homework and creating a disturbance in class were no longer present. Currently he was having problems with the content in his English class. In all other classes he was receiving passing grades. Mrs. Evans was pleased that the number of weak areas had decreased in number again. The PET had determined that Randy's problems were not due to skill deficits. His failure in school was primarily a result of his attitude and behavior problems.

The next section of the IEP to be reviewed contained the long-term goals and short-term objectives. Again, as the teachers had carefully documented Randy's progress on the IEP, the team was able to see which goals and objectives had been met and to identify new goals and objectives for the coming year. Randy's goals and objectives on his old IEP appear in Figure 17.4.

Examination of the data related to the goals and short-term objectives showed that Randy had mastered every objective except 1.1. He still had an apparent problem in passing English tests. Currently these problems were due to skill deficits in identifying parts of speech, using correct footnotes, and using punctuation. His reading had showed a dramatic gain of two years, but he was still one year below his expected level. By carefully examining the

Old IEP	New IEP
Present Level of Performance	**Strengths and Weaknesses Section**

Strengths

A. Willingly follows directions in the classroom.

B. Is a leader in physical education class.

C. Frequently contributes to class discussions.

Weaknesses

1. Has a difficult time receiving passing grades on tests in history, English, and math classes.

2. Frequently is unprepared on assignments.

3. Has "angry episodes" in class when frustrated.

4. Reads two years below grade level.

Strengths

A. Is a good student in classes.

B. Tries hard in all classes.

C. Frequently contributes to class discussions.

Weaknesses

1. Reads one year below grade level.

2. Needs to improve achievement level in English grammar.

FIGURE 17.3
Changes in the IEP

FIGURE 17.4
Randy Miner's old IEP of goals and objectives

Long-Term Goal 1

Randy will receive a 70% or better average on his end-of-term exams in all academic classes by April, 1980.

Short-Term Objectives

	1st-term average	2nd-term average	3rd-term average	4th-term average	Person responsible
1.1 Randy will pass history exams with a 70% or above average	72%	84%	82%		Oldroyd
1.2 Randy will pass reading exams with a 70% or above average	75%	90%	92%		Day
1.3 Randy will pass English exams with a 70% or above average	62%	60%	55%		Levine
1.4 Randy will pass mathematics exams with a 70% or above average	81%	76%	84%		Garcia

Long-Term Goal 2

Randy will have homework completed at least 90% of the time in all of his classes by the end of each academic term.

Short-Term Objectives

	1st-term average	2nd-term average	3rd-term average	4th-term average	Person responsible
2.1 Randy will complete homework assignment at a 90% level in history	95%	100%	100%		Oldroyd

Short-Term Objectives

	1st-term average	2nd-term average	3rd-term average	4th-term average	Person responsible
2.2 Randy will complete reading homework at a 90% level	100%	100%	100%		Day
2.3 Randy will complete English homework at a 90% level	80%	100%	100%		Levine
2.4 Randy will complete math homework at a 90% level	90%	100%	98%		Garcia

Long-Term Goal 3

Randy will decrease the number of inappropriate behavior incidents in potentially frustrating situations in class by May, 1980.

Short-Term Objectives

3.1 Randy will reduce the incidence of throwing objects to zero by October, 1979. (Mrs. Dunham)

3.2 Randy will reduce swearing to no more than one incident per month by January, 1980. (Mrs. Dunham)

3.3 Randy will follow teacher directions in all classes for two consecutive weeks by January, 1980

Long-Term Goal 4

Randy will improve his reading skills by two years to the seventh-grade level as measured by the Spache Diagnostic Reading Scales by May, 1980.

(continued)

FIGURE 17.4 (Continued)

Short-Term Objectives

4.1 Randy will read and comprehend material at the 6th-grade level as measured by the Diagnostic Reading Scales. (Mr. Day) (passed January 4, 1980).

4.2 Randy will read and comprehend material at the 7th-grade level as measured by the Diagnostic Reading Scales. (Mr. Day) (passed May 1, 1980.)

data, new goals and objectives were identified (Figure 17.5) that focused on his present strengths and weaknesses.

Goals and objectives were devised that reflected his two remaining weak areas in reading and grammar. Mrs. Dunham, the resource teacher, and Mr. Day, the reading teacher, were designated as the persons responsible for insuring that Randy received the help he needed and the necessary data were collected to insure accountability. By making sure that an individual was identified to oversee particular objectives, the plan complied with the law and was more certain to be used by the teachers as the basis for Randy's program. At this meeting, each teacher reported on Randy's progress on the specific objectives for which he or she was designated as the "person responsible."

The next part of the IEP under review was the Program Description section. The purpose of this section is to provide a precise description of the services and materials used. The first plan for Randy had contained a description of an elaborate contract system to deal with inappropriate angry episodes and chronic unpreparedness on out-of-class assignments. Further, a special study skills program had been designed and carried out by the resource teacher. All regular class teachers had also participated by providing a weekly report card to Randy's parents. Apparently, all of these accommodations had worked; only two weak areas remained. He had made a lot of progress this past year.

After some deliberation it was decided that special accommodations in the classroom, behavioral contracts, etc., were

FIGURE 17.5
New goals and objectives

Long-Term Goal 1

Randy will receive an 80% or better average on his first term exam in English class by October 15th, 1981 (Mrs. Dunham)

Short-Term Objectives

1.1 Randy will recognize the parts of speech at an 80% level as measured by written unit tests.

1.2 Randy will write a brief research paper containing correct footnotes at the 80% level.

1.3 Randy will correctly use standard punctuation in the punctuation exercises in the 9th-grade text, chapter 7, 8, and 9 exercises) at the 80% level.

Long-Term Goal 2

Randy will improve his reading level to the 9th-grade level as measured by the Stanford Achievement Test, May, 1982 (Mrs. Day)

Short-Term Objectives

2.1 Randy will read and provide a two-paragraph synopsis of one library book per week. Difficulty levels of the books will increase from an 8th-grade to a 9th-grade level by the end of the year.

2.2 Randy will read, spell, and define at least ten new words a week at 100% accuracy.

2.3 Randy will provide a written summary of main ideas contained in each weekly history text reading assignment with at least 90% accuracy.

no longer necessary. The new program description section (Figure 17.6) was filled out to reflect Randy's less severe needs.

The Program Description section provides documentation of all specific aspects of the educational program that have been made in order to insure that the goals and objectives can be met.

FIGURE 17.6
Program description

Special Services

1. Randy will attend the resource room during his study hall period for 45 minutes each day during the school year for the purpose of working on his English objectives. (September 3 through June 12.)

2. Randy will continue to receive reading instruction one period per day from Mrs. Day, to work on reading in the content areas.

Materials

Materials used will be the same as those used in the regular class.

Special Accommodations

1. In case behavior problems reappear or if academic performance drops below the passing level, the teacher observing the problem is to call Mr. and Mrs. Miner at 555-2017.

2. If Randy receives a grade below a C in any of his classes, in any one marking period, a special P.E.T. meeting will be convened to review the problem.

FIGURE 17.7
Evaluation plan

Person responsible	Data source	When collected
Mrs. Durham		
Objective		
1.1	Textbook tests % correct	Weekly 1st term
1.2	Research paper	by October 1, 1981
1.3	Textbook % correct	by September 30, 1981
Mr. Day		
Objective		
2.1	Weekly book report	Weekly (Friday)
2.2	Weekly vocabulary quiz	Weekly (Friday)
2.3	Oral quiz on history chapter	Weekly
	Stanford Achievement Test	May, 1982

The Program Description should precisely identify services
necessary to insure that the student's deficits receive proper
attention. The program description may be viewed as an
instructional plan designated to capitalize on strengths and
overcome the weaknesses of a particular student. To determine
what kinds of services, materials, and other accommodations are
appropriate, the teachers used the data collected on Randy's
behavior and academic growth. If his problems had been more
severe, a more detailed program description would likely have
resulted.

The final section of the IEP is called the Evaluation Plan. The purpose of this section is to document how progress for each long-term goal and short-term objectives are measurable, the PET needs to make three decisions: (1) what kind of test or measure of the student's performance on a goal or objective will be made; (2) when the measures of the skill or behavior will take place; and (3) who will measure the skill or behavior. In Randy's case, the persons responsible for teaching the goals and objectives were also designated as being responsible for evaluating progress. The final plan is shown in Figure 17.7.

When the time comes for the next review of Randy's progress, each teacher will have recorded in the records data that reflect the evaluation plan. Again, by deciding who is to do what, the progress on each objective is carefully monitored throughout the coming year. The Evaluation Plan should be designed so that the student's progress can be evaluated at any time during the year. By collecting data on the student's performance at regular intervals, the appropriateness of the program can be determined on an ongoing basis. Without continuous evaluation, it is possible that a student might go on for a long period of time with an inappropriate program before it was realized that changes were necessary.

In Randy Miner's case, careful design of IEPs throughout a four-year period had resulted in his overcoming what initially was a severe behavior and learning problem and developing the skills and behaviors necessary to be successful with little specialized assistance.

The IEP should be viewed as a blueprint that leads the student closer and closer to success as each year passes. By carefully identifying weaknesses, selecting goals and objectives that reflect these weaknesses, designing a program that focuses on mastering the goals and objectives, and designing a workable evaluation plan, the PET assures the student with special needs a degree of success. The IEP, then, becomes the basis for insuring that learning and positive behavior changes take place.

A final word about Randy's IEP: The Individual Education Plan in this case was the result of a team effort. Each member of the team contributed suggestions and willingly shouldered some of the responsibility for planning data collection and carrying out the program. Everyone, including the parents, was involved in the problem solving and decision process. Because everyone "owned" a piece of the plan, they were committed to carrying out their share of the roles and responsibilities. The plan clearly identified what each person was to do, so the plan was efficiently carried out. Randy's presence at the meeting helped him understand what was happening to him and assisted him to understand the efforts and dedication each teacher was prepared to offer. It is not always practical to have students attend their own PET meetings. Sometimes students might misunderstand what is taking place or may be incapable of contributing to the proceedings. In any case, the PET process should be carefully planned and orchestrated to produce the desired outcomes. In Randy's case, it was decided that he should continue in the reading class and that the behavioral programs should be dropped. Each decision was based on data presented by the teachers at the meeting. By systematically following the problem-solving model they were able to identify strengths, weaknesses, goals and objectives, and determine the best way to teach Randy to overcome his learning and behavioral problems and to evaluate the success of their efforts.

The Role of the Teacher as a Problem-Solver

Helping students overcome their educational and behavioral deficits and being a part of the team charged with the responsibility to make important decisions about the lives of students is an exciting challenge. It is also an important responsibility. Given this charge it is imperative that you learn how to help the PET make good decisions that will lead to effective teaching. We believe that good decisions are those based on knowledge of handicapping conditions and data collected by the classroom teacher. We have, in this text, collected and presented what we believe to be the knowledge necessary to understand exceptionality. We have also described a problem-solving model whereby you can use your knowledge and data to help make good decisions for educating students with learning and behavioral problems.

You may have determined by now that we do not believe in some special technique or method that works only for exceptional children. Our approach reflects the belief that good teaching works to everyone's advantage. By finding the answers to the questions implied by the four steps in the model, you can find the most appropriate educational plan for any student.

1. *What are this student's educational and behavioral needs?* Needs can be determined, in part, from the type and degree of the handicap. Students who are gifted, visually impaired, retarded, emotionally disturbed, or who possess other handicaps often share some common general needs. More specific needs, however, must be identified through the process of assessment to measure needs in learning and/or behavior. Despite the fact that types of handicaps differ, most school-related problems can be described in terms of behavior in school and mastery of academic skills.

2. *What should I teach this student?* Once the deficits and strengths have been identified, a decision has to be made to select appropriate goals and objectives. Again, data are used to identify what you will teach. You

You have the opportunity to teach a wide variety of students and experience the joy of being a positive influence in their lives.

may consider type of exceptionality, degree of exceptionality, level of present functioning, or any other information you consider to be pertinent to the case. You identify measurable goals and objectives because they help you focus your teaching efforts precisely on a program and be accountable for progress the student makes. In many cases what you teach the handicapped student will not be different from what you teach other students.

3. *How should I teach this student?* The "how" of teaching requires many decisions. What methods should be used? What materials are appropriate? How frequently should instruction be given and for how long? Should a behavior management program be used? Finally, how should the classroom space be utilized? It should be apparent that selecting the best way to teach the student requires knowledge. The good teacher needs to be aware of alternatives. By knowing the student and available methods and materials, you can match the student with the most appropriate educational program. Many of the changes in the instructional process can lead to more effective teaching of all students in your classes.

4. *Have I successfully taught the skills and behaviors?* Once the teaching program has been designed and is in the process of being carried out, you will need to know if it is working or not. By building in data

collection procedures, you can, at any time, measure whether or not the student is moving towards mastery of the goals and objectives. Ongoing evaluation of an educational program is essential if you are to be sure you are using an appropriate IEP. Evaluation of measurable objectives with measurable data takes the guesswork out of education. It helps you to be more sure of yourself and accountable for student progress.

Summary

The passage of legislation mandating appropriate education programs for all handicapped students has not resulted in a mass migration of severely handicapped students into the regular classroom. Instead, teachers are now receiving help with many students they had taught in the past without supportive services. Many students who formerly were labeled "slow" or as having a "behavior problem" can now be recognized as being learning disabled, retarded, or emotionally disturbed, and supportive services can be provided.

Many teachers are learning that exceptional students "mainstreamed" into the class do not *take away* from the class but *add to it*.

The diversity and examples of individual courage that exceptional students offer can result in other students' learning to understand and accept differences. They may also learn by example how to adapt the challenges they may experience in other areas.

Your role as classroom teacher in meeting the needs of exceptional students is to recognize and carry out your responsibilities as a part of the Pupil Evaluation Team. The problem-solving model requires that all professionals use their collective wisdom to devise an appropriate educational experience for all exceptional students. In this chapter the problem-solving model was described in detail. The following major ideas were presented:

1. The problem-solving model consists of four major steps: assessing students, establishing goals and objectives, identifying methods, and evaluating learning.

2. The problem-solving model is a step-by-step procedure by which the successful completion of one step leads to the next one until an effective educational program is developed.

3. The problem-solving model can be directly applied to formulating an Individualized Education Program. By going through the four steps, the IEP can be systematically and logically developed.

4. You can play an important role in the development and carrying out of an IEP. This is a responsibility that requires knowledge of handicapping conditions and how to assess and teach new skills and behaviors.

5. The use of the problem-solving model and continuous data collection results in an IEP that can be adapted to the changing needs of the student throughout the year.

After you have read this text, it is our hope that you will come to recognize yourself as a *special teacher* in the sense that you are now trained to teach a wide variety of students and to experience the joys that come from being a positive influence in all students' lives.

Activities

1. Using the problem-solving process, construct an IEP for a hypothetical student. Share your program with others in your class.

2. Divide your class into two groups. Have one group find research and opinion articles that support the concept of mainstreaming and the other group articles that do not support it. Have the class debate the mainstreaming issue.

3. Design a classroom environment in which exceptional as well as nonexceptional students could be educated. Determine how the teacher might meet the needs of all students.

Study Questions

1. The problem-solving process has four steps. What general question must be answered at each step?

2. What are the five major components that must be included in every IEP?

3. Why is an agenda an important consideration in the PET process?

4. Why is it important for everyone to participate in the PET? Why wouldn't it be better for specialists to devise the plan?

5. Why is the evaluation section an important part of the IEP?

Questions for Further Thought

1. Since the IEP helps teachers provide an appropriate education program for handicapped students, why not require one for all children?

2. Why is it a good idea to provide an opportunity for nonhandicapped and handicapped students to share social and education experiences?

3. The modern teacher must be knowledgeable if he/she is to succeed in the classroom. In your opinion, do teachers have to be better prepared today than they did thirty years ago? Explain your answer.

Additional Resources

BOOKS

Lerner, J., Dawson, D., and Horvath, L. *Cases in learning and behavior problems: A guide to individualized education programs.* Boston: Houghton Mifflin, 1980.

Lowenbraun, S., and Affleck, J. Q. *Teaching mildly handicapped children in the regular classes.* Columbus, Ohio: Charles E. Merrill, 1976.

Mann, P. H., Suiter, P. A., and McClung, R. M. *Handbook in diagnostic-prescriptive teaching.* Boston: Allyn and Bacon, 1979.

Piazza, R., and Newman, I. *Readings in individualized educational programs.* Guilford, Connecticut: Special Learning Corporation, 1978.

Turnbull, A. P., Strickland, B. B., and Brantley, J. C. *Developing and implementing individualized education programs.* Columbus, Ohio: Charles E. Merrill, 1978.

Bibliography

Adler, S. Behavior management: A nutritional approach to the behaviorally disordered and learning disabled child. *Journal of Learning Disabilities*, 1978, *11* (10), 49–54.

American Association on Mental Deficiency. *AAMD Adaptive Behavior Rating Scale — Public School Version.* Washington, DC: American Association on Mental Deficiency, 1977.

Anderson, R. D., and Faust, G. W. *Educational psychology: The science of instruction and learning.* New York: Dodd, Mead & Co., 1973.

Aronson, E., Blaney, N., Sikes, J., Stephan, C., and Snapp, M. Busing and racial tension: The jigsaw route to learning and liking. *Psychology Today*, 1975, *8* (9), 43–50.

Becker, W. C. *Parents are teachers.* Champaign, IL: Research Press, 1971.

Becker, W. C., Engelmann, S., and Thomas, D. R. *Teaching 2: Cognitive learning and instruction.* Chicago: Science Research Associates, 1975.

Bender, L. *Bender Visual-Motor Gestalt Test.* New York: American Orthopsychiatric Association, 1938.

Berkowitz, P. H., and Rothman, E. P. *The disturbed child: Recognition and psychoeducational therapy in the classroom.* New York: New York University Press, 1960.

Bessell, H. *Methods in human development.* La Mesa, CA: Human Development Training Institute, Inc., 1972.

Best, G. A. *Individuals with physical disabilities — an introduction for educators.* St. Louis: C. V. Mosby Co., 1978.

Bettelheim, B. *Love is not enough.* New York: Macmillan, 1950.

Blake, K. *Educating exceptional pupils.* Reading, MA: Addison-Wesley Publishing Co., 1981.

Block, S. H., and Anderson, L. W. *Mastery learning in classroom instruction.* New York: Macmillan, 1975.

Bloom, B. S. *Human characteristics and school learning.* New York: McGraw-Hill Book Co., 1976.

Bloom, B. S. Learning for mastery. In B. S. Bloom, J. T. Hastings, & G. F. Madaus (Eds.), *Handbook on formative and summative evaluation of student learning.* New York: McGraw-Hill Book Co., 1971.

Boehm, A. E. *Boehm Test of Basic Concepts Manual.* New York: Psychological Corporation, 1971.

Bower, E. M. *Early identification of emotionally handicapped children in school* (2nd ed.). Springfield, IL: Charles C. Thomas, 1969.

Bower, E. M., and Lambert, N. M. A process for in-school screening of children with emotional handicaps. Princeton, N.J.: Educational Testing Service, 1962.

Bowermaster, M. Peer tutoring. *The Clearing House,* 1978, *52* (2), 59–60.

Bryan, T., and Bryan, J. *Understanding learning disabilities.* Sherman Oaks, CA: Alfred Publishing Co., Inc., 1978.

Bureau of Education for the Handicapped. *Progress toward a free appropriate public education: A report to congress on the implementation of Public Law 94-142, the Education for All Handicapped Children Act.* Washington, DC: U.S. Department of Health, Education, and Welfare, Office of Education, 1979.

CTB/McGraw-Hill. *The California Achievement Tests.* Monterey, CA: CTB/McGraw-Hill, 1977.

Callahan, C. *Developing creativity in the gifted and talented.* Reston, VA: Council for Exceptional Children, 1978.

Cattell, R., Eber, H., and Tatsuoka, M. *Sixteen personality factor questionnaire.* Champaign, IL: Institute for Personality and Ability Testing, 1970.

Charles, C. M. *Building classroom discipline: From models to practice.* New York: Longman, Inc., 1981.

Charles, C. M. *Individualizing instruction.* (2nd ed.). St. Louis, MO: The C. V. Mosby Co., 1980.

Charles, C. M. *Individualizing instruction.* St. Louis, MO: The C. V. Mosby Co., 1976.

Chinn, P. C. The exceptional minority child: Issues and some answers. *Exceptional children,* 1979, *45* (7), 532–536.

Chinn, P. C., Drew, C. S., and Logan, D. R. *Mental retardation: A life cycle approach* (2nd ed.). St. Louis, MO: The C. V. Mosby Co., 1979.

Christopolos, G., and Renz, P. A critical examination of special education programs. *The Journal of Special Education,* 1969, *3* (4), 371–379.

Connors, C. K. A teacher rating scale for use in drug studies with children. *American Journal of Psychiatry,* 1969, *126,* 884–888.

Connors, C. K., Goyette, C. H., Southwick, D. A., Lees, J. M., and Andrulonis, P. A. Food additives and hyperkinesis: A controlled double-blind experiment. *Pediatrics,* 1976, *58,* 154–156.

Cruickshank, W., Bentzen, F., Ratzburg, F., and Tannhauser, M. *A teaching method for brain-injured and hyperactive children.* Syracuse, NY: Syracuse University Press, 1961.

Curran, T. J., and Algozzine, B. Ecological disturbance: A test of the matching hypothesis. *Behavioral Disorders,* 1980, *5* (3), 169–174.

Dale, E., and Chall, J. S. A formula for predicting readability. *Educational Research Bulletin,* 1948, *27* (1), 11–20.

Deno, E. *Instructional alternatives for exceptional children.* Reston, VA: Council for Exceptional Children, 1973.

Deno, E. Special education as developmental capital. *Exceptional Children,* 1970, *37* (3), 229–237.

Dineen, J., Clark, H., and Risley, T. Peer tutoring among elementary students: Educational benefits to the tutor. *Journal of Applied Behavior Analysis*, 1977, *10* (2), 231–238.

Dunn, L. M. *Peabody Picture Vocabulary Test* (2nd ed.). Circle Pines, MN: American Guidance Service, 1980.

Dunn, L. M. *Exceptional children in the schools — special education in transition* (2nd ed.). New York: Holt, Rinehart and Winston, Inc., 1973.

Dunn, L. M. Special education for the mildly retarded — is much of it justifiable? *Exceptional Children*, 1968, *35* (1), 5–22.

Dunn, L. M., and Markwardt, F. C. *The Peabody Individual Achievement Test*. Circle Pines, MN: American Guidance Service, 1970.

Durost, W. N., Bixler, H. H., Wrightstone, J. W., Prescott, G. A., and Balow, I. H. *Metropolitan Achievement Test*. New York: Harcourt Brace Jovanovich, 1971.

Elias, M. Helping emotionally disturbed children through prosocial television. *Exceptional Children*, 1979, *46* (3), 217–218.

Epilepsy Foundation of America. *Answers to most frequent questions people ask about epilepsy*. Washington, DC: Epilepsy Foundation, 1977.

Erikson, E. H. *Childhood and society* (2nd ed.). New York: W. W. Norton & Company, Inc., 1963.

Fagan, S. A., Long, N. S., and Stevens, D. J. *Teaching children self control*. Columbus, OH: Charles E. Merrill, 1975.

Federal Register, August 23, 1977, 42478.

Feingold, B. F. *Why your child is hyperactive*. New York: Random House, 1975.

Feingold, B. F. Hyperkinesis and learning disabilities linked to the ingestion of artificial food colors and flavors. *Journal of Learning Disabilities*, 1976, *9* (9), 551–559.

Folio, M. R., and Norman, A. Toward more success in mainstreaming: A peer approach to physical education. *Teaching Exceptional Children*, 1981, *13* (3), 110–114.

Frostig, M., Maslow, P., Lefever, D. W., and Whittlesey, J. R. *The Marianne Frostig Developmental Test of Visual Perception: 1963 standardization*. Palo Alto, CA: . Consulting Psychologists Press, 1964.

Fry, E. A readability formula that saves time. *Journal of Reading*, 1968, *11* (4), 513–16, 575–78.

Gadow, K. D. *Children on medication: A primer for school personnel*. Reston, VA: Council for Exceptional Children, 1979.

Gallagher, J. J. *Teaching the gifted child* (2nd ed.). Boston: Allyn and Bacon, Inc., 1975.

Gast, D. L., and Nelson, C. M. Time out in the classroom: Implications for special education. *Exceptional Children*, 1977, *43* (7), 461–464.

Gearheart, B. R. *Learning disabilities: Educational strategies*. St. Louis, MO: The C. V. Mosby Co., 1977.

George, C., and Main, M. Social interactions of young abused children: Approach, avoidance, and aggression. *Child Development*, 1979, *50* (2), 306–318.

Gillung, T. B., and Rucker, C. N. Labels and teacher expectations. *Exceptional Children*, 1977, *43* (7), 464–465.

Glasser, W. *Reality therapy: A new approach to psychiatry*. New York: Harper & Row, 1965.

Glasser, W. *Schools without failure*. New York: Harper & Row, 1965.

Goldman, R., and Fristoe, M. *Goldman-Fristoe Test of Articulation*. Circle Pines, MN: American Guidance Service, 1969.

Gordon, T. *Parent effectiveness training.* New York: Peter H. Wyden, 1970.

Graham, F., and Kendall, B. *Memory-For-Designs Test.* Missoula, MT: Psychological Test Specialty, 1960.

Graham, S., Burly, N. B., Hudson, F., and Carpenter, D. Educational personnel's perceptions of mainstreaming and resource room effectiveness. *Psychology in the Schools,* 1980, *17* (1), 128–134.

Grossman, H. *Manual on terminology and classification in mental retardation* (rev. ed.). Washington, DC: American Association on Mental Deficiency, 1977.

Guilford, J. P. Intellect and the gifted. In J. C. Gowan, J. Khatena, and E. P. Torrance (Eds.), *Educating the ablest: A book on readings on the education of gifted children.* Ifasca, IL: F. E. Peacock Publishers, Inc., 1979.

Hallihan, D., and Cruickshank, W. *Psychoeducational foundations of learning disabilities.* Englewood Cliffs, NJ: Prentice-Hall, Inc., 1973.

Haslam, R. H., and Valletutti, P. J. (Eds.). *Medical problems in the classroom — the teacher's role in diagnosis and management.* Baltimore: University Park Press, 1975.

Hammill, D. D. Assessing and training perceptual-motor processes. In D. D. Hammill and N. R. Bartel (Eds.), *Teaching children with learning and behavioral problems.* Boston: Allyn & Bacon, 1975.

Heward, W., and Orlansky, M. *Exceptional children.* Columbus, OH: Bell and Howell Co., 1980.

Hewett, F. M., and Forness, S. R. *Education of exceptional learners* (2nd ed.). Boston: Allyn and Bacon, 1977.

Hewett, F. M., and Forness, S. R. *Education of exceptional learners.* Boston: Allyn and Bacon, 1974.

Hewett, F. M., and Taylor, F. *The emotionally disturbed child in the classroom.* Boston: Allyn and Bacon, 1980.

Hieronymus, A. N., Lindquist, E. F., and Hoover, H. D. *Iowa Test of Basic Skills.* Lombard, IL: Riverside Publishing Company, 1978.

Hirshey, G. Family Circle guide to learning disabilities. *Family Circle,* 1978, *91* (1), 20, 68–70.

Huberty, T., Koller, J., and Ten Brink, T. Adaptive behavior in the definition of mental retardation. *Exceptional Children,* 1980, *46* (4), 256–261.

Hudson, F., Graham, S., and Warner, M. Mainstreaming: An examination of the attitudes and needs of regular classroom teachers. *Learning Disabilities Quarterly,* 1979, *2* (3), 58–62.

Hutt, M. L., and Gibby, R. G. *The mentally retarded child: Development, education and treatment* (3rd ed.). Boston: Allyn and Bacon, Inc., 1976.

Imber, S. C., Imber, R. B., and Rothstein, C. Modifying independent work habits: An effective teacher-parent communication program. *Exceptional Children,* 1979, *46* (3), 218–221.

Itard, J. M. *The wild boy of Aveyron.* (G. Humphrey and M. Humphrey, trans.) New York: Appleton-Century-Crofts, 1932.

Jastak, J. F., Bijou, S. W., and Jastak, S. *The Wide Range Achievement Test.* Wilmington, DL: Jastak Associates, 1978.

Johnson, D. W., and Johnson, R. T. Integrating handicapped students into the mainstream. *Exceptional Children,* 1980, *42* (2), 90–98.

Johnson, S. W., and Morasky, R. L. *Learning disabilities.* Boston: Allyn and Bacon, Inc., 1977.

Joint Study Committee of the American School Health Association and the National Society for the *Prevention* of Blindness, Inc. *Teaching about vision.* New York: National Society for the *Prevention* of Blindness, 1972.

Jones, T., Sowell, V., Jones, J., & Butler, L. Changing children's perceptions of handicapped people. *Exceptional Children*, 1981, *47* (5), 365–368.

Jones, T. P. *Creative learning in perspective.* New York: Wiley, 1972.

Kauffman, J. M. *Characteristics of children's behavior disorders.* Columbus, OH: Charles E. Merrill, 1981.

Kavanaugh, E. A classroom teacher looks at mainstreaming. *Elementary School Journal*, 1977, *77* (4), 318–322.

Kelly, T., Bullock, L., and Dykes, M. Behavioral disorders: Teacher's perceptions. *Exceptional Children*, 1977, *43* (5), 316–318.

Kephart, N. C. *The slow learner in the classroom.* Columbus, OH: Charles E. Merrill, 1971.

Kerr, M. M., and Raglund, E. Pow wow: A group procedure for reducing classroom behavior problems. *The Pointer*, 1979, *24* (1), 92–96.

Khatena, J. *The creatively gifted child: Suggestions for parents and teachers.* New York: Vantage Press, 1978.

Khatena, J. The gifted child in the United States and abroad. *Gifted Child Quarterly*, 1977, *21* (3), 372–387.

Kirk, S. A., and Gallagher, J. *Educating exceptional children* (3rd ed.). Boston: Houghton Mifflin Co., 1979.

Kirk, S. A., McCarthy, J. J., and Kirk, W. D. *The Illinois Test of Psycholinguistic Abilities.* Urbana, IL: University of Illinois Press, 1968.

Krager, J. M., Safer, D. S., and Earhardt, J. *Medication used to treat hyperactive children: Follow up survey results.* Unpublished manuscript, 1977.

Kübler-Ross, E. *On death and dying.* New York: Macmillan, 1969.

Lambert, N. M., Hartsough, C. S., and Bower, E. M. *Pupil Behavior Rating Scale.* Monterey, CA: Publishers Test Service, CTB/McGraw Hill, 1978.

Laycock, F. *Gifted children.* Glenview, IL: Scott, Foresman and Co., 1979.

Lee, L. *Developmental Sentence Analysis.* Evanston, IL: Northwestern University Press, 1974.

Lerner, J., Dawson, D., and Horvath, L. *Cases in learning and behavior problems.* Boston: Houghton Mifflin Company, 1980.

Leyser, Y., and Gottleib, J. Improving social status of rejected pupils. *Exceptional Children*, 1980, *46* (6), 459–461.

Lilly, M. S. A training based model for special education. *Exceptional Children*, 1971, *37* (10), 745–749.

Litton, F., Banbury, M., and Harris, K. Materials for educating non-handicapped students about their handicapped peers. *Teaching Exceptional Children*, 1980, *13* (1), 39–43.

Long, N. S., Alpher, R., Butt, F., and Cully, M. Helping children cope with feelings. In N. S. Long, W. C. Morse, and R. G. Newman (Eds.), *Conflict in the classroom* (2nd ed.). Belmont, CA: Wadsworth Publishing Co., 1971.

Long, N. S., and Dufner, B. The stress cycle or the coping cycle? The impact of home and school stresses on pupil's classroom behavior. In N. S. Long, W. C. Morse, and R. G. Newman (Eds.), *Conflict in the classroom* (4th ed.). Belmont, CA: Wadsworth Publishing Co., 1980.

Long, N. S., and Newman, R. G. Managing surface behavior of children in school. In N. S. Long, W. C. Morse, & R. G. Newman (Eds.), *Conflict in the classroom* (4th ed.). Belmont, CA: Wadsworth Publishing Co., 1980.

Lyons, H. Our most neglected natural resource. *Today's Education*, 1981, *70* (1), 14–20.

Mackie, R. P. *Special education in the United States: Statistics, 1946–66.* New York: Teachers College Press, Columbia University, 1969.

Madden, R., Gardner, E. F., Rudman, H. C., Karlsen, B., and Merwin, J. C. *Stanford Achievement Tests.* New York: Harcourt Brace Jovanovich, Inc., 1973.

Maine Council for Learning Disabilities. *Newsletter.* Augusta, ME: Maine Council for Learning Disabilities, Summer, 1981.

Marishima, A. Another Van Gogh of Japan: The superior artwork of a retarded boy. *Exceptional Children*, 1974, *41* (2), 92–96.

Martino, L., and Johnson, D. W. Effects of cooperative versus individualistic instruction in interaction between normal progress and learning disabled students. *Journal of Social Psychology*, 1979, *107*, 177–183.

Maslow, A. H. A theory of human motivation. *Psychological Review*, 1943, *50* (4), 370–396.

McCarthy, R., and Stodden, R. Mainstreaming secondary students: A peer tutoring model. *Teaching Exceptional Children*, 1979, *11* (4), 162–163.

Mercer, C. D., and Mercer, A. R. *Teaching students with learning problems.* Columbus, OH: Charles E. Merrill Publishing Co., 1981.

Mercer, J. R. *Labeling the mentally retarded.* Berkeley, CA: University of California Press, 1973.

Mitchell, P., and Erickson, D. The education of gifted and talented children: A status report. *Exceptional Children*, 1978, *45* (1), 12–16.

Morse, W. C. The crisis or helping teacher. In N. S. Long, W. C. Morse, and R. G. Newman (Eds.), *Conflict in the classroom* (2nd ed.). Belmont, CA: Wadsworth Publishing Co., 1971.

Morse, W., Cutler, R., and Fink, A. *Public school classes for the emotionally handicapped: A research analysis.* Reston, VA: The Council for Exceptional Children, 1964.

Murray, H. *Thematic Apperception Test.* Cambridge, MA: Harvard University Press, 1943.

Myers, B. The child with a chronic illness. In R. H. Haslam & P. J. Valletutti (Eds.), *Medical problems in the classroom.* Baltimore, MD: University Park Press, 1975.

Newcomer, P., and Hammill, D. *Test of Language Development (TOLD).* Austin, TX: Empiric Press, 1977.

Newland, T. E. *The gifted in socioeducational perspective.* Englewood Cliffs, NJ: Prentice-Hall, Inc., 1976.

Ohleson, E. L. *Identification of specific learning disabilities.* Champaign, IL: Research Press, 1978.

O'Leary, K. D., and O'Leary, S. S. (Eds.). *Classroom management: The successful use of behavior modification.* New York: Pergamon Press, Inc., 1972.

Orton, S. *Reading, writing, and speech problems in children.* New York: W. W. Norton, 1937.

Palomares, U., and Logan, B. *A curriculum on conflict management.* La Mesa, CA: Human Development Training Institute, 1975.

Patterson, G. F., Reid, J. B., Jones, R. R., and Conger, R. E. *A social learning approach to family intervention: Vol. 1, Families with aggressive children.* Eugene, OR: Castalia, 1975.

Payne, J. S., & Patton, J. R. *Mental retardation.* Columbus, OH: Charles E. Merrill Publishing Co., 1981.

Payne, J. S., Polloway, E. A., Smith, J. E., and Payne, R. A. *Strategies for teaching the mentally retarded* (2nd ed.). Columbus, OH: Charles E. Merrill Publishing Co., 1981.

Peterson, R. M., and Cleveland, J. O. (Eds.). *Medical problems in the classroom — An educator's guide.* Springfield, IL: Charles C. Thomas, 1975.

Poorman, C. Mainstreaming in reverse with a special friend. *Teaching Exceptional Children*, 1980, *12* (4), 136–142.

Prescott, G. A., Balow, I. H., Hogan, T. P., and Farr, R. C. *Metropolitan Achievement Tests: Survey Battery*. New York: Psychological Corporation, 1978.

Price, M., and Goodman, L. Individualized education programs: A cost study. *Exceptional Children*, 1980, *46* (6), 446–454.

Pulvino, C., and Lupton, P. Superior students: Family size, birth order, and intellectual ability. *Gifted Child Quarterly*, 1978, *22* (2), 212–216.

Quay, H. C., and Peterson, D. R. *Manual for the Behavior Problem Checklist*. Mimeographed, Champaign, IL: University of Illinois, 1967.

Rapp, D. Does diet affect hyperactivity? *Journal of Learning Disabilities*, 1978, *11* (6), 56–62.

Redl, F. The concept of the life space interview. In N. S. Long, W. C. Morse, and R. G. Newman (Eds.). *Conflict in the classroom* (4th ed.). Belmont, CA: Wadsworth Publishing Co., 1971.

Redl, F., and Wineman, D. *Children who hate*. New York: Free Press, 1951.

Redl, F., and Wineman, D. *Controls from within*. New York: Free Press, 1952.

Renzulli, J. S. *The enrichment triad model*. Mansfield Center, CT: Creative Learning Press, 1977.

Renzulli, J., and Smith, L. *A guidebook for developing individualized education programs for gifted and talented students*. Mansfield Center, CT: Creative Learning Press, 1979.

Reynolds, M. C., and Birch, J. W. *Teaching exceptional children in all America's schools*. Reston, VA: The Council for Exceptional Children, 1977.

Rhodes, W. C. A community participation analysis of emotional disturbance. *Exceptional Children*, 1970, *37* (5), 309–314.

Rhodes, W. C. The disturbing child. A problem of ecological management. *Exceptional Children*, 1967, *33* (7), 449–455.

Ritvo, E. R. Biochemical studies of children with syndromes of autism, childhood schizophrenia, and related developmental disabilities: A review. *Journal of Child Psychology and Psychiatry*, 1977, *18* (4), 373–379.

Roach, E., and Kephart, N. C. *The Purdue Perceptual Motor Survey*. Columbus, OH: Charles E. Merrill, 1966.

Rogers, C. R. *Freedom to learn*. Columbus, OH: Charles E. Merrill, 1969.

Rorschach, A. *Rorschach Ink Blot Test*. New York: Grune and Stratton, 1966.

Rosen, S., Powell, E., and Rollins, P. Competence and tutorial role as status variables affecting peer tutoring outcomes in public school settings. *Journal of Educational Psychology*, 1978, *70* (4), 602–612.

Rubin, R., and Balow, B. Prevalence of teacher identified behavior problems: A longitudinal study. *Exceptional Children*, 1978, *45* (2), 102–111.

Salvia, J., and Ysseldyke, J. E. *Assessment in special and remedial education*. Boston: Houghton Mifflin Co., 1978.

Schifani, J. W., Anderson, R. M., and Odle, S. J. (Eds.). *Implementing learning in the least restrictive environment: Handicapped children in the mainstream*. Baltimore, MD: University Park Press, 1980.

Schultz, E., Hirshoren, A., Manton, A., and Henderson, R. Special education for the emotionally disturbed. *Exceptional Children*, 1971, *38* (4), 313–320.

Schuncke, G. Action approaches to learning. *Social Studies*, 1978, *69* (5), 212–217.

Sevort, R. A secondary school resource room makes mainstreaming work. *Teaching Exceptional Children*, 1979, *11* (3), 77–79.

Slosson, R. L. *Slosson Intelligence Test* (2nd ed.). East Aurora, NY: Slosson Educational Publications, 1981.

Smith, J., and Schneider, J. Certification requirements of general educators concerning exceptional pupils. *Exceptional Children*, 1980, *46* (5), 394–396.

Spache, G. D. A new readability formula for primary grade reading materials. *Elementary School Journal*, 1953, *53* (3), 410–413.

Spivack, G., and Spotts, J. *Devereaux Child Behavior Rating Scale*. Devon, PA: Devereaux Foundation Press, 1966.

Spivack, G., Spotts, J., and Haimes, T. *Devereaux Adolescent Behavior Rating Scale*. Devon, PA: Deveraux Foundation Press, 1967.

Spivack, G., and Swift, M. The Hahnemann High School Behavior (HHSB) Rating Scale. *Journal of Abnormal Child Psychology*, 1971, *5*, 299–307.

Stephens, T. M., and Braun, B. L. Measures of regular classroom teachers' attitudes toward handicapped children. *Exceptional Children*, 1980, *46* (4), 292–294.

Strauss, A., and Lehtinen, L. *Psychopathology and education of the brain-injured child*. New York: Grune & Stratton, Inc., 1947.

Swap, S. Disturbing classroom behaviors: A developmental and ecological view. *Exceptional Children*, 1974, *41* (3), 163–172.

Swart, R. A secondary-school resource room makes mainstreaming work. *Teaching Exceptional Children*, 1979, *11* (2), 77–79.

Tarjan, G., Wright, S. W., Eyman, R. K., and Keeran, D. V. Natural history of retardation: Some aspects of epidemiology. *American Journal of Mental Deficiency*, 1973, *77* (4), 369–79.

Terman, L. M., and Merrill, M. A. *Stanford-Binet Intelligence Scale*. Boston: Houghton Mifflin, 1960.

Thomas, A., Chess, S., and Birch, H. G. *Temperament and behavior disorders in children*. New York: New York University Press, 1968.

Torrance, E. P. *Torrance Tests of Creative Thinking*. Princeton, NJ: Personnel Press, 1966.

Tuttle, F. *Gifted and talented students*. Washington, DC: National Education Association, 1978.

Tuttle, F. B., and Becker, L. *Characteristics and identification of gifted and talented students*. Washington, DC: National Education Association, 1980.

Urban, W. *Draw-a-Person*. Los Angeles, CA: Western Psychological Services, 1963.

Van Riper, C. *Speech correction — principles and methods* (5th ed.). Englewood Cliffs, NJ: Prentice-Hall, Inc., 1972.

Walker, H. *Walker Problem Behavior Checklist*. Los Angeles, CA: Western Psychological Services, 1970.

Walker, J. E., and Shea, T. M. *Behavior modification* (2nd ed.). St. Louis, MO: The C. V. Mosby Co., 1980.

Wechsler, D. *Wechsler Intelligence Scale for Children* (rev. ed.). New York: Psychological Corporation, 1974.

Weiss, C. E., and Lillywhite, H. S. *A handbook for prevention and early intervention — Communicative disorders*. St. Louis, MO: The C. V. Mosby Co., 1976.

Wickman, E. K. *Children's behavior and teacher's attitudes*. New York: The Commonwealth Fund, Division of Publications, 1929.

Witty, E. Equal educational opportunity for gifted minority children: Promise or possibility? *Gifted Child Quarterly*, 1978, *22* (3), 344–352.

Wixson, S. E. Two resource room models for serving learning and behavior disordered pupils. *Behavioral Disorders*, 1980, *5* (2), 116–125.

Index

Numbers in *italics* refer to tables and figures.